# Schoenberg's Atonal Music

Award-winning author Jack Boss returns with the "prequel" to *Schoenberg's Twelve Tone Music* (Cambridge, 2014) demonstrating that the term "atonal" is meaningful in describing Schoenberg's music from 1908 to 1921. This book shows how Schoenberg's atonal music can be understood in terms of successions of pitch and rhythmic motives and pitch-class sets that flesh out the large frameworks of "musical idea" and "basic image." It also explains how tonality, after losing its structural role in Schoenberg's music after 1908, begins to reappear not long after as an occasional expressive device. Like its predecessor, *Schoenberg's Atonal Music* contains close readings of representative works, including the Op. 11 and Op. 19 Piano Pieces, the Op. 15 *George-Lieder*, the monodrama *Erwartung*, and *Pierrot lunaire*. These analyses are illustrated by richly detailed music examples, revealing the underlying logic of some of Schoenberg's most difficult pieces of music.

JACK BOSS is Professor of Music Theory and Composition at the University of Oregon. His previous book, *Schoenberg's Twelve-Tone Music: Symmetry and the Musical Idea* (Cambridge, 2014) received the Wallace Berry Award from the Society for Music Theory in 2015. His articles can be found in the *Journal of Music Theory, Music Theory Spectrum, Perspectives of New Music, Music Theory Online, Music Analysis, Intégral,* and *Gamut.*

Music Since 1900

GENERAL EDITOR    Arnold Whittall

This series – formerly *Music in the Twentieth Century* – offers a wide perspective on music and musical life since the end of the nineteenth century. Books included range from historical and biographical studies concentrating particularly on the context and circumstances in which composers were writing, to analytical and critical studies concerned with the nature of musical language and questions of compositional process. The importance given to context will also be reflected in studies dealing with, for example, the patronage, publishing, and promotion of new music, and in accounts of the musical life of particular countries.

*Titles in the series*

**Jonathan Cross**
The Stravinsky Legacy

**Michael Nyman**
Experimental Music: Cage and Beyond

**Jennifer Doctor**
The BBC and Ultra-Modern Music, 1922–1936

**Robert Adlington**
The Music of Harrison Birtwistle

**Keith Potter**
Four Musical Minimalists: La Monte Young, Terry Riley, Steve Reich, Philip Glass

**Carlo Caballero**
Fauré and French Musical Aesthetics

**Peter Burt**
The Music of Toru Takemitsu

**David Clarke**
The Music and Thought of Michael Tippett: Modern Times and Metaphysics

**M. J. Grant**
Serial Music, Serial Aesthetics: Compositional Theory in Post-War Europe

**Philip Rupprecht**
Britten's Musical Language

**Mark Carroll**
Music and Ideology in Cold War Europe

**Adrian Thomas**
Polish Music since Szymanowski

# Schoenberg's Atonal Music

## Musical Idea, Basic Image, and Specters of Tonal Function

Jack Boss

*University of Oregon*

CAMBRIDGE
UNIVERSITY PRESS

# CAMBRIDGE
## UNIVERSITY PRESS

University Printing House, Cambridge CB2 8BS, United Kingdom

One Liberty Plaza, 20th Floor, New York, NY 10006, USA

477 Williamstown Road, Port Melbourne, VIC 3207, Australia

314–321, 3rd Floor, Plot 3, Splendor Forum, Jasola District Centre, New Delhi – 110025, India

79 Anson Road, #06–04/06, Singapore 079906

Cambridge University Press is part of the University of Cambridge.

It furthers the University's mission by disseminating knowledge in the pursuit of education, learning, and research at the highest international levels of excellence.

www.cambridge.org
Information on this title: www.cambridge.org/9781108419130
DOI: 10.1017/9781108296991

© Jack Boss 2019

First published 2019

Printed in the United Kingdom by TJ International Ltd, Padstow Cornwall

*A catalogue record for this publication is available from the British Library.*

*Library of Congress Cataloging-in-Publication Data*
Names: Boss, Jack Forrest author.
Title: Schoenberg's atonal music : musical idea, basic image and specters of tonal function / Jack Boss.
Description: New York, NY : Cambridge University Press : Cambridge, United Kingdom, 2019. | Series: Music since 1900 | Includes bibliographical references and index.
Identifiers: LCCN 2019008714 | ISBN 9781108419130 (alk. paper)
Subjects: LCSH: Schoenberg, Arnold, 1874–1951 – Criticism and interpretation. | Music – 20th century–History and criticism. | Music – 20th century – Analysis, appreciation. | Atonality.
Classification: LCC ML410.S283 B66 2019 | DDC 780.92–dc23
LC record available at https://lccn.loc.gov/2019008714

ISBN 978-1-108-41913-0 Hardback

*For SunHwa*

# Contents

# Music Examples

# Acknowledgments

It seems that with children of the mind, just like with physical children, the second child is easier to deliver than the first. Though this book only needed four years to come into being, a much shorter gestation period than its older sibling's (*Schoenberg's Twelve-Tone Music*) thirteen years, there was still a large number of people who assisted and encouraged me as it took shape, and others who served as inspirations for me.

I would first like to thank the publishers, individuals and organizations that gave me permission to reproduce Schoenberg's score excerpts and sketches: Richard Birnbach (Berlin), Meisel Music (Berlin), Universal Edition AG Vienna, Belmont Music Publishers, the Arnold Schönberg Center, *Perspectives of New Music*, Claudio Spies, and Hal Leonard LLC (for Edition Wilhelm Hansen).

At Cambridge University Press, Kate Brett, Eilidh Burrett, and Lisa Sinclair, were patient and enthusiastic guides through the process of proposing, commissioning, vetting, and finally producing the book. Arnold Whittall, the series editor, and I had an enlightening discussion about the book's contents via email that resulted in several substantial improvements. Janice Baiton refined my presentation with her careful copyediting, and Varun Kumar Marimuthu and Puviarassy Kalieperumal were efficient and helpful partners in the "nuts and bolts" of production and proofreading. My deans at the University of Oregon School of Music and Dance, Brad Foley and Sabrina Madison-Cannon, together with my colleagues there, were more than willing to listen to my detailed reports of progress on the book, and served as sources of encouragement. Marc Levy of the SOMD Instructional Technology staff was helpful in procuring the software I needed to design the book's music examples myself.

All of my students at the University of Oregon since the mid-1990s have contributed to this book in larger and smaller ways; even before I began planning the book in 2015, I had already presented many of its analyses in my bi-annual post-tonal theory courses, and made small adjustments based on my students' feedback. But I would like to single out seven students who went through it with me, chapter by chapter, in a doctoral seminar in fall 2018, testing the analyses for coherence and clear presentation. These are Zachary Boyt, Michael Dekovich, Andrew Eason, JP Lempke, John King,

Stephen Medlar, and Joy Schroeder. Joy Schroeder also helped me construct the book's index.

The reader will not go very far through this book before encountering the names of two Yale professors who not only served as the dual inspirations for it, but also are primarily responsible for giving me the training and analytic "equipment" I needed to complete this task. When I entered Yale in 1984, my main objective was to study with Allen Forte and David Lewin. I only had a year of coursework with Prof. Lewin, as he moved on to found the music theory graduate program at Harvard in fall 1985, but my connection and friendship with Prof. Forte continued on through my doctoral dissertation and far beyond that. It would not be too fanciful, I think, to understand the analyses I have presented here as the discussions I would have had with David Lewin and Allen Forte about these pieces 34 years ago, if I had known a little more and been a bit more confident back then (indeed, many of the analyses seem to carry on a running dialogue with published works of Lewin).

Just as she did for *Schoenberg's Twelve-Tone Music*, my daughter, Christine Boss, provided me with a painting for the cover that perfectly captures the spirit of the book. Last but certainly not least, my wife, SunHwa Lee Boss, was my greatest source of encouragement during the past four years, a willing listener to my detailed accounts of the joys and struggles of creating this book and designing its examples. She also provided motivation for me by promising to take me out for Orange Mocha Mousse Cake every time I finished a chapter. As she always does, she made the journey that was writing this book much sweeter.

Jack Boss
Eugene, Oregon

# Abbreviations and Notational Conventions

| | |
|---|---|
| CHROM | the chromatic collection |
| DIA, G major or DIA (G) | the G major diatonic collection (not necessarily established through traditional chord progressions) |
| $HEX_{a,b}$ | a transposition of the hexatonic collection; the numbers in subscript indicate the two starting pitch classes of the particular transposition (in normal form) |
| $I_x$, $T_xI$, or I, t = x | inversion of a pitch class or set of pcs around pitch-class 0 (accomplished by subtracting the original pitch class(es) from 12), followed by transposition "up" x number of half-steps in pitch-class space |
| ic | interval class |
| LH | left hand (of the piano) |
| $OCT_{a,b}$ | a transposition of the octatonic collection; the numbers in subscript indicate the two starting pitch classes of the particular transposition (in normal form) |
| P | passing tone |
| $P_x$, $I_x$, $R_x$, $RI_x$ | prime, inversion, retrograde, retrograde inversion. These four symbols identify some succession of twelve or fewer notes as one of the four "canonical" transformations of a source row. The number in the subscript signifies the first pitch class of a prime or inversion, and the last pitch class of a retrograde or retrograde inversion |
| N | neighboring tone |
| n-1 invariance | where two pitch-class sets hold all but one pitch class in common, for example {0, 1, 3} and {0, 1, 4} |
| pc/PC | pitch class |
| pcs/PCs | pitch classes |
| RH | right hand (of the piano) |
| SC | set class |
| Strong Rp {3, 6, 7} | two four-note pc sets have the three pcs 3, 6, and 7 in common |

| | |
|---|---|
| $T_x$ or $t = x$ | transposition "up" x number of half-steps in pitch-class space (can be understood most easily as rotating a group of pitch classes x spaces clockwise on the "pitch-class clock," an arrangement of the twelve pitch classes in a circle with 0 at the top) |
| Weak Rp<br>3-5 (016) | two four-note pc sets do not literally have three pcs in common, but could share three pcs if one set were transposed and/or inverted. The three common pcs would belong to SC 3-5 |
| $WT_x$ | a transposition of the whole-tone collection; the number in subscript indicates the starting pitch class of the particular transposition (in normal form) |

Pitches are indicated using the registral designations recommended by the Acoustical Society of America, in which middle C is designated as C4, the octave above as C5, etc.

Successions of pitch classes or intervals are enclosed in angle brackets, unordered sets in curly brackets.

A vertical dyad of pitch classes is indicated as "11-above-0."

Horizontal successions of ordered pitch intervals are indicated as follows: <+1, –3> (plus signs represent ascent in half-steps, minus signs descent in half-steps); vertical stacks of unordered pitch intervals (usually counted up from the bottom of a chord) are indicated as follows: <5, 6>.

Ordered pitch-class intervals between the adjacent pitch classes of a prime or normal form are indicated by bold numbers below and between the pitch-class numbers of the prime or normal form:

(014)

**1 3**

Set classes are indicated using both their Forte name and prime form, for example 3-3 (014).

Interval vectors are enclosed in square brackets.

Pitch-class numbers are not given in bold, order numbers are given in bold.

Vertical pitch symmetry is represented by the name of the pitch axis in bold, with vertical arrows extending up and down from that axis.

Pitch-class symmetry is represented by the name of the pitch-class axis in bold (no registral designation), with vertical arrows extending up and down.

## Instruments

Woodwinds (WW): fl. (flute), picc. (piccolo), ob. (oboe), E.H. (English horn), cl. (clarinet), bass cl. or b. cl. (bass clarinet), E♭ cl. (E♭ clarinet), D cl. (D clarinet), bsn. (bassoon), cbsn. (contrabassoon).

Brass: hn. (horn), tpt. (trumpet), tb. (trombone), ta. (tuba).

Strings: vn. (violin), 1st vn. (first violin), 2nd vn. (second violin), va. (viola), vcl. or 'cello (violoncello), cb. (contrabass).

Percussion: timp. (timpani), cel. (celesta), glock. (glockenspiel), xyl. (xylophone)

Hp. (harp).

# 1 Tonal oder Atonal?

*The Complicated, Contradictory Nature of Schoenberg's Middle-Period Music (Op. 11, No. 1)*

Any study of the music of Arnold Schoenberg's middle period (traditionally understood as beginning around the time of the Op. 15 songs and the last two movements of the Op. 10 String Quartet and ending after the Op. 22 songs) must begin by reconsidering the label that has traditionally been assigned to it in literature on music: "atonal." It is well known that Schoenberg himself detested this label, protesting that the only music that could be rightly called "atonal" would be music that lacked tones altogether. He preferred to call his music "pantonal," a music that gave equal status to every tonality.[1] And Ethan Haimo, following the composer, claims that it is counterproductive, at least, to subject Schoenberg's music to the binary opposition that "tonal" and "atonal" represent, suggesting instead that we understand the middle period (the first part of it, at least) as moving incrementally away from traditional means of pitch organization. He argues for a long transition from chromatic tonality in 1899 to the music of 1908–09, a sudden break with tradition that he calls "New Music" in August 1909, followed by a recapturing of an older means of organization after 1911.[2]

Still, despite Schoenberg's and Haimo's aversion to the label "atonal," it persists. One reason may be that it does represent, quite well, two radical changes that Schoenberg's middle-period music made in the realm of pitch organization and that he acknowledged. Haimo is justified in arguing that

[1] Two similar expressions of Schoenberg's distaste for the term "atonal" can be found in his *Theory of Harmony*, trans. Roy E. Carter (Berkeley and Los Angeles: University of California Press, 1978), pp. 432–33; and the essay "Hauer's Theories," in *Style and Idea*, ed. Leonard Stein, trans. Leo Black (Berkeley and Los Angeles: University of California Press, 1984), pp. 210–11. It is interesting that both of these passages make reference to Josef Matthias Hauer. According to Bryan Simms, Schoenberg, or at least his followers, may actually have *approved* of the term "atonal" until 1920, when Hauer used it in *Vom Wesen des Musikalischen* to describe his own music. Simms shows clearly that Schoenberg was always careful to make a clear distinction between his own style and traditional tonality, using the term *Tonart* (key) to represent the traditional notion, and *Tonalität* to represent a broad spectrum of ways of organizing tones, including his own later approaches that did not admit a central tone. See Simms, *The Atonal Music of Arnold Schoenberg 1908–1923* (New York: Oxford University Press, 2000), pp. 8–10.

[2] Ethan Haimo, *Schoenberg's Transformation of Musical Language* (Cambridge: Cambridge University Press, 2006), ch. 1, pp. 1–7, conclusion, pp. 351–56.

these changes were accomplished gradually between 1899 and 1908. Even
so, by the time Schoenberg reaches his Op. 15 songs, final movements of his
Op. 10 String Quartet, and Op. 11 Piano Pieces, there are two basic features
in his music that abrogate the principal tenets of traditional tonality to such
an extent that a label representing a diametric opposition becomes appropriate. First, he replaces the basic harmonic elements of tonal music, triads
and seventh chords, with a much larger variety of sonorities that are mostly
more dissonant (it is true that conventional triads and seventh chords still
appear occasionally, but not often enough to be heard as basic elements).
This is a move that Schoenberg explained and justified not long after the
beginning of his atonal period in the seventeenth chapter of his
*Harmonielehre* (1911), on "Non-Harmonic Tones":

> There are no non-harmonic tones whenever one discovers such principles. For
> the natural prototype, the tone [Schoenberg has been speaking of the overtone
> series in the preceding paragraphs], can be used to explain, as chords, still other
> harmonic combinations entirely different from these simple ones. And our
> relation to this prototype is that of the analyst, of the seeker; in imitating it, we
> discover more or fewer of its truths. The creative spirit strives for more, more
> and more; those who merely seek enjoyment are satisfied with fewer.[3]

Rather than treat every chord of the vast, dissonant spectrum equally,
however, in his middle-period music Schoenberg tends to favor families of
chords that grow out of certain pairs of intervals. Chief among these are the
half-step and minor third and the half-step and major third. When both
intervals have the same direction, the former pair creates set class 3-3 (014)
and the latter 3-4 (015). These set classes, supersets of them such as set class
4-19 (0148), 5-21 (01458), and 6-Z19 (013478), and the symmetrical "hexatonic" collection that is created by alternating half-steps and minor thirds,
6-20 (014589), are all basic elements in his atonal chord repertory. Another
family that plays a crucial role is the one stemming from the Viennese
Trichord, a combination of a perfect fourth with a tritone. Schoenberg
often uses the chord in that particular voicing (as does Webern, hence the
name), but also reorders and transposes its notes to form different members
of set class 3-5 (016), and adds notes to 3-5 to form supersets such as 4-8
(0156) and 4-9 (0167). I will also touch on several other groups of chords,
some associated with other large collections such as octatonic and whole
tone, in the analyses that make up the body of my book.[4]

---

[3] Schoenberg, *Theory of Harmony*, p. 319.

[4] Bryan Simms has a different (but perhaps complementary) description of, and rationale
for, the chord vocabulary of Schoenberg's early atonal music from mine. He suggests that
Schoenberg was attracted to four-note supersets of the major and minor triads, and

In addition to replacing the old repertory of chords with a new one, the second sea change that occurs by the time Schoenberg's middle period begins has to do with the ways chords are combined into larger patterns. In the music leading up to Schoenberg by composers he emulated (Wagner, Brahms, Mahler, Strauss), and in Schoenberg's own music during his first period, the familiar progressions of diatonic triads and seventh chords around a tonal center had been deemphasized, to the point where they generally emerged only at phrase endings. Alternatively, one could say that late nineteenth-century German music preserves the contrapuntal structures of traditional harmony (well-supported Schenkerian 3- and 5-lines, linear intervallic patterns and the like), but fills them in with unexpected chords. In some of Schoenberg's first-period music, the tonal cadences are spaced even more widely than his immediate predecessors, sometimes disappearing for many measures (Haimo illustrates this effectively using the string sextet, *Verklärte Nacht*).[5] But by the time Schoenberg reaches his middle period, these rare tonal pillars are omitted altogether, the contrapuntal structures that linked them disappear, and the organizational functions of those elements are taken up by different kinds of procedures. Nevertheless, most of these procedures, formal and motivic ones, are borrowed from tonal music. Schoenberg described this state of affairs in his essay from *Style and Idea*, "Problems of Harmony":

> We further conclude that the manner of composition of a piece abandoning tonality in the traditional sense must be different from that in which tonality is followed. From this angle tonality is seen as *one of the means* which facilitates the unifying comprehension of a thought and satisfies the feeling for form. But since this means alone does not achieve the goal, it may be said that tonality accomplishes but a part of the purpose. If the function of tonality be dispensed with, but the same consideration be given to unity and feeling of form, this effect must be achieved by some other function. (italics are Schoenberg's)[6]

Now, an analyst can still find chord or note progressions that invoke tonic, dominant and predominant in Schoenberg's atonal music. In fact, beginning with his monodrama *Erwartung*, Op. 17, we hear occasional

---

particularly the minor triad with added major seventh, which forms set class 4-19. The examples in Schoenberg's chapter on non-harmonic tones in his *Theory of Harmony* are full of such sonorities. Simms, however, asserts that Schoenberg moved away from this chord repertoire later in his career, which does not seem to agree with the evidence – 4-19 and other chords with triad subsets will continue to play central roles in all of the analyses in this book. See Simms, *The Atonal Music of Arnold Schoenberg*, pp. 16–19.

[5] Haimo, *Schoenberg's Transformation*, ch. 3, pp. 23–41.

[6] Schoenberg, *Style and Idea*, pp. 284–85.

segments of music that unmistakably function within some key for a brief moment within a larger atonal context. The passages in *Erwartung*, as we will see in Chapter 4, are quotations from a D minor song, "Am Wegrand," Op. 6, No. 6 – the first in E♭ minor and the second in the song's original key. These quotations have a text-painting function; the ultimate arrival in D minor representing a woman's final realization that her beloved is dead. In the music after *Erwartung*, we begin to hear brief tonal segments that attempt to resolve in a key but are thwarted by the surrounding music – these also will be shown either to have text-painting significance or to contribute to a more abstract kind of narrative. I will discuss three examples in Chapter 5 in my analysis of Op. 19, Nos. 3 and 6, and several more in Chapter 6 in my analysis of "O alter Duft," the final recitation of *Pierrot lunaire*.[7]

Therefore, my main argument regarding functional tonality in Schoenberg's middle-period music is that tonality relinquishes its role as guarantor of large-scale coherence around the time of the first *George-Lieder* Op. 15 (in early 1908), and only later begins to reappear in a much more limited role as occasional expressive devices – the "specters" of my sub-title. Much more central to any of Schoenberg's atonal pieces is a combination of all or some of the following procedures, which can be shown to have their origin in Schoenberg's own tonal musical language and that of his predecessors, but are realized through non-tonal pitch structures:

1.  A large narrative of conflict, elaboration of that conflict, and resolution, expressed intervallically and rhythmically, which Schoenberg called the "musical idea."[8]
2.  The "basic image" (my term; though it is similar in concept to Kathryn Bailey Puffett's "structural imagery"): a visual and/or aural pattern

---

[7] Michael Cherlin discusses the phenomenon of tonal fragments in a larger atonal context in Schoenberg's music in "Schoenberg and *Das Unheimliche*: Spectres of Tonality," *Journal of Musicology* 11/3 (Summer 1993): 357–73. He compares it to Freud's concept of "das Unheimliche": something familiar and old that had been repressed, but recurs briefly, in a dream or work of literature. Cherlin's concept is a little broader than mine in that he allows pitch-class successions that are removed from their original harmonic context to serve as "spectres of tonality." I will limit my discussion to brief segments of music that are more or less completely controlled by traditional tonal harmonic functions in all their voices: thus my term "specters of tonal *function*."

[8] In Chapter 1 of my book, *Schoenberg's Twelve-Tone Music: Symmetry and the Musical Idea* (Cambridge: Cambridge University Press, 2014), I introduce Schoenberg's concept of "musical idea" in much more detail, through copious quotations from his writings, and careful consideration of the "idea's" cultural and philosophical forebears.

summarizing the text of a vocal piece, which is translated into intervals and rhythms.[9]

3. Tonal conventions of motivic process (such as the incremental expansion or contraction of intervals), phrasing and musical form.

I plan to show that these procedures carry over from piece to piece, and in this way my book will also push back against the notion of "contextuality" in Schoenberg's atonal music – I claim that there are indeed structural features, as well as harmonic and motivic ones, that are *not* unique to individual works, but span the entire period.[10]

I will now illustrate those features that enable one to identify a Schoenberg piece as "atonal" by comparing one of his tonal songs, the Op. 2 song "Jesus bettelt (Schenk mir deinen goldenen Kamm)," with the opening and closing sections of what has become his best-known atonal piece, the first Piano Piece, Op. 11. "Jesus bettelt" is Haimo's example of the beginning stages of Schoenberg's incremental process of change in *Schoenberg's Transformation of Musical Language*. I will approach it through a Schenkerian voice-leading graph to show how the song can be understood (more conservatively than Haimo does) in terms of traditional contrapuntal structures ornamented by voice-leading patterns, especially linear intervallic patterns. The opening and closing sections of Op. 11, No. 1 will also be approached using a voice-leading graph, which will

[9] Bailey Puffett introduces her notion of "structural imagery" in two articles describing the three melodramas in *Pierrot lunaire* that are heavily dependent on traditional contrapuntal devices such as canon and fugue: No. 8, "Nacht," No. 17, "Parodie," and No. 18, "Der Mondfleck." (Kathryn Bailey, "Formal Organization and Structural Imagery in Schoenberg's *Pierrot lunaire*," *Studies in Music from the University of Western Ontario* 2/1 (1977): 93–107; and Kathryn Bailey Puffett, "Structural Imagery: *Pierrot lunaire* Revisited," *Tempo* 60/237 (2006): 2–22.) She argues that the choice and use of such contrapuntal devices that structure the pieces as wholes, in addition to other aspects of the music, can be heard as determined by images that summarize the text. My concept of "basic image" extends the same notion to pieces within *Pierrot lunaire* that do not involve traditional contrapuntal devices, and to other Schoenberg opus numbers as well. I want to show that images summarizing the text can be heard as driving musical structure in a variety of ways from the beginning of Schoenberg's middle period (the Op. 15 songs) all the way through to Op. 22.

[10] The notion of Schoenberg's atonal music as contextual, that is, without "self-consistent, generally applicable compositional procedures," was put forward by George Perle in his *Serial Composition and Atonality* (Berkeley: University of California Press, 1962), p. 9, and was adopted by numerous other scholars, including some who disagree on most other aspects of Schoenberg's music, such as Ethan Haimo, *Schoenberg's Serial Odyssey: The Evolution of his Twelve-Tone Method* (Oxford: Clarendon Press, 1990), p. 69, and Martha Hyde, "Musical Form and the Development of Schoenberg's Twelve-Tone Method," *Journal of Music Theory* 29/1 (Spring 1985): 98.

ultimately prove to be unsuccessful – I want to demonstrate visually just how tonality "relinquishes its role as guarantor of long-range coherence." Then a motivic and set-class analysis will account for the changes that have taken place in its chord repertory, and its large organization will be explained through parallels to tonal motivic process, phrasing, form, and "musical idea," in the absence of a Schenkerian contrapuntal structure.

But before embarking on my comparison of Op. 2, No. 2 with Op. 11, No. 1, I would like to address a question that those familiar with recent books on the "extended common practice" (Dmitri Tymoczko's term) may be asking. Namely, why use an older analytic method like Schenker as a yardstick to distinguish between Schoenberg's tonal and atonal music, when newer, finer, measures have been proposed by Tymoczko and Daniel Harrison to distinguish the many varieties of late nineteenth-, twentieth-, and early twenty-first-century tonal music from each other, as well as from atonality?[11]

My answer would be that Schoenberg's tonal music before 1908 is something essentially different from Prokofiev's, Hindemith's, or Brian Wilson's (a few of the many "extended" tonal composers Tymoczko and Harrison discuss). As I have asserted already, it is very much late nineteenth-century German/Austrian music. Like his predecessors Wagner, Brahms, and Mahler (as well as his mentor Alexander von Zemlinsky), Schoenberg's tonal music "preserves the contrapuntal structures of traditional harmony (well-supported Schenkerian 3- and 5-lines, linear intervallic patterns, and the like), but fills them in with unexpected chords" (see page 3). These unexpected harmonies generally do not appear at the beginnings or ends of contrapuntal structures (i.e., beginnings or ends of formal sections and subsections), but in the middles.

What we are about to see and hear in the top voice of "Jesus bettelt," therefore, is not merely the "conjunct melodic motion" that Tymoczko proposes as a tonality-defining feature, nor even Harrison's "S-lines" (S for Schenker), which move by step in a single direction, beginning and ending on notes of the underlying chord.[12] Instead, Schoenberg's tonal song is filled with lines that descend stepwise from scale degrees $\hat{5}$ or $\hat{3}$, which are ornamented by other stepwise lines, chord skips, and stepwise neighbor motions. Likewise, the harmonic progression of Op. 2, No. 2 does not

---

[11] Dmitri Tymoczko, *A Geometry of Music: Harmony and Counterpoint in the Extended Common Practice* (New York: Oxford University Press, 2011); Daniel Harrison, *Pieces of Tradition: An Analysis of Contemporary Tonal Music* (New York: Oxford University Press, 2016).

[12] Tymoczko, *A Geometry of Music*, p. 5; Harrison, *Pieces of Tradition*, pp. 83–84.

merely surround its tonic with some orderly pattern of "harmonic fluctuation" (Harrison, after Hindemith), nor does it only display "harmonic consistency" (Tymoczko),[13] but its soprano and bass come together consistently to outline harmonic progressions that feature traditional tonic–predominant–dominant–tonic sequences at their beginnings and ends, and incorporate different inner voices and (less often) chromatically altered bass notes in their middles.

A related question the reader might also ask is "why use Schenker as a measuring stick to distinguish Schoenberg's tonal music from his atonal music, when Schoenberg had his own, well worked-out, theory of tonal harmony, introduced in the *Theory of Harmony* (original edition, 1911) and updated for his American students in the *Structural Functions of Harmony* (original edition, 1954)?"[14] And, though Schoenberg's tonal theories have many interesting points of contact with his tonal music, the answer must be the same as before: Schoenberg's tonal music has multiple melodic, contrapuntal, and harmonic features that align with Schenker's conception of tonal structure, and some of those features (particularly the melodic and contrapuntal ones) are more completely described using Schenker's method than the composer's. In my opinion, this is because Schoenberg's books were not principally intended to function as analytic introductions to his *own* harmonic and melodic practice, at least not in the sections where he discusses tonal harmony (however, some of the passages where he discusses dissonance and its treatment, like the famous seventeenth chapter of *Theory of Harmony* on "nonharmonic tones," can be read as apologetics for his turn to atonality (as I suggested on page 2). Rather, Schoenberg's books on tonal harmony were guides for his students to help them make good harmonic and voice-leading choices in *their* compositions.

Understanding Schoenberg's harmony books as primarily pedagogic rather than analytic explains why the section on "connection of the diatonic primary and secondary triads,"[15] seems to prefer the progressions I–iii–V–I and I–IV–ii–V–I to more normative progressions such as I–ii–V–I and I–IV–V–I: the first two progressions are easier for students to voice lead, owing to their common tones. (However, the more normative progressions do begin to appear more frequently in *Theory of Harmony* after Chapter 7, "Directions for Better Progressions.") By way

---

[13]  Harrison, *Pieces of Tradition*, pp. 45–68; Tymoczko, *A Geometry of Music*, p. 6.

[14]  Schoenberg, *Theory of Harmony*; Schoenberg, *Structural Functions of Harmony*, rev. ed. Leonard Stein (New York: Norton, 1969).

[15]  Schoenberg, *Theory of Harmony*, pp. 38–46.

of contrast, the most common underlying progression in the first 100 measures of Schoenberg's tonal masterpiece, *Verklärte Nacht*, is not I–IV–ii–V–I, but i–ii°7–V–i and its incomplete version, i–ii°7–V (mostly in D minor), thus without the intervening iv and with ii°7 often inverted; where it appears, this progression invariably can be read as supporting scale-degree descents such as $\hat{3} - \hat{2} - \hat{1}$ or $\hat{3} - \hat{2}$.[16]

One of the very few places Schoenberg analyzes his own tonal music in his harmony books is the final two pages of Chapter 10, "Extended Tonality," in *Structural Functions*.[17] His account of the first eleven measures of his Op. 6, No. 8 song, "Der Wanderer," seems to support my point about the good fit between his tonal music and Schenker's theories. It is a Roman numeral analysis consisting mostly of diatonic and altered I, ii, IV, and V chords, in the tonic (D major), flat mediant, and flat submediant regions. The chords combine into normative I–ii–V and I–IV–V progressions (which usually modulate after stopping at the V), but more importantly for my argument, they do not account for every verticality in the passage. As Schoenberg himself puts it, there are "apparently free passing notes and suspensions . . . [that are] merely melodic but not harmonic."[18] Thus it could be argued that Schoenberg's harmonic analysis of his tonal song makes use of the Schenkerian concept of middleground harmonic progression (though he probably did not think of it as such). And it would be possible, I think, to tease out middleground melodic lines (consisting mainly of $\hat{3} - \hat{2}$ interruptions in the various regions Schoenberg indicates) and bass lines to create an underlying contrapuntal structure, on the basis of Schoenberg's analysis – but, because *Structural Functions* is a harmony book, he has not suggested anything like that (except for a few roots as bass notes in parentheses).

There are numerous other examples I could provide of the close fit between Schoenberg's tonal music and Schenker's concept of tonality, but that topic could fill up its own book (and perhaps will someday). For now, let us proceed to the Schenkerian analysis of Op. 2, No. 2. In his discussion of "Jesus bettelt," Ethan Haimo comments on its "almost uninterrupted succession of seventh chords" and suggests two quite unusual basic principles for chord progression (among others). First, "adjacent chords are rarely answerable to a single diatonic collection," and, probably as a corollary, "the circulation of the total chromatic is common within

---

[16] Instances of the i–ii°7–V–I and i–ii°7–V progressions (sometimes missing the initial tonic) may be found at mm. 25–29, 33–34, 35–36, 37–38, 53–54 (in E♭ minor), 69–72 (in F minor), 73–74, and 100–05 (in E major).

[17] Schoenberg, *Structural Functions of Harmony*, pp. 110–11.      [18] Ibid., p. 110.

phrases."[19] But such a characterization of Schoenberg's chord progressions is subject to the same criticism Haimo directs at the term "atonal": it attempts to define them in terms of what they do *not* do (stay within the same diatonic scale, as all the voices progress from chord to chord). It seems better to take the approach suggested by Walter Frisch in his analysis of the same song: understanding the chord successions as "basic cadential succession[s], in which ... the diatonic *Stufen* are harmonized with vagrant chords."[20] A Schenkerian analysis of the song, like the one I provide in Examples 1.1–1.3, is bound by its nature to emphasize the conventional contrapuntal structures that Schoenberg fills in in unconventional ways.

For example, consider measures 1–7, the opening phrase, sketched in Example 1.1.

An F♯ minor tonic chord progresses via three chromatic or almost-chromatic lines, F♯–E–E♭–D (bass), C♯–C–B (tenor and soprano), and F♯–G–A♭ (alto, which in the full score transfers down to the tenor), to arrive at a chord with B, the fourth scale degree, in the soprano and bass D in m. 2. But instead of the diatonic iv$^6$ that would normally fill in such a counterpoint, Schoenberg chooses a fully diminished iv$^{o6}_5$, no doubt under the influence of the chromatic line in the alto that has landed on A♭. Here, a conventional tonal contrapuntal structure, C♯–B supported by F♯–D, is being filled in with an unusual chord. The remainder of the phrase can be understood similarly: Schoenberg spells A♯, the third scale degree in F♯ major, enharmonically as B♭ in the second half of m. 2, and harmonizes it, unconventionally, with a minor seventh chord on ♭II. This chord then gives rise to a 10–7–6–7 linear intervallic pattern in mm. 3–5 that prolongs an interval of the ♭II chord in the soprano, B♭–G. Though Schoenberg harmonizes the 10–7 part of the pattern in the usual way as dominant and minor seventh chords with roots moving down by fifth, the fact that it starts on ♭II minor 7 makes it seem like a foreign object in an F♯ minor or major context. After the linear intervallic pattern completes itself in m. 5, Schoenberg again moves chromatically in the soprano, G–F♯–E♯, and ascends by third in the bass, A–C♯, to arrive back at a dominant seventh chord that resolves to the tonic. Though some of the chords and the internal linear intervallic pattern seem at odds with it, the underlying skeleton of this opening phrase is still, essentially, a descending 5-line in F♯ with harmonic support of i–iv$^6$–♭II–V$^7$–I.

---

[19] Haimo, *Schoenberg's Transformation*, pp. 11, 21–22.

[20] Walter Frisch, *The Early Works of Arnold Schoenberg, 1893–1908* (Berkeley: University of California Press, 1993), p. 102.

Example 1.1 Score and Schenkerian analysis for Schoenberg, "Jesus bettelt," Op. 2, No. 2, mm. 1–7. Copyright © 1903 by Dreililien Verlag. All rights reserved. Used by permission of Dreililien Verlag, Richard Birnbach, Berlin

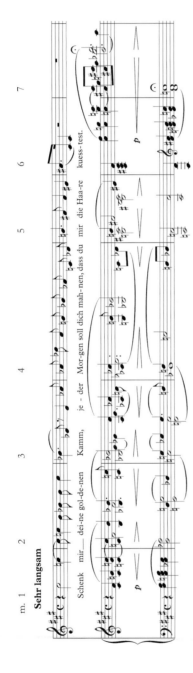

Translation: Give me your golden comb, every morning will remind you that once you kissed my hair.

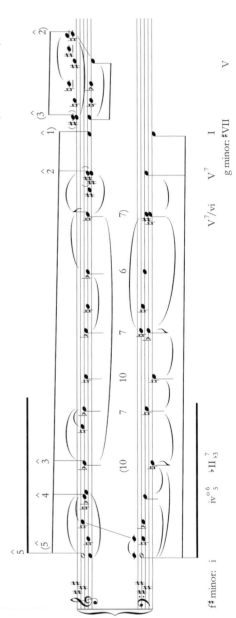

Another passage in "Jesus bettelt" brought forward by Haimo as an example of Schoenberg's incremental motion away from tonality (and in the direction of cycling through the aggregate) can be understood similarly, as a typical tonal contrapuntal structure filled in with unusual harmonies. I am speaking of mm. 37–38, which Haimo explains as a "cadence [in m. 38] articulated with a non-traditional (and non-consonant) sonority."[21] Haimo's choice of the D augmented triad in m. 38 as "cadential" is no doubt influenced by the fermata under its bass note. But it is also possible to understand this chord as a passing motion in the bass from a deceptive cadence on a diatonic vi chord (D♯ minor) that happened a measure earlier, as my graph in Example 1.2 does.

My reading incorporates the augmented chord on D♮ into a larger structure in mm. 34–39 that harmonizes scale degrees $\hat{3}$, $\hat{2}$, and $\hat{1}$ in the soprano with F♯, G♯, C♯, D♯, and F♯ in the bass. This would have the potential to be harmonized as i–ii°–V7–vi–i in F♯ minor, a conventional deceptive cadence followed immediately by the tonic. Instead, Schoenberg chooses a half-diminished chord on the initial F♯, what Frisch calls a "whole-tone chord" on the G♯, retains the dominant seventh on C♯ and minor vi chord on D♯ (resolving into the fifth of the vi chord by 6-5 suspension).[22] Then, he holds the upper voices while the bass passes down by half-step chromatically in m. 38 to a C♯ that appears an octave higher (through register transfer) as part of the major tonic in m. 39. The fact that the D♮ has a fermata does not require the listener to treat it as a cadence, particularly because of its chordal and contrapuntal context. Actually, understanding the D augmented triad as a passing motion that is suspended in time instead fits the accompanying text well – it is the question at the end of the second stanza, where Jesus asks Mary Magdalene: "will you not also lay your heart on my head, Magdalene?"

One last example of Schoenberg filling in a conventional contrapuntal structure with unexpected chords (and, in addition, changing one note of the bass) is the song's final cadence, mm. 39–44, given to the piano alone. This is analyzed in Example 1.3. Here, the descending 5-line from the song's opening returns to serve as its final descent (except that its opening C♯ no longer appears as C♯5, since the piano plays alone). The descent's first two notes receive a similar I–iv°$^6_5$ progression in the same voicing as in mm. 1–2. But at m. 41, the A♯ enharmonically spelled as B♭ and supported by G♮, which had been associated with ♭II before, receives

---

[21] Haimo, *Schoenberg's Transformation*, p. 17.
[22] Frisch discusses the "whole-tone chord" in *The Early Works of Arnold Schoenberg*, pp. 103–04.

Example 1.2 Score and Schenkerian analysis for Schoenberg, "Jesus bettelt," Op. 2, No. 2, mm. 34–39. Used by permission of Dreililien Verlag, Richard Birnbach, Berlin

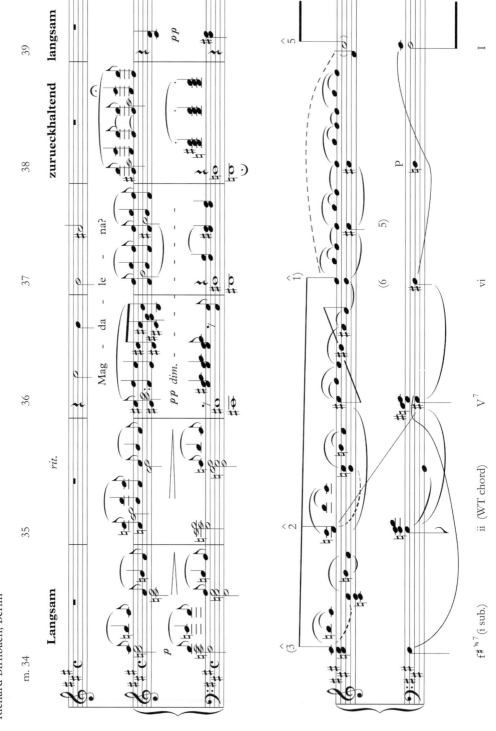

Example 1.3  Score and Schenkerian analysis for Schoenberg, "Jesus bettelt," Op. 2, No. 2, mm. 39–44. Used by permission of Dreililien Verlag, Richard Birnbach, Berlin

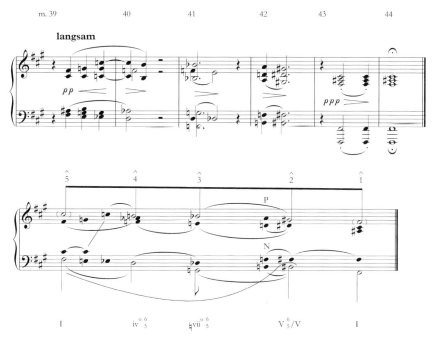

a different harmony – a fully diminished natural vii°⁶₅ with E as root. And the harmony supporting scale degree $\hat{2}$, G♯, goes a step further: it replaces the dominant seventh chord with its own dominant seventh, in ⁶₅ position, meaning that the expected bass note C♯ is supplanted by B♯. Still, it is reasonable to understand this passage as a conventional contrapuntal structure that has been harmonically altered, not as a turning away from "norms of harmonic syntax" toward cadences that are defined by locally emphasized chords.[23]

A completely different result is obtained when we try to apply the same Schenkerian analytic tools to the opening measures of Schoenberg's Piano Piece, Op. 11, No. 1, a work that stands near the endpoint of Schoenberg's process of incremental innovation toward atonal music. This attempt is made in Example 1.4. With the aid of one of the oldest analyses of Op. 11, No. 1, Edwin von der Nüll's *Moderne Harmonik* (1932), I propose Roman numerals and figured bass for mm. 1–11.[24] But, as the reader can see from

[23] Haimo, *Schoenberg's Transformation*, p. 15.
[24] Edwin von der Nüll, *Moderne Harmonik* (Leipzig: F. Kistner & C.F.W. Siegel, 1932), pp. 102–03.

Example 1.4  Score and Schenkerian analysis for Schoenberg, Piano Piece Op. 11, No. 1, mm. 1–12a. Drei Klavierstücke Op. 11. Copyright © 1910, 1938 by Universal Edition AG Vienna, UE 2991. All rights reserved. Used by permission of Belmont Music Publishers and Universal Edition AG Vienna, UE 2991. All rights reserved. Used by permission of Belmont Music Publishers and Universal Edition

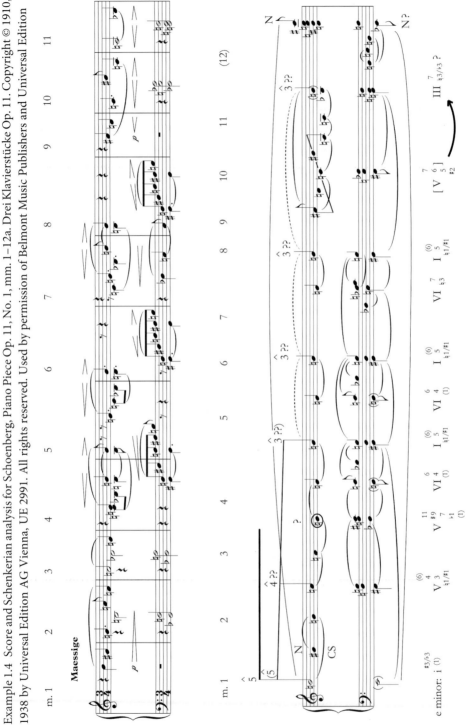

my painstakingly complete figured bass symbols, every chord in this tonal account of the piece except for one is missing at least one crucial note (indicated by figures in parentheses) and has at least one added tone. This seems like a much more severely altered harmonic vocabulary than the occasional passing augmented triads and whole-tone ii chords of "Jesus bettelt." The tonic chord in measure 1 lacks its root and adds its major third to the minor third (unlike von der Nüll, who analyzed the piece in E major–minor, I am treating the minor mode as referential). The dominant seventh in measure 2 lacks its third, D♯, and adds a second version of its fifth, F♮, to the diatonic F♯ in the bass. The prolongation of the dominant seventh in m. 3 adds a ninth, C♯, and an eleventh, E, while replacing the root with the note a half-step below, B♭. And so on. Faced with a situation like this, the analyst is sorely tempted to give up trying to find conventional triads and seventh chords, and look instead for a repertory of chords that is based on different principles.

In addition, a number of the chords I identified in Example 1.4 are subject to challenges. Some of the notes I identified as chord tones (again, under the influence of von der Nüll in many cases), because of their rhythmic positions in context, would better have been understood as non-harmonic tones. The A in m. 2, for example, strongly resembles an incomplete neighbor from the preceding G, since G rests on the downbeat with a dotted quarter note, and A follows it with an eighth note on the second half of beat 2. But to treat G as the chord tone instead of A would be replacing the seventh of the V7 chord in m. 2 with the flat sixth above the root, an interval that obscures the harmonic function even further than it already has been, and it would make it impossible for me to read A as scale degree $\hat{4}$ in the $\hat{5} - \hat{4} - \hat{3}$ descent that spans the opening eleven measures.

It is that proposed middleground structure to which I would like to turn our attention now. Example 1.4 reads the soprano as scale degrees $\hat{5} - \hat{4} - \hat{3}$ with the third scale degree sustained in mm. 4–8 through three consonant skips from E, the tonic, and in mm. 8–11 through a neighbor to F♯ that in turn unfolds down to A through a D secondary-dominant seventh chord. Like "Jesus bettelt," the beginning of Op. 11, No. 1 could be said to have a conventional *Urlinie* transference in the soprano voice. But this soprano is accompanied by a bass line that includes numerous alterations, as opposed to only two, the G♮ and B♯, at the final cadence of "Jesus bettelt" (mm. 41–42 in Example 1.3). And, while those two bass notes had made consonant intervals with the third and second scale degrees in the soprano, most of the bass alterations in Example 1.4 either withhold the bass note altogether or change it by half-step to create dissonances with the soprano.

The root E in m. 1 is withheld (my graph provides it in parentheses). The expected F♯ bass for $V_3^4$ is provided in m. 2, albeit enharmonically spelled as G♭, and with the F♮ added tone a diminished octave higher. The B♮ that would have formed the root for the prolongation of V7 in m. 3 is replaced by B♭. M. 4, second beat, lacks a bass note again: I suggested a G♮ that belongs to the VI chord and creates a lower neighbor to the G♯ on the third beat. But that G♯ is itself a problem, because it creates a diminished octave with the G♮ in the soprano. So many altered, dissonant notes make it impossible for the bass to fulfill its usual function of harmonic support, which would be necessary for a Schenkerian analyst to confirm certain notes in the soprano as structural. And so, in addition to the scale degree $\hat{4}$ in m. 2 that we already challenged on rhythmic grounds, we can also dispute the scale degree $\hat{3}$ in mm. 5, 6, and 8 because of its lack of consonant support (that is why these scale degrees are also labeled with question marks in the example).

After m. 9, the underlying tonal counterpoint seems a little more clear, but still has some problems. Mm. 9 and 10 could be understood as an unfolded D dominant in $_5^6$ position with two added notes, a relatively innocuous major ninth E, and a much more daring flat fifth or raised fourth A♭/G♯ (together with the natural fifth A). My reading departs from von der Null at this point, who reads these measures as a ii half-diminished seventh chord. I chose the D $_5^6$ because it functions as a secondary dominant seventh to G, which follows immediately, after a retardation, A–B♭, in m. 11. This III seventh chord, like the tonic at the beginning of the passage, has both major and minor thirds, so that even though the bass support is consonant (octaves), the chords under both F♯ and G have dissonant added tones. In addition, the seventh weakens the G chord's role as a resolution of the preceding dominant unfolding.

If the first eleven measures of Op. 11, No. 1 yield a conventional tonal soprano voice (albeit one poorly supported by its bass and chords, opening many of the soprano notes' functions to serious challenges), what follows immediately presents an even cloudier picture. Mm. 12 and following have been recognized by Haimo and others as a point of extreme contrast.[25] Nevertheless, my attempt to make a Schenkerian graph of mm. 12–18 is provided in Example 1.5. Von der Null calls our attention to the E♭2 at the

---

[25] Haimo, *Schoenberg's Transformation*, p. 303; others include Bryan Simms, *The Atonal Music of Arnold Schoenberg*, p. 63, and Reinhold Brinkmann, who calls m. 12 a "radical upheaval of the whole musical structure" (*Arnold Schönberg, Drei Klavierstücke Op. 11: Studien zur Frühen Atonalität bei Schönberg*, vol. 7 of Beihefte zum Archiv für Musikwissenschaft (Wiesbaden: Franz Steiner Verlag, 1969), p. 60).

Example 1.5  Score and Schenkerian analysis for Schoenberg, Piano Piece Op. 11, No. 1, mm. 12–18. Used by permission of Belmont Music Publishers and Universal Edition

bottom of the ascending arpeggio in m. 12, and the F♯1 on the downbeat of m. 13 that ends the descending arpeggio, and claims that they both point to E2 on the second half of beat 3, measure 13, as two members of the B dominant chord resolving back to tonic (he respells E♭ as D♯, as I did in my graph). I also added C♯6, the prominent note at the top of the ascending arpeggio, as a major ninth to the B7 chord in m. 12. As before, this reading consigns much of the content of m. 12's ascending arpeggio to dissonant added tone status – the A3 fits as seventh, but the D♮4, G♯4, C5, and E5 are outliers, hard to explain as diminutions since they form an arpeggio. The descending arpeggio could be justified as a chromatic descent with register transfer, from A♯5 (another added tone, ♯5 above the bass) to the chord tone F♯ on the downbeat of m. 13. And the first few notes on and after the second beat of m. 13 could be read as D♯2 and B2 in the left hand and D♯3 in the right hand. After that, however, relatively few of the notes outside the D♯/E♭2 are members of the E-minor V♯9 chord (the dissonant notes of m. 13 are circled on my graph).

The arrival of E on the second half of m. 13's third beat that von der Null remarks on is also problematic, since the right hand only provides notes for the soprano, F♯4 and F5, that are increasingly dissonant against the root. I implied a scale degree $\hat{5}$ above the second bass E2 on the third sixteenth of m. 14, but the pitch class B is completely absent from the texture, so this reading seems forced. E4 and G♯5, scale degrees $\hat{1}$ and $\hat{3}$, do make their appearance later, on and just after the downbeat of m. 15 (the E4 as a piano harmonic), but by that time the bass has shifted to F♮2, an upper neighbor to the tonic chord, with a harmony (F A C♯E) that is hard to explain in an E minor context (its significance in a different context, in which interval successions create a conflict, will be explained later). In m. 17, the same D secondary dominant seventh chord that we heard back at mm. 9–10 returns. But instead of leading to III7 as it had before, it slips back down to F♮ in m. 18, which supports a dominant seventh with added minor third as G had in the previous passage – a ♮II7.

The first part of Example 1.5, mm. 12–13, could be interpreted as inverting the situation we found in mm. 1–11: this time, the bass alone projects a conventional tonal contrapuntal voice (a lower neighbor figure D♯2–E2 with decorative consonant skip F♯1), where it had been the soprano in the previous example. But after m. 13, the two outer voices seem to be completely at odds. Where the bass arrives at E2 (m. 13, second half of beat 3), the soprano holds on to F♯4 from the previous chord. And by the time the soprano finds tonic triad members in m. 15, the bass has moved ahead to an upper neighbor. Meanwhile, the majority of the chords are still shot through with dissonant added tones. Op. 11, No. 1 can no longer be understood as a conventional contrapuntal structure that is filled in with unusual chords.

In "Jesus bettelt," the final cadence fulfilled its customary role of bringing the *Urlinie* down from scale degree $\hat{5}$ to $\hat{1}$, supported by consonant bass notes all the way, though two of them were harmonized by unexpected chords, the third scale degree by $\natural$ vii$^{\circ 6}_{5}$ and the second scale degree by V/V in the place of the dominant. Perhaps if we could find a similar descent in the closing measures of Op. 11, No. 1, it would make up for the serious deformities in the opening measures' contrapuntal structures. Example 1.6 provides my attempt to make a Schenkerian graph of mm. 53–64.

The closing passage begins as a varied return of the opening, with the melody from mm. 1–3, <B, G♯, G, A, F, F, E>, voiced mostly in octaves in mm. 53–55, and the arpeggio from mm. 4–8's left hand returning underneath it as harmonic support in m. 54. Because of this, I feel somewhat confident in reading B5 and A5 in measures 53–54 as scale degrees $\hat{5}$ and $\hat{4}$, and the left-hand arpeggio as a I$^6$ chord with multiple added notes, in similar ways to my analysis of the opening passage (see mm. 1–2 and 5 in Example 1.4).[26] But after that point, the contrapuntal structure begins to fade from view, as it had in previous passages from Op. 11, No. 1. Rather than moving on to repeated <E, G> motives as it had in mm. 4–8, establishing scale degree $\hat{3}$, the melody in mm. 54–58 continues down the chromatic scale from F5, stopping at D5, or scale degree $\natural\hat{7}$. However, this sustained D5 is supported by a bass note, the octave G2-G3, that *does* fulfill the need for a third scale degree, and it has a strong motivic affinity with the soprano of mm. 4–8, since it is approached by E♭2-E♭3 three times. For this reason, my *Urlinie* descends into the bass at m. 56, a common enough device in nineteenth-century music.[27]

But, after mm. 56–58, it becomes next to impossible to pull out anything resembling a traditional *Urlinie*, bass line, or chord progression. The chord progression in mm. 59–64 is perhaps closest to being normative: it could be heard as a deformed plagal cadence, with a subdominant containing multiple added notes and chromatic inner voice progressions in mm. 59–62 progressing to a two-note arpeggiation of the Neapolitan in m. 63, and an even more sketchy allusion to the tonic in the bass on the third beat of the same measure. But then, Schoenberg moves on quickly to the lower

[26] Von der Null also suggests reading mm. 53–55 as a reprise of the piece's beginning in the key of E major/minor. See *Moderne Harmonik*, p. 105.

[27] An interesting study of this phenomenon in the music of Chopin (among others) is provided by Eric Wen, "Bass-Line Articulations of the *Urlinie*," in *Schenker Studies 2*, ed. Carl Schachter and Hedi Siegel (Cambridge: Cambridge University Press, 1999), pp. 276–97.

Example 1.6 Score and Schenkerian analysis for Schoenberg, Piano Piece Op. 11, No. 1, mm. 53–64. Used by permission of Belmont Music Publishers and Universal Edition

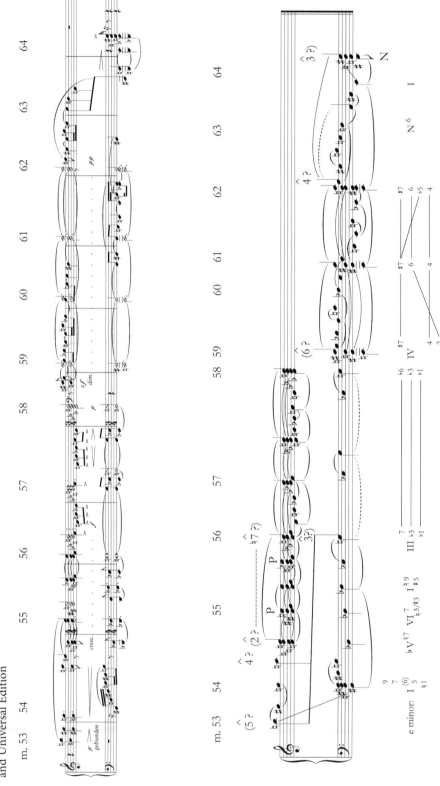

neighbor E♭1-E♭2 to finish the piece.[28] Melodically, we cannot find any substantive occurrences of scale degrees $\hat{2}$ and $\hat{1}$ in these same measures. F♯3 appears in m. 61 at the end of one of the chromatic descents, and sustains until m. 62, but because of the underlying subdominant, it is hard to understand this note as a well-supported scale degree: it makes more sense to read it as an added sixth, a chordal dissonance. So, instead, I chose scale degree $\hat{6}$, then $\hat{4}$ for the soprano during the subdominant prolongation, which resolves to $\hat{3}$ above the final chord – unfortunately, the bass slips down to E♭ at that same point (m. 64 second beat; spelled as D♯ in my graph), preventing the consonant support that would have enabled us to hear a cadence of some sort.

As they had at the beginning of the piece, traditional contrapuntal structures at the end of Op. 11, No. 1 appear briefly and then melt into the thin, dissonant air. This situation constitutes something substantially different from the melodic structures in Op. 2, No. 2 that are complete and well supported by the bass, but harmonized with unusual chords. Even though Schoenberg may have progressed from the former kind of piece to the latter in a gradual, step-by-step fashion (or even two steps forward, one step back as Haimo seems to characterize it), the pitch organization of Op. 11, No. 1 is different enough that it deserves a new label – "atonal."[29]

However, this does not mean that other principles characteristic of tonal music are completely absent in the Piano Piece. In fact, I can demonstrate that important components of tonal composition *as Schoenberg understood it* can be used to account for this piece's elements and processes with

---

[28] Von der Nüll's Roman numeral analysis of mm. 59 to the end follows almost the same outline as mine, but he adds a chord: he reads an "organ point" on the subdominant A, a Neapolitan chord skip, A♯ as lower neighbor, representing the dominant scale step B, and finally E, which is quickly displaced by E♭. See *Moderne Harmonik*, pp. 105–06.

[29] Though I used Edwin von der Nüll's very early attempt at finding an underlying tonal structure in Schoenberg's Op. 11, No. 1 as my guide, there are a number of other analytic studies that approach the piece in similar ways. A few of them orient themselves toward the same tonal centers as von der Nüll's analysis, most use different centers. Three notable examples are Brinkmann, *Arnold Schönberg, Drei Klavierstücke Op. 11*, pp. 60–96; Dieter Gostomsky, "Tonalität – Atonalität: Zur Harmonik von Schönbergs Klavierstück Op. 11, Nr. 1," *Zeitschrift für Musiktheorie* 7/1 (1976): 54–71; and Will Ogdon, "How Tonality Functions in Schoenberg's Opus 11, Number 1," *Journal of the Arnold Schoenberg Institute* 5/2 (1981): 169–81. Brinkmann, like von der Nüll, orients the piece toward E at beginning and end, and calls attention to the bass lower neighbor in mm. 12–13 (though he spells it as E♭–E). Gostomsky reads the first eleven measures as (potentially) a modulation from A minor to A♭ major, and the final chord as a neighboring chord either to A major or E♭ major. And Ogdon claims that the piece opens in G major, with m. 12 beginning an "episode" in E♭ minor. He hears the closing measures as suggesting both G and E♭ major simultaneously, although G has priority.

remarkable detail. These consist of, first, the compositional dialectic that he called "musical idea," second, a technique of varying motives incrementally by expanding or contracting their intervals and set classes, which constitutes a kind of "developing variation," and, finally, the repetition schemes of sonata-rondo form. My approach to Op. 11, No. 1 seems to bear out Schoenberg's claim (quoted on p. 3) that "other means" (that had been originally associated with tonality) could serve the purposes of unity and form in tonality's absence. I will now provide motivic (by which I mean pitch-interval succession) and chordal (set-class) analyses that illustrate "developing variation" within the context of an all-embracing "musical idea," a conflict and resolution, in Examples 1.7, 1.8, and 1.9. Examples 1.7 and 1.8 (as did 1.4 and 1.5 in the foregoing Schenkerian graphs) represent the first eighteen measures, and Example 1.9 reaches from m. 50, third beat, to m. 64 (a slightly longer passage than Example 1.6).

Example 1.7 portrays the first eleven measures as an amalgamation of a motivic process that expands its intervals incrementally, with chordal processes that first contract ordered pitch-class intervals, then expand them at the end, all in the service of outlining the small three-part form of the opening section. (I understand mm. 1–11's three-part form as the first A section of a truncated sonata-rondo form, A–B–A'–developmental C–A", with the other refrains coming at m. 17 and m. 53, the B section at m. 12, and the development at m. 34.) The large motivic expansion takes place in the right hand of the small a and a' sections: the opening motive *a1* in mm. 1–2, <–3, –1>, progresses to an expansion of its first ordered pitch interval, <–4, –1>, in mm. 2–3 (*a2*), and then to an expansion of both of its intervals, <–4, –2>, in mm. 9–10 (*a3*). What follows is a more extensive and less incremental interval expansion, <+8, –11>, in m. 10 (which I call *a4* because it retains the same total interval content and set class as *a1*), leading on to <–11, +1> in mm. 10–11 (which is called *y2*, because it can be understood as an octave complementation of one of the motives appearing in the b section).

The b section, mm. 4–8, does not participate in the overall interval expansion, but presents a different motivic picture. The piano's right hand combines two motives: the soprano states E4-G4 and then repeats it twice. This can be understood as a reduction of *a* to its minor third component, –3, which is inverted (or retrograded). The alto, meanwhile, provides a transposed retrograde, <–2, +1>, of an interval succession that had originally linked *a1* and *a2* together, which I call *x1*: <–1, +2>. Even though the right hand is combining motives in counterpoint rather than expanding their intervals incrementally, the contour of *reduced a* and *x2* together forms an outward-opening wedge. The left hand in the b section,

Example 1.7 Motivic and chordal analysis for Schoenberg, Piano Piece Op. 11, No. 1, mm. 1–11

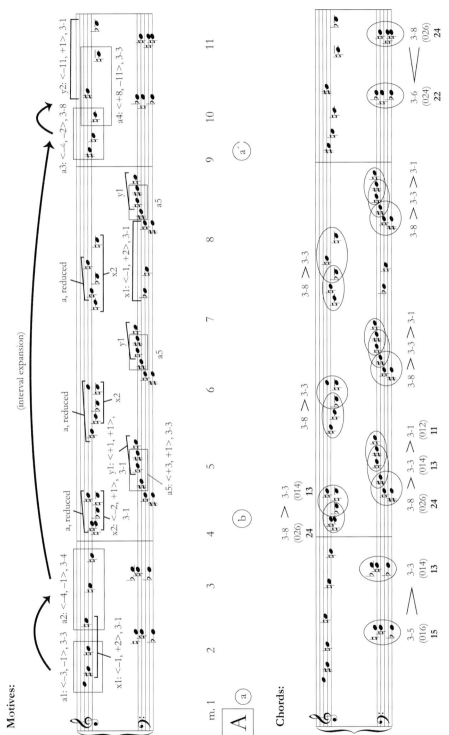

following directly after the right, produces a third contrapuntal line, <+4, +3, +1, +1>, which contains another version of the *a* motive, the complete inversion *a5* (<+3, +1>), overlapping with <+1, +1>, the *y1* motive that will be octave-complemented later in mm. 10–11. On the third repetition of the left hand's figure in mm. 7–8, we hear the extra notes D♭3 and C3, forming another version of *x1*. As a whole, the b section is not concerned with expanding pitch intervals incrementally, but rather searches for new ways to transform, reduce, and combine the motives already attained in section a. In this way, it provides a motivic contrast, helping it to fulfill its unique formal function with respect to a and a′.[30]

If we now look at the supporting chords of mm. 1–11, including some of the ones that are formed between contrapuntal lines in the b section, we find a number of chord progressions that contract rather than expand, creating a foil to the motivic activity in the right hand of mm. 1–3 and 9–11. (In this analysis, I am building on definitions of and distinctions between "motive" and "chord" that I suggested years ago in my article on Schoenberg's Op. 22 radio talk.[31] Essentially, "motives" are pitch-interval successions that appear either horizontally or vertically (reckoned up from the lowest voice). "Chords" are set classes (or unordered pitch-class sets) that also can be projected either vertically or horizontally, or as some combination of the two. The greater abstraction of the set class encourages me to understand it as something akin to a Roman numeral, which after all can be voiced in a nearly infinite variety of ways without changing its

---

[30] My motivic analysis of mm. 1–11 has a number of details in common with that presented by Ethan Haimo in *Schoenberg's Transformation of Musical Language*, pp. 297–302. His *a* motive is identical to mine, and he labels my *x* as *b* and my *y* as *c*. There are a number of important differences, however: he claims that what I call *a3* appears in the b section as a composite line between soprano and alto voices, which it does in the second repetition of b's material in m. 5, but not in the other two repetitions. In his thinking, then, the b section does participate in the overall process of expansion. Finally, and most importantly, he defines his motives much more broadly than I do – so that (it seems) any combination of two intervals moving in the same direction can be labeled *a*, and any combination of two intervals moving in opposite directions can be labeled *b* (whereas my *a* label, except for a4, is limited to a chain of motives occurring through small interval expansions and my *x* label is limited to retrogrades and inversions of the original *x1* motive).

    Another motivic analysis of mm. 1–11 that is particularly notable for its detailed account of the b section, which describes the numerous pitch-class links between sections a and b, is Brinkmann's account in *Arnold Schönberg, Drei Klavierstücke Op. 11*, pp. 62–72.

[31] Jack Boss, "Schoenberg's Op. 22 Radio Talk and Developing Variation in Atonal Music," *Music Theory Spectrum* 14/2 (Fall 1992): 145.

identity, while the pitch-interval succession is immediate enough to qualify as motivic.)

In the a section, mm. 1–3, the two left-hand chords produce set classes 3-5 (016) and 3-3 (014). The ordered pitch-class intervals between the pcs in the two prime forms are **1, 5** and **1, 3** respectively, which I am asserting to be a kind of contraction (in reality, we hear it as a shift from a chord that contains the tritone and perfect fourth, or their complements or compounds, to a chord that contains major and minor thirds, or their complements or compounds, so that even though all the pitch intervals do not literally contract, we do hear a progression to a different pair of interval classes that could be understood – in an abstract way – as "smaller"). The b section follows with contractions of the same sort in both the right and the left hands. In the right hand, 3-8 (026) progresses to 3-3 (014), producing ordered pitch-class interval progressions that contract from **2, 4** to **1, 3** (reversing the set classes of the interval expansion from *a1* to *a3* in the right hand); and the left hand follows 3-8 with 3-3 and 3-1 (012), creating a contraction from **2, 4** to **1, 3,** followed by **1, 1**.

Finally, in the a′ section, mm. 9–11, set class 3-6 (024) progresses to 3-8 (026), resulting in an ordered pitch-class interval expansion in the prime forms from **2, 2** to **2, 4**. This more abstract expansion reinforces the more immediate ordered pitch-interval expansion from *a3* to *a4* to *y2* that is happening directly above it.[32]

In all, the motives and chords of mm. 1–11 are varied in such ways that they either change incrementally in a particular direction (toward expansion or contraction), or create new kinds of transformations and combinations, to signal a contrasting section. Schoenberg appears to illustrate the principles of "developing variation" in these measures: by creating successions of motives that often develop in a direction, and always delimit and characterize parts of the form by the kind of development they undergo (whether it is directed development or combining motives in new ways).[33]

---

[32] The notions of contracting and expanding ordered pitch-class intervals between prime forms of consecutive set classes will be important tools in my analyses of all three pieces of Op. 11, in both this chapter and Chapter 2. I will refer to them as "set-class contraction" and "set-class expansion." Several other theorists have made use of similar processes in the past: Miguel Roig-Francolí writes about "linear transformation of set classes" and Joseph Straus about "parsimonious voice leading between set classes." See Roig-Francolí, "A Theory of Pitch-Class Set Extension in Atonal Music," *College Music Symposium* 41 (2001): 57–90; and Straus, "Voice Leading in Set-Class Space," *Journal of Music Theory* 49/1 (Spring 2005): 45–108.

[33] In "Schoenberg's Op. 22 Radio Talk," p. 129, I defined developing variation along similar lines:

As we progress to mm. 12–18, however, we find sudden changes in numerous aspects of the piece: rhythm, tempo, heard meter (or lack of it), dynamics, timbre, etc. In Reinhold Brinkmann's words (my translation): "after the rounded structure of the first eleven measures comes a seemingly abrupt contrasting outbreak: a clearly entrenched, orderly course is almost violently interrupted by something foreign to it."[34] At first, the motivic elements are not all that different from the previous measures, but very soon a new motive leaps onto the stage and is increasingly emphasized. This creates a conflict in the motivic realm to match the other kinds of upheaval, but as we shall see, the conflict is resolved in three different ways near the piece's end – two more obvious, one more subtle. The first piano piece of Op. 11 thus can be interpreted as manifesting Schoenberg's concept of "musical idea."

Example 1.8 illustrates mm. 12–18, the large B section (12–16) and the beginning of the refrain, A′, in mm. 17–18. Measure 12 begins with the succession <+1, −1, −8>, which, although it produces a new ordered pitch-interval combination, can be understood as derived from the initial motive *a1*, since it belongs to the same set class, 3-3. (Indeed, if we were to remove the first B2 of the succession and replace it with an E♭3, an octave above the final note, the first two intervals would be <−3, −1>.) Therefore, I call this motive *a6*. It overlaps with two instances of what at first seems to be a new motive, *b*, consisting of the intervals <+18, +5> and <+5, +6>, combinations of a compound or simple tritone with a perfect fourth; that is, two representations of the Viennese Trichord mentioned at the beginning of the chapter. Though we have not heard that particular interval combination (at least not emphasized) yet in Op. 11, its set class is a familiar one, 3-5 (016) – it appeared as the accompanying chord in m. 2. Motive *b* will continue to be an important component of the piece, emerging again as the top three notes of the final chord, m. 64.

But what follows the two overlapped *b* motives, the interval sequence <+4, +4, +9> that reaches to the top of the run, strikes my ear as something completely foreign. Most of the motives in the first eleven measures had

---

According to *Fundamentals [of Musical Composition]* and other writings of Schoenberg, a "succession of motive-forms produced through variation of the basic motive" performs two functions that make it developmental. It fulfills implications of the original motive, and it delimits a segment of the musical form and characterizes that segment in such a way that it can carry out its role within the form.

[34] Brinkmann, *Schönberg: Drei Klavierstücke Op. 11*, p. 60. Ethan Haimo likewise characterizes m. 12 as "a sudden eruptive burst [where] everything changes. So much so that mm. 12–13 appear to be unlike anything we have heard so far in the composition" (Haimo, *Schoenberg's Transformation*, p. 303).

Example 1.8 Motivic and chordal analysis for Schoenberg, Piano Piece Op. 11, No. 1, mm. 12–18

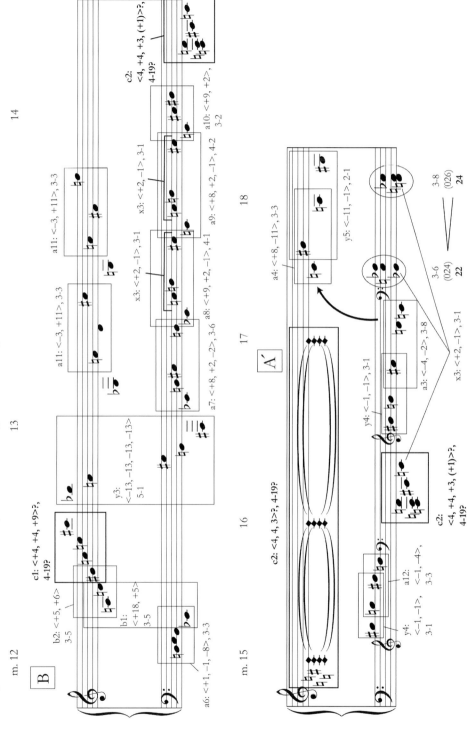

combined larger intervals with half-steps or whole steps, or consisted entirely of steps, but this succession, motive *c*, rockets through three relatively large intervals, the largest at the top. A question could be said to arise, which I believe is reinforced by all the drastic changes in other musical parameters in m. 12: how should we understand the relationship between this bit of new material and what has come before? The answer to that question will not become completely clear until the piece's final measures.[35]

M. 12's upward run is balanced by something more familiar, a downward plunge that can be heard as a transformation of motive *y* through interval compounding: <–13, –13, –13, –13>. What follows in mm. 13–14a is harder to interpret motivically, but perhaps we can read the left hand as four retrogrades of the motive that had opened the B section, <+1, –1, –8>, which either expand their intervals or raise their starting pitches, and incorporate the *x* motive as a subset as they do so. Motive *a7* on E♭2, <+8, +2, –2>, leads to motive *a8* on the same starting pitch, <+9, +2, –1>, then *a9* on E2, <+8, +2, –1>, and finally the incomplete *a10* on E2, <+9, +2>. The right-hand part in these measures forms the interval sequence <+14, –3, +11> twice, the last two intervals of which can be heard as *a1* with an octave compounding, or *a11*.

The last half of m. 14 introduces another element that sounds foreign in its immediate context, but at the same time it seems related to the four notes at the top of the run in m. 12. This is the piano harmonic chord, a new timbre as well as ordered and unordered pitch-interval combination, <4, +4, +3> reckoned up from the bottom. An inspection of all the interval classes within this chord yields the interval vector [101310], the same total interval content as <+4, +4, +9>, which means in this case that they share the same set class, 4-19 (0148). The set-class identity here corresponds to an audible connection: both of these chords are built up from augmented triads, and their final note creates a half-step (in pitch-class space) with one of the notes of the augmented triad. Again one is tempted to ask: how do these foreign sounds relate back to section A?

The question of connection to section A is answered in an inconclusive way in mm. 15–17, as a motive similar to motive *a2*, <–1, –4> or *a12*, and the original *a3*, <–4, –2>, re-enter over the sustained 4-19 chord (both *a12*

---

[35] I give a much more detailed account of the various appearances of motive *c* and its set class 4-19 throughout the piece in my article "'Musical Idea' and Motivic Structure in Schoenberg's Op. 11, No. 1," in *Musical Currents from the Left Coast*, ed. Jack Boss and Bruce Quaglia (Newcastle-upon-Tyne: Cambridge Scholars, 2008), pp. 260–71. As my article's title suggests, the appearances of the motive create a conflict that is elaborated and then resolved, which I will discuss in somewhat less detail in the present chapter.

and *a3* are preceded by the inversion of *y1*, the descending chromatic fragment *y4*). Motive *a3* continues on into *a4*, followed by a motive that can be related to y through turning the first interval in the opposite direction and octave complementation, <–11, –1>. Underneath them we hear the chords of mm. 10–11, set classes 3-6 (at the same pitch level as m. 10) and 3-8 (a step lower than m. 11), which means that the link back to the refrain is being accomplished through its ending measures, rather than its beginning ones.

Though section A has returned, the question about how the foreign interval succession and chord belonging to set class 4-19 can be understood as relating to the piece's opening still remains unanswered. If we are to grasp this piece in terms of a Schoenbergian "musical idea," the conclusion of the piece ought to explain just how <+4, +4, +9> and <4, +4, +3> function within a motivic context created by expansions of <–3, –1>. My analysis in Example 1.9 shows that it does just that.

Examples 1.9a and b, the motivic and chordal analysis of the final fourteen measures, perform what Reinhold Brinkmann has called an "integration" of the elements preceding m. 11 with those following m. 12.[36] I want to focus on how these measures complete the musical idea, by explaining what had been heard as foreign as related to the piece's opening material. First, Schoenberg presents motives and chords from section A in counterpoint with those from section B in mm. 50–52 (see Example 1.9a, top half). The right hand's top line consists of *a2* <–4, –1> and *a1* <–3, –1> side-by-side, in almost the same rhythm as their original appearance in mm. 1–3 (shifted one beat forward), but in reverse order.

Underneath the last two notes of *a2* in the right hand's lower voices in m. 51, the set-class progression from mm. 2–3 recurs, 3-5 followed by 3-3. In mm. 51–52, this is followed by three set-class sequences from 3-3 to 3-8, which reverse part of the thrice-repeated set-class succession in the left hand from mm. 4–8.

Underneath these motives and set-class progressions from section A, in the left hand we hear an arpeggio in m. 50 that brings together three different versions of the *b* motive first introduced in m. 12, followed by the last two intervals of *c1*, <+4, +9>. Motive *c1* had been the principal "foreign" element back in m. 12, but here its final two intervals by themselves form the set class 3-3, suggesting a connection with the material of section A. But in mm. 51 and 52, the left hand locks into the last five intervals of the ascending run of m. 12 that cast the music headlong into contrasting section B, <+5, +6, +4, +4, +9>, presented at two pitch levels. As Example 1.9a shows, this fragment

---

[36] Brinkmann, *Schönberg: Drei Klavierstücke Op. 11*, pp. 61 and 91.

Example 1.9a Motivic and chordal analysis for Schoenberg, Piano Piece Op. 11, No. 1, mm. 50–58

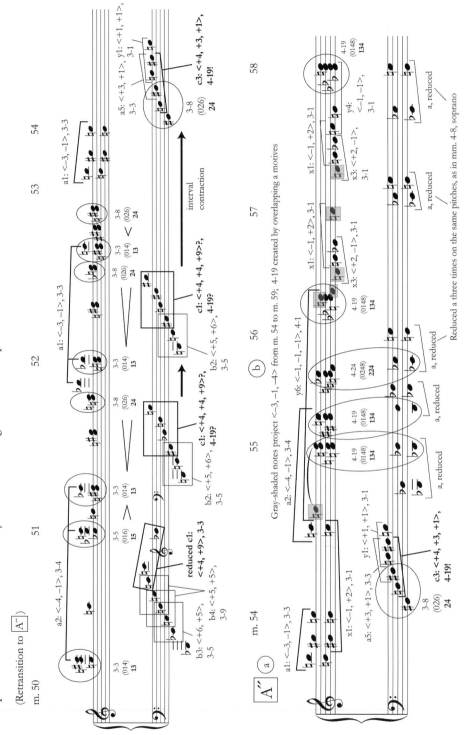

preserves one of the set class 3–5s and the <+4, +4, +9> succession that was marked as foreign in the earlier appearance.

After Schoenberg presents motives and chords from A and B in counter-point, the second step in his integration process is to change the left hand's arpeggios from intervals characteristic of B, through contraction, to intervals familiar from section A. Thus <+5, +6, +4, +4, +9> in m. 52 becomes <+6, +4, +3, +1, +1> in m. 54, through removing the initial +5 and contracting almost everything else. In addition, the new interval succession is set at a pitch level (beginning on G♯2) that reveals it as a direct quotation of the thrice-repeated left-hand arpeggio in mm. 4–8 – in this way, contraction helps us to recognize the "foreign" upward arpeggio as a close relative of the familiar A section material. In addition, part of m. 54's arpeggio, <+4, +3, +1>, produces the same set class, 4-19, as the <+4, +4, +9> that had seemed so new in its original context in m. 12, and hearing these two fragments next to one another in mm. 52–54 enables the listener to recognize the similarity between them that comes from having the same total interval content.

While the left hand is converting section B's interval successions back into those of A, the right hand follows the slightly altered version of mm. 1–3's melody it had stated in mm. 50–52 with a rhythmically and intervallically correct one (now in octaves) in mm. 53–55, returning the music formally to the last iteration of the refrain, A (see the bottom half of Example 1.9a). (We can understand mm. 50–52 as the final measures of a retransition, precisely because of the different ways they prepare for A material, consid-ered above.) In this final statement of the refrain, however, the opening phrase in the soprano continues on past the F–E (now F5–E5) with which it had ended in m. 3. It makes a chromatic descent all the way down to D5 in m. 56 and then remains there for almost three measures, while the alto voice retraces the motion from F to D an octave lower twice, touching on several renditions of the *x* motive along the way, and ending with a *y4* <–1, –1> leading into the downbeat of m. 58. All the Fs and Ds in both octaves are marked with gray shading in Example 1.9a, for a reason that will be discussed below. The bass line in mm. 55–58, meanwhile, repeats E♭2/3–G2/3 three times, recalling the soprano of mm. 4–8. Because of this, we can perhaps understand mm. 55–58, with its *x* motives in the alto and *reduced a* motives in the bass, as a varied return of the original b subsection of A, following mm. 53–55, which evoke the original a subsection.

But let us return to the multiple Fs and Ds that I shaded in mm. 54–57. Why are those notes, and the motion from F to D (and back), given such prominence? One possible reason could be what follows in mm. 58–59 (see the motivic analysis in the top half of Example 1.9b): a right-hand chord with C♯4 on top followed immediately by a major seventh in the bass built on A1.

Example 1.9b Motivic and chordal analysis for Schoenberg, Piano Piece Op. 11, No. 1, mm. 58–64

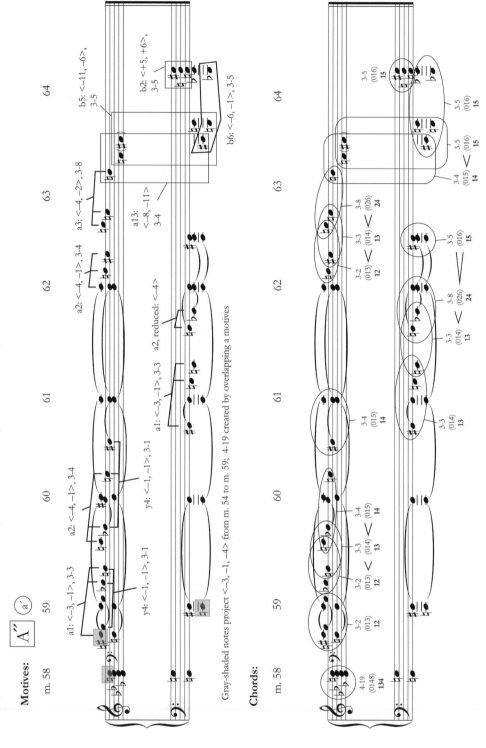

(Both of these notes are also shaded in gray.) I argued in my previous essay on Op. 11, No. 1 that the succession F5–D5–C♯4–A1, if reduced to a single octave (F4–D4–C♯4–A3, for example), produces the ordered pitch-interval succession <−3, −1, −4>.[37] This succession belongs to set class 4-19, the same one that had contained the foreign elements from the B section such as <+4, +4, +9> and <4, +4, +3>, but projects the set class in such a way that it can be understood as the *a1* motive <−3, −1> overlapped with an expansion of itself <−1, −4>. Thus, in a way far more subtle than the left-hand arpeggios of mm. 51–54, the foreign interval successions of B are explained as derivable from familiar motivic material through their set class.

Skeptics may want to accuse me of picking notes from the texture to create an interval succession that serves my analytical purpose here; but it seems incontrovertible that the progression of F to D (and back) is highlighted in mm. 54–58. If a pianist is willing to weight C♯4 at the end of m. 58 and A1 on the downbeat of m. 59 a little more heavily (giving emphasis to the outer voices, in other words), the succession I am asserting becomes audible, though it is certainly behind the surface. (A closely related motive, <−4, −1, −3>, has a similar "explanatory" function in the third movement of Op. 11, as we shall see in Chapter 2.) In any case, such an explanation could also account for Schoenberg using set class 4-19 no fewer than four times as a chord in mm. 55–58, circled in Example 1.9a, with the intervals from the bottom – <16, 4, 5, 3>, <19, 4, 4>, <1, 4, 4>, and <3, 4, 4> – giving a few more opportunities for the set class to continue to sound "foreign" as an augmented triad with a half-step added in pitch-class space, before it is explained for the final time. (Set class 4-19 ceases to be heard prominently after m. 59.)[38]

Mm. 59–64, coming after the three-stage resolution of the preceding measures, seem to have two functions: they serve as a kind of extended reprise of *a′*, to go with mm. 55–58's b and the a section of mm. 53–55; and

[37] Boss, "'Musical Idea' and Motivic Structure in Schoenberg's Op. 11, No. 1," pp. 269–71.

[38] It is interesting to note that Ethan Haimo's account of the motivic processes at work in Op, 11, No. 1 are, like mine, organized around a dialectic of conflict and resolution. However, the principal synthesis that he chooses to illustrate in detail comes not at the piece's end, but at the first return of the A section, mm. 19–24. He describes the first return of A in very similar terms to my description of the final return:

> Thus we see that the motivic material of mm. 19–24 is rooted equally strongly in mm. 4–8 and mm. 12–13. This illustrates a crucial aspect of the formal process: Schoenberg works toward a reconciliation of what had originally been two profoundly contrasting ideas. At their inception the ideas of mm. 4–8 and 12 had seemed mutually incompatible and apparently irreconcilable. That incompatibility created a formal tension – how could these contrasting elements coexist in the same piece? By drawing on motives from one and pitch-collections from the other, Schoenberg is revealing to us that common ground can be found. (*Schoenberg's Transformation*, p. 307)

they continue to relate materials that had been introduced as foreign in the B section to the piece's opening measures. One of the reasons I hear the final six measures as reminiscent of a' is motivic – the lines that move against the sustained chords retrace the path from *a1* to *a2* in mm. 59–60, right hand, from *a1* to an incomplete *a2* in mm. 61–62, left hand, and finally from *a2* to *a3* in the right hand of mm. 62–63. This sequence of motives represents not just subsection a', but the entire incremental interval expansion that characterized subsections a and a' together.[39]

But the expanding of ordered pitch intervals does not stop with m. 63. Indeed, the last three bass notes of the piece trace the interval succession <-6, -1>, from A♯1 to E1 to E♭1. This can be heard as a continuation of the expansion process, <-3, -1>, <-4, -1>, <-4,-2>, <-6, -1>, and the set class <-6, -1> forms is 3-5 (016). Meanwhile, the final right-hand chord that enters together with the low E♭1 and its octave doubling E♭2 also projects 3-5, but does so as a Viennese Trichord, <5, 6> from the bottom. This same interval succession had been another one of the foreign elements first heard in m. 12's arpeggio (it is an octave below the three notes marked as *b2* in Example 1.8), which means that we can understand the final cadence as another explanation of something foreign – by means of <5, 6> having the same set class as a more familiar element, <-6, -1>.

The other reason I hear mm. 59–64 as an extension of the original a' is the "chord progression" formed by its sequence of set classes, illustrated in the bottom half of Example 1.9b. I pointed out above that the set classes in mm. 10–11 expand from 3-6 (024) to 3-8 (026), and a look at the set-class progressions in the lower half of Example 1.9b, mm. 59–64, shows that they consist mostly of similar incremental expansions of the ordered pitch-class intervals of prime forms. First, in mm. 59–61, right hand, we find 3-2 (013), 3-2, 3-3 (014), 3-4 (015), 3-4, or a progression from ordered pitch intervals **1, 2** (twice) to **1, 3** and on to **1, 4** (twice). The left hand of mm. 61–62 answers with 3-3, 3-3, 3-8 (026), 3-5 (016), where the second ordered pitch interval expands from **3** to **4** to **5** (the first ordered pitch interval fluctuates between **1** and **2**). Finally, the right hand in mm. 62–63 and left hand in 63–64 complete the piece with 3-2, 3-3, 3-8, 3-4, 3-5, an incremental journey from **1, 2** to **1, 3** to **2, 4,** contracting for a moment to **1, 4** and finally

---

[39] My explanation of mm. 53–64 as a variation of mm. 1–11's three-part structure, a, b, a', agrees completely with Allen Forte's form chart in "The Magical Kaleidoscope: Schoenberg's First Atonal Masterwork, Opus 11, Number 1," *Journal of the Arnold Schoenberg Institute* 5/2 (1981): 131. He, however, characterizes my large A″ as the recapitulation of a sonata form, not the final refrain of an abbreviated sonata-rondo. My A, B, and A' together make up his exposition, and we also agree to understand mm. 34–52, C, as developmental, ending with a retransition in mm. 50–52.

expanding again to **1, 5**. Again, the sense of incremental expansion in the set-class realm may not be as immediate as the motivic expansions from *a1* to *a2* and *a3* happening at the same time. But one does certainly hear a change in types of interval from chord to chord – minor thirds (or their complements) are replaced by major thirds, which give way to perfect fourths or fifths and eventually tritones, while the half-step continues on as an important element. These more audible features are dependent on the total interval contents that are nearly always associated with a particular set class.

Thus, although Op. 11, No. 1 fails to sustain a traditional contrapuntal structure, and because of that ought to be labeled as something different from tonal music (according to my principal argument in this chapter), it still adheres to conventions of motivic process, form, and "musical idea" that were all important components of tonal music as Schoenberg understood it. This atonal piece can be explained in terms of motivic progressions that either expand their intervals incrementally or present reductions, transpositions, inversions, etc. in a free counterpoint; and whether they do the former or latter can be justified by the location of the motives in the overall form. As a whole, the piece presents foreign motives and chords in its second large section (m. 12ff.), and then connects that material back to the motives of mm. 1–11 in mm. 50–59, by presenting foreign and familiar elements in counterpoint, by gradually changing strange to familiar intervals through contraction, and finally by demonstrating that what had sounded foreign actually has the same interval content (belongs to the same set class) as familiar material. In these ways, it manifests a "musical idea" through conflict and resolution of its musical elements. Rather than arguing whether it should be labeled "atonal," it seems more fruitful to me to acknowledge that it has, in fact, "abandoned tonality" (using Schoenberg's own phrase from my earlier quotation on p. 3), and instead look for the "other functions," many of them borrowed from tonal music, that create "unity and feeling of form."[40]

---

[40] The view of Schoenberg's Op. 11, No. 1 presented here contrasts sharply in its aesthetic perspective, choice of analytical methods, and results with that propounded by Dmitri Tymoczko in *A Geometry of Music*. Tymoczko points out (pp. 162–63) that Op. 11, No. 1 exhausts the full range of twelve pitch classes early on (it presents eleven of them by m. 4, reserving the twelfth, E♭, until m. 12). Thereafter, it continues to cycle quickly through the aggregate, unlike functional-harmonic and scale-based pieces that limit themselves to one or another group of five, six, seven, or eight pitches for longer periods of time. In Tymoczko's words, Op. 11, No. 1 has a "high rate of pitch-class circulation." He goes on (pp. 164–67) to measure the total distribution of six- and seven-note set classes in Schoenberg's piece, showing that it is relatively even. Though there are small peaks in the seven-note graph at 7-3 (0123458) and 7-21 (0124589), the distribution is considerably more even than a tonal piece with frequent modulations (John Coltrane's "Giant Steps"), where 7-35 (013568T), the diatonic scale, is the dominant collection.

The reader will no doubt have noticed that my description of Schoenberg's atonal Piano Piece relied heavily on the concept of "set class," the central concept of pitch-class set analysis. This concept and method were developed by Allen Forte in the 1960s and 1970s, building on the work of Milton Babbitt and David Lewin.[41] Since its invention, both the concept and the ways it is used in analysis have been subject to steady and often dismissive criticism. Some question whether "set class" is appropriate for the analysis of Schoenberg's music at all. As Ethan Haimo argues in *Schoenberg's Transformation of Musical Language*:

> Pitch-class set analysis – as preached and practiced by Allen Forte and his followers – is not an acceptable tool for the understanding of Schoenberg's works.[42]

Later in the same book, Haimo considers whether a "limited" version of pitch-class set analysis (which does not insist that every note be a member

---

Later in the book (pp. 183–86), Tymoczko compares his pitch-class circulation and six-note chord distribution graphs for Op. 11, No. 1 to those for a randomly generated sequence of pitches, claiming that the graphs are "nearly indistinguishable." From that, he goes on to conclude that "atonal music is often remarkably similar to random notes," and, though he adds a disclaimer that he is not making an aesthetic judgment, he finishes his discussion by characterizing atonal music as a rather strange acquired taste, like "the taste for clam chowder ice cream."

But, as my preceding analysis has shown, what seems random if measured one way can be understood as carefully patterned if measured a different way. If Tymoczko had been willing to shift his attention from counting pitch classes to identifying ordered pitch intervals between adjacent notes, he would have discovered patterns of interval expansion, fragmentation, inversion, and retrograde in the first eleven measures of Op. 11, No. 1 that are certainly audible, and that contribute to expressing the passage's three-part form, together with texture and rhythm. And, if he had only paid attention to the progressions of three-note set classes, rather than counting how many times each seven-note set class appears in the whole piece, he would have recognized sequences of set-class contraction that *do* give the opening measures a harmonic consistency only a little less audible than the motivic transformations, as they progress from sets with more open intervals like 3-8 (026) to more closed ones like 3-3 (014) and 3-1 (012).

It would be possible, I suppose, to characterize even a Mozart piano sonata as "random," if one chose the "right" kind of measure – for example, counting up how many times notes appear on each line and space of the five-line staff (without regard to clefs or accidentals). But what would be the point of such an exercise?

[41] The classic presentation of "set class" and the whole system of pitch-class set analysis is found in Allen Forte, *The Structure of Atonal Music* (New Haven: Yale University Press, 1973). But it was a Lewin article from the early 1960s that introduced the concepts underlying "set class" (as a transpositional or inversional equivalence in pitch-class space) and "total interval content," and considered what we now call the Z-relation, situations where two sets are not T- or I-equivalent and still have the same interval content. See Lewin, "Re: The Intervallic Content of a Collection of Notes, Intervallic Relations between a Collection of Notes and Its Complement: An Application to Schoenberg's Hexachordal Pieces," *Journal of Music Theory* 4/1 (Spring 1960): 98–101.

[42] Haimo, *Schoenberg's Transformation*, p. 292.

of some pitch-class set, or a version that focuses on trichords and tetra-chords to the exclusion of larger sets, as mine does) could be useful for analyzing Schoenberg. The answer to that question is, again, negative:

> Although I acknowledge its ability to identify and describe certain types of relationships with great precision, I have doubts about the value of limited pitch-class set analysis as the sole, or even the principal, analytical tool for Schoenberg's music ... In some ways, it is less successful.[43]

Haimo's aversion to set class seems at least partially grounded in his sense that it does not match any of the categories that Schoenberg himself would have been familiar with or would have called on in the act of composing. He presents this argument in a well-known article, "Atonality, Analysis and the Intentional Fallacy":

> The conclusion is unequivocal. There is no evidence of any sort in Schoenberg's manuscripts or writings, or those of his students, that would support the contention that composition with pitch-class sets was a conscious, intentional act by Schoenberg. We have failed to find any such evidence in spite of the fact that we had ample resources at our disposal. If Schoenberg had made any conscious use of pitch-class sets in composing, surely some evidence would have remained. There is none.[44]

And Haimo is right in arguing that Schoenberg's sketches show no evidence of his familiarity with the concept of set class or anything like it, as he demonstrates in his article with the composer's "continuity draft" for Op. 11, No. 1: no interval classes are computed on the sketch, no collections are circled, nor are any arrows drawn from one chord to another to show set-class identity.[45] Schoenberg's atonal sketches are indeed notorious for their lack of analytic overlay: by themselves, they sometimes seem to suggest that the music was freely improvised without any conscious thought process at all.

But Haimo may be going a bit too far when he claims that "there is no evidence of any sort in Schoenberg's ... *writings*" for the composer's con-sciousness of the set-class concept. I have claimed previously that I believe he may have been familiar with the notion, and that he, understandably, called it by a different name – to Schoenberg, what we call "set-class equivalence" today would have been comprehended as a motive varied so substantially that it only retains its notes or its intervals (in a different arrangement). My corroboration for such a belief comes from his music examples in the analysis of the Op. 22 songs that he drafted in 1932 to read on the Frankfurt

---

[43] Ibid., p. 294.
[44] Ethan Haimo, "Atonality, Analysis and the Intentional Fallacy," *Music Theory Spectrum* 18/2 (Fall 1996): 176.
[45] Ibid., 170.

Example 1.10a Example Nos. 16a and b from Schoenberg's Op. 22 radio talk. Copyright © 1965 *Perspectives of New Music*. Used by permission of *Perspectives of New Music* and Claudio Spies. This article first appeared in *Perspectives of New Music*, 3(2), 1965

and that, furthermore, a small phrase makes its appearance twice in succession at the end, in the accompaniment for celli:

No. 16a (Vlc. m. 16)    No. 16b (Vlc. m. 17)

The first three notes are once again in the sequence of minor second and third that we have heard before. It is to play an important role in what

Example 1.10b Example Nos. 32a and b from Schoenberg's Op. 22 radio talk. Used by permission of *Perspectives of New Music* and Claudio Spies

From the final section and its orchestral conclusion, I would like first to show you that the initial motif returns in the voice in the form of a chain of motifs.

No. 32a (Piano)

The motif is included six times:

No. 32b (Piano)

Radio (but, unfortunately, he was never able to deliver the talk himself).[46] Two of these are reproduced as Examples 1.10a and b.

Schoenberg tells us in the commentary on Example 1.10b that the "initial motive," which had been defined in Examples 16a and b in the talk as a sequence of minor second and third, both ascending (creating members of set class 3-3 (014)), returns in the final stanza of the song in the form of a "chain of motives." As his Example 32b shows, in this chain the original

---

[46] The radio talk was translated by Claudio Spies as "Analysis of the Four Orchestral Songs Op. 22" in *Perspectives of New Music* 3/2 (Spring–Summer 1965): 1–21, and I used it as the basis of an analytic method for the first song, "Seraphita," in my article "Schoenberg's Op. 22 Radio Talk and Developing Variation in Atonal Music." The examples in question, Nos. 16a and b, come from p. 6 of Spies's translation, and Nos. 32a and b from p. 10.

motive is transformed in a variety of ways, including making the minor second and third progress in opposite directions in the first, fourth, and fifth members of the chain (which creates a new set class, 3-2 (013)), expanding the second interval from a minor third to a major third and inverting, in the chain's second member (which creates 3-4 (015)), and placing the minor third before the minor second in the chain's sixth member (which preserves the original set class, 3-3).

All of these transformations seem to suggest that Schoenberg's "motive" was something different from the concept of set class we know today, since one motive contains at least three set classes. But the third link in the chain of motives leads me to the conclusion that the larger category "motive" actually included "set class" as a subcategory in his thinking. Schoenberg asserts that the sequence E5–C5–E♭5 manifests the same "motive" as C♯4–D4–F4. Unlike the other motives in the chain, the third link in Example 32b can only be derived from its predecessor in Example 16a by a process of inverting C♯4–D4–F4 to C♯4–C4–A3, transposing that up to E5–E♭5–C5 and reordering that in turn to E5–C5–E♭5. Such a multiple transformation can no longer be explained in terms of changing the directions of the intervals or expanding them, because it preserves only one feature of the original motive; namely, its membership in the equivalence class of twelve transpositions and twelve inversions of unordered pitch-class sets that we know today as set class 3-3. In at least one case, what Schoenberg identified as motivic equivalence corresponds exactly to what we call set-class equivalence.

Because I believe that the concept of set class (by a different name) was indeed part of Schoenberg's composing arsenal, and, more importantly, because it is an indispensable tool to me in constructing analyses to demonstrate that his atonal music illustrates concepts of developing variation, musical idea, and form that he borrowed from tonal music, I will continue to use it liberally in the remainder of this book.[47] But the reader should be warned that my use of the concept will not normally take the

---

[47] I should point out here that, despite his protests to the contrary, Ethan Haimo in his analyses in *Schoenberg's Transformation of Musical Language* also makes use of equivalence relations that correspond to the notion of "unordered pitch-class set," though, like Schoenberg, he does not call them by that name. On pp. 305–07, he brackets the two left-hand chords in mm. 19–20 of Op. 11, No. 1 and labels them as "motive Q." He then points out that the same six pitch classes, in a different order and higher registers, had constituted the middle part of the ascending and descending flourish in m. 12. In Haimo's reading, measures 19–24 creates a synthesis in the sense that it brings back the six pitch classes from m. 12 (the contrasting section) with motives from mm. 4–8 of the opening section (which appear, mostly, in the right hand of mm. 19–24). But the connection between the Q motive in m. 12 and the one in mm. 19–20 is an unordered pitch-class set equivalence, with its free changes in order and register. It is not that much of a step further

same shape as Allen Forte's classic analyses in *The Structure of Atonal Music* and elsewhere.[48] For the most part, I will avoid sets larger than hexachords in my analyses (although, from time to time, I will remark on the larger sets that contain motivic sets or significant chords, or are complements of them), and I am not interested in finding connected structures around a nexus set. Instead, as my Op. 11, No. 1 analysis demonstrated, I am more concerned with using the set class (and the unordered pitch-class set as well) as a kind of equivalence that contributes to the manifestation of a musical idea (as in my claim that the contrasting interval successions <+4, +4, +9> and <−3, −1, −4> belong to the same set class, and that constitutes an explanatory motivic relationship between them). Or, I use it as a tool to describe successive sonorities as a sequence of elements connected by a process of developing variation (as in my assertion of three such successions in mm. 59–64 that "develop" in the sense that the adjacent ordered pitch intervals in their prime forms expand incrementally).

It is impossible in a book this size to analyze every atonal piece Schoenberg wrote exhaustively, but through detailed analyses of a number of pieces and excerpts, I aim to show that there is a strong thread of coherence from piece to piece through "musical idea," "basic image," and other conventions of musical form and motivic process that Schoenberg seems to have carried over from tonal music. These few pieces will also show how tonality itself reemerges as an expressive device, after losing its traditional coherence-producing function. Instead of asking "Tonal oder atonal?," I would like to proclaim "Atonal *und* tonal," and then show in what ways this fascinating and perpetually misunderstood music blends new motivic and chordal elements as well as old ones, with traditional ways of organizing them.

---

to claim motivic or chordal identity on the basis of set-class equivalence, as Schoenberg does in his radio talk, and as I am doing and will do in my analyses.

[48]  Forte's published analysis of Op. 11, No. 1 itself is remarkable for his focus on large sets: primarily hexachords, but some larger sets as well. He refers to the trichords I have mentioned, as well as set class 4-19, frequently, but comprehends these elements as subsets of and intersections between the larger sets that are his main concern. He is generally not interested in describing processes that connect smaller sets. See Forte, "The Magical Kaleidoscope," 132–68.

## 2  Piano Pieces Op. 11, Nos. 2 and 3

*The Latter Movements of a Remarkably Progressive Cycle*

Most scholars who survey the three Piano Pieces, Op. 11 usually emphasize the fact that, according to the dates marked on Schoenberg's first
draft for the three pieces, the first two of them were composed relatively
close to each other in February 1909, and the third did not emerge until
several months later, in August 1909.[1] Writers such as Ethan Haimo,
Bryan Simms, and Reinhold Brinkmann go on to argue that
Schoenberg's compositional approach went through a sudden, drastic
conversion during the intervening spring and summer. In a matter of
months, he apparently transformed himself from a composer who
adapted traditional musical forms and created clear motivic processes
on both the smaller and larger scale, to a writer of stream-of-
consciousness pieces consisting of small, unrelated episodes separated
by violent disjunctions. Haimo's characterization of Schoenberg's make-
over is typical:

> We come now to one of the most perplexing and mysterious junctures in
> Schoenberg's compositional career. In the span of only a few short days,
> a central aspect of Schoenberg's compositional language underwent a radical
> transformation, perhaps the most dramatic, abrupt, and far-reaching trans-
> formation of his entire career. Before this point Schoenberg's music had
> changed constantly and relentlessly, but always gradually. Not here. With
> little warning and with minimal precedent, Schoenberg went from writing
> intensely motivic music to writing music in which there were no repeated
> themes, no recurrent motives, and a complete avoidance of learned devices . . .
> Is it really possible that . . . the composer of Op. 11, No. 1 is the same as Op. 11,
> No. 3?[2]

Bryan Simms describes a similar abrupt change with regard to
Schoenberg's handling of form:

---

[1] The first draft can be found on the Schönberg Center website, at the address: www
.schoenberg.at/compositions/manuskripte.php?werke_id=190&id_quelle=505&id_gat
t=&id_untergatt=&herkunft=allewerke (accessed September 4, 2015). It is unusually close
to the finished version, with the only major change coming at the end of m. 4 in the third
piece (Brinkmann discusses this revision at length on pp. 122–26 of *Drei Klavierstücke
Op. 11*).

[2] Haimo, *Schoenberg's Transformation*, p. 318.

> In his atonal instrumental music composed prior to August 1909, Schoenberg
> used forms unmistakably derived from classical models. These works are
> subdivided into sections linked together by their expository, developmental,
> or recapitulatory treatment of a common group of themes, phrases or
> motives ... Piece No. 3 is very different, since traditional thematic develop-
> ment and recapitulation does not occur ... The listener to Piece No. 3 notices,
> first of all, a succession of brief, clearly contrasted sections, set off from one
> another by silences, changes in dynamic level and tempo, and sudden shifts in
> surface rhythm and textural design.[3]

In my experience of the Three Piano Pieces over the years, however, I have
always had the strong sense that the "conventional wisdom" exaggerates
the differences between the third piece and the first two. I hear and see
similar motives and chords, and even some of the same progressions
connecting those motives and chords, in all three pieces. My purpose,
then, in considering Piano Pieces 2 and 3 in close proximity to one another
within this chapter, and directly after our discussion of Piece No. 1 in the
first chapter, will be to show in what ways all three of them are linked
together by individual motives and chords and short- and long-range
motivic and formal processes. Despite the assertions made by Haimo and
Simms, I want to argue that Schoenberg's Op. 11 is, in fact, a *cycle*.[4] Even
though the third piece's musical form is more fragmented than either of the
first two, the second can also be understood as more fragmented than the
first, creating an incremental dissolution of large formal units. And,
the second and third pieces take up and continue motives and motivic
developments (as well as chords and chordal developments) that were
introduced in the first.

   The three main processes that we will trace through all three pieces have
been discussed already in the first chapter: (1) the incremental interval
expansion of the first piece's opening motive, $<–3, –1>$; (2) the abstraction
of the first process to an incremental expansion of the ordered pitch-class
intervals in prime forms of set classes, which typically features the set classes
3-2, 3-3, 3-4, 3-8, and 3-5 (usually in that order); and (3) processes by which
foreign interval successions belonging to set classes 4-19, 3-5, and others are
"explained" by following them immediately with renditions of the same set

---

[3] Simms, *The Atonal Music of Arnold Schoenberg*, pp. 66–67. Brinkmann's account of the
   third piece's features that differentiate it from the other two may be found on pp. 109–14 of
   *Drei Klavierstücke Op. 11*, and his comments about the third piece's chronological
   separation from the other two on pp. 114–18.

[4] I am not the first to make such an assertion. David Lewin's brief article on Op. 11, "Some
   Notes on Schoenberg's Opus 11," *In Theory Only* 3/1 (April 1977): 3–7, focuses on larger
   pitch-class sets, which, appearing at the same transpositional level, connect all three pieces.

class that are clearly derivable from <–3, –1>. These processes, and their developments and extensions, trace the clear outline of a musical idea (on multiple levels) in the second piece, as they did in the first: conflict, elaboration, and resolution. In the third piece, the conflict between explanatory and expanding processes is elaborated, but not resolved – the interval and prime form expansions simply crowd out "explanations" of set class 4-19.

## Op. 11, No. 2

The second of the Three Piano Pieces has several features that connect it to traditional tonality more closely than the first piece: it begins with an ostinato on the pitches D2 and F2, and sustains that ostinato for ten of the first fifteen measures. For much of mm. 29–39 (what we will call the opening measures of the B section), the bass line cycles through D3, B♭2, A2, and back to D3. And near the end, in what we will call A′, mm. 55–63, the same cycle returns in the bass in an elongated form, half of it an octave lower: D2, B♭1, A2, D3. All of these patterns point to a reading in D minor, which was Schoenberg's favorite key in his more traditionally tonal music.

Howard Cinnamon is emboldened by these strong tonal markers to produce a Schenkerian graph for the second piece similar in many ways to the one that I attempted for Op. 11, No. 1 in Chapter 1.[5] Not surprisingly, he runs up against many of the same problems I did: most of the chords have dissonant added tones, often half-steps or major sevenths or their compounds, and sometimes omit their roots, and often only a single outer voice has a recognizable middleground pattern, while the other outer voice creates dissonant intervals against it. Instead of giving up the attempt as I did, however, Cinnamon excuses the unusual chords by calling them a "logical extension" of Schoenberg's claim about the non-existence of non-harmonic tones in Chapter 17 of his *Theory of Harmony*.[6] Cinnamon understands the dissonant middleground lines as arpeggiations prolonging a dissonant sonority, in much the same way that a consonant sonority would be prolonged in a traditional Schenkerian analysis, and he justifies the lack of anything resembling a traditional *Urlinie* by the assertion that neighbor figures serve the corresponding function of long-range melodic coherence.[7]

[5] Howard Cinnamon, "Tonal Elements and Unfolding Nontriadic Harmonies in the Second of Schoenberg's *Drei Klavierstücke*, Op. 11," *Theory and Practice* 18/2 (1993): 127–70.

[6] Ibid., 137.

[7] Cinnamon's comments about the lack of an *Urlinie* are on p. 150 of "Tonal Elements," while the principle that dissonant chords may be prolonged at the middleground is demonstrated by many of the graphs in the article. One prominent example is his graph that shows a prolonged B♭ major seventh chord with split third through m. 16, on p. 139.

Nevertheless, even with these adjustments to the traditional approach, Cinnamon has to admit that there are numerous places in the second Piano Piece that are resistant to tonal analysis. In his words: "it is obvious that many passages cannot be adequately explained by tonal means alone."[8] In response to this problem, he goes on to explain such passages through a pitch-class set analysis of the piece built around 5-16 (01347) and 5-Z18 (01457), as well as their tetrachord subsets and six- and seven-note supersets.[9] But there are numerous other important patterns and processes involving ordered pitch-interval motives and the recurrence of pitch-class sets at specific transpositions with different ordered pitch intervals, which Cinnamon's analysis does not touch on. These patterns and processes create a large-scale conflict, elaboration of that conflict, and resolution, a musical idea, and several more local conflicts and resolutions; thus they will form the basis of my account of Op. 11, No. 2 below.

As I will do for all my analyses in this book, I would like to begin with a formal overview of the piece (provided in Example 2.1). My form chart follows the large outline provided by Brinkmann and Cinnamon of a three-part song form, but I have further subdivided the large A section in ways different from them.[10] I broke it up into smaller sections – subsections a, b, a, and c – to highlight the consequences of understanding mm. 1–4a and 4b–5 (which Reinhold Brinkmann calls themes a and b) as creating a conflict through their contrasting natures. Brinkmann understands them this way; in his words (my translation):

> A and b are distinguished in character by nuances: a is a self-oscillating, uniform melody without strong developmental tendencies and with weak thematic contours: b, through its rising and sinking back, is restless, urgent and conclusive at the same time.[11]

---

[8] Cinnamon, "Tonal Elements," 152.

[9] Olli Väisälä deals with the problem of Op. 11, No. 2's skewed relationship to traditional tonal hierarchies in a different, inventive way: he also claims that the piece is prolongational, but that it prolongs dissonant pitch-class sets, which are often (not always) presented in consistent registral orderings. His main element for the piece is the pitch-class set {2, 3, 6, 9, 10} and two subsets of its T11 transposition, {1, 2, 5, 8} and {1, 2, 5, 9}, which are given their principal registral orderings of ordered pc intervals <3, 11, 7> and <3, 11, 6> figured from the bass D2 in mm. 2–3. See Väisälä, "Concepts of Harmony and Prolongation in Schoenberg's Op. 19/2," *Music Theory Spectrum* 21/2 (Fall 1999): 252–59.

[10] Brinkmann's comments about the large form can be found in *Drei Klavierstücke Op. 11*, p. 97, and Cinnamon provides a form chart in "Tonal Elements," p. 143. Cinnamon's chart diverges from both Brinkmann's and my accounts of the large form: he places large B at m. 40 rather than m. 29, probably because he understands the beginning of m. 39 as a large tonic cadence, and because of the dotted quarter of rest within m. 39. But I side with Brinkmann in his claim that the cessation of the triplet ostinato in m. 29 is form-defining.

[11] Brinkmann, *Drei Klavierstücke Op. 11*, p. 98.

Example 2.1  Form chart for Schoenberg, Piano Piece Op. 11, No. 2

## A  mm. 1–28

**a**

mm. 1–4a
presents a material; motives *d1* and *d2*, D–F ostinato, set class 3-3 (014)

mm. 13b–15
repeats a material with displacement between hands

mm. 16–19
combines b with a material and motives from Op. 11/1; in RH of m. 16, *d1* is followed by melodic versions of subsets of b chords; in m. 18, the pcs of motive *a1* from Op. 11/1 appear, next to 3 pcs from b chord 1

**b**

Stage I, mm. 4b–5a
presents b material; motives *e* and *f*; three b chords: b chord 1, {4, 6, 9, 10}; b chord 2, {2, 3, 7, 9}; b chord 3, {0, 1, 3, 8, 9}

Stage II, mm. 5b–9a
combines b with a material; b chords 3, 1, 2, 3 in RH leading to motive *d* at phrase's end; in LH, D–F ostinato, 3-3, motive from Op. 11/1

Stage III, mm. 9b–13a (Chorale)
mostly b material; b chords 1 and 2 sequenced up a fourth (with expansion), leading to a passage that seems diffuse harmonically and unrelated to prior music, but connects to it through "strong isograph."

**c**

Stage II, mm. 20–24
combines a material with Op. 11/1 material; ostinato returns on B♭–G♭ in RH; LH alters motive *d1* so that it produces <A, F, E>, motive *a2* from mm. 2–3 of Op. 11/1

Stage III, mm. 25–28
combines b with a material; m. 25 "inverts" b chords 1 and 2 for RH and adopts b chord 3 for LH; 26-28 combines the b chords in RH with C♯–F♯ ostinato in LH

## B  mm. 29–54

Stage I, mm. 29–32
combines a and b material; introduces motive *g*, a horizontal version of b chord 2's set class (4-16) with three common pcs. Its contour resembles *d1*

Stage II, mm. 33–37
begins with motive *g*, moves on in mm. 34–37 to project pitch classes of b chord 1 in a context that highlights motives *g* and *d*

Stage III (climax), mm. 38–49
combines a and b material with motive *g*, from Op. 11/1; begins with motive *g*, in m. 39 presents the set class of motive *d2*, 3–8, as <4, –2, –2>, *a3* from Opus 11/1. In m. 43 begins a climactic passage based solely on b chords, first b chord 3, then b chords 1 and 2. <4, –2> returns as "cadence" in mm. 48–49

Stage IV, mm. 50–54
combines a and b material with motive from Op. 11/1; begins with motive *g*, continues its LH chords under a RH that includes <–1, –3> from C. p. 11/1 and the RH of mm. 45–49's "cadential" chord

## A´  mm. 55–66

Stage I, mm. 55–58
repeats and extends motivic and chordal material of subsection a

Stage II (synthesis), mm. 59–61a
combines material from a, b, c, as well as Op. 11/1; RH presents motive *a1* from Op. 11/1, variations of motive *d1*, and a horizontal version of b chord 1, <4, 10, 9, 6>, overlapped together, highlighting their similarities

Stage III, mm. 61b–66
juxtaposes material from a, b, and B, as well as Op. 11/1, in a "montage"; begins with b chord 3 and ends with b chords 1, 2 and 3

As my more detailed analysis on the following pages will show, the function of large section A is to first contrast the material of subsection a with the material of subsection b, then demonstrate in continually changing ways how these contrasting materials relate to each other, and also to the motives and chords of Op. 11, No. 1 that are the ultimate source for the second piece's motives and chords. It goes through the process twice, revealing a few connections between a and b in mm. 5–9, and more connections between a, b, and motives of the first Piano Piece in mm. 16–28.

The large B section initially seems like completely new music (Brinkmann points out its main distinguishing quality, the cessation of the constant eighth-note ostinato),[12] but its motto, which we will call motive *g1*, is actually a subtle blending of the motivic contour of the a subsection with the pitch-class and set-class content of the b subsection. As the large B section progresses, Schoenberg continues to find new ways to combine material from subsections a and b, and to show that the roots of both subsections can be found in Op. 11, No. 1. In the midst of the section, we hear a climactic passage (the end of my Stage III, mm. 43–47), where he abandons synthesis momentarily, to focus on sequencing the components of the b subsection (three chords, which we will call b chords 1, 2, and 3). This passage could be understood as the place where the piece's conflicts are brought to a peak.

In section A′, then, the main function is to provide a convincing, all-embracing synthesis between subsections a and b and the Op. 11, No. 1 motives that underlie them. Schoenberg does this throughout most of the section, but the highlight is mm. 59–61a, my stage II, where the soprano voice presents two motives in succession: motive *a1*, the opening motive from Op. 11, No. 1, at its original pitch level (<B4, G♯4, G4>), and a slightly ornamented horizontal rendition of b chord 2 (<E5, A♯4, A5, F♯4>) directly after it. These mottos of the second piece's b subsection and the first piece's opening are linked by three variations of the opening motive from subsection a of the second piece. After this high point, motives from all parts of the form appear in a new ordering to close the piece.

Thus, Op. 11, No. 2, like its predecessor, demonstrates the conflict and resolution that defines Schoenberg's "musical idea" at two levels: within sections such as the two halves of the large A section, a b and a c, but also over the span of the whole piece, with mm. 43–47's climax consisting of b chord materials presented by themselves, followed eventually by mm. 59–61's synthesis of the second b chord with materials from subsection a and the first piece. But, it must be reiterated that the second piece projects conflict and resolution in a different way from Op. 11, No. 1, in that the

---

[12] Ibid., p. 97.

motivic elements that conflict and are brought together are more fragmentary. Op. 11, No. 2 no longer includes an eleven-measure theme that returns,
transformed, but complete, at the end of the piece, as its predecessor had.
Instead, we will be considering motivic materials that are never longer than
three measures, and most often constitute only part of a measure. The second
piece's fragmentation of its basic elements from themes to motives then
accelerates in Op. 11, No. 3, where the motives themselves become even
more fragmentary (but, *pace* Haimo, do not disappear completely).

## A Section: Subsections A and B

I will now present more detailed analyses of certain sections of Op. 11,
No. 2, with illustrations. Examples 2.2a, b, and c illustrate the two conflicting phrases at the opening – what I call subsection a, mm. 1–4a, and the
first stage of subsection b, mm. 4b–5a.

As Example 2.2a shows, subsection a opens with an alternation between
D2 and F2 in the left hand, doubled an octave lower by F1. The resulting
pitch-interval succession <–3, +3, –3, +3, etc.> recalls the soprano voice
in mm. 4–8 of Op. 11, No. 1, what we had labeled in Chapter 1 as "*reduced a.*"
(The large curved arrow connecting the two motives in the example indicates the ultimate source of the second piece's ostinato in the first piece.)
When the right hand enters, its first pitch is D♭3, forming with the left hand
a member of set class 3-3 (014): {1, 2, 5} in normal form. This set class, of
course, originated with the opening motive of Op. 11, No. 1, motive *a1*; and
as the quotation from the right hand of mm. 1–3 of the first piece in
Example 2.2a shows, m. 3 of that piece produces a second version of 3-3,
{1, **4,** 5}, that is similar in pitch-class content to the opening trichord of Op.
11, No. 2. Thus, the opening gestures of the second piece recall first the
middle section, then the opening, of the first piece's three-part A section.

As the right-hand part in Op. 11, No. 2 unfolds, however, it begins to
produce interval successions unfamiliar to the first piece. My analysis
follows Schoenberg's phrase markings to break off the first trichord as
motive *d1*: <+8, –6>. The second phrase, five notes in length, can be heard
as overlapping two trichords, motive *d2* <–6, –2> and motive *d3* <+3, –2>.
I assigned motives *d1* and *d2* the same letter because they project two
interval successions within the same set class, 3-8 (026), thus we can grasp
*d2* as a variation of *d1*. As for motive d3, it forms a new set class, 3-2 (013),
but its interval succession contracts both intervals of *d1*, from +8 to +3
and –6 to –2, preserving *d1*'s overall contour.

Since motives *d1* and *d2* both project set class 3-8, there is a subtle way in
which the unfamiliarity of their intervals with respect to piece No. 1 is

Example 2.2a Schoenberg, Piano Piece Op. 11, No. 2, mm. 1–4 (theme a). Copyright © 1910, 1938 by Universal Edition AG Vienna, UE 2991. All rights reserved. Used by permission of Belmont Music Publishers and Universal Edition

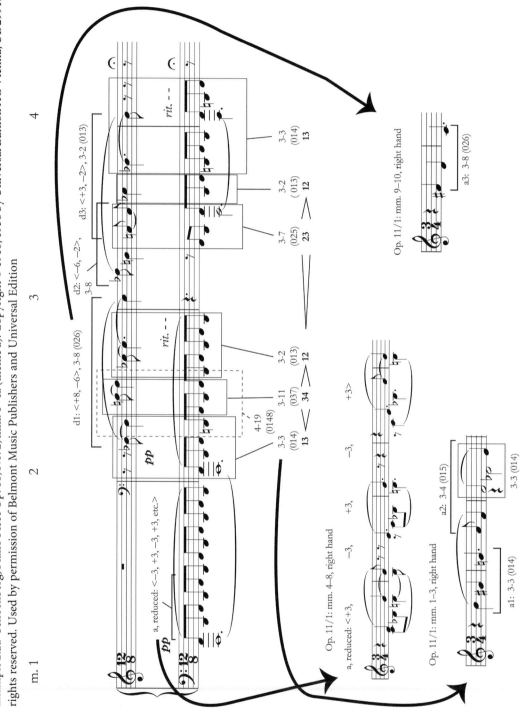

Example 2.2b  Schoenberg, Piano Piece Op. 11, No. 2, mm. 4b–5a (theme b; b subsection, stage I). Used by permission of Belmont Music Publishers and Universal Edition

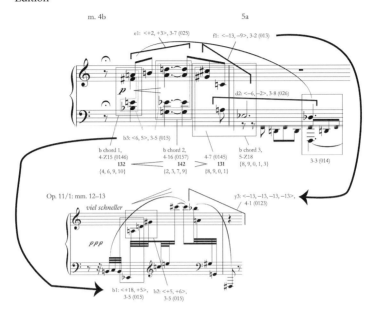

mitigated. SC 3-8 was the set class associated with motive *a3* in mm. 9–10 of the first piece, <–4, –2>. Because of this, theme a in piece No. 2 can be understood as projecting Op. 11, No. 1's opening interval expansion from <–3, –1> (3-3) to <–4, –2> (3-8) in a different way, generalizing it to set classes, which are then represented by new interval successions. It also changes the opening expansion of piece No. 1 to a small arch form in piece No. 2, since set class 3-3 as a chord at the beginning of m. 2 expands out to set class 3-8 in the right hand's motives in mm. 2–3, and then collapses back in to the 3-3 chord, at the same pitches {D♭3, D2, F2}, as the a subsection's second phrase comes to a close in m. 4. The supporting chords in mm. 2–4 duplicate this little arch on the level of adjacent chords: in m. 2, the progression goes 3-3, 3-11 (037), 3-2, with adjacent ordered pitch class intervals **1, 3**, expanding to **3, 4**, then contracting back to **1, 2**. (The first two chords combine to form set class 4-19, enclosed with a dotted line, that certainly lies beneath the surface in mm. 2–3, but will become much more prominent in the b subsection.)

This ingenious rewrite of parts of Op. 11, No. 1's opening to form the opening of piece No. 2 then gives way to a fermata in the middle of m. 4. After the fermata comes music that is marked as a contrast to what came before, in a number of ways – the texture is more vertical after the counterpoint of the opening, the dynamic ratchets up one level from *pp* to *p*, and Schoenberg abandons the low register momentarily for the sake of the closely spaced chords. Motivically and harmonically, the music of m. 4 also seems to introduce something new: consult Example 2.2b for a detailed analysis of subsection b's first stage. We hear two more trichord motives, *e1* and *f1*: the former consists of the pitch intervals <+2, +3>, which, although they resemble somewhat the variations of motive *a* in Op. 11, No. 1, were never actually given in that form in the opening measures of the first piece. Motive *f1*, <–13, –9>, calls to mind a similar motive in the contrasting B section of the first piece, the variation of *y*, <–13, –13, –13, –13>, which I called *y3* in Example 1.8.

The three chords underlying motives *e1* and *f1* are pervasive throughout Op. 11, No. 2 as pitch-class sets *and* as set classes, and as such they merit their own labels: I will call them b chords 1, 2, and 3. The first two belong to set classes that were not really salient in the first piece. Pitch classes {4, 6, 9, 10} in b chord 1 form set class 4-Z15 (0146) and pitch classes {2, 3, 7, 9} in b chord 2 form set class 4-16 (0157). As the consecutive Forte numbers suggest, the second b chord can be heard as an expansion of the adjacent ordered pitch class intervals of the first, **1, 3, 2** to **1, 4, 2**; and in this particular instance the expansion is portrayed strongly by the outward wedge contour between right and left hands. B chord 3, in contrast to the first two, does not appear vertically, but could be thought of as an arpeggiated chord. Its first four pitch classes, {8, 9, 0, 1}, form set class 4-7 (0145), which was more common in piece No. 1 (one prominent occurrence there was the third beat of m. 49, {3, 4, 7, 8}). The 4-7's adjacent ordered pitch-class intervals can be thought of as a contraction of those of 4-16: **1, 4, 2** to **1, 3, 1**, so that the b chords create another arch in the set-class realm (and the downward plunge of b chord 3's soprano strongly portrays the completion of the arch). When we add E♭, pitch class 3, the pitch-class set of the full b chord 3 extends itself to {8, 9, 0, 1, 3}, which belongs to set class 5-Z18 (01457), one of the two principal sets of Cinnamon's analysis.

The reader may wonder why it is I am emphasizing unordered pitch-class sets in the case of these three b chords, when most of the previous references to "chords" in this book have dealt with set classes. We will see later on in the analysis that Schoenberg uses specifically the *pitch-class* content (not just the interval content) of these chords to create syntheses of a and b material, solutions to the problem posed by the juxtaposition of themes a and b; most often by clothing the pitch classes of b chords in contours and rhythms that evoke the motives of subsection a, and placing them in close contact with motives of that subsection.

It is not just the use of a fermata and textural, dynamic, and rhythmic changes that set the music of mm. 4b–5a off as something completely different from the previous music. As the lower half of Example 2.2b shows, the b chords also echo prominent motives of the contrasting B section in Op. 11, No. 1,

Example 2.2c  From Lewin's Example 2, showing the connection back from sub-section b to subsection a of Op. 11, No. 2, through b chords 1 and 2

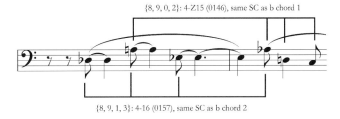

{8, 9, 0, 2}: 4-Z15 (0146), same SC as b chord 1

{8, 9, 1, 3}: 4-16 (0157), same SC as b chord 2

which means they can be heard as evoking the first piece's contrasting material in the same way that the first four measures of piece 2 evoked the first eleven measures of piece 1. Both b chords 1 and 2 contain a prominent three-note subset that consists of the unordered pitch intervals <6, 5>: the soprano, tenor, and bass of the first b chord create a Viennese Trichord with the tritone below the perfect fourth, as do the top three notes of the second b chord. The curved arrow extending down from these subsets in Example 2.2b shows their ante-cedents in the upward arpeggio of m. 12 of Op. 11, No. 1: the two motives that we had called *b1* and *b2* in Chapter 1. And I already observed that the falling part of the arch in mm. 4–5, motive *f1*, in the second piece resembles motive *y3* in mm. 12–13 of the first piece, another precipitous descent. Indeed, the main contour of the initial contrasting material in Op. 11, No. 1 was a large arch, and the contrasting material in Op. 11, No. 2 creates a smaller arch, bringing back several of the interval patterns of its predecessor.[13]

Even though the first stage of subsection b creates a marked contrast to subsection a, there is a subtle way in which the subsections connect to each other through their set classes, which will lead to more obvious syntheses as Op. 11, No. 2 progresses. David Lewin pointed out the connections between the melody of subsection a and the first two b chords that are illustrated in my Example 2.2c (which is adapted from his Example 2a in "A Tutorial on Klumpenhouwer Networks, Using the Chorale in Schoenberg's Op. 11, No. 2").[14] The first four notes of the melody of

---

[13] Joshua Banks Mailman's analysis of Op. 11, No. 2 in *Music Theory Spectrum* singles out the arch of mm. 4–5, showing that it is adumbrated by what I call motive d1 in m. 2, and that the whole arch or fragments of it repeat throughout the first nineteen measures. He gives special attention to the chords that are formed at the registral "peak" of the arches or fragments, showing that they create an intervallic conflict that resolves, "in a sense." See Mailman, "Schoenberg's Chordal Experimentalism Revealed through Representational Hierarchy Association (RHA), Contour Motives, and Binary-State Switching," *Music Theory Spectrum* 37/2 (Fall 2015): 234–43.

[14] *Journal of Music Theory* 38/1 (Spring 1994): 81.

Example 2.3  Schoenberg, Piano Piece Op. 11, No. 2, mm. 5b–9a (b subsection, stage II). Used by permission of Belmont Music Publishers and Universal Edition

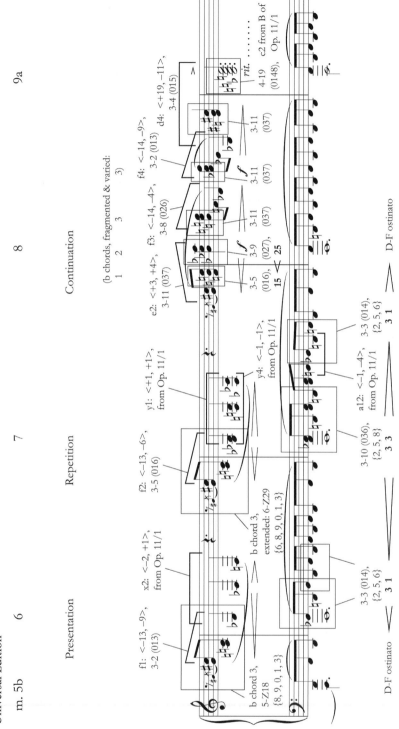

a produce the set class of b chord 2, 4-16; while the top two notes taken together with the last two notes yield the set class of b chord 1, 4-Z15.

The b subsection's connection with theme a is made even more tangible at the close of theme b by the reappearance of motive *d2*, <–6, –2>, after the pickup to m. 5 (refer back to Example 2.2b). The motive is transposed a half-step above its original appearance in m. 3, so that it ends on D♭3, combining with the reappearance of the D2-F2 ostinato to form the pitches that began the a theme.

Stage II of the b subsection continues the work of drawing connections between themes a and b that was already started at the end of Stage I. It is illustrated in Example 2.3. In Stage II, Schoenberg returns to the method of bringing contrasting materials together that he had employed in mm. 50–54 of the first movement – the contrasting elements are juxtaposed against one another in the two hands of the piano. The left hand recaptures and makes small changes to the ostinato from theme a, as the right hand repeats and develops the three b chords, adding to them material that first recalls Op. 11, No. 1's opening, and then the first piece's contrasting B section.

The right hand's development of b material begins with two reiterations of the arpeggiated b chord 3, mostly unchanged, but with appendages. These appendages, the first three quarter notes in both mm. 6 and 7, begin the process of synthesis by recalling motives from Op. 11, No. 1: m. 6 yields an *x2* motive, which had been featured in the alto voice in mm. 4–8 of the first piece, and m. 7 presents *y* motives in contrary motion, *y1* <+1, +1> and *y4* <–1, –1>. The *y1* motive had been prominent in the tenor in mm. 4–8 of the first piece. As the right hand progresses into mm. 7b and 8, the focus shifts back onto development of b material through fragmentation, so that mm. 7b–9a could perhaps be heard as a "continuation" to mm. 5b–6a's "presentation" and mm. 6b–7a's "repetition," creating a sentence structure. We hear first an expanded version of motive *e1: e2*, <+3, +4>, which forms an enharmonic minor triad, set class 3-11. Then the fragmentation begins, through repeating and expanding the intervals of motive *f1*. Motive *f3* expands the first interval by half-step from the previous *f* motives, <–14, –4>, and *f4* follows with an expansion of the second interval of *f3*, <–14, –9>. At the end, however, the continuation culminates (with a wedge accent and a decrease in tempo) in a radically expanded version of motive *d, d4*: <+19, –11>. The final note of the d chord on the downbeat of m. 9, interestingly, is harmonized with a familiar tetrachord, unordered pitch intervals <4, 4, 3> from the bottom up. This is the *c2* piano harmonic motive from mm. 14–17 of Op. 11, No. 1, which had been one of the more "foreign" sounding elements in that piece. Thus, the development of b material in mm. 5–9 of Op. 11, No. 2 incorporates recognizable motivic material from both the opening and the contrasting sections of the first piece, as it simultaneously turns back toward the opening motive of its own a subsection at the end.

The left hand's motivic content in these measures shows a similar tendency to turn back toward material reminiscent of Op. 11, No. 1. In the middle of m. 7, the eighth-note line briefly descends through a chromatic scale before dropping to D again to restart the ostinato. This results in a <–1, –4> succession, motive *a12*, recalling motive *a2* (<–4, –1>) from the first piece as its retrograde inversion. Meanwhile, the chords (set classes) formed by the ostinato, as well as those in the right hand, create patterns that resemble the arch forms and expansions of the previous measures of Op. 11, No. 2. Set class 3-3, {2, 5, 6}, formed by the addition of G♭ to the ostinato in m. 6, leads on the downbeat of m. 7 to 3-10 (036) as {2, 5, 8}. In both the set class and the pitch-class set realms, this yields an adjacent interval expansion: **3, 1** to **3, 3** between intervals of the pc sets, **1, 3** to **3, 3** between those of the set classes. As the third beat of m. 7 closes back into {2, 5, 6} and set class 3-3 in the left hand, the arch descends, followed by a further contraction to the D-F in mm. 8 and 9, which had also been the starting point of the passage in m. 5b.

The third stage of the b subsection, mm. 9b–13a, is shown in Example 2.4. These measures constitute the "chorale" Lewin referred to in his analysis (mentioned previously on pp. 51–53); they also can be understood as a second sentence structure, with a short phrase that is first sequenced and then extended into a longer third phrase. The first two phrases of Stage III can clearly be understood as developing b chords 1 and 2, but the third phrase consists of a number of chords and melodic motives that seem unrelated to prior material. I will use portions of Lewin's analysis to show how the continuation, despite its apparent strangeness, actually does perform a synthesis: it connects the foreign 4-19 chord of m. 9a's downbeat to b chords 1 and 2 in subtle, yet audible ways.

Measures 9b–11a present a return of the first two chords of the b theme at their original pitch, followed by a repetition that expands them both motivically and harmonically. The motivic expansion changes *e1*, <+2, +3>, into *e3*: <+2, +4>. Motive *e3* is a member of set class 3-8, the same class that had contained motives *d1* and *d2* in the a subsection of Op. 11, No. 2. Not only that, but it projects 3-8 with intervals that recall the *a* motives of Op. 11, No. 1: <+2, +4> is the retrograde of <–4, –2>, the *a3* motive that culminated the gradual interval expansion in mm. 9–10 of the first piece. Thus, the interval expansion beginning Example 2.4 connects the motivic material of the second piece's b theme back to the same piece's

Example 2.4 Schoenberg, Piano Piece Op. 11, No. 2, mm. 9–13a (b subsection, stage III). Used by permission of Belmont Music Publishers and Universal Edition

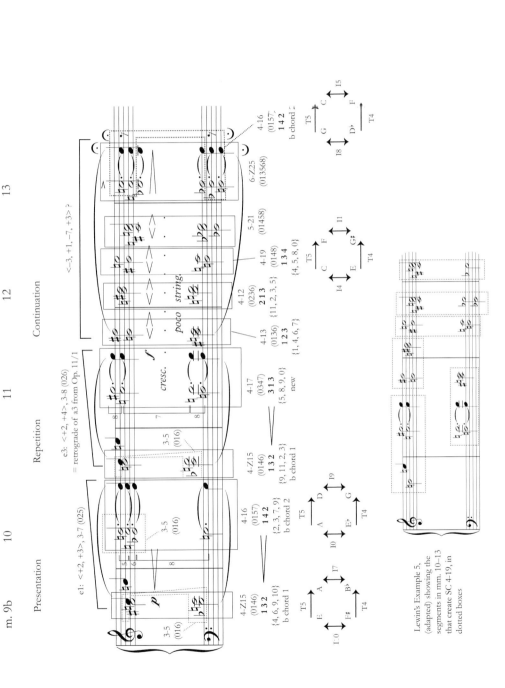

Lewin's Example 5, (adapted) showing the segments in mm. 10–13 that create SC 4-19, in dotted boxes

a subsection, and also connects both sections to the opening motivic progression of the first piece.

As for the chord progressions in mm. 9b–11a, the presentation is a literal repeat of the first two b chords, 4-Z15 with adjacent ordered pitch-class intervals **1, 3, 2** expanding out to 4-16 with ordered pitch-class intervals **1, 4, 2**. Like the original version in mm. 4b–5a, the abstract ordered pc interval expansion is made more concrete here through outward contrary motion in the two hands of the piano. In this context, the repetition in mm. 10b–11a should be understood as an expansion one step further, from 4-Z15 (transposed up a perfect fourth) to 4-17. The ordered pitch-class interval successions of these chords, **1, 3, 2** and **3, 1, 3**, do not consistently expand each corresponding interval: the middle interval contracts. But there is enough evidence to read this pair of chords as expanding out further: the bass line descends a tritone instead of a minor third, the soprano yields the expansion from <+2, +3> to <+2, +4> remarked on above, and the unordered pitch intervals between the elements of the second chord of the repetition fan out to 8, 7, 8, a symmetrical shape, as opposed to the more condensed 8, 6, 5 of the presentation's second chord.

In this context, the music that follows, mm. 11b–13a, seems anomalous. We have an interval succession on top, <–3, +1, –7, +3>, which does not have any obvious connection to the motives earlier in the second piece or the first piece. And the succession of chords presents many elements that are new, such as set classes 4-13 (0136) and 4-12 (0236), before settling back on 4-19 (0148), the same set class as the foreign chord on the downbeat of m. 9. 4-19 is followed by its superset 5-21 (01458) on the third half note of m. 12, leading to 6-Z25 (013568) in m. 13. What to make of this chord succession?

David Lewin in his "Tutorial on Klumpenhouwer Networks, Using the Chorale in Schoenberg's Opus 11, No. 2" reads the repetition and continuation as projecting not one member of set class 4-19, but *six*. An adaptation of his Example 5 from that article can be found at the bottom of my Example 2.4.[15] Since Lewin reads the last part of the chorale as a developing variation of m. 9's contrasting chord (which, in turn, had evoked the piano harmonic chord from Op. 11, No. 1), the question arises: how is all this contrasting material pulled back into a relationship with the rest of the second piece? Lewin poses it this way: "Agenda 1: To formulate an overall view of the chorale, we must somehow relate the 4-19 sets of its middle to the 4 -16s and 4-Z15s of its opening."[16]

---

[15] Lewin, "A Tutorial on Klumpenhouwer Networks," 83.      [16] Ibid., 86.

His way of relating the contrasting <4, 4, 3> from m. 9 and other members of its set class back to b chords 1 and 2 is through using the Klumpenhouwer networks referenced in his article's title. The middle level of my Example 2.4 provides four of them; the network for 4-19 on the second half note of m. 12, those for b chords 1 and 2 in mm. 9b–10a, and the one for the top two and bottom two notes of the chorale's final six-note chord in m. 13a (which is a member of set class 4-16, like b chord 2). All four of these tetrachords may be arranged in a square format where the top row of pitch classes is connected by a forward-pointing T5 relation, the bottom row of pitch classes by a forward-pointing T4 relation, and the two columns of the square are related by two inversions, the first of which is three units larger than the second (for example, $I_{10}$ and $I_7$, or $I_4$ and $I_1$). Because of these identities and similarities, all four of these tetrachords are "positively isographic" to one another, and Lewin's analysis demonstrates that four of the other five instantiations of 4-19 shown in his Example 5 can also be arranged as positively isographic Klumpenhouwer networks to these and to each other.[17] This provides a way to relate the 4-19 sets of the chorale to b chords 1 and 2, and through them the <4, 4, 3> collection on the downbeat of m. 9 and its predecessor in the piano harmonic of Op. 11, No. 1 can also be connected with the first two b chords.[18]

The reader could certainly respond to my (and Lewin's) connecting 4-19 back to the first two b chords through Klumpenhouwer networks with skepticism about the audibility of these connections. Since these networks are arranged visually for the express purpose of highlighting isographies (rather than on the basis of register, instrumentation, or some other audible feature), one could wonder to what extent we actually hear these isographies. But in this particular instance, the way Schoenberg voices three of the four chords in question, particularly his representation of the T5 and T4 relationships within each chord, does indeed provide an audible link between 4-Z15, 4-16, and 4-19. The first two b chords each contain a prominent perfect fourth (T5) and minor sixth (T4). In b chord 1, the fourth E4-A4 and the sixth Bb3-F♯4 (spelled enharmonically) overlap one another, but as Schoenberg expands the voices out to b chord 2, the two

---

[17] Ibid., 86–88.

[18] Mailman's analysis of Op. 11, No. 2 in "Schoenberg's Chordal Experimentalism" takes up Lewin's positively isographic Klumpenhouwer networks that manifest as squares with T5 on top, T4 on the bottom, and an I on the left side that is three units higher than the one on the right (like those shown in my Example 2.4), and demonstrates that they can account for many (but not all) of the sonorities in the b theme, mm. 4b–5a – not only b chords 1 and 2. Thus the 4-19 chords of the chorale are more closely tied to the preceding b theme than even Lewin recognized. See Mailman, 244.

components stack on top of one another vertically, the sixth G3-E♭4 below, the fourth A4-D5 above. In the 4-19 chord on the second half note of m. 12, then, two similar or identical intervals are found one above the other: the fourth is now inverted to a perfect fifth F3-C4 in the left hand, and the minor sixth occurs above it as G♯4-E5 in the right. In other words, the same intervals return and make audible connections from the contrasting 4-19 chord to b chords 1 and 2, enabling the chorale to serve its synthesizing function.

To provide a quick review of subsections a and b: they first present a and b themes separately to highlight the contrast between them, then juxtapose the two kinds of music (b motives and chords in the right hand, a ostinati in the left), then begin to suggest ways that b material can be derived not only from a material, but from the motives and chords of Op. 11, No. 1. In m. 9, a contrasting element from the first piece makes its return, <4, 4, 3>, but then the following measures (the chorale) begin to explain its relationship to the opening chords of b.

## A Section: Subsections A and C

The work of connecting the b theme to the a theme and also to motives and chords of Op. 11, No. 1 has begun, but there is much more to do in the remaining parts of the piece. Example 2.5 illustrates the beginning and end of the c subsection's first stage, mm. 16–19, which arrives after a brief return of the a theme in mm. 13b–15.

Mm. 16 and 18–19 have similar functions, but the latter passage continues the motivic and chordal processes of the former and takes them several steps further. The first passage returns to the strategy of juxtaposing a theme and b theme materials vertically that we saw in mm. 5b–9a, but now the melody of a (rather than the ostinato) appears in the right hand and a 3-5 (016) arpeggio with the pitch intervals <+7, +6> sounds twice in the left. (The first two notes of the first 3-5 arpeggio form set class 4-19 with the first two notes of the a melody, so that the foreign element from subsection b also appears, generated by a and b themes together.)

More specifically, the pitch class and ordered pitch-interval successions of motive *d1* return in the soprano voice of m. 16, <1, 9, 3> and <+8, −6>: the only differences from m. 2's right hand are the higher register and rhythm. Motive *d1* in m. 16, like its predecessor in m. 2, gives way to a descending step and leap – rather than the <−6, −2> of m. 3, however, we now have a contracted version that switches the order of the step and leap, <−1, −5>. This creates the same set class as the left-hand arpeggio, 3-5, another link with the left hand. Overlapping with this soprano descent, we

Example 2.5  Schoenberg, Piano Piece Op. 11, No. 2, mm. 16 and 18–19
(c subsection, stage I, beginning and end). Used by permission of Belmont Music
Publishers and Universal Edition

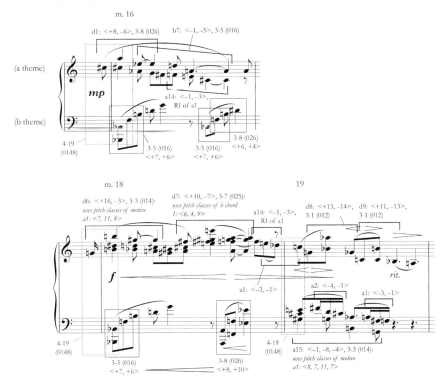

find <–1, –3> in the alto voice, the retrograde inversion of Op. 11, No. 1's
opening motto. As in subsection b, a combination of a and b motives from
the second piece gives way to a motive that recalls the first piece. And, since
the <–1, –3> in the alto is proximate to the <–1, –5> that preceded it in the
soprano, we can argue that the foreign element 3-5 is being explained here
as an expansion of a motive related to the first piece's opening motto,
a similar strategy to the presentation of 3-5 as <–6, –1> in the bass line of
the first piece's final cadence (discussed in Chapter 1, p. 34).

   As I suggested earlier, the last two measures of the c subsection's stage
I extend and intensify the process introduced in its first measure. The right
hand of mm. 18 and 19 presents a number of motives that share the
contour of motive *d1*, but expand its intervals to <+16, –3>, <+10, –7>,
<+13, –14>, and <+11, –13>. The first of these is notable for its link to Op.
11, No. 1 that is stronger yet than that of m. 16: it presents <7, 11, 8>, the
pitch classes of the first piece's opening motto (in a rotation of the original
version, <11, 8, 7>). The second motive in the series, *d7*, then introduces

three of the pitch classes of the original b chord 1 in the same contour and approximate rhythm as the first. (This setting together of b chord 1 pitch classes with motive *a1* from Op. 11, No. 1, under the umbrella of motive *d*, adumbrates the final synthesis of the second piece, which will occur at mm. 60–61.) Other, intervallic, reminders of the first piece appear between the second and third *d* motives in the soprano, <–1, –3> and <–3, –1> in the alto linking m. 18 to m. 19, and a reversal of the first step in Op. 11, No. 1's interval expansion – <–4, –1>, motive *a2*, leading to <–3, –1>, motive *a1*, in the tenor voice of m. 19. (This same reversal, motive *a2* progressing to *a1*, had characterized the return of large A in the first piece of Op. 11 at mm. 50–52 in Example 1.9a.)

Meanwhile, the left hand of mm. 18–19 begins exactly where it had in m. 16 and gradually creates its own path toward a reiteration of the pitch classes of the first piece's motto. We hear the 3-5 arpeggio reminiscent of the b theme on the downbeat of m. 18 (whose first note forms 4-19 with the right hand's chord in a similar way to the beginning of m. 16). The next arpeggio, on the third and fourth dotted quarter beats, expands the intervals of the first to create a member of set class 3-8, the set class associated with the *d1* and *d2* motives in the a theme. Then, the bass line in m. 19 projects pitch classes <8, 7, 11, 7> to recapture the pitch classes of the opening motto of Op. 11, No. 1. The overall progression is from a b-theme set class to an a-theme set class of the second piece, and then beyond to the specific pitch-class set that began the first piece – again linking the b theme to its more immediate predecessor and then its more distant one.

Specific pitch-class and ordered pitch-interval references to the first piece continue in the following measures, the second stage of the c subsection. Its first four measures are given in Example 2.6. Already in the ostinato that begins in m. 20, Schoenberg hints at <–1, –3> again, an important component of the preceding stage that had evoked the beginning of Op. 11, No. 1 by providing the retrograde inversion of motive a1, <–3, –1>.

This is followed immediately, however, by an even more obvious reference to the first piece, in the bass voice. After a motive, *d10*: <+16, –4>, that again expands the intervals of motive *d1*, we hear <–4, –1>, motive *a2*, set to its original pitch class succession from mm. 2–3 of Op. 11, No. 1, <9, 5, 4>. This overlaps with the largest expansion of motive *d* we have heard yet, <+24, –4>, giving way in turn to a repetition of motives *d10* and *a2*, <9, 5, 4>, and an even wider expansion of motive *d*, <+31, –3>. In mm. 16–22, the intervallic references to the *a* motives of the first piece (including transposed forms of *a1* and *a2*) lead inexorably to the pitch-class set of motive *a1*, reordered from its original version, and finally to motive *a2* in its original ordering and transposition.

Example 2.6  Schoenberg, Piano Piece Op. 11, No. 2, mm. 20–23a (c subsection, stage II). Used by permission of Belmont Music Publishers and Universal Edition

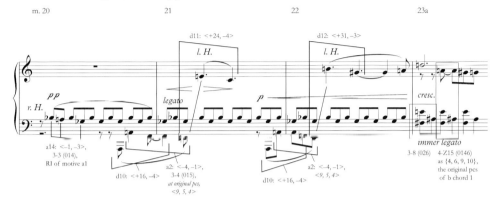

In m. 23, the focus turns away from making connections with Op. 11, No. 1, back toward linking the a and b themes of Op. 11, No. 2. The ostinato first creates set class 3-8 of the a theme from pitch classes 4, 6, and 10, then adds PC 9 in the alto voice to complete the pitch-class content of b chord 1, {4, 6, 9, 10}. The following passage, mm. 25–28, portrayed in Example 2.7, is likewise concerned mainly with developing the three b chords, though a few references to Op. 11, No. 1's motives and chords persist. We begin with m. 25, which consists of two passages that gradually draw closer to retrograding the first two chords of the b theme. The first half of m. 25 progresses from a 4-16 (0157) set class to a 4-18 (0147) set class under a soprano motive that descends rather than ascends: <–1, –5>. This is the same motive that explained set class 3-5 in m. 16 as a close relative of the a motives. The 4-16 that opens the progression is the correct set class for b chord 2, but is arranged differently from the original prototype in its intervals (from the bottom): <6, 5, 5>. Its successor, 4-18 (0147), has not been associated with the b theme before, but does contain 3-5 as <5, 6> in its top three notes, a Viennese Trichord that is similar to the important subset of both b chords 1 and 2 in m. 4. A descending arpeggio follows in the left hand, which forms set class 4-9 (0167) and resembles b chord 3 in its initial and second intervals as well as its rhythm and precipitous descent. (The initial interval +5 here horizontalizes what had been a harmonic interval with grace note in the original b chord 3, and the second interval –11 is similar to the original –13.)

The second half of m. 25 comes a bit closer to retrograding the original b theme beginning. Now 4-16 (again as <6, 5, 5>) progresses to 4-Z15 with b chord 1's original pitch classes in a different voicing: {4, 6, 9, 10} with PC 6

Example 2.7 Schoenberg, Piano Piece Op. 11, No. 2, mm. 25–28 (c subsection, stage III). Used by permission of Belmont Music Publishers and Universal Edition

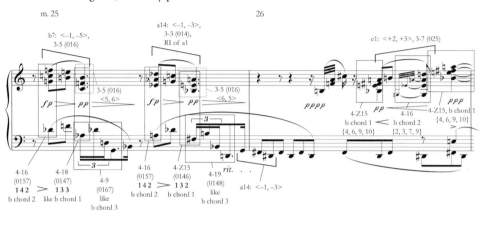

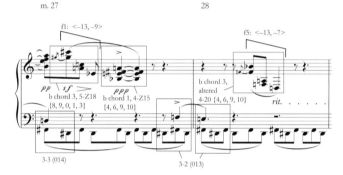

in the bass rather than 10. The soprano motive that connects these two chords continues Schoenberg's explanation of how 3-5 relates to the *a* motives of Op. 11, No. 1, because it follows <–1, –5> with <–1, –3>. And a version of b chord 3 overlaps this chord with intervals <+5, –13, –8>: the middle interval as well as the first conforms to the original b chord 3 succession.

The right hand in the rest of stage III of subsection c then follows these approximations of b-theme elements in m. 25 with more faithful renderings, some in different orderings from the original. B chords 1 and 2 and soprano motive *e1* appear on the third and fourth beats of m. 26, the latter chord arpeggiated upwards. B chord 1 returns an octave higher to end the measure, leading in m. 27 to a repetition of b chord 3 an octave higher and an accented b chord 1 (in the original octave). Finally, we hear an echo of b chord 3 in m. 28, with both the upper voice motive and the set class slightly changed: 4-20 (0158) and <–13, –7>.

While the right hand is focusing on the development of the three b chords, the left hand reintroduces its ostinato in m. 26, which returns Op. 11, No. 2

to the same condition as the music in mm. 5b–9a. The a and b themes again develop separately from one another – b in the right hand, a in the left – so that their relation reverts to one of juxtaposition. After the multiple connections that were drawn in previous measures, the music seems to be taking a step back from synthesizing – perhaps to prepare for the onset of the large B section in m. 29 with its new kinds of syntheses. Still, it is worthwhile to remark on the multiple formations of set classes 3-3 and 3-2 between the bass ostinato and a slower-moving tenor voice, and the <–1, –3> motive that leads into the ostinato over the barline from m. 25 to m. 26.

## B Section

My form chart in Example 2.1 splits the large B section into four subsections, each of which begins with motive *g1*, intervals <+4, +7, –5> realized as <B♭4, D5, A5, E5>, harmonized by a chord progression that expands from 4-18 (0147) to 4-19 (0148) and then contracts back to 4-13 (0136), forming yet another ordered pc interval arch. (The adjacent ordered pitch class intervals involved are **1, 3, 3; 1, 3, 4**; and **1, 2, 3**.) The set class of motive *g1* itself is of interest: it is set class 4-16, which has been associated with b chord 2, but also is formed by the first four notes of the a theme (as shown by Example 2.2c). Not only that, but the specific pitch class collection of motive *g1* contains three members of the original b chord 1: 4, 9, and 10. The last three pitches of motive *g1*, D5, A5, and E5, create an ordered pitch interval sequence that is a half-step smaller than motive *d1*, <+7, –5> rather than <+8, –6>, and at the same time is a subset of b chord 2's 4-16. Finally, the D5 and A5 participate in set class 4-19 with the chord harmonizing them, {D3, F3, C♯4}. Thus the opening of the a theme, the pitch classes of b chord 1, the set class of b chord 2, and the "foreign" set class of m. 9 within subsection b of large A are all brought together by motive *g1* and its accompaniment, and this little motive repeats that synthesis four times at mm. 29, 33, 38, and 51.

I will limit my detailed analysis to two parts of the large B section: the second stage, mm. 33–37, which not only brings together b chords 1 and 2 with motive *d1* but also goes on to reiterate all four pitch classes of b chord 1 in a context that evokes the a theme; and the final measures of the third stage, mm. 43–49, which a number of authors have recognized as the work's climax. Like the measures just preceding the onset of large B, this climax turns its attention away from synthesis to focus more narrowly on the elements of the b theme in new combinations.

Stage II of the large B section is portrayed in Example 2.8. After the motto, motive *g1*, with its expanding and contracting accompaniment

Example 2.8 Schoenberg, Piano Piece Op. 11, No. 2, mm. 33–37 (B section, stage II). Used by permission of Belmont Music Publishers and Universal Edition

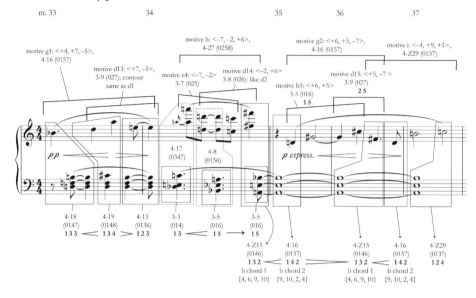

in m. 33, m. 34 introduces a new melodic idea in octaves, motive *h*, which has ties to both motive *e1* from the b theme and motive *d2* from the a theme, thus continuing the synthesis of b and a. The first two intervals of motive *h* are <–7, –2>, forming set class 3-7 (025), the set class of motive *e1*, and the first two pitch classes of *h*, 9 and 2, remind the listener of *e1*'s pitch-class succession, <9, 11, 2>. The last two intervals of *h*, <–2, +6>, recall the pitch intervals of the second motive of theme a, <–6, –2>, and share the earlier motive's set class, 3-8 (026). Meanwhile, the chord progression beneath motive *h* constitutes one of the many ordered pitch-class interval expansions of Op. 11: a move from 3-3 (014) to two versions of 3-5 (016). The ordered pc intervals between the prime forms of the first two chords, as we have discussed before (and will discuss again) are **1, 3** and **1, 5**. And the voicing of the two 3-5s themselves reinforces the general expanding contour: unordered pitch intervals (from the bottom) <5, 6> open out to <7, 6> (We will encounter almost exactly the same voice leading and vertical intervals in the middle line of mm. 2–3 of Op. 11, No. 3, one of the numerous motivic links between second and third pieces).

What follows in mm. 35–37 is a simplified texture we have not heard before in Op. 11, No. 2: a held chord in the left hand against a single-line melody in the right. This simplification calls our attention to the pitch classes of the held chord: they are 4, 9, and 10. They remind us quite strongly of the b theme: not only because of their set class (3-5) and their pitch intervals from the bottom (<7, 6>, similar to the Viennese Trichord), but mainly because they comprise a pitch-class subset of b chord 1: {4, 6, 9, 10}. As the melody in mm. 33–37 ranges through its pitch-class collection, at two points it reaches F♯, pitch class 6 (the last beat of m. 34 and third beat of m. 36): this brings back all four pcs of b chord 1. In two other places, the melody touches on D2: with 4, 9, and 10 this forms set class 4-16, representing b chord 2 (but not at the original pc level).

I mentioned above that the pitch classes of b chord 1 are recaptured here "in a context that evokes the a theme," and part of that has to do with the texture: the single-line melody with held chord in mm. 35–37 is not much different from a single line with left-hand ostinato and held note in the bass. But certain qualities of the pitch classes and intervals in the right hand also recall theme a. The set class of the first tetrachord, motive *g2*, forms set class 4-16, just like the first four pitch classes of theme a (and the four pcs of motive *g1* a few measures earlier). And the last two intervals of motive *g2*, <+5, −7>, recreate the up-down contour of motive *d1*. After the first tetra-chord, however, the right hand seems to take a different direction, with the intervals <−4, +9, +1> in motive *i*. This forms set class 4-Z29 (0137), which we have not encountered yet in Op. 11, No. 2; and the C5 that ends motive *i* forms another version of the same set class with the held chord beneath. Even though the second stage of Section B, in similar ways to the stages preceding and following it, comes up with a number of creative ways to bring b theme materials, and especially the specific pitch classes of b chord 1, into relation with the a theme, stage II ends by introducing more foreign material.

The third stage of B, after a few introductory measures, then produces the work's climax as well as a brief *denouement*, represented in Examples 2.9a and b. Mm. 43–47 alternate long stretches that develop b theme material exclusively with shorter passages that suggest connections between b and a themes: either by transforming b fragments so that they take on character-istics of a, or by placing b and a fragments with common features in close proximity. The climax first presents b chord 3 at a *forte* dynamic, a half-step down (and octave higher) from the original pitch level in mm. 4–5, followed by a transformation of b chord 3 at the new pitch level into a horizontal succession by arpeggiating its two dyads: <+5, −13, −3, −6>, at a *pp* dynamic. This in turn gives way to a sequence of the same arpeggio twice by half-step in the right hand while the left creates a stretto that ascends by half-step from F♯3, increasing steadily in loudness as it does. At the beginning of m. 44, the stretto begins to liquidate the arpeggio by turning its last two pitches into a vertical dyad, continuing to ascend by steps and half-steps in both hands while maintaining the *crescendo*. As the measure progresses, the liquidation process takes a step further, by cutting the right hand down to the first two

Example 2.9a  Schoenberg, Piano Piece Op. 11, No. 2, mm. 42b–47 (B section, stage III, climax). Used by permission of Belmont Music Publishers and Universal Edition

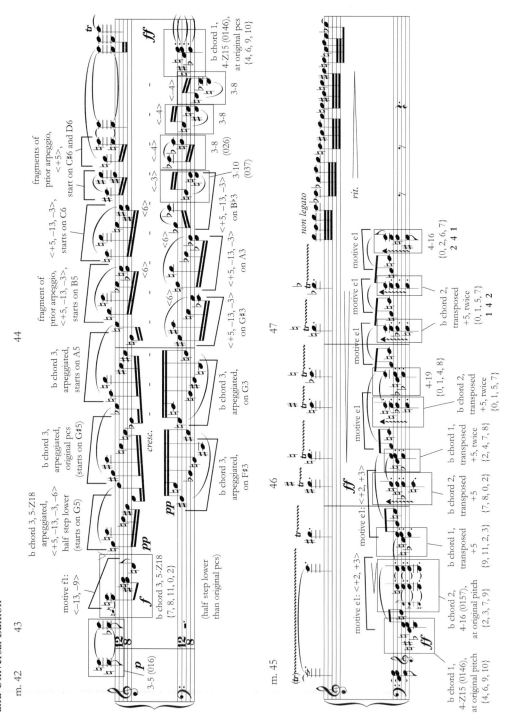

sixteenths of the pattern and the left hand to the last two sixteenths, while both continue to ascend by half-step (in pitch or pitch-class space) and *crescendo*. With this final step in the liquidation of b chord 3, however, an interesting change occurs in the left hand – an interval expansion that changes the ordered pitch interval −3 that had led into the vertical tritone into −4. This changes what had been set class 3-10 into 3-8, the principal trichord of theme a's right hand.

But this brief connection with the a theme is abandoned for the *ff* chord on the last dotted quarter beat of m. 44: the left hand brings back b chord 1, an octave beneath its original appearance at m. 4. This leads directly in m. 45 to b chords 1 and 2 in the original octave (and rhythm) in the left hand, and then a sequence of these two chords, to balance the sequences of arpeggiated b chord 3 that had dominated the texture in mm. 43–44. B chords 1 and 2 as a pair first move up one perfect 4th under the sustained F♯6 in mm. 45b–46a, and then up another perfect 4th under the descending chromatic line F6-E6. Then, a small adjustment gives rise to a new set class. The passage had been alternating 4-Z15 and 4-16 in accordance with the b chord 1 and 2 sequences, but on the last dotted quarter of m. 46, Schoenberg sustains the C6 in the top voice, bringing in a repetition of most of the sequenced b chord 1 <A♭4, D♭5, E5> underneath it. (The original chord had had D♮5 rather than D♭5.) Pitch classes {0, 1, 4, 8} result, giving rise to set class 4-19 (0148), and in this way the foreign chord of m. 9 is explained as a suspension over one of the b chords. This gives way in m. 47 to repetitions of b chord 2 at its highest transposition and a revoicing of that chord.

A *ritardando* and *decrescendo* then brings us down from the work's registral, textural, and dynamic high point, as the top voice continues its chromatic descent. What follows in mm. 48–49 is an interesting passage, illustrated in Example 2.9b. Part of its interest lies in the fact that it repeats earlier music from m. 39, and it will be repeated again near the end of the piece at m. 65. Howard Cinnamon attaches importance to the fact that the beginning chord of the two sixteenth-note groups and their elongated successor contains (from the bottom) F♯, D, F♮, and A. If we understand the piece as prolonging D minor (as he does), this would signify a tonic triad with split third (and the E♭5 could serve as a flat ninth or frozen neighbor note).[19] Cinnamon goes on to interpret these tonics as cadences that close the three large sections of the piece; the principal reason that his overall ABA form has different dimensions than mine.[20]

---

[19]  Cinnamon, "Tonal Elements and Unfolding Nontriadic Harmonies," p. 138.

[20]  Ibid., pp. 140–43. I mentioned above in footnote 10 that Cinnamon places the onset of the large B section in m. 40 rather than m. 29, where I have it: this is because he reads m. 39 as

Example 2.9b Schoenberg, Piano Piece Op. 11, No. 2, mm. 48–49 (B section, stage III, ending measures). Used by permission of Belmont Music Publishers and Universal Edition

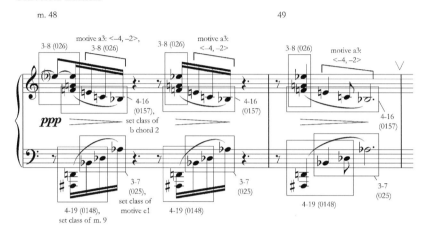

But my preference is to seek motivic significance in mm. 48–49: namely, the thrice-repeated configuration brings motives and chords from a and b themes into close proximity, and shows that the 4-16 set class that encompassed b chord 2, a source of conflict in m. 4, has a 3-8 subset that ties it not only to Op. 11, No. 2's theme a, but a specific intervallic manifestation of 3-8 that points back further to Op. 11, No. 1. More specifically, the opening chord in the right hand of all three repetitions forms set class 3-8, one of the principal harmonies of theme a. From the F4 of this chord follow E4, C4, and B♭3, completing the set class 4-16 discussed above. Its last three notes form 3-8, but do so using ordered pitch intervals <–4, –2>: these of course are identical to the intervals of motive a3, the endpoint of the expansion process in mm. 1–10 of the first piece. The left hand, meanwhile, can be broken into segments that bring two more elements from theme b into the orbit of 4-16 and its explanatory 3-8/<–4, –2> – set classes 4-19 (the foreign chord from m. 9 and Op. 11, No. 1) and 3-7 (the set class of theme b's soprano motive, e1).

## A' Section

The final large section of Op. 11, No. 2, after an extended return of the a theme with further development of motives d1, d2, and d3 (mm. 55–58),

a large tonic cadence for the A section. But the change in texture at m. 29 and the fact that mm. 29–54 contains four subsections that all begin with the same motto (motive g1) support my reading.

leads into the passage portrayed in Example 2.10. In measure 59 we return
to the texture, rhythm, and motives of subsection c in the right hand
against the D2-F2 ostinato in the left (now with B♭1 below), but after one
measure, other motives are presented that provide what I think is the
work's most convincing synthesis of motivic material from the b theme
with that of the a theme. Not only that, but the motivic connections reach
back and link the material of the second piece with the opening motto of
Op. 11, No. 1 in a conclusive way.

Here is how it works, step by step: at the pickup to m. 60, we hear motive
*d17*, <+11, –3>, a contour that recalls motive *d1*, <+8, –6>. The last two pitches
of this motive are B4 and G♯4, and these lead immediately to G4 to complete
the opening motto of the first piece, motive *a1*, at original pitch. After motive
*d* from the second piece and motive *a* from the first piece are placed in such
close proximity, the same G4 that had ended motive *a1* begins another version
of motive *d*, <+9, –3>, making the connection even more firm (we will call it
*d18*). Directly afterward, the pickup to m. 61 begins a third derivative of
motive *d*, which I call *d19*: <+11, –15>. This motive consists of the pitch classes
10, 9, and 6, constituents of b chord 1, which had just been emphasized so
strongly in the piece's climax. (In addition, the last two of them, 9 and 6, are
harmonized by set classes 3-5 voiced as Viennese Trichords, recalling b chords
1 and 2.) It would even be possible for a listener to hook pitch classes 10, 9, and
6 up with the prominent E5 on the third beat of m. 60, to form the entire pitch-
class content of b chord 1, {4, 6, 9, 10}. In this way, motives and chords that call
to mind the a and b themes of the second piece and the opening motto of the
first piece are linked together in a tight chain, while the ostinato characteristic
of theme a continues underneath.

What happens directly after, from m. 61b to the end of the piece, seems
to step back from this important synthesis. The final measures of the piece,
illustrated in Example 2.11, make relatively few new connections between
motives and chords from themes a and b of the second piece and the
opening of the first piece. Instead, they mostly repeat fragments of material
already presented, in an order that follows the trajectory of the whole piece
at the beginning, but turns toward randomness at the end. Even though
these fragments do remind us of syntheses previously made in a few places,
by the final measure elements of theme b take over, to the exclusion of all
else. Reinhold Brinkmann describes the "montage" quality of this ending
(my translation):

> It is more a gathered montage of "citations" than a closing succession. Even
> though it could be understood as a summary of the whole, it scarcely has the
> "reprise" character of the close of Opus 11, No. 1. Even the manner of its
> implementation, a mere connecting, not a continuation by means of

Example 2.10 Schoenberg, Piano Piece Op. 11, No. 2, mm. 59–61 (A' section, stage II, synthesis). Used by permission of Belmont Music Publishers and Universal Edition

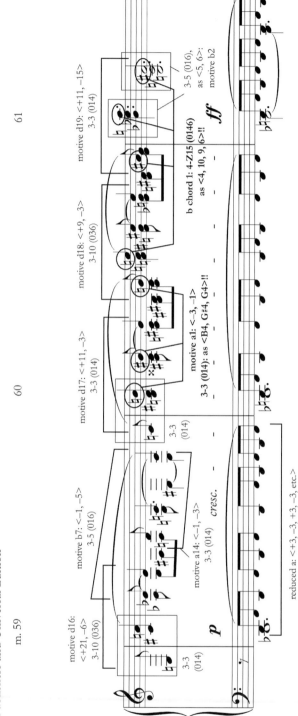

Example 2.11 Schoenberg, Piano Piece Op. 11, No. 2, mm. 61b–66 (A′ section, stage III, conclusion). Used by permission of Belmont Music Publishers and Universal Edition

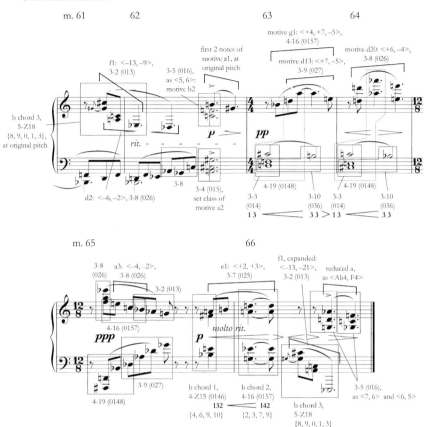

a necessary completion of something longed for, distinguishes it from the corresponding passage in the first piece: there the culmination of a reprise was brought about, here the repetition only comes about after the large crescendo has subsided. And this repetition does not have the function of summing things up, rather one could describe its formal idea as "remembering" . . . By the passing-by of these thoughts, the history of the whole is reviewed.[21]

These "passing thoughts" from earlier in the piece begin with b chord 3 in the right hand against the D-F ostinato in the left. This gives way on the third dotted quarter beat of m. 62 to a right-hand chord that combines the Viennese Trichord related to b chords 1 and 2, set class 3-5, with the soprano fragment B4-G♯4, suggesting motive *a1* from the first piece. But

[21] Brinkmann, *Drei Klavierstücke Op. 11*, pp. 100–01.

this fleeting association of b theme material with Op. 11, No. 1 in m. 62 is supplanted by motive *g1* from the second piece's large B section in the following measure. The latter two pitch intervals of *g1*, <+7, –5>, shrink to <+6, –4> in the soprano of m. 64, forming a trichord that belongs to set class 3-8, making a further connection between motive *g1* and the a theme of Op. 11, No. 2. Meanwhile, in the left-hand part, trichords 3-3 and 3-10 alternate, calling to mind the expanding and contracting ordered pitch-class intervals that had occurred in the left hand at mm. 5b–7 (return to Example 2.3). At m. 65 follows a quotation from the final measures of the B section: mm. 48–49's configuration is brought back and extended, reminding the listener of the way in which it connects set class 3-8 as a chord and as <–4, –2> to set class 4-16, linking the a and b themes together, and both of them to motive *a3* from the first piece.

So far, mm. 61b–65 could be heard as a motivic "flyover" of the large A and B sections of the piece: one of the b chords first appears against the ostinato and then theme b is brought into relationship with theme a, followed by motive *g1*, which leads to its own synthesis of 4-16 from b chord 2, {4, 9, 10} from b chord 1, and 3-8 from the a theme and the first piece. But the final phrase goes off in a completely different direction, and that is what makes the end sound random to me: the pickups to m. 66 begin a literal repetition of b chords 1, 2, and 3, with the final interval of motive *f1* extended by an octave. Why we do not hear some sort of large, overarching synthesis here, or at the very least a return to theme a to round off the piece, is a mystery. It is true that the final two chords associate two set classes 3-5 (one of them voiced as the ubiquitous Viennese Trichord <6, 5>) with the descending minor third characteristic of Op. 11, No. 1's *reduced a* motive. But this particular descending minor third is <A♭4, F4>, not pitch classes that evoke the first piece in any significant way. Instead, the music simply seems to turn toward the b theme in its final measure and then stops.

## *Busoni's Arrangement of Op. 11, No. 2*

Before moving on to Op. 11, No. 3, I would like to show how certain aspects of my analysis can be used to understand and justify Schoenberg's reactions to Ferruccio Busoni's arrangement of the second movement. The two musicians carried on a correspondence from July 1909 to July 1910 that was initiated by Schoenberg, a relatively little-known composer, in the hope that Busoni, the world's most formidable pianist in that time, would perform the Op. 11 pieces in public. Instead, Busoni made an arrangement of the second piece that adhered to romantic notions of piano writing to a greater extent than the original, and added repetitions and developments of certain motives, setting off an exchange of letters where Busoni attempted to justify the edits for pianistic reasons and Schoenberg in turn justified his (mostly negative) reactions for compositional reasons.[22] Their correspondence is famous for Schoenberg's letter of August 13, 1909 with its exclamation: "Away from motivic working," which I will address in much more detail in my analysis of Op. 11, No. 3 below.

An excerpt from the Busoni arrangement, mm. 4b–11, corresponding to the passages discussed in Examples 2.2b and 2.3 (originally mm. 4b–9), is given as Example 2.12.

Busoni's rendition of Schoenberg's theme a in the published version is identical to Schoenberg's original. But at the onset of theme b, Busoni begins to repeat thematic elements and make additions and changes that upset Schoenberg's balance between introducing new motives and making connections back to previous music. For example, he repeats b chords 1 and 2 an octave higher, followed by b chord 3 in the higher octave, b chord 2 again, and b chord 3 in the original octave. Busoni stretches out Schoenberg's compact arch to almost two measures, changing the balance of power between themes a and b to sustain the conflicting material of b for a much longer time than originally intended.

This tendency to stretch out the contrasting material, and give it too much developmental emphasis too soon, continues in Busoni's reworking of the following measures. Like Schoenberg, he places theme a material in the left hand and runs a synthesis of motives from themes b and Op. 11, No. 1 against it in the right: b chord 3 followed by the *x2* and *y* motives from the first piece. But Busoni's second b chord 3 in m. 7b undergoes the same arpeggiation that Schoenberg himself had held back until the climax of Op. 11, No. 2 in m. 43. (Schoenberg calls this point to Busoni's attention in a letter of July 3, 1910, writing "if the sixteenth-note figure represents the further developed form [of b chord 3], then surely the original form from which it is derived should not be missing.")[23] Busoni's drawing-out process

---

[22] The complete correspondence is translated into English in *Ferruccio Busoni: Selected Letters*, trans., ed., and with an introduction by Antony Beaumont (New York: Columbia University Press, 1987), pp. 379–423. It is discussed at length in a number of articles, including Daniel M. Raessler, "Schoenberg and Busoni: Aspects of Their Relationship," *Journal of the Arnold Schoenberg Institute* 7/1 (1983): 7–27, and Jutta Theurich, "Der Briefwechsel zwischen Arnold Schönberg und Ferruccio Busoni," in *Arnold Schönberg – 1874 bis 1951: Zum 25. Todestag des Komponisten*, ed. Mathias Hansen and Christa Müller (Akademie der Künste der DDR, 1976), pp. 55–58.

[23] Schoenberg letter to Busoni of July 3, 1910, translated by Beaumont in *Ferruccio Busoni: Selected Letters*, p. 404.

Example 2.12 Busoni's arrangement of Schoenberg, Piano Piece Op. 11, No. 2, mm. 4–11a. Used by permission of Belmont Music Publishers and Universal Edition

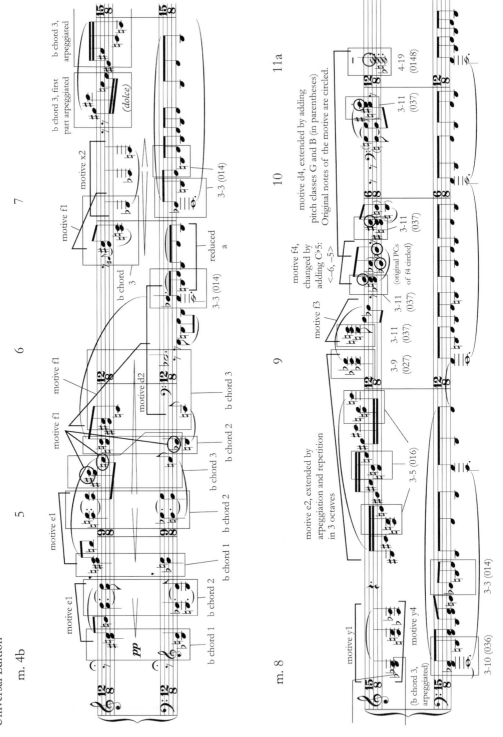

then continues with what had been the last two eighth notes of Schoenberg's m. 7, the beginning of motive e2, which Busoni elongates to six eighth notes by arpeggiation and repetition in three octaves. And Schoenberg's m. 8 and first part of m. 9, in which he had presented two variations of the *f* motive, linking to a concluding statement of the *d* motive and the foreign set class 4-19 in six dotted quarter notes, is stretched out by Busoni to eight dotted quarters (mm. 9–11). He does this by adding notes to Schoenberg's original *f1* motive (C♭5) and *d4* motive (two G-B dyads) and repeating the C♯ minor chord that had appeared once in Schoenberg's setting, in two octaves.

Schoenberg's original version of Op. 11, No. 2 is replete with his own motivic processes, many of which I have just described in detail. But it seems obvious that Busoni's additional "motivic working" in the revision was too much for Schoenberg, as it allowed contrasting b theme material to dominate the texture of mm. 4b–11, rather than using those measures to highlight connections between themes b, a, and the first Piano Piece, as the composer seems to have intended. Although Schoenberg's famous exclamation to Busoni, "Away from motivic working," was part of a letter of August 13, 1909, almost a year before Schoenberg saw Busoni's transcription, it seems that Schoenberg's later negative reactions in the correspondence came about as a result of *too much* motivic working in Busoni's transcription. As a result, the concision of Schoenberg's original, as well as its balance between motivic processes, is lost.[24]

---

[24] Daniel Harrison engages in a similar comparison of Schoenberg's original for Op. 11, No. 2 with Busoni's rewrite, but focuses on the closing measures, mm. 63–66, rather than the opening measures as I did. Harrison shows how Busoni alleviates somewhat the sense of randomness in Schoenberg's closing (caused by, as we saw, the motivic "flyover" of the piece turning suddenly toward a repeat of the b chord sequence). Busoni does this by repeating the music of m. 65a (which had originally come from mm. 48–49) and sequencing it down by octave twice, and by stating the sequence of b chords 1 and 2 in mm. 65b–66a only once, softening the suddenness of the two b chords a little by placing less developmental emphasis on them (though he doubles their note values). Busoni then subjects the first two verticals of b chord 3 in m. 66b to another downward sequence by octave (four times), with some octave complementation of individual intervals. Harrison points out that these revisions lend Schoenberg's music a sense of "traditional [ending] rhetoric" by fragmenting and sequencing material in the manner of a sentential continuation, or a *rallentando* preparing for the final cadence. But in m. 66b, Busoni takes a step further, repeating Schoenberg's bass E♭1 five times in four octaves, making what had been a tonally ambiguous ending gravitate strongly toward E♭ as tonic. This must have been troublesome to Schoenberg, for reasons other than the motivic ones I highlighted. See Harrison, *Pieces of Tradition*, pp. 42–45.

## Op. 11, No. 3

Now we come to the third piece of Schoenberg's Op. 11, which, as I pointed out earlier, is absolutely notorious for its fragmentation of form and its apparent lack of themes, motives, and processes that organize them. Indeed, the third piece has been the focus of an international controversy among scholars, which I portrayed in a *Music Theory Online* article in 2015. English-speaking authors such as Joseph Auner, Áine Heneghan, and two of the writers I quoted at the beginning of this chapter, Ethan Haimo and Bryan Simms, associate it with a very short period of Schoenberg's career, from 1909 to 1911 or 1912, marked, according to them, by an "intuitive aesthetic" (Auner's term).[25] As Haimo and Simms characterize it in my quotations, Schoenberg's intuitive music completely lacks "repeated themes, recurrent motives and learned devices," replacing form-defining thematic and motivic repetition with a "succession of brief, clearly contrasted sections, set off from one another by silences, changes in dynamic level and tempo, and sudden shifts in surface rhythm and textural design."[26]

Those who argue for the "intuitive aesthetic" invariably call on a passage from Schoenberg's August 13, 1909 letter to Ferruccio Busoni for support (the same letter from which I quoted on p. 73 in our discussion of Busoni's edits to Op. 11, No. 2). A larger excerpt is given below (translated by Antony Beaumont from Schoenberg's original German; italics correspond to Schoenberg's underlining).[27]

---

[25] Jack Boss, "'Away with Motivic Working'? Not So Fast: Motivic Processes in Schoenberg's Op. 11, No. 3," *Music Theory Online* 21/3 (September 2015); Joseph Auner, "Schoenberg's Aesthetic Transformations and the Evolution of Form in *Die glückliche Hand*," *Journal of the Arnold Schoenberg Institute* 12/2 (November 1989): 103–28; Áine Heneghan, "Schoenberg's Compositional Philosophy, the Three Piano Pieces, and his Subsequent *Volte-Face*," in *Musical Currents from the Left Coast*, ed. Jack Boss and Bruce Quaglia (Newcastle-upon-Tyne: Cambridge Scholars, 2008), pp. 299–314; Haimo, *Schoenberg's Transformation of Musical Language*, pp. 332–56; Simms, *Schoenberg's Atonal Music*, pp. 59–71.

[26] William Benjamin offers a different analytic take on the "intuitive" music in "Abstract Polyphonies: The Music of Schoenberg's Nietzschean Moment," in *Political and Religious Ideas in the Works of Arnold Schoenberg*, ed. Charlotte M. Cross and Russell A. Berman (New York: Garland, 2000), pp. 1–39. Benjamin portrays the first seventeen measures of the last of the Orchestral Pieces Op. 16, the "obbligato recitative," not as disconnected small sections, but as multiple metric and harmonic layers. These layers have traditional tonal and metric long-range continuity within themselves, but cancel out each other's coherence.

[27] Beaumont, *Ferruccio Busoni: Selected Letters*, p. 389. A photocopy of Schoenberg's original handwritten letter to Busoni can be found in the archive of the Arnold Schönberg Center, in SatColl D2, folder 2. Its finding element is 1909.08.13.

I want to declare my intentions (encouraged by your comment: my music affects you because you envisage something of the kind as the goal of our immediate developments).

> I strive for: complete liberation from all forms
> from all symbols
> of cohesion and
> of logic.

> Thus:
> away with "motivic working out."
> Away with harmony as
> cement or bricks of a building.

> Harmony is *expression*
> and nothing else.

> Then:
> Away with Pathos!
> Away with protracted ten-ton scores, from erected or constructed
> towers, rocks and other massive claptrap.
> My music must be
> brief.

> Concise! In two notes: not built, but "*expressed*"!!

As Haimo puts it, "nothing could highlight more clearly the suddenness of the transformation in Schoenberg's compositional approach than this letter."[28] But should we really understand the letter as a compositional manifesto, one that celebrates the expungment of "motivic work" from Schoenberg's music altogether (together with form, harmony, logic, and pathos)? I made the argument in my 2015 *Music Theory Online* article that Beaumont's translation of the key phrase is a little too strong.[29] What Schoenberg actually wrote was "also: weg von der 'motivischen arbeit'." Now, we do not know for sure whether the difference between "weg mit" (away with) and "weg von" (away from) was the same in Schoenberg's 1909 Viennese dialect as it is today. But, in modern German, while the first definitely has the connotation of suddenly and violently casting something unwanted to the side,[30] the second is a little more gentle and gradual. I think Daniel Raessler's translation possibly captures the intention of the original

---

[28] Haimo, *Schoenberg's Transformation*, p. 348.
[29] Boss, "'Away with Motivic Working'?," paragraphs 10 and 11.
[30] A Google search of "weg mit" (accessed January 6, 2016), for example, brought up a fitness website that exhorted its readers: "Weg mit den Rettungsringen" (Away with the "lifebuoys" or "love handles").

phrase better: "Let's get away from motivic working out."[31] An even better way
to translate it might be: "I've been trying to get away from motivic working
lately, but I haven't been entirely successful yet" – given the three paragraphs
of Schoenberg's August 13 letter to Busoni that immediately precede the above
quotation. As they are crucial to my argument, I would like to quote them as
a whole (from Beaumont's translation; italics are mine):[32]

> To close, I must add that I was overjoyed to hear that you already like the one
> piece [Op. 11, No. 2]. And I really hope that you will later come to like the
> other one [No. 1]. Earlier I also preferred the 12/8 one (which I composed
> second) to the first. But recently I looked at the first one again: I almost believe
> that what I had conceived in terms of freedom and variegation of expression,
> of unshackled flexibility of form uninhibited by "logic," is much more evident
> in the first than the second.
>
> What I had visualized has been attained in neither. *Perhaps, indeed defi-
> nitely also not in the third, which will soon be finished.* In a few orchestral
> pieces which I wrote very recently [Op. 16, Nos. 3, 4, and 5], I have in certain
> respects come closer, but again in others have turned far from what
> I considered already achieved.
>
> *Perhaps this is not yet graspable.* It will perhaps take a long time before I can
> write the music I feel urged to, of which I have had an inkling for several years,
> *but which, for the time being, I cannot express.*

This is far from a proclamation of a sudden change in Schoenberg's style.
Instead, the immediate context of "Away from motivic working" in his letter
expresses frustration that none of the three pieces of Op. 11 attain the ideal that
he claims to be working toward: freeing pure expression and intuition from the
shackles of form, motivic working, etc. It is also interesting to note that he
describes the *first* piece of Op. 11, which has typically been understood by
modern scholars as the most motivically dense and worked-out of the three, as
closer to his ideal (before claiming at the beginning of the following paragraph
that neither it, nor the second nor third piece, actually reach that ideal).

So what was Schoenberg trying to communicate in his August 13 letter,
if not an announcement of his abandonment of motivic working in Op. 11,
No. 3? I believe it is essential to keep in mind the underlying purpose of
Schoenberg's correspondence with Busoni. As I pointed out previously (see
pp. 72–73), he was trying to convince Busoni, a prominent pianist in Berlin
at that time, to perform the first two pieces of Op. 11 in public. He made his
original request in a letter of July 13, 1909, and Busoni responded three
days later asking for the scores. Schoenberg sent them on July 20, and on

---

[31] Raessler, "Schoenberg and Busoni: Aspects of Their Relationship," p. 14.
[32] Beaumont, *Ferruccio Busoni: Selected Letters*, pp. 388–89.

the 26th, a response came from Busoni that surely caused anxiety for Schoenberg. Busoni praised Schoenberg's aesthetics effusively, but quibbled about his piano writing (from Beaumont's translation, italics are Busoni's, bold is mine).[33]

> Your piano pieces came as no surprise to me – that is: I happened to know what I could expect. **It was therefore self-evident that I should find a subjective, individual art based on emotion** – and that you would make me acquainted with refined artistic entities.
>
> All this has come to pass, and I rejoice heartily over such a phenomenon.
>
> My impression as a pianist, which I cannot overlook – be it due to upbringing or professional considerations – is otherwise. My first qualification of your music '*as a piano piece*' is the limited range of the textures in time and space.
>
> ... I believe I have grasped your intentions and feel confident, after some preparation, to produce sonorities and atmospheres according to your expectations. But the task is hindered by their excessive *conciseness* (that is the word).

To his letter, Busoni appended a revision of m. 40 of Op. 11, No. 2 (not included in my earlier examples from No. 2), where he changed the register of one left-hand figure from low to high, doubled another at the octave below, and repeated one of the right hand's intervals in a higher register, in an attempt to thicken the piece's texture and extend its register in both directions.

Schoenberg responded, apparently a few days later (the letter is undated), in a respectful tone ("from a certain standpoint, you are absolutely right") but asserting that his original textures and registers were essential to the expression of the second piece as well as the first ("particularly these two pieces, whose sombre, compressed colours are a constituent feature, would not stand a texture whose effect on one's tonal palate ... was all too flattering").[34] However, encouraged by Schoenberg's respectful tone, Busoni continued his rewrite of No. 2. He announced to Schoenberg in a letter of August 2: "I have (with total lack of modesty) 'rescored' your piece." (This is the version that we discussed on pp. 72–75.)

Such news must have caused great alarm for Schoenberg, even though he had not yet seen any of Busoni's rewrite besides m. 40. On the one hand, he was desperately hoping for a premiere by a performer of Busoni's stature: that would boost his standing in Viennese musical culture, and perhaps even lead to a publication contract for the piano pieces (which now included No. 3). On the other hand, allowing Busoni's rewrite of No. 2 to take the place of the original in the premiere would compromise his standards as an artist, and perhaps even tarnish his reputation. It seems that his only recourse in the famous letter of August 13 was to assure

---

[33] Ibid., pp. 384–85.    [34] Ibid., p. 385.

Busoni that he had understood Schoenberg's aesthetics rightly: his art was indeed "subjective" and "individual," and his ultimate goal as a composer was to keep logic, form, motivic working, and the like from interfering with his free, unadulterated expression of emotion. Therefore, Busoni would gain much from performing the pieces of Op. 11, because they embodied, even though imperfectly, those qualities of Schoenberg's aesthetic for which the pianist had expressed admiration. But, at the same time, it was essential for him to play them *as written* without adding edits, because Schoenberg's "limited" textures and concision were crucial means to the end of pure emotional expression. I believe this is the true context and significance of Schoenberg's phrase "Away from motivic working," something very different from an announcement that Schoenberg had suddenly banished motives and motivic processes from his music.

But, of course, my assertion ultimately must be supported by close analysis of the music of Op. 11, No. 3. I will attempt that shortly, but first I would like to consider the other side of the "international controversy" I mentioned, for such approaches to the third piece provide motivic and harmonic groundwork for the approach I will take. If we consider the German-language analytical writings on Op. 11, No. 3, we encounter either strong disagreement or ambivalence toward the very notion of "away with motivic working." Christian Raff, for example, challenges as "one-sided" and "inaccurate" the idea that Schoenberg suddenly abandoned motives and motivic networks in Op. 11, No. 3.[35] Christoph Neidhöfer asserts the existence of harmonic processes in the third piece, drawing together a number of its harmonies into Lewinian transformational networks. Not only that, but he shows that the same transformations yield networks in the first as well as the third pieces of the set, supporting Lewin's and my readings of them as related to one another cyclically.[36] Finally, an older analysis that no doubt influenced both of theirs (as well as my own), Reinhold Brinkmann's in his 1969 book on the three pieces of Op. 11, seems to express ambivalence about whether motivic working exists or not in the third piece, within a clear depiction of its fragmentation of form.[37]

---

[35] Christian Raff, *Gestaltete Freiheit: Studien zur Analyse der frei atonalen Kompositionen A. Schönbergs – auf der Grundlage seiner Begriffe*. Sinefonia, vol. 5 (Hofheim: Wolke, 2006), pp. 233–65.

[36] Christoph Neidhöfer, "Atonalität und Transformational Analysis: Zu einigen verborgenen (und nicht so verborgenen) Strukturen in Schönbergs Klavierstück op. 11, 3," in Jahrbuch 2008/09 des Staatlichen Instituts für Musikforschung Preußischer Kulturbesitz, ed. Simone Hohmaier (Mainz: Schott, 2009), pp. 53–73.

[37] Brinkmann, *Drei Klavierstücke Op. 11*, pp. 109–29. Another, slightly less older (1980), account that advocates for melodic and harmonic motivic working in the first two

The reader should consult my 2015 *Music Theory Online* article for a more detailed description of Brinkmann's approach to Op. 11, No. 3.[38] Here, let it suffice to say that he begins his analysis by strongly asserting the disappearance of "melodic correspondences,"[39] but as he continues, he gives an increasing number of illustrations of what he calls the "remnants of motivic working" (*Reste motivischer Arbeit*), eventually describing and illustrating a larger motivic network that spans most of the piece, as well as a local one that accounts for much of the opening five measures.[40]

My analysis of the third piece, then, will build on the work of my Central European predecessors in two ways. First, I want to show that, despite its fragmentary form, Op. 11, No. 3 is held together by something stronger than motivic networks: motivic *processes*. In other words, its diachronic motive and chord progressions are not only connected, but also can be heard as generated by a small number of definable procedures. Second, the motivic (as well as harmonic) procedures that saturate the third piece are the same as those that we encountered in the first two pieces: incremental pitch-intervallic expansion that generalizes to expansion of ordered pc intervals in prime forms, and processes that "explain" set classes such as 4-19 and 3-5, first using intervals foreign to the opening of Op. 11, No. 1, and following those with other interval successions within the same set classes that are closely related to the opening motives. The third piece does, however, differ from the first two motivically and harmonically in one important way – it has no climactic, culminating resolution near the end that connects new and foreign elements back to Op. 11's beginning (such as mm. 60–61 in the second piece or mm. 50–64 in the first). Instead, the principal "explanatory" progression disappears relatively early in the third piece, "submerged" as it were by a proliferation of expanding processes. (One could make the argument that a second explanatory progression appears near the end, but it is not salient enough to be heard as a major resolution.) Because of this, Op. 11, No. 3, unlike its predecessors, does not have the profile of a complete musical idea.

Example 2.13 provides a form chart for the third piece. To represent that aspect of its nature that manifests as a series of fragmentary phrases, I label

---

measures of Op. 11, No. 3 is Carl Dahlhaus's analysis at the end of *Nineteenth-Century Music*, which concludes by asserting "we have little cause to speak of random sonorities." See Dahlhaus, *Nineteenth-Century Music*, trans. J. Bradford Robinson (Berkeley and Los Angeles: University of California Press, 1989), pp. 387–88; originally published as *Die Musik des 19. Jahrhunderts*, vol. 6 of *Neues Handbuch der Musikwissenschaft* (Wiesbaden: Akademische Verlagsgesellschaft Athenaion, 1980).

[38] Boss, "'Away with Motivic Working'?," paragraphs 13–18.
[39] Brinkmann, *Drei Klavierstücke Op. 11*, p. 110.      [40] Ibid., pp. 120–22.

Example 2.13 Form chart for Schoenberg, Piano Piece Op. 11, No. 3

# A1   mm. 1–9

## A (*Grundgestalt*)
mm. 1–5a

Set-class expansions (3-3, 3-4, 3-5) whose unordered pitch intervals simultaneously contract, culminating in "Viennese Trichords." In mm. 2–3, RH, an "explanatory succession" of 4-19 set classes followed by <–4, –1, –3> arises (twice)

## B
mm. 5b–6a

develops the ordered pitch interval stack <8, 4>, a close relative of <9, 4> and <7, 4> in m. 1, RH of A.

## C
m. 6b

Set-class expansion (3-1, 3-7, 3-8); the last two set classes also feature expansion of pitch intervals

## D
m. 7a

Set-class expansion (3-4, 3-4, 3-8), using unordered pc interval stacks from A

## E
mm. 8–9

Includes a SC expansion (3-5, 3-4, 3-8): the first two 3-5s use pc interval stacks <6, 5> to <6, 7>; reversing a progression from m. 3 of A. Also introduces elements from Op. 11/1 and 2

# A2   mm. 10–20

## F
mm. 10–11a

Set-class expansion (3-3, 3-4, 3-5) whose unordered pitch intervals contract, culminating in a Viennese Trichord. This, and the rhythm, contour and dynamics, recall the opening

## G
mm. 11b–13

"Thematic" according to Brinkmann; both hands feature pitch interval expansions; RH begins with <+3, +1>, inversion of motive a1 and <+1, –2>, motive x, from Op. 11/1

## H
mm. 14–16a

Both measures 14 and 15 combine SC expansions with an unexplained form of 4-19 (something other than <–4, –1, –3>). Melodic motives from SC 3-5 dominate mm. 15b–16

## I
mm. 16b–19a

Tentative return of the explanatory progression from mm. 2–3. Outer voices project 3-3, 3-4, 3-5, while inner voices yield a series of unexplained 4-19s, followed by <–3, –1, **–3**> (the explanatory motive falls short)

## K (retransition?)
mm. 19b–20

returns to section A by presenting its characteristic SCs and unordered pitch intervals as verticals, but not in expanding (or contracting) order. The contour of m. 1's alto returns in m. 20

# A3  mm. 21–35

## L
### m. 21

Set-class expansion (3-3, 3-4, 3-5, 3-8, 3-12), some using familiar unordered pitch intervals from A (<9, 4> and <6, 5>). This, and the opening wedge contour between hands, the descending bass, and the dynamics, all recall the opening, even more clearly than section F

## M
### mm. 22–24a

Brinkmann calls this *ppp* section "field-like." It has few SC expansions, but recalls motives (<+6, +2>, <–13, –9>) and chords (4-13) of Op. 11/2's small b section

## N
### m. 24b–26a

This *forte* "thematic" section again features SC expansions: 3-3, 3-7, 3-9, and 3-3, 3-7, 3-5, within a rhythmic context that strongly evokes Op. 11/1, mm. 53–54

## O
### m. 26b

Continues the recall of Op. 11/1's first theme into that piece's b section with two *reduced a* motives; but breaks them up using other material, including a SC expansion: 3-3, 3-5, and an upper neighbor figure

## P
### mm. 27–29

Characteristic SCs (3-4, 3-5) and interval stacks (<7, 4>, <8, 5>, <6, 5>, <5, 6>, <6, 7>) alternating as verticals. In m. 28, the LH creates a pitch-interval expansion, based on section O's upper neighbor figure, while the RH recalls interval patterns and rhythms from mm. 2–3's "explanatory" music, without ever reaching <4, –1, –3>.

## Q (Climax)
### mm. 30–31

After P's set-class expansion from 3-3 (014) to 3-7 (025), we hear whole-tone tetrachords containing 3-8 (026) prominently in m. 30, possibly another way to project SC expansion. Then m. 31 creates an expansion of not only SCs but also topmost intervals in the RH: the most obvious and marked expanding wedge in the piece!

## R
### mm. 32–33

Repeats 3-5 and <6, 5>, the endpoints of section Q's set-class expansion (and many other SC expansions throughout the piece) as an exclamation point

## S (Codetta)
### mm. 34–35

One last unordered pitch interval expansion: from <12, 11, 12> to <12, 22>, to remind the listener of the piece's primary process

the various sections with Brinkmann's letters: A through S (he excludes J). However, two of these sections, F and L, contain pitch-interval patterns, textures, rhythms, and contours at their beginnings that strongly recall the opening five measures, Section A – so I have used these almost-thematic returns to subsume Brinkmann's chart under a larger one consisting of A1, A2, and A3.[41] The piece has some features in common with rondo form, but its fragmentation and persistent extreme contrasts between the non-refrain sections make me reluctant to label it as such.

As I already asserted, however, the fragments induced by abrupt changes in texture, rhythm, register, and dynamics in the third piece are at the same time knit together by motivic processes to create a pattern that spans the entire work. The opening section, A, serves as a *Grundgestalt* in that it introduces the two competing motivic and chordal processes Piece No. 3 carries over from its predecessors. The first consists of a familiar set-class expansion, 3-3 (014), 3-4 (015), 3-5 (016), in the pickup measure and measure 1, which is (interestingly) projected in the unordered pitch interval realm as stacks of intervals that gradually contract: <11, 4>, <9, 4>, <7, 4>, <6, 5>. A second process breaks in in the top staff of mm. 2–3, by which a series of 4-19 chords using unordered pitch-interval patterns reminiscent of the foreign chords of m. 14 in the first piece and m. 9 in the second piece, <3, 4, 4> and <4, 4, 5>, is supplanted immediately by another member of that set class that "explains" the foreign intervals by using ordered pitch intervals reminiscent of the opening motives of the first piece: <–4, –1, –3>.

After the two competing processes are introduced, section B works with the unordered pitch-interval stack <8, 4>, a close relative of the <9, 4> and <7, 4> stacks of the opening measure, and sections C–E, as *pianissimo* interludes, develop both unordered pitch interval and set-class elements of the opening set-class expansion. Certain interval successions of section E begin to recall the openings of Op. 11, Nos. 1 and 2. But these are rudely interrupted by section F in m. 10, the first of the two sections that recalls the piece's opening, through its set-class expansion (coupled again with an

---

[41] Ethan Haimo also recognizes the second of these, section L at m. 21, as a return to the beginning, but qualifies his description to convince the reader that this falls short of a true thematic return: "One can scarcely point to anything in m. 21 that is identical to anything in [mm. 1–3] … All the same, there are similarities … Throughout the work, one is constantly struck by the feeling that a given passage sounds vaguely like things we have heard before." (*Schoenberg's Transformation of Musical Language*, p. 344). Reinhold Brinkmann characterizes the relationship between A and L with less qualification: "an even clearer relationship [to the opening measures] in all the voices" (*Drei Klavierstücke Op. 11*, p. 120). My analysis of m. 21, as well as that of mm. 10–11a, will point out several features that are indeed identical to the opening (while others are varied).

unordered pitch-interval contraction), its rising contour, emphasis on dotted rhythms, and *crescendo* starting at *forte*.

Section F gives way to a pair of passages, G and H, which combine distant reminiscences of earlier material in the cycle with reworkings of elements from the beginning of the third piece. Section G evokes the ♩. ♪ ♩ rhythm of Op. 11, No. 1 in both hands while beginning its right hand with two fixed pitches familiar from the first piece's opening, G♯4 and B4. The right hand produces a series of descending pitch intervals that expand, while the left hand turns the third piece's beginning formula upside-down: a gradual *expansion* in ordered pitch intervals together with a set-class *contraction*. The following section, H, then returns to working with the unordered pitch intervals and set classes of the third piece's opening.

To this point, the subsections gathered under large section A2 have concerned themselves exclusively with set-class expansions (and one SC contraction). But with section I, the focus briefly turns back to the progression that "explained" set class 4-19 back in measures 2–3. This progression begins its course in m. 17, but ultimately dies away (not only procedurally but also dynamically) at the bar line between mm. 17 and 18, under a sustained 3-5 with unordered pitch intervals <5, 6>, similar to the endpoint of many of the set-class successions of the previous music. And the explanatory succession, with its <–4, –1, –3> or <–3, –1, –4> following a series of 4-19 chords, is never heard from again in Op. 11, No. 3 – one might say that it is submerged under the weight of first set-class, then eventually pitch-interval, expansions.

That submerging process begins in earnest in section K, which I read as a retransition back to the return of the third piece's opening material at m. 21. It places the listener's focus back on the trichord set classes of the opening, 3-3, 3-4, and 3-5, now not in simple increasing order, but nevertheless culminating in 3-5 as <5, 6>. Several of the opening's other unordered pitch-interval stacks return as well, particularly those that had been associated with set class 3-3.

Section L begins the third major section of the piece, A3, in m. 21 with a more thorough recall of the piece's opening than the one provided by mm. 10–11. Not only a set-class expansion from 3-3 to 3-5 (together with an unordered pitch-interval contraction from <11, 4> to <6, 5>), but also texture and contour (an outward wedge shape opening up between the two hands) and a *crescendo* from double to triple *f* work together to evoke the music of mm. 1–2.

As was the case with section F, the next few sections after section L are marked by a drastic softening (*ff* to *p* in m. 11b, *fff* to *ppp* here in m. 22), followed by a recall of motives from Op. 11, Nos. 1 and 2, which are promptly buried under a crowding in of set-class expansions. No obvious synthesis is made between the set-class expansions and the material from previous pieces; the expansions simply take over. Section M combines rhythms and textures that suggest subsection b of Op. 11, No. 2 (mm. 4b–13a of that piece) with specific pitch motives from it, such as <+6, +2> and <–13, –2>, and specific pitch-class sets such as 4-13. Section N, again *forte*, turns its attention to rhythms and contours that evoke Op. 11, No. 1's final return of the A section (mm. 53–54 in that piece), but the pitch-interval expansions and syntheses of those measures are replaced by a set-class expansion that brings in different set classes: 3-7 and 3-9. The recall of Op. 11, No. 1 continues in section O, but more tentatively, as two *reduced-a* motives are surrounded by yet another set-class expansion.

The chords resulting from set-class expansion in Op. 11, No. 3 again come to the fore in mm. 27 and 29: 3-4 and 3-5 as verticals in m. 27, and two 3-7 arpeggios in m. 29. Between these bookends of section P, m. 28 combines a pitch-interval expansion in the left hand with a rhythmic and contour reminiscence of the "explanatory" music from mm. 2–3. But 4-19 does not figure prominently in this measure, nor does the explanatory succession, <–4, –1, –3>, make any appearance – as I suggested above, the explanatory process has been swallowed up by set-class expansions at this point in the piece.

Section Q, mm. 30–31, constitutes the dynamic and articulative climax of Op. 11, No. 3: the marking *ffff* appears for the first and only time, together with a pedal marking (rare for this piece) and multiple wedge accents in m. 31. But there is no synthesis of motivic materials here, as in Op. 11, Nos. 1 and 2. Instead, m. 30 continues the set-class expansion of mm. 27–29 with whole-tone tetrachords 4-24 and 4-25 (each containing 3-8 as a subset). The following measure brings the expanding process even closer to the surface in the right hand, with a set-class expansion (3-1, 3-2, 3-3, 3-5), in which the top pitch intervals of the trichords also expand, <1, 2, 3, 6>.

The endpoint of m. 31's expansion then echoes for two measures in section R, set class 3-5 rendered as <–5, –6> and <+6, +5>. In this way, mm. 31–33 could be understood as representing and summarizing numerous set-class expansions throughout the third piece that all ended in forms of the Viennese Trichord. The codetta to the piece, section S, then reminds the listener of the importance of expansion one final time, by presenting two unordered pitch-interval stacks that expand, <12, 11, 12> to <12, 22>.

My general overview of Op. 11, No. 3 has demonstrated how motivic and chordal elements and processes introduced by the first two pieces of Op. 11 give the third piece coherence, in the absence of a traditional form. To show more thoroughly and convincingly the dependence of No. 3 on such elements and processes, I would now like to offer a section-by-section analysis. My discussion (as always) will be accompanied by detailed music examples.

Example 2.14 illustrates the A section, which serves as the third piece's *Grundgestalt* in the sense that it introduces the two motivic processes with which the piece will work.

They are a set-class expansion expressed as an unordered pitch-interval contraction, and the "explanatory" process. The pickup measure and m. 1's first dotted quarter contains a set-class expansion in the top staff that moves initially from 3-3, the set class of motive *a1* in Op. 11, No. 1, to 3-4, the set class of motive *a2*. (Return to Example 1.7 to see how these same set classes were projected as a pitch-interval expansion in the opening of the first piece.) The prime form of set class 3-3 (014) has the adjacent ordered pitch-class intervals **1, 3**, and that of 3-4 (015) the intervals **1, 4**, so they relate to one another as an expansion of adjacent pc intervals in prime forms. The expansion then continues on to set class 3-5 (016), having the adjacent pc intervals **1, 5**. Set class 3-5 had been associated with contrasting material in both of the first two pieces (motives *b1* and *b2* in m. 12 of the first piece, see Example 1.8; and the prominent trichord subsets of b chords 1 and 2 in m. 4b of the second piece, see Example 2.2b). In effect, the motivic expansion and conflict of the first two pieces is being summarized in the abstract by a single three-step expansion in the third.

While the intervals between the adjacent pitch classes in the prime forms expand incrementally in the opening chords of the right hand, the vertical stacks of unordered pitch intervals that realize 3-3, 3-3, 3-4, and 3-5 (given below the chords in Example 2.14) do the opposite, mostly: <11, 4> (figured from the bottom up) shrinks to <9, 4>, then <7, 4>. The progression completes itself with a contraction of the bottom interval and expansion of the top one to yield <6, 5>, a form of the Viennese Trichord that was prevalent in the first two pieces.

This four-chord progression of expanding set classes and shrinking unordered pitch-interval stacks ending with a Viennese Trichord becomes a motive itself in Op. 11, No. 3. A variation of it is presented immediately on the fourth and fifth eighth notes of m. 1 in the top two staves: its set classes are 3-3, 3-3, 3-3, and 3-5, and its unordered pitch-interval stacks start the same way as previously: <11, 4> and <9, 4>, but then contract and reverse the larger and smaller intervals, <3, 8>, finishing again with a Viennese Trichord: <5, 6>. The bass line in octaves under the four-chord progression and its variation, meanwhile, creates its own pitch-interval expansion. Its first four-note rhythmic group overlaps <–1, –6> and <–6, –2> (motive *d2* from m. 3 of Op. 11, No. 2), and the second three-note group expands out considerably to <+11, –16>. It is interesting to

Example 2.14 Schoenberg, Piano Piece Op. 11, No. 3, mm. 1–5a, section A. Copyright © 1910, 1938 by Universal Edition AG Vienna, UE 2991.

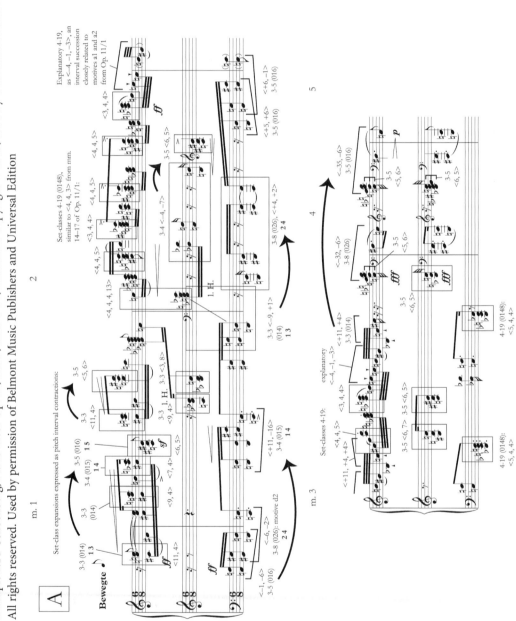

notice that the set classes created by the last two of these motives trace a contraction: set class 3-8 has the ordered pitch-class intervals **2, 4** in its prime form, while the subsequent 3-4 has **1, 4**. Expanding set classes are realized by contracting intervals in the right hand, while the opposite situation occurs in the left hand.

With m. 2 in the right hand, as mentioned above, the focus turns from expanding set classes and intervals to the process that explains set class 4-19 as an overlapping of versions of motives *a1* and *a2*. We encountered the "explanatory" process for the first time in Op. 11, No. 1 – 4-19 burst forth in that piece's B section, mm. 12ff, as a disruptive conflict, and was characterized there by the piano harmonic chord sustained from m. 14 to m. 17, consisting of the unordered pitch-interval stack <4, 4, 3> reckoned from the bottom up (refer back to Example 1.8). I argued in Chapter 1 that this strange element was reconciled to the motivic world of Op. 11, No. 1 later on in the piece at mm. 54–59, by projecting its set class as the intervals <–3, –1, –4>, an overlap of motive *a1* with a close relative of motive *a2* (see again the gray-shaded notes in Examples 1.9a and b). The right hand in mm. 2–3 of Op. 11, No. 3 can be heard as an accelerated rendition of the same explanatory process. A series of chords containing the unordered pitch intervals <3, 4, 4> or <4, 4, 5>, both close relatives of the piano harmonic chord of Op. 11, No. 1, gives way to a briefly flashing melodic motive in thirty-seconds, <–4, –1, –3>, which reverses the intervals of the first piece's explanatory motive. This process happens twice for emphasis, once in m. 2 and again in m. 3.

While "explanation" occurs in the top stave, the bottom two staves of mm. 2–3 continue and extend gestures established in the opening measures, namely set-class expansions that culminate in Viennese Trichords or their set class, 3-5. The bass line of m. 1, as it crosses the barline into m. 2 (and jumps up into the middle staff), projects set class 3-3, followed by 3-8 directly after. The middle staff of m. 2 continues with a 3-4 that horizontalizes the interval stack from m. 1's fourth sixteenth, <7, 4>, as <–4, –7>, and like its predecessor, this 3-4 leads directly to a Viennese Trichord, <6, 5>. At the end of m. 2, the bass line presents overlapping motives that belong to 3-5, the first of them an arpeggiation of the ubiquitous chord, <+5, +6>. The lower staves of m. 3 present different versions of the Viennese Trichord together with the "unexplained" 4-19 interval stack, <5, 4, 4>. The Viennese Trichords in the middle staff are remarkable in that they create a voice exchange A-G♯/G♯-A between top and bottom voices of the interval stacks <6, 7> and <6, 5>, a pattern that will return later in the piece.

Section A ends in mm. 3b–5a with a pair of descending gestures consisting of a thirty-second-note chord followed by a dotted rhythm in octaves. The top line of the large chords, together with that of the octave dotted rhythms, can be understood as yet one more set-class expansion, this one coordinated with a pitch-interval expansion. If we begin with the right hand motive <+11, +4> on the fourth and fifth eighths of m. 3, that progresses to <–32, –6> on the pickup and first two eighths of m. 4, and finally <–35, –6> on the thirty-second and dotted quarter in m. 4b and eighth note in m. 5. This consistent expansion of pitch intervals (which begins as extreme, then becomes more incremental) projects the set classes 3-3, 3-8, and 3-5, the first two of which relate by expansion. The culminating 3-5 also occurs several times as a subset of the large thirty-second-note chords in mm. 3b–4. This reminds the listener of b chords 1 and 2 in Op. 11, No. 2, which have prominent Viennese Trichord subsets.

Our consideration of the A section has focused mainly on motivic and chordal processes that derive ultimately from the first two pieces of Op. 11, and, as we will see, are repeated and developed with multiple variations in the remainder of the third piece. But it is also worthwhile to step back and view Example 2.14 from the vantage point of its repertory of chords. Not every possible set class is circled or bracketed in these 4 measures and one eighth note, but the majority of the obvious vertical and horizontal groupings are (some in more ways than one), and it is remarkable that they limit themselves to four trichords and one tetrachord. It is even more remarkable that this chord vocabulary is the same as the most prominent chords in Op. 11, No. 1: 3-3, 3-4, and 3-8 from the A section's opening pitch expansion, and 3-5 and 4-19 from its contrasting B section. When Ethan Haimo remarks that "one is constantly struck by the feeling that a given passage sounds vaguely like things we have heard before," or, for that matter, when Bryan Simms explains that coherence in Op. 11, No. 3 is dependent on "the free and sporadic return of *motivic particles*, that is, small and usually nondistinctive figures that lack a memorable rhythm or shape," I suspect that they may be hearing the set-class (as well as some of the intervallic) connections within the third piece and between it and its predecessors.[42]

Example 2.15 illustrates Sections B through E. Brinkmann's division into four small sections represents well the fact that dynamics, tempo, or texture change abruptly after just about every measure or partial measure, giving the music its characteristic fragmented sound. Measures 5b–6a contain a loud, crashing descent to a sustained eighth-note chord that yields suddenly (on the third eighth of m. 6) to a quickly passing triplet figure at one of the softest dynamics. M. 7 introduces a stream of dyads and undergoes a pronounced lag in tempo, culminating in another sustained chord, all still soft. Finally,

[42] Haimo, *Schoenberg's Transformation of Musical Language*, p. 344; Simms, *The Atonal Music of Arnold Schoenberg*, p. 67.

Example 2.15  Schoenberg, Piano Piece Op. 11, No. 3, mm. 5–9, sections B–E. Used by permission of Belmont Music Publishers and Universal Edition

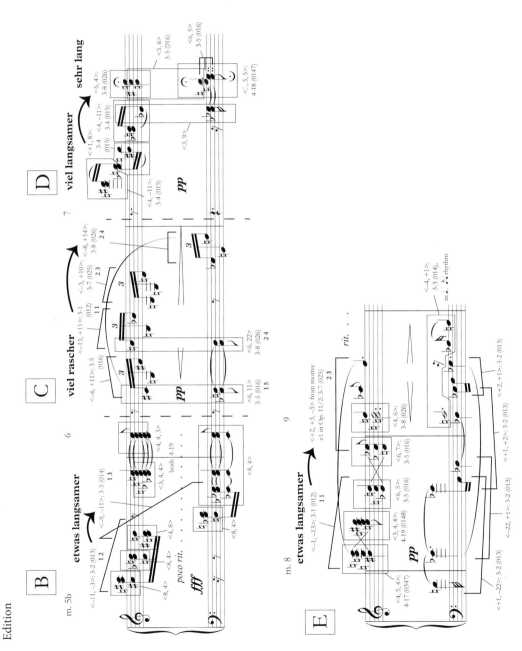

after a single measure, the direction changes yet again – now two parts are heard, a single line in the left hand and a stream of three or four notes in the right, which breaks up into soprano, chord, and perhaps tenor in m. 9.

But despite all the sudden (and some gradual) changes, there is a strong sense of continuity within the passage and between it and section A, for which Brinkmann's analysis does not account. Each of sections B, C, D, and E can be understood as developing motivic or chordal elements or progressions introduced in the opening measures. Section B slightly adjusts the unordered pitch-interval stacks that were widespread in m. 1, such as <9, 4> and <7, 4>, to a descending stream of four <8, 4>s and a single reversal, <4, 8>. The intervals of descent between these stacks are also noteworthy – the first three descend by the pitch intervals <–11, –3>, a member of set class 3-2 (013), in their outer voices, and the third through fifth descend <–9, –11>, 3-3 (014), constituting both a pitch-interval and a set-class expansion. And the culminating sonority on the fifth and sixth eighth notes of m. 5 contains as its upper five voices a stack of intervals <3, 4, 4, 3>, which can be heard as overlapping <3, 4, 4>, one of the 4-19 chords of mm. 2–3, with a reversal of itself. Section B places the elements of m. 1 and those of mm. 2–3 up against one another, not really a synthesis but a juxtaposition.

With its abrupt changes in dynamics and tempo, section C seems to usher in a new sound world. But that world is, again, built out of developments of the elements and processes of section A. The rushing triplet arpeggios begin with set class 3-5 and then trace a set-class expansion, 3-1 (012), 3-7 (025), 3-8 (026), creating ordered pitch class intervals **1, 1** to **2, 3** to **2, 4**. Unlike many of the progressions at the beginning of the piece, this set-class expansion also manifests as a pitch-interval expansion, when we compare the first to the second triplet, <–6, +11> and <–13, +11>, as well as the third to the fourth triplet, <–3, +10> and <–8, +14>. Even the few verticals we can find in the measure participate in the expanding process: the 3-5 (016) on the third eighth of m. 6 leads to 3-8 (026) on the fourth eighth, with unordered pitch intervals <6, 11> and <6, 22>.

Section D slows down appreciably and thickens the texture from one voice to two, three, and finally seven. But the set-class expansion process still governs here – this time, three consecutive 3-4s lead to a 3-8, yielding the ordered pitch class intervals **1, 4** to **2, 4**. The boxed three-note groupings that produce these set classes resemble the interval stacks from m. 1 in that they combine a small interval, often unordered pitch interval 4, with a larger one, such as ordered pitch interval –11. And, like their predecessors in m. 1, these interval configurations contract when one compares the first and second, <4, –11> and <+1, 8>, as well as the third and fourth, <4, –11> and <6, 4>. The only component of the third piece's signature gesture that is missing here is the Viennese Trichord at the end – instead of <6, 5> we hear <6, 4>, forming the aforementioned set class 3-8. But 3-5, as <5, 6> and <6, 5>, appears twice in the lower voices of section D's culminating seven-note chord.

In section E, for the first time, the focus seems to turn away from set-class and interval expanding processes. But the right hand of m. 8 still concerns itself with set classes, unordered pitch-interval stacks, and even a voice leading taken from the first three measures of Op. 11, No. 3. It begins with set class 4-17 as <4, 5, 4> leading to 4-19 as <3, 4, 4>, the second of which was an important component of mm. 2–3. But this pair of chords also has a voice leading in common with the opening measures: its top and bottom voices create a voice exchange, D♯5-E5 in the lowest voice against E6-D♯6 in the highest voice. This reminds the listener of the middle staff of m. 3, second and third eighth notes, where G♯3-A3 and A4-G♯4 had participated in a similar voice exchange. As if to confirm the listener's recall of the earlier voice leading, the second half of m. 8's right hand produces a transposed (T6) retrograde of it, three voices with E♭4-D4 in the lowest and D5-E♭5 in the highest voice. The set classes of m. 8b (both 3-5s) and unordered pitch-interval stacks (<6, 5> and <6, 7>) are identical to those in m. 3 (though reversed). And the two 3-5s resulting from the voice exchange progress on the downbeat of m. 9 to 3-8, forming one of the section's few set-class expansions. Another may be found when considering the ordered pitch intervals projected by the top voice in mm. 8–9; the first three notes yield <–1, –13>, a member of set class 3-1 (012) with adjacent ordered pitch-class intervals **1, 1**, and the last four produce <+2, +3, –3>, a member of set class 3-7 (025) with adjacent pc intervals **2, 3**.

Part of the second group of notes just mentioned stands out for a completely different reason. The ordered pitch intervals <+2, +3> recall one of the main motives of Op. 11, No. 2, motive *e1* in m. 4b of that piece (compare Example 2.15 with Example 2.2b). The pitch succession here in the third piece, <E♭5, F5, A♭5>, is a transposition up a tritone of the original motive *e1*, <A4, B4, D5>. This evocation of an earlier piece of Op. 11 in the soprano voice pairs with another motivic recall in the tenor of m. 9 (highest voice in the left hand), consisting of the sustained C4 on the downbeat followed at the end of the measure by an A♭3 sixteenth and an A3 quarter note. Not only the set class, 3-3, but also the ordered pitch-interval motive, <–4, +1>, and even the rhythm, which reduces to ♩.. ♪ ♩, all remind the listener of aspects of the opening of Op. 11, No. 1.

To review the larger scheme tying together sections B–E, we can claim that three sections devoted mainly to different kinds of expanding processes (B, C, D) give way in the fourth section to reminiscences of not only chords and progressions from the "explanatory" part of section A, mm. 2–3, but also motives from earlier pieces in the cycle. This same pattern, multiple

Example 2.16 Schoenberg, Piano Piece Op. 11, No. 3, mm. 10–11a, section F. Used by permission of Belmont Music Publishers and Universal Edition

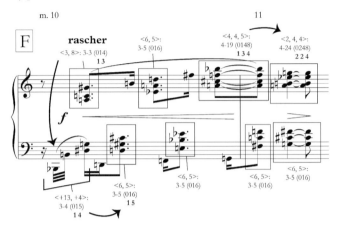

expansions together with references to the explanatory progression and/or earlier movements of Op. 11, will return later in the third piece. But first, section F produces a brief recall of the opening of section A, initiating the second large section of the piece, A2. It is portrayed in Example 2.16. When one considers the bracketed figure and boxed sonorities in the example, which constitute most of the prominent elements in mm. 10–11a, another set-class expansion and unordered pitch-interval contraction emerges. This begins with the initial motive in the bass <+13, +4>, a member of set class 3-4 (015) that resembles the pitch-interval profile of some of the opening chords of m. 1 (<11, 4> for example), and a vertical unordered pitch-interval stack <3, 8> in the right hand, belonging to set class 3-3 (014). The SC expansion/pitch-interval contraction then immediately progresses to a series of unordered pitch-interval stacks <6, 5>, the culminating element of the opening progression in m. 1, belonging to set class 3-5 (016). As section F progresses to its end, the right hand begins to present stacks of three unordered pitch intervals, <4, 4, 5>, one of the prominent manifestations of set class 4-19 (0148) in mm. 2–3, and <2, 4, 4>, a member of set class 4-24 (0248). The contraction in unordered pitch intervals is clear, but the set-class relationship is harder to characterize as an expansion – adjacent ordered pc intervals **1, 3, 4** move to **2, 2, 4**. One could make the claim, perhaps, that the interval content is becoming more even to create a whole-tone scale subset, a move that Schoenberg will make several times in the following measures, including the climax of the piece, section Q in m. 30.

The repeat of the set-class expansion and unordered pitch-interval contraction that characterized the opening measure is not the only characteristic

Example 2.17  Schoenberg, Piano Piece Op. 11, No. 3, mm. 11b–16a, sections G–H.
Used by permission of Belmont Music Publishers and Universal Edition

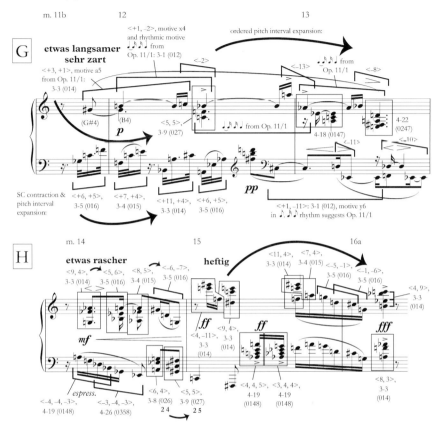

of section F that recalls the beginning, however. In addition, the increase in
tempo, the rising contour, the texture that alternates three-voice chords with
single notes, the dotted rhythm, and the dynamic increase from *forte* all call
to mind the pickup measure and m. 1, and clearly mark section F as the
beginning of a varied reprise. The next four sections G, H, I, and K also
resemble sections B–E in that they combine set-class expansions, unordered
pitch-interval contractions, variations on these processes, and the individual
elements of both processes with a reminiscence of not only the "explanatory"
process of mm. 2–3 but also veiled recalls of earlier pieces in the Op. 11 cycle.
Example 2.17 contains the first two sections, G and H.

   Section G is one of those sections that Reinhold Brinkmann labels
"thematic."[43] And, indeed, the right hand in mm. 11b–13 introduces

43  Brinkmann, *Drei Klavierstücke Op. 11*, p. 112.

a number of features that recall the theme of the first piece of Op. 11. First we hear the pitches G♯4 and B4, that piece's opening sounds, which grow out into the succession <+3, +1>, motive *a5* from the first piece, interlocking with a new version of motive *x* from that piece, which we will call *x4*: <+1, −2>. Finally, the continuation of the right-hand line consists of the rhythm ♩ ♪ ♪ ♩, stated three times, a variation of the ♩. ♪ ♩ that had served as a motto for piece No. 1.

The right hand in mm. 11b–13 also participates in expressing the expanding process, in a more concrete way than the previous expansions in the set-class realm: a series of sixteenth-note pickups to longer notes in both right and left hands presents a series of descending pitch intervals that expands, contracts, and expands again. The <−2> in m. 12 leads to <−13> from m. 12 across the barline into m. 13, then <−11> in the left hand on the second and third eighths of m. 13 (this instance associates with ♪ ♪♪, a reduction in half of ♩. ♪♪). The series continues in the right hand with <−8> on the third and fourth eighths of m. 13, and completes itself with <−10> in the left hand (in a different rhythm) in the latter half of m. 13. Though this series of motives manifests the third piece's signature expanding process, one could also hear it as repeatedly echoing a motive from the first piece of Op. 11, the first two notes of motive *a2* in m. 2, <A4, F4>, which had the same short–long rhythm. The right hand of mm. 11b–12 also manifests a set-class expansion, from the 3-3 (014) containing motive *a5* to the unordered pitch-interval stack <5, 5> in the second half of m. 12, a member of set class 3-9 (027). This is the farthest yet we have expanded: from **1, 3** out to **2, 5**. The left hand of these same measures, even more interestingly, presents a set-class *contraction* together with an ordered pitch interval expansion, a reversal of the usual process. The first three bracketed motives read <+6, +5>, <+7, +4>, and <+11, +4>: horizontalized versions of three of Op. 11, No. 3's opening right-hand chords, but in retrograde. Their associated set classes, 3-5, 3-4, and 3-3, create the set-class contraction, which then reverts to its original state with another <+6, +5>: 3-5.

Section H, steadily growing louder after the few measures of *p* in the previous section, abandons all references to Op. 11, No. 1 to focus again on set-class expansion and the juxtaposition of chords from m. 1 of the third piece with those of mm. 2–3. In this way, elements from both expanding and "explanatory" processes mingle, but the latter process is represented only by 4-19 chords in their unexplained form. M. 14 includes three pairs of trichords whose set classes expand and unordered pitch-interval stacks partially contract: in the right hand 3-3 (014) as <9, 4> leading to 3-5 (016) as <5, 6>, followed by 3-4 (015) as <8, 5> leading to 3-5 as <−6, −7>.

The last two chords in the left hand consist of 3-8 (026) projected by <6, 4> and 3-9 (027) as <5, 5>. The left hand in the first part of m. 14, meanwhile, draws its material from a different source: the first of its overlapped tetrachords is set class 4-19 as <−4, −4, −3>, a horizontal version of one of m. 2's most prominent motives. The second tetrachord is 4-26 (0358) as <−3, −4, −3>, continuing the descent in major and minor thirds. (The progression 4-19 to 4-26, like that of mm. 10–11, looks forward to the piece's climax in m. 30.)

The remainder of section H, mm. 15–16a, continues to juxtapose familiar set-class progressions from 3-3 to 3-4 to 3-5 with unordered pitch-interval stacks belonging to set class 4-19 from mm. 2–3. The right hand at the beginning of m. 15 and both hands on the last two eighth notes of that measure, going forward into m. 16, present the same three set classes and pitch-interval stacks that opened the third piece in the right hand, in a similar order. Example 2.14 had labeled the piece's first four boxed chords in the right hand as 3-3 <11, 4>, 3-3 <9, 4>, 3-4 <7, 4>, and 3-5 <6, 5>. In m. 15, the second eighth presents 3-3 as <4, −11>, the third and fourth eighths 3-3 as <9, 4>, and the fifth eighth two chords, 3-3 as <11, 4> and 3-4 as <7, 4>. The last chord of mm. 0–1's opening progression, <6, 5>, becomes in mm. 15–16 a pair of overlapping motives, <−5, −1> and <−1, −6>, both members of the same set class, 3-5. On the second and third eighths of m. 16, section H ends with prominent 3-3s in both hands: <8, 3> in the left and <4, 9> in the right. Prominent members of set class 4-19 also appear in m. 15, on the fourth eighth note in the left hand: both of the interval stacks are characteristic motives of mm. 2–3.

As mentioned above, all three of the 4-19 set classes in section H are of the "unexplained" variety. The last two of them are the unordered pitch-interval stacks <4, 4, 5> and <3, 4, 4>: close relatives of the foreign chords in m. 14 of Op. 11, No. 1 and m. 9 of Op. 11, No. 2 (both of these had consisted of the intervals <4, 4, 3>). Section I, shown together with section K in Example 2.18, makes an attempt for the first time since m. 3 to explain 4-19's close relation to the opening motto of Op. 11 by projecting it as <−3, −1, −4>. But this attempt ultimately fails.

The first part of section I, from m. 16b to the third eighth note of m. 18, breaks up into two streams: the held chords at the registral extremes, which consist of 3-3 as <3, 8> and 3-4 as <4, 7> on the pickup to m. 17, and 3-5 as <5, 6> on the fifth eighth note of that measure, holding over into m. 18. Not only do the set classes bring back the three-chord expanding sequence from the opening of Op. 11, No. 3 (which also had been emphasized in the previous section, H) but also two of the opening's unordered pitch-interval stacks (inverted), <4, 7> and <5, 6>. The other

Example 2.18 Schoenberg, Piano Piece Op. 11, No. 3, mm. 16b–20, sections I–K.
Used by permission of Belmont Music Publishers and Universal Edition

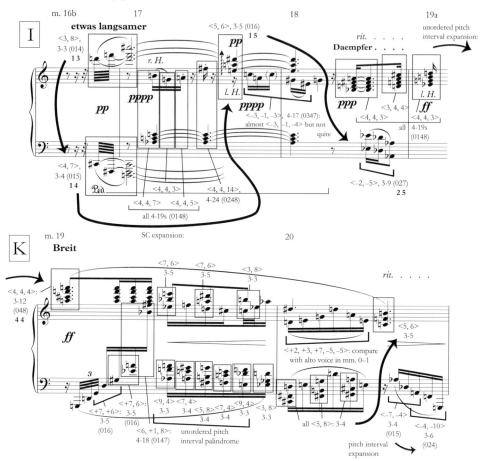

stream, in the inner voices, is where the explanation of 4-19 peters out.
In m. 17, a sustained augmented triad <4, 4> with a three-note fragment
above it, played *pppp* (as if to mark it as less important than the
surrounding expansion), creates three unexplained 4-19s in a row,
<4, 4, 7>, <4, 4, 3>, and <4, 4, 5>. (A fourth vertical yields set class
4-24, producing the piece's second 4-19 to 4-24 progression.) The end
of m. 17 begins with ordered pitch interval –3, C5-A4, which (after what
I interpret as a decorative repeat of the first note) continues –1, A4-G♯4.
But, the final –4 never appears to complete the explanatory motive –
instead the melody continues on with –3, G♯4-E♯4, and adds another +2
(G4) before it disappears completely. Thus, what had started with
the promise of a motivic explanation of set class 4-19 similar to the two

<-4, -1, -3>s in mm. 2–3, or the middleground motive <-3, -1, -4> in mm. 54–59 of Op. 11, No. 1, falls one interval short, almost inaudibly.

After the middle voices fail to produce an explanation of 4-19, the right hand presents a few more uninterpreted versions of it in the remainder of m. 18 and downbeat of m. 19. Unordered pitch-interval stacks <4, 4, 3>, <3, 4, 4> and <4, 4, 3> seem to demonstrate for the listener that 4-19 remains problematic. Underneath them in the left hand, <-2, -5> appears, a member of set class 3-9 (027): providing a fourth element for section I's series of expanding trichords, that is, 3-3 (014), 3-4 (015), 3-5 (016), 3-9 (027), as well as a bridge to the next section, K. Section K's right hand, as shown on the bottom half of Example 2.18, begins with 3-12 (048), a further expansion of the ordered pc intervals in 3-9's prime form (2, 5 to 4, 4). And this specific 3-12 is expressed as <4, 4, 4>, so that it expands something else as well: the <4, 4, 3> unordered pitch-interval stacks that end section I.

As section K continues, the emphasis shifts from set class 4-19 and the explanatory process, to the elements of the set-class expansion process. There are relatively few expansions per se in the section: one could point out the presence of three 3-4 chords on the first, third, and fifth sixteenths of m. 20 in the left hand, all with unordered pitch intervals <5, 8>: moving on to 3-5 as <5, 6> on the second half of the measure in the right hand. Underneath this Viennese Trichord, the left hand overlaps two motives whose intervals expand: 3-4 as <-7, -4> to 3-6 as <-4, -10>. But most of m. 19 is filled with familiar trichords and unordered pitch-interval stacks jumbled together without much in the way of clear ordering: 3-3 as <9, 4> and <3, 8>, 3-4 as <7, 4>, 3-5 as <7, 6> or <+7, +6>. (There is, however, a palindrome of set classes and interval stacks among the first five sixteenth notes in the left hand of m. 19b.) Section K is perhaps the most deserving of the label "intuitive" among the parts of Op. 11, No. 3 we have heard thus far – but even here, just about every chordal and motivic element can be traced back to earlier sections of Op. 11, No. 3, particularly the opening. This includes not only the pitch-interval stacks discussed above, but also the alto line in m. 20a, consisting of ordered pitch intervals <+2, +3, +7, -5, -5>: it has the same contour and rhythm and some of the same intervals (and pitches) as the alto in mm. 0–1, <+2, +3, +2, +6, -1, -5>.

Section K can be heard as a retransition for two reasons. First, it contains numerous elements borrowed from the opening, as we have seen; and second, it leads, after a brief *ritard*, to the second section that produces a varied reprise of the opening measures. This is section L, shown in Example 2.19. Section L has numerous non-pitch qualities that evoke the third piece's beginning: the opening texture and rhythm (two streams in the right hand, the higher consisting of dyad eighths, the lower a single line

Example 2.19 Schoenberg, Piano Piece Op. 11, No. 3, m. 21, section L. Used by permission of Belmont Music Publishers and Universal Edition

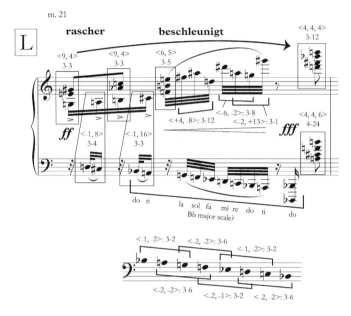

in sixteenths, and a single line in the left hand), the outward-wedge contour, and the dynamic increase from *ff* to *fff*. The first five chords in m. 21 also create the pattern that by now has become quite familiar: set classes 3-3 and 3-4 leading to set class 3-5 at the end of a gesture. Two of the unordered pitch-interval stacks associated with this set-class expansion are also customary, <9, 4> for 3-3 and the Viennese Trichord <6, 5> for 3-5, with a new configuration for 3-4, <–1, 8>.

But what comes after the 3-5 beginning the third eighth of the measure is something new. In the right hand, we hear three trichords overlapping, followed after an eighth rest by a fourth. Their set classes are mostly further expansions from the 3-3/3-4/3-5 formula that we heard at the beginning of the measure: 3-8 (026) and 3-12 (048). But the sequence also includes the set-class with the narrowest possible ordered pc intervals, 3-1 (012), and the order of set classes does not express an incremental expansion at all: 3-5, 3-12, 3-8, 3-1, 3-12. As for ordered pitch-interval motives, these also expand generally but not incrementally: <+4, –8> goes to <–6, –2> (motive *d2* from Op. 11, No. 2) and on to <–2, +13>. The unordered pitch-interval stack at section L's cadence in the right hand is <4, 4, 4>, which could be understood as expanding the <4, 4, 3> stacks that had been heard two measures prior at the end of section I.

If the right hand of the latter parts of m. 21 seems anomalous, the left hand is even more so. We hear, in effect, a descending B♭ major scale with do–ti–do at the end. B♭ is not suggested as a key area anywhere else in Op. 11, No. 3, so a tonal interpretation is probably out of the question (there are no B♭s in the final section, S, for example). Maybe the only way to understand this intrusion is to parse the scale into its component trichords, which twice manifest an expansion from set class 3-2 (013) as <–2, –1> or <–1, –2> to set class 3-6 (024) as <–2, –2>. (This is shown directly below the score excerpt in Example 2.19.) The left hand ends with the unordered pitch-interval stack <4, 4, 6>, which could be heard as an expanded version of the <4, 4, 4> directly above it.

Like the immediately previous section, there is a certain random quality to section L, although, considered in context, the hard-to-explain chords and progressions in the middle and end of m. 21 seem to participate in an overall gesture that begins along the same lines as the third piece's opening measures, but quickly flies off into other realms as the measure continues to expand in register, grow louder, and take on smaller note values. The following section, M, just like sections E and G before it, pulls back, not only to a softer dynamic but also to reminiscences of motives and chords from an earlier part of Op. 11. It is shown in Example 2.20, together with section N.

Section M includes numerous set classes, motives, and rhythmic and contour gestures that point back to Op. 11, No. 2. But the section begins by recalling the opening of the third piece once again, with an expansion of both pitch intervals and set classes, 3-4 to 3-5, in the left hand (the intervals in the two ordered pitch-interval successions also repeat interval pairs typical of the opening measures, <–4, –7> and <–7, –6>). But beginning on the fourth eighth note of m. 22, the left hand plays a motive, <+6, +2>, that strongly evokes motive *d2* from Op. 11, No. 2, as its pitch-interval inversion (compare Example 2.20 with Example 2.2a, m. 3). The right hand directly above it presents two gestures that, with their double grace notes and upward arpeggios, also hark back to the second piece, particularly the opening three notes of its theme b, motive *e1* in m. 4b, and later versions of that figure that add the ascending arpeggio to the final chord (see Example 2.2b, m. 4b, and Example 2.9a, mm. 45–47). The set classes found in m. 22 of piece No. 3 are different from b chords 1 and 2: the first upward arpeggio yields 4-13 (0136) and the second 4-24 (0248). But 4-13 had been a prominent chord later in subsection b of Op. 11, No. 2 (in the chorale at m. 11, see Example 2.4), and here in Op. 11, No. 3 it does a set-class expansion into the 4-24 of the second chord, uniting a characteristic chord of the second piece with the main chordal process of the third piece.

Measure 23 turns its attention from the beginning of theme b in Op. 11, No. 2 to its middle measures, presenting – twice – a variation of what we

Example 2.20 Schoenberg, Piano Piece Op. 11, No. 3, mm. 22–26a, sections M–N. Used by permission of Belmont Music Publishers and Universal Edition

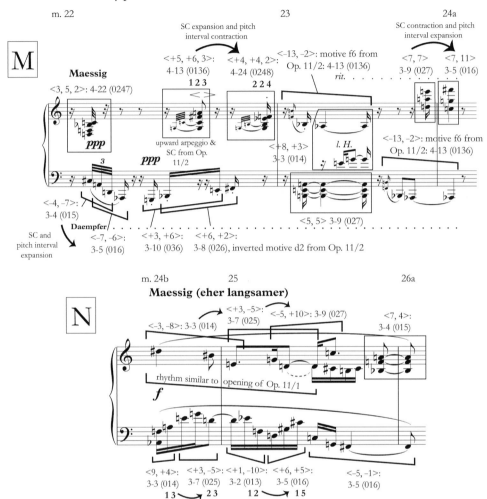

had called motive *f1* (refer back to Example 2.3, mm. 5b–6). This variation, which we will call *f6*, contracts the ordered pitch intervals of the original from <–13, –9> to <–13, –2>, and changes the surrounding set class from 5-Z18 (01457), b chord 3, to 4-13 (0136). Nevertheless, coming as it does after the references to the first part of the second piece's b theme in m. 22, m. 23 seems to complete a summary of that part of the earlier movement. Other elements prominent in m. 23 include a succession of three unordered pitch-interval stacks moving from the low register to the upper registers: 3-9 as <5, 5>, 3-9 as <7, 7>, and 3-5 as <7, 11>. Both set classes are familiar from earlier music, as is the first interval stack <5, 5>.

Section N follows M's evocation of Op. 11, No. 2 with its own recollection of elements from the first piece. The rhythm and contour in the right hand, ♩ ♪ ♪ ♪♪, mainly descending, varies the opening two measures of Op. 11, No. 1, and that in the left hand, with its ascending sixteenths to a longer note, recalls mm. 53–54 in the first piece – that place where the opening motives of section A and the motives of section B were brought together, first in counterpoint and eventually in a kind of synthesis through the <–3, –1, –4> explanatory motive in the middleground. And some of the set classes and pitch-interval motives associated with the earlier passage return as well – the right hand begins section N with 3-3 and ends with 3-4, the set classes of Op. 11, No. 1's motives *a1* and *a2*, and the left hand ends the section with two motives belonging to set class 3-5: a pitch-interval motive that recalls contrasting section B in the first piece (<+6, +5>, a close relative of motive *b1*, <+18, +5> from Example 1.8), followed by a motive, <–5, –1>, that recalls the "explanation" of set class 3-5 in mm. 63–64, the final cadence of the first piece (refer to Example 1.9b).

At the same time, section N puts these reminders of Op. 11, No. 1 in a context where set-class expansions, the hallmark of piece No. 3, are more strongly emphasized than in the first piece. The first three trichord motives in the right hand, which overlap with one another, create set classes 3-3, 3-7, and 3-9, yielding an expansion in the ordered pc intervals of the prime forms from **1, 3** to **2, 3** and finally to **2, 5**. The left hand begins with two pairs of trichords, each of which expand. The first follows 3-3 with 3-7, imitating the beginning of the right hand's progression (this correspondence is strengthened by the left hand's 3-7 using the same ordered pitch intervals and pitches as the right hand's, <+3, –5>). The second pair of set classes progresses from 3-2 to the first of the two 3-5s mentioned above, an ordered pc expansion of **1, 2** to **1, 5**.

The modus operandi of piece No. 3 to this point has been to feature incremental set-class expansions in strongly marked sections that create large *crescendos*, and then either allude to the "explanatory" process or recall material from earlier pieces in sections that are softer in dynamic and sometimes more diffuse sounding. We have seen this pattern repeatedly, with section A followed by E, section F followed by G, and H followed by I (which is particularly diffuse), and section L followed by sections M (also diffuse) and N. Afterward, what the listener would most likely expect is another large *crescendo* featuring set-class expansions, perhaps to a climax, followed by a decrease in intensity to end the piece. What happens in sections O through S is exactly that: the piece's largest *crescendo*, which begins by using set classes and pitch-interval stacks from the expanding sections that have come before, organized more or less randomly, and gradually pieces them together into set-class and pitch-interval successions that expand, then finally reaches (at the climax in section Q) an expanding succession of unordered pitch intervals, making the sense of expansion as concrete as it ever had been.

The first two stages of the large *crescendo* are portrayed in Example 2.21, sections O and P. Section O combines three components that look backward as well as forward.

The first involves references to and variations of the ascending minor third from subsection b of Op. 11, No. 1, the *"reduced a motive"* as we called it in Chapter 1 (this motive first appeared in mm. 4–8 of that piece and returned in mm. 54–58, where it expanded from a minor third to a major third (see Examples 1.7 and 1.9a)). This motive follows naturally from section N's allusions to mm. 1–3 of the first piece (and also to their return in mm. 53–55 of that piece). Measure 26 begins with two major thirds in the outer voices that ascend and descend in the manner of a voice exchange, E5-G♯5 and G♯3-E3 (doubled an octave lower). At the end of the measure, this contracts to the minor third B2-D3 (again doubled). Because of their short–long rhythms, both the major and minor thirds strongly evoke the first piece's *reduced a* motive.

The second component is brought to the fore through Schoenberg's *crescendo* and accent markings; the three-note motive, D4-E♭4-D4, <+1, –1>, in the middle of the measure. This motive was highlighted at times in Op. 11, No. 1; the same pitch classes an octave lower were a prominent motive in m. 41 of that piece, for example. But, more importantly for the present context, D–E♭–D sets off a chain of upper neighbors in mm. 28–29 of the P section that submit to interval expansion, clearly manifesting the third piece's main process. Finally, Section O contains a set-class expansion/pitch-interval contraction consisting of two chords, set classes 3-3 and 3-5 with unordered pitch intervals <8, 3> and <6, 5>. Both the set classes and pitch intervals remind us of earlier expanding processes in Op. 11, No. 3 (such as the one at mm. 16b–17 that consisted of pitch intervals <3, 8> and <5, 6>: see Example 2.18).

As the music moves on into section P, set classes and pitch-interval stacks from earlier in the third piece continue to dominate the texture. Two motives appear, formed by the top voice in first the left hand, <–2, –4> or set class 3-8, and then the right hand, <–1, –4> or set class 3-4. These versions of the *a* motive from Op. 11, No. 1, called *a16* and *a12*, contract both their ordered pc intervals and their pitch intervals. But the vast majority of ingredients of m. 27 are chords alternating between two set classes, 3-4 and 3-5, in a variety of pitch-interval voicings that we have heard before: <6, 5>, <5, 6>, <6, 7>, <7, 6>, <4, 7>, <7, 4>. These chords do not seem to project any long range-motion from 3-4 to 3-5 or vice versa; they simply

Example 2.21  Schoenberg, Piano Piece Op. 11, No. 3, mm. 26b–29, sections O–P. Used by permission of Belmont Music Publishers and Universal Edition

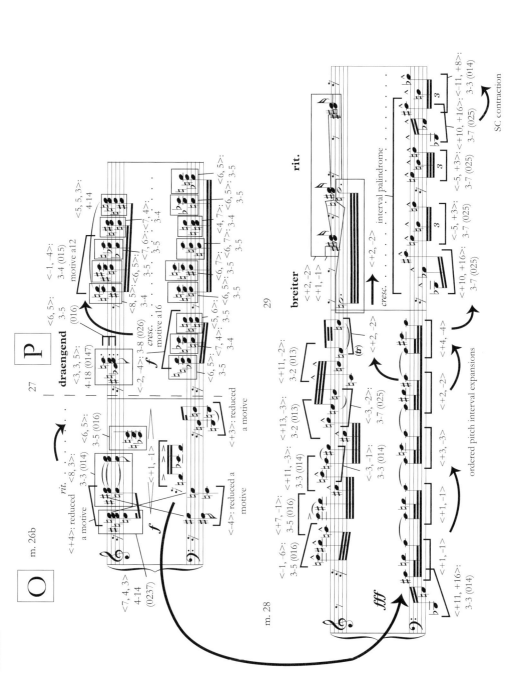

alternate, as the piece continues to grow louder toward the climax. In the following measure, 28, we begin to hear incremental expansion again, in the left hand. The motive <+11, +16>, a member of set class 3-3 that uses a pitch-interval succession similar to the stack that opened Op. 11, No. 3 in the right hand, <11, 4> (and that had also appeared as <+11, +4> on the same pitch classes at the end of the thirty-second note run in the right hand of m. 3), calls forth a series of neighbor figures that expands in two stages: from <+1, −1> to <+3, −3> and from <+2, −2> to <+4, −4>. This could be a veiled reference to the interval expansion that began Op. 11, No. 1: motive *a1*, <−3, −1>, followed eventually by motive *a3*, <−4, −2>. But in any case, it is a clear pitch-interval expansion. It is followed in both hands of m. 29 by further developments of its elements (the arrows in Example 2.21 indicate the lines of development). The left hand forms a palindromic interval contraction and expansion with two elements: a slight variation of the <+11, +16> that began the previous measure, <+10, +16>: 3-7, and a second motive, <−5, +3>, also forming set class 3-7. The contraction and expansion of intervals in the left hand of m. 29 could also be heard as a kind of neighbor motion, and since the ordered pitch intervals there are generally larger than those of m. 28's left hand, there is a large interval expansion spanning the pair of measures. (Also, if we compare the left hand of m. 29 with the *right* hand of m. 28, which we are about to discuss below, the repeated 3-7s of the latter measure produce a set-class expansion from the 3-2s and 3-3s of the former.) Meanwhile, the right hand in m. 29 combines <+2, −2> and <+1, −1> in a three-voice counterpoint of upper neighbors.

The right hand of m. 28 is the only passage that does not participate in the gradually increasing cascade of neighbors. In rhythm, contour, and articulation, it seems to hark back to mm. 2 and 3, the last place where the explanatory process stood its ground against set-class expansion. But we have already heard the demise of <−4, −1, −3> and <−3, −1, −4> in section I, mm. 17 and 18, so here there are no interval combinations that recall the explanatory motive or its set class, 4-19. Instead, the same segments that yielded <−4, −1, −3> in the earlier passage, the last two or three thirty-seconds of each group and first two thirty-seconds of the next, when split into trichords, produce a set-class contraction from 3-5 to 3-3 to 3-2, interrupted by a single set class 3-7. These segments' interval successions begin with a steady expansion, <−1, −6> to <+7, −1> to <+11, −3>, but then waver back and forth between smaller and larger intervals.

Finally, the dynamic climax of the piece is reached at m. 30, the beginning of section Q. (The final three sections, Q, R, and S, are portrayed as Example 2.22.)

Example 2.22  Schoenberg, Piano Piece Op. 11, No. 3, mm. 30–32, sections
Q (climax), R–S. Used by permission of Belmont Music Publishers and Universal
Edition

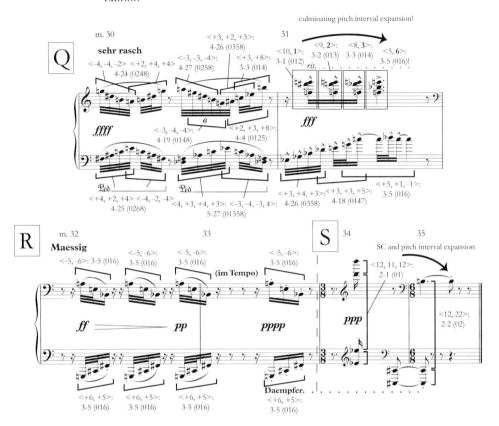

Q begins by carrying over the palindromic structuring that had appeared
at the end of P: both right and left hands play palindromes at the piece's
loudest dynamic, *ffff*. The right-hand mirror produces set class 4-24 as
<−4, −4, −2> and <+2, +4, +4>, while the left-hand one yields 4-25 as <+4,
+2, +4> and <−4, −2, −4>. These two whole-tone tetrachords were pre-
dicted by motions from 4-19 to 4-24 earlier in the third piece (mm. 11 and
17) (which I commented on in our discussions on pp. 94 and 98). I argued
there that even though set classes 4-19 to 4-24 (ordered pc intervals 1, 3, 4
to 2, 2, 4) do not literally constitute an expansion, they could be thought of
as doing something related to expanding: evening out the interval content
to move the music in the direction of the whole-tone collection.
The opening of section Q seems to confirm that motion toward even
intervals has a similar function to expansion, and perhaps it can be understood generally as a second step in the process that Op. 11, No. 3 associates

with its large *crescendos*. (It is worth mentioning here that both 4-24 and 4-25 contain set class 3-8 as a subset, and both ordered pitch-interval successions <-4, -4, -2> and <-4, -2, -4> contain <-4, -2> as a subset. So another way to interpret m. 30a's whole-tone tetrachords is as extensions of 3-8 <-4, -2>, motive *a3*, the endpoint of the original expanding process at the outset of Op. 11, No. 1.)

The latter half of m. 30 then turns its focus back to the actual expansion of pitch intervals, particularly in the left hand. The bass had alternated pitch intervals 2 and 4 in m. 30a's palindrome, now in 30b it alternates pitch intervals 3 and 4 (some ordered, some unordered). The right hand is more complicated: one of its sequences, <-3, -4, -4> produces set class 4-19, showing that, in the pitch-interval realm, 4-19 can arise from 4-24 through expansion. But as it continues, it first contracts its intervals, alternating pitch interval 3 with 2, then expands dramatically again at the end to form <+3, +8>, a projection of set class 3-3 whose pitch intervals are familiar from earlier in the third piece.

If m. 30 is Piece No. 3's dynamic climax, then the following measure can be heard as its motivic climax. For at this point, we hear – *fff*, accented, and gradually slowing for emphasis, in the top two voices of the right hand – an incrementally expanding series of pitch intervals: <1, 2, 3, 6>. I call this the "motivic climax" because it culminates the large arc of the third piece, which began in section A with expanding and explanatory processes side-by-side, then allowed the expanding process to develop and increase (and continue to associate itself with large *crescendos*) while the explanatory process dwindled away at extremely soft dynamic levels (in section I). M. 31 serves as an exclamation point to set-class expansion's assertion of its triumph over not only the explanatory process, but also the motivic and chordal references to the first and second pieces. It brings expansion up onto the more concrete, audible level of pitch intervals, yet at the same time preserves it in the set-class realm: set class 3-1 moves to 3-2, 3-3, and finally 3-5. And the last two set classes are given unordered pitch-interval stacks that have both become mottos for piece No. 3: <8, 3> for 3-3 and <5, 6> for 3-5. The left-hand accompaniment in m. 31, meanwhile, also progresses to and highlights set class 3-5, presenting it as <+5, +1, -1>: perhaps we can understand this as an "explanation" of what had been a foreign element in Op. 11, for <+5, +1> is an expanded version of <+3, +1>. (A similar explanation of 3-5 as <-6, -1> had occurred in the final three bass notes of Op. 11, No. 1: we discussed this on p. 34 and it is illustrated in Example 1.9b.)

As if to reinforce the 3-5 <5, 6> in the right hand of m. 31b as the third piece's exclamation point and the culmination of all its set-class and interval expansions, the following section, R, echoes it for two measures. It does so by projecting its intervals several octaves lower, as <+6, +5> in the left hand and <–5, –6> in the right, and gradually decreasing in volume. This brings the piece to its final section, S, now at ***ppp***. Section S seems to take the music in a new direction (as do several of the final sections of other Schoenberg atonal works we will study, as well as the codas in some of his twelve-tone pieces). It does not project familiar set classes or interval stacks. Its main connection to the rest of the piece is its increase in the size of unordered pitch intervals from <12, 11, 12> to <12, 22>, bringing the piece to a close with one final unordered pitch interval and set-class expansion.

My detailed account of the third piece of Schoenberg's Op. 11 has shown that it is neither completely "intuitive" nor improvisatory. It is full of motivic and chordal repetition on the levels of set class, unordered pitch-interval stack, and even ordered pitch-interval motive. Such repetition not only manifests itself from beginning to end of the third piece, but also reaches back into the first and second pieces, making Op. 11 a cycle. And, if one traces the motivic and chordal progressions of the third piece carefully, it becomes clear that No. 3 indeed has a large plan that involves the interaction of two processes carried over from Nos. 1 and 2. The first process, defined at the beginning of Op. 11, No. 3 by set classes that expand while the unordered pitch intervals projecting them contract (usually culminating in set class 3-5 as <5, 6>), is initially interrupted by a second process that "explains" set class 4-19 as <–4, –1, –3>, as well as by reminiscences of the first two pieces. But it roughly pushes these interruptions aside, as it continually gains strength in passages that increase in dynamic and registral span, and eventually the set-class expansions give rise to something more concrete: a pitch-interval expansion ending in <5, 6> in m. 31. After this motivic climax, there is nothing left for the piece to do but repeat the intervals 5 and 6, then expand further, as it dies away. Op. 11, No. 3 is a masterpiece in the way it combines motivic and harmonic integration and a clear large organizational scheme with its strong expression of formal fragmentation and abruptness.

This large plan is, of course, something different from the conflict and resolution schemes projected by Op. 11, Nos. 1 and 2, their manifestations of "musical idea." The third piece's relentless drive toward the triumph of set-class expansion and (eventually) interval expansion fits well with the fragmentary nature of its form relative to the other pieces, just as their abbreviated sonata-rondo and ABA forms supported their focus on resolving the differences between their A and B sections or a and b themes. Even though Schoenberg by no means abandoned motivic working in the summer of 1909, it does seem clear that by this point in his composing career he had become interested in creating large schemes for pieces that were different from the problem-solution dialectic. I believe that he was experimenting with other ways to create large-scale coherence from the very beginning of his atonal period (and probably well before that, though to demonstrate that would go beyond the scope of this book). In Chapter 3, we will explore two songs from Op. 15, the *George-Lieder*, written prior to Op. 11, and thus among Schoenberg's first atonal pieces. Op. 15, Nos. 7 and 11 both will illustrate his use of what I call the "basic image" – a visual image abstracted from the text that controls not only every aspect of pitch and rhythm, but also other features of the music.

# 3 *Das Buch der hängenden Gärten*, Op. 15, Nos. 7 and 11

## *Basic Images in Two of the Earliest Atonal Pieces*

The fifteen songs of Op. 15, on poems from Stefan George's collection *Das Buch der hängenden Gärten*, were singled out by Schoenberg as the first of his compositions to abandon tonality as a structure-producing device altogether. As he wrote in his program notes for the premiere performance in 1910:

> With the George songs I have for the first time succeeded in approaching an ideal of expression and form which has been in my mind for years. Until now, I lacked the strength and confidence to make it a reality. But now that I have set out along this path once and for all, I am conscious of having broken through every restriction of a bygone aesthetic; and though the goal towards which I am striving appears to me a certain one, I am, nonetheless, already feeling the resistance I shall have to overcome.[1]

As is the case with most Schoenbergian "firsts," however, the picture is more complex than it initially seems. For one thing, the composition of Op. 15 apparently was spread over more than a year's time, from March 1908 to spring 1909, and its gestation overlapped with two other opus numbers: the final three movements of the Second String Quartet Op. 10, and the first two of the Three Pieces, Op. 11 (which we discussed in Chapters 1 and 2). The most careful accounts of the chronology of Op. 15, such as those found in Bryan Simms's *The Atonal Music of Arnold Schoenberg*, Ethan Haimo's *Schoenberg's Transformation of Musical Language*, and Jan Maegaard's *Entwicklung des dodekaphonen Satzes bei Arnold Schönberg*, tell us that he finished writing the first drafts for four songs, Nos. 4, 5, 3, and 8, in "*Sammelhandschrift* Nr. 10" (Manuscript Collection No. 10), in March and April 1908, confirmed by the dates Schoenberg wrote at the end of these drafts. He then added one more song, No. 7, and a sketch for No. 6, in April 1908 in a second *Sammelhandschrift*, No. 14 (only No. 7 is dated, April 28, 1908). During the summer of 1908 (the summer of his marital crisis, which we will consider in detail later), he apparently set the Op. 15 songs aside to complete the second movement of the Op. 10 String Quartet and write the third and fourth. He picked up the song cycle again in September 1908 in *Sammelhandschrift*

---

[1] Schoenberg, cited in Willi Reich, *Schoenberg: A Critical Biography*, trans. Leo Black (New York: Praeger, 1971), p. 49.

No. 22, completing a first draft for Song No. 13 (dated September 27, 1908) and making sketches for Nos. 14 and 15. In February 1909, he turned to composing the first two Piano Pieces of Op. 11, the first of which was dated February 19 at its end and the second February 22 at its beginning. Then, directly afterward, in *Sammelhandschrift* No. 23, he made another sketch for Song No. 14 and finished drafting No. 15 (dated February 28, 1909). The other Hanging Gardens songs have no dated first drafts that have survived, so that they could have appeared at any point between the beginning of Schoenberg's work on the cycle and spring 1909. Thus, the only songs in Op. 15 that truly have a claim to being the "first atonal pieces" are Nos. 3, 4, 5, 7, and 8.[2] (We will explore No. 7 in detail later as a representative of this first stage of the work's genesis.)

A second qualifier to Schoenberg's assertion about the priority of his Op. 15 songs is the sense that some of them do not step completely over the atonal "line." Certain songs in the collection have been shown in whole or in part to have underlying large-scale functional-tonal structures; interestingly, they do not include the songs written in the first creative wave of spring 1908, but instead are limited to songs that were (possibly) composed later. One thinks of Steve Larson's Schenkerian sketch of No. 2, "Hain in diesen Paradiesen," where Larson connects a simple i–ii–V–i progression in D minor (only the bass line, there is no conventional *Urlinie*) to Schoenberg's piece through no less than eleven levels. As he works his way gradually down to the surface of the piece, Larson encounters many of the same issues I faced in my Schenkerian graph of Op. 11, No. 1 in Chapter 1 – dissonant added notes, rhythmic displacements that prevent the outer voices from being consonant, missing chord tones, and numerous pitches that seem to be more easily explained through motivic, intervallic means. But the principal four chords of the underlying progression do sound prominently enough: at the beginning, middle, and end of the song.[3] Another passage with strong tonal resonances, according to Bryan Simms, is the piano introduction to No. 10, "Das schöne Beet." As Simms describes it:

> Schoenberg's music is unique in the entire cycle as it makes a startling return to the late romantic style, the post-Tristanesque language of Eros. A lengthy and impassioned piano prelude begins in the key of D major and minor, the

---

[2] Simms, *The Atonal Music of Arnold Schoenberg*, pp. 47–49; Haimo, *Schoenberg's Transformation of Musical Language*, pp. 244–45; Jan Maegaard, *Studien zur Entwicklung des dodekaphonen Satzes bei Arnold Schönberg*, 3 vols. (Copenhagen: Wilhelm Hansen, 1972), I, pp. 61–63. The majority of surviving manuscripts for Op. 15 can be viewed online at www.schoenberg.at.

[3] Steve Larson, "A Tonal Model of an 'Atonal' Piece: Schönberg's Opus 15, Number 2," *Perspectives of New Music* 25/1–2 (Winter–Summer 1987): 418–33.

key extended to its very limits of perceptibility by free linear motions in multiple parts ... The opening measures adumbrate a D triad, and the introduction concludes in measures 9–10 with a similarly veiled dominant chord in this key. The voice then enters, briefly repeats the piano's opening music, but then moves effortlessly back into the atonal style.[4]

Interestingly, the key suggested in No. 10 is D, the same key that Larson asserts as the basis for No. 2. But attempts to grasp the rest of the cycle in D minor or major, related keys, or any other keys for that matter meet with even more insurmountable obstacles, as we will see in our detailed analyses of Nos. 7 and 11.

Before discussing those two songs, a few words are in order about the texts of the cycle, and what they may have signified for their poet on the one hand and their composer on the other. Schoenberg set fifteen of the thirty-one poems in Stefan George's *Das Buch der hängenden Gärten*, the third of three books of poems published in 1895: *Die Bücher der Hirten- und Preisgedichte, der Sagen und Sänge, und der hängenden Gärten* (The Books of Eclogues and Eulogies, of Legends and Lays, and of the Hanging Gardens). The poetry of *Das Buch der hängenden Gärten* is notoriously vague in its outline and suggestive of various interpretations; those familiar with George's poetry will recognize these features as characteristic elements of his strong early debt to the French symbolist poets. Nevertheless, an attempt at a brief synopsis of the text of *Das Buch* follows, representing some of the interpretations suggested to me as I read through the cycle and two of its critiques – Ulrich Goldsmith and Robert Norton.[5] The speaking character is a young king – according to Goldsmith it is George's projection of himself into ancient Babylon in his childhood or adolescent dreams.[6] In the poems prior to the ones Schoenberg set, the dream-ruler leads his armies in triumph over a foreign people and lifts his sword against their god, then gathers his people around him and teaches them. Eventually he becomes involved in an affair forbidden by his culture, described in a sub-collection of fifteen poems, the ones Schoenberg set in his Op. 15. They set the stage for and describe a furtive, increasingly fervent courtship of an uncertain length (corresponding to the ten poems in the

---

[4] Simms, *The Atonal Music of Arnold Schoenberg*, pp. 50–51.

[5] Ulrich K. Goldsmith, *Stefan George: A Study of His Early Work* (Boulder, CO: University of Colorado Press, 1959), pp. 64–71; and Robert E. Norton, *Secret Germany: Stefan George and His Circle* (Ithaca: Cornell University Press, 2002), pp. 177–82. An English translation of the cycle can be found in Stefan George's *The Works of Stefan George Rendered into English*, trans. Olga Marx and Ernst Morwitz (Chapel Hill, NC: University of North Carolina Press, 1949), pp. 71–75.

[6] Goldsmith, *Stefan George: A Study of His Early Work*, p. 64.

group preceding Song 11), which possibly culminates in sex at a time prior to Song 11. In the five poems beginning with Song 11, the affair dies down, and the object of the affair (who remains silent throughout the cycle) leaves (or is banished?). One of the strengths of the fifteen poems describing the affair is George's effective use of "growth" images from plant life, such as a gate blooming with flowers, to parallel the growth of the affair, and images of plant decay – windblown leaves, withered grass – to portray the dissipation of the affair.[7]

The person who is the object of the king's tryst is vague in gender. On the one hand, it could be a young woman to whom sexual access is not permitted. Lines 2 and 3 of Song 4 suggest (to me) a female member of the harem of the young king's father, and this interpretation is strengthened by the fact that Songs 5 and 15 use the word "she" to refer to the silent character. But this person could also be a boy, given George's own sexual inclinations and his framing of the cycle as autobiographical. Goldsmith claims the *Hanging Gardens* poems are "[George's] only artistic record of a satisfactory relationship with the other sex" and suggests a female model for the cycle's "other": Ida Coblenz, whose six-year friendship with George overlapped with the time period in which he wrote the *Hanging Gardens* poems as well as *Das Jahr der Seele*.[8] Norton, in contrast, argues for a same-sex interpretation, based on the reasons given above and the paucity of uses of the pronoun "sie" in the cycle.[9]

It seems that Schoenberg, for his part, can be interpreted as making this story coherent in a way meaningful to him and translating it into music in ways typical for him: the "basic image" and "musical idea." Schoenberg's concern, as far as I know, was not with portraying an affair between man and boy. But there was a forbidden relationship of a different kind that was preying on his mind at the times he wrote his settings of *Das Buch der hängenden Gärten*. In 1907 Schoenberg and his first wife, Mathilde (Alexander von Zemlinsky's sister), made the acquaintance of a young painter, Richard Gerstl, who served as painting tutor to both of them.

---

[7] The reader should compare my synopsis of the text at this point with Bryan Simms's lengthy overview of the text and music in *The Atonal Music of Arnold Schoenberg*, pp. 49–52. Simms also suggests an overall increase and decrease in intensity, but following Theodor W. Adorno's essay "Zu den Georgeliedern" and reacting (like Adorno) to certain musical characteristics of Schoenberg's setting, he claims that the decrease begins at Song No. 9. Adorno's essay can be found as an appendix to Schoenberg's *Arnold Schönberg, Fünfzehn Gedichte aus "Das Buch der hängenden Gärten" von Stefan George. Für Gesang und Klavier* (Wiesbaden: Insel-Bücherei no. 683, 1959), pp. 76–83.

[8] Goldsmith, *Stefan George: A Study of His Early Work*, pp. 71 and 80.

[9] Norton, *Secret Germany*, pp. 179–80.

During that year and the first part of 1908 (as Schoenberg was beginning to
compose Op. 15), the friendship between Mathilde Schoenberg and
Richard Gerstl developed into an affair, and in the summer of 1908,
Mathilde left Schoenberg and their children to live with her new lover.
After a short time, Anton Webern and other friends persuaded Mathilde to
return, and in November 1908 Gerstl committed suicide after destroying
his documents and works.[10] Joseph Auner's anthology of Schoenberg's
writings reproduces a draft of Schoenberg's Last Will and Testament that
he made right after Mathilde's betrayal. This document portrays, rather
starkly, Schoenberg's emotional disassociation from her ("My wife can
only be faithful. Therefore she was not my wife"), and in another place
expresses his uncertainty that the marriage ever happened (or perhaps his
wish that it never had).[11] It is not entirely fanciful, then, to imagine that
Schoenberg interpreted George's poetry in terms of a heterosexual marriage relationship that created increasing anxiety, together with hope and
desire, as his wife's faithfulness came under suspicion, and eventually was
destroyed (or at least irreparably damaged) by the affair. In the aftermath,
the betrayed partner tries to recall specific sensations, emotional as well as
sexual, from the relationship he once had with his wife, but other, stronger
images associated with the betrayal crowd in and prevent him from
doing so.[12]

[10] A detailed narrative of the occurrences surrounding Mathilde Schoenberg's and Richard
Gerstl's affair can be found in Hans Heinz Stuckenschmidt, *Schoenberg: His Life, World
and Work*, trans. Humphrey Searle (New York: Schirmer Books, 1978), pp. 93–97.

[11] Joseph Auner, *A Schoenberg Reader: Documents of a Life* (New Haven: Yale University
Press, 2003), pp. 52–56.

[12] My analyses will proceed from similar assumptions to Allen Forte's massive survey of the
Op. 15 songs, "Concepts of Linearity in Schoenberg's Atonal Music: A Study of the Opus
15 Song Cycle," *Journal of Music Theory* 36/2 (1992): 285–382. Forte's main concern is to
show how numerous linear entities in the songs are derived from pitch motives in Song 1
through pitch and order transformations. But he also claims that several of these lines, as
well as certain individual pitch classes, are ciphers for "Arnold Schoenberg," "Mathilde,"
and "Richard Gerstl."

My interpretation therefore takes what at first seems to be an opposing position to
Ethan Haimo's in *Schoenberg's Transformation*, about the influence or lack of it that
Schoenberg's personal issues exerted on his compositional choices. Haimo's protests have
to do with claims other scholars have made about the String Quartet Op. 10. On
pp. 227–30, for example, he argues against the notion that Schoenberg's choice to quote
"O du lieber Augustin" in the second movement of the quartet had anything to do with his
marriage. And on pp. 269–79 he disputes the claims (common in the literature) that
Schoenberg's marital crisis influenced him to stop work on the quartet in fall 1907 before
the third and fourth movements were written and return to them in summer 1908, to add
the voice part for those movements, to choose texts from George's *Siebente Ring* for them,
and finally to adopt either a less functionally tonal harmonic style than his works before

## "Angst und Hoffen," Op. 15, No. 7

As mentioned previously, Song No. 7 will serve as my representative of those Op. 15 songs written in spring 1908, demonstrating the extent to which Schoenberg had already crossed over the line in one of his first atonal works. But even more importantly, I want to show that this song can be analyzed fruitfully, demonstrating relationships between text and music on multiple levels, by abstracting a visual image from the poem's first two lines and showing how pitch, interval, rhythm, phrasing, and form all manifest this image in different ways. This will be the first of many analyses in this book that demonstrates the concept of the "basic image," a notion that will prove useful again and again in later chapters (particularly in the analyses of Op. 21, *Pierrot lunaire*, in Chapter 6).

The original text is given below, with my own English translation:

| | |
|---|---|
| Angst und hoffen wechselnd mich beklemmen, | Fear and hope in turn constrict me, |
| Meine worte sich in seufzer dehnen, | My words expand into sighs, |
| Mich bedrängt so ungestümes sehnen, | Such impetuous longing afflicts me |
| Daß ich mich an rast und schlaf nicht kehre, | That I pay no mind to rest or sleep, |
| Daß mein lager tränen schwemmen, | That my bed is soaked with tears, |
| Daß ich jede freude von mir wehre, | That I repel every joy from me, |
| Daß ich keines freundes trost begehre. | That I ask for no friend's consolation. |

I translated the poem myself in order to use "constrict" and "expand" instead of the other synonyms that could have represented George's "beklemmen" and "dehnen." (For example, David Lewin's choices in his detailed analysis of Song No. 7 are "seize" and "trail off"; others might have chosen the standard dictionary translations "oppress" and

---

1907 (according to many writers) or a more functionally tonal one than Op. 15 (according to Bryan Simms).

   Though his analyses of Op. 15 do not broach the issue, I have the strong sense that Haimo would also argue against any assertion that Mathilde and Gerstl inspired Schoenberg's choice of *Das Buch der hängenden Gärten* for his texts, or that the marital crisis motivated Schoenberg to push his harmonic language over the line into atonality in the first wave of Op. 15 songs. I too believe Schoenberg probably was inspired to use George for positive reasons (namely, a deep interest in and appreciation for his poetry), and that he was motivated to advance his harmonic language out of a compulsion to move musical culture forward (as he himself claimed repeatedly). But my claim is a less sweeping one: essentially, that the "basic images" one might abstract from George's texts, which, as I will show, serve as effective frameworks for the pitch, intervallic, and rhythmic relationships in the two songs we will study, are indeed consistent with Schoenberg's personal experiences.

"stretch."[13]) Key words and phrases from the first two lines, "Fear and hope in turn," "constrict," and "expand," together suggest a visual image in motion, which could be expressed perhaps as the face of the poet turning first one way (downward, toward fear) and then the opposite way (upward, toward hope), again and again, while his whole body is pressed down or constricted, then expands itself, taking in the air necessary to emit longer and longer sighs. The construction of such an image seems to me at least partly consistent with Schoenberg's assertion in "The Relationship to the Text" that "inspired by the sound of the first words of the text, I had composed many of my songs straight through to the end without troubling myself in the slightest about the continuation of the poetic events."[14] My basic image visualizes the first two lines of "Angst und Hoffen," but does not respond to the rest of the poem in any significant way. And, we might go a step further to imagine the composer himself as the one whose face turns alternately toward fear (that Mathilde would abandon him) and hope (that she would remain faithful) as his whole body constricts, then expands to emit longer and longer sighs. A passage from his Last Will and Testament describes similar behaviors:

> Now, it certainly cannot be denied that I am extremely unhappy about her breach of faith. I have cried, have behaved like someone in despair, have made decisions and then rejected them, have had thoughts of suicide and almost carried them out, have plunged from one madness into another – in a word, I am totally broken.[15]

The reader should be assured I am not claiming with any certainty that my basic image accurately describes Schoenberg's physical or mental state in spring 1908, or that Song No. 7 documents real experiences he had – such claims would only be provable beyond doubt if I were able to time travel, to Schoenberg's study during those days, or even to the inner reaches of his mind. There are no drawings among Schoenberg's sketches for the work that portray objects alternating, contracting, or expanding, as far as I know. Yet, I believe I can still make the assertion that the construction of such an image provides me as analyst with a useful framework on which to hang my own observations (and those of others) about musical features and

---

[13] David Lewin, "A Way into Schoenberg's Opus 15, Number 7," *In Theory Only* 6/1 (November 1981): 3–24.

[14] Arnold Schoenberg, "The Relationship to the Text" (1912), in *Style and Idea* (1984), p. 144. We will discuss later, in Chapter 6, why I interpret this quotation in terms of Schoenberg drawing visual images from the *meaning*, as well as the sheer sound, of the opening lines of text.

[15] Auner, *A Schoenberg Reader*, p. 55.

Example 3.1 Schoenberg, "Angst und Hoffen," Op. 15, No. 7, mm. 1–3a. Copyright © 1914, 1941 by Universal Edition AG Vienna, UE 5338. All rights reserved. Used by permission of Belmont Music Publishers and Universal Edition

processes and their relationships to the text. This framework has the further advantage of agreeing in part with Schoenberg's own remarks about how he set texts. I will now proceed to describe in detail exactly how Song No. 7 represents the alternation of fear and hope, and how it is constricted (i.e., contracts) and expands in multiple ways and directions.

At least two writers on this song have labeled the two initial chords, 3-12 (048) and 3-5 (016), which set the words "Angst" and "Hoffen," as the "Angst" and "Hoffen" chords.[16] (See Example 3.1, the musical setting of the first line of the poem.)

We saw in Chapters 1 and 2 that both chords are widespread in the three Op. 11 Piano Pieces (written about a year after this song); 3-12 usually as a subset of 4-19 (0148), but also as an entity in itself, and 3-5 in its two Viennese Trichord voicings, <5, 6> and <6, 5>. Whether 3-12 as <4, 4> represents fear in "Angst und Hoffen" and 3-5 as <6, 5> represents hope is

---

[16] Lewin, "A Way into Schoenberg's Opus 15, Number 7," 8; Robert Falck, "'Fear and Hope': A Look at Schoenberg's Op. 15, No. VII," *Canadian Association of University Schools of Music Journal* 7 (1977): 93.

not as crucial as recognizing that these two chords do, indeed, alternate with one another throughout the song, providing a musical correspondence to the "Fear and hope in turn" part of the basic image. Alternations of 3-12 and 3-5 (always in the same order, 3-12 first) recur at mm. 3, 4, 7, 8, 14, 15–16, 17, and 18–19. In addition, a passage featuring 4-24 (0248), a superset (one might even call it an expansion) of 3-12, in mm. 5–6 precedes another passage in mm. 9–11 where 3-5 appears multiple times, creating alternation on a higher level. It is important to recognize that these alternations of the "fear" and "hope" chords most often do *not* preserve the specific pitches, pitch classes, and unordered pitch intervals of m. 1. For example, the pair in m. 3a (included at the end of Example 3.1) presents the pitch classes <C, E, A♭> and <A♭, D♭, G> reckoned from the bottom (rather than the original forms <G♭, B♭, D> and <F♭, B♭, E♭>), and their unordered pitch intervals consist of <4, 4> and <5, 6>, the second different from the original form in m. 1b. Many of the subsequent 3-12/3-5 pairs continue transposing pitch classes and reversing intervals, until the original chords return in mm. 18 and 19. So to speak of persistent alternation between fear and hope through the piece, we must have recourse to the notion of set class.

The "constricting" or contracting and "expanding" of the first two lines of the poem also have clear portrayals in the ordered pitch and pitch-interval sequences of the first line. Richard Domek recognizes that the soloist's line can be partitioned in the manner of a compound melody into two strands that progress up from D5 to E♭5 to F♭5, and down from G♭4 to F♭4 to E♭4, creating an overall expansion.[17] The stems and beams applied to the voice part in the lower half of Example 3.1 make this outward wedge more obvious – however, I must emphasize that these are not used in the typical way as Schenkerian symbols, but simply as visual aids to highlight the component voices in the compound melody. Since none of the intervals between the notes of these voices, an augmented fifth, a major seventh, and a minor ninth, are consonant, these stems and beams cannot signify a tonal contrapuntal structure, like those in my analysis of Op. 2, No. 2 in Chapter 1 had. Instead, they indicate a crossing of the line into atonality, already in March 1908. In the first half of m. 2, there are four notes in the voice unaccounted for by the previously described compound melody. Domek reads these as compound melody also: of the thirds C5-A4 and A♭4-C♭5 (which appear as verticals in the piano part directly below). What he does not point out is that with respect to the overall pattern in mm. 1–3, this pair of thirds in the compound melody creates a contraction as the singer moves

---

[17] Richard Domek, "Some Aspects of Organization in Schoenberg's *Book of the Hanging Gardens*, Opus 15," *College Music Symposium* 19/2 (Fall 1979): 120–21.

over the barline from m. 1 to m. 2 and an expansion from m. 2a to 2b (highlighted by my arrows in Example 3.1's bottom half). The rhythms also contract and expand in exactly the same places: after the downbeat of m. 2, we hear quadruplet sixteenths, and in the second half of m. 2 a return to m. 1's rhythm, quarter tied to a sixteenth followed by another sixteenth. Both the overall expansion and the interpolated contraction of m. 2a are represented in the ordered pitch-interval sequence of the line (above the music in the top half of Example 3.1), by the circled intervals that progress <−8, −11, −13>, as well as the boxed <−3, +1, −3> interrupting the overall expansion at m. 2.

At the same time, the piano accompaniment, for right hand alone, creates several expansions and contractions of its own. Its opening sonorities grow larger registrally in m. 1b, then smaller in m. 2a (which can be accounted for, of course, by the fact that the piano is duplicating as verticals what the voice sings as leaps in these measures). But even after the piano breaks away from doubling the singer in mm. 2b and 3a, it gives the sense that it is being pushed down, while expanding out at the same time. The downward motion comes from the top line's pitch-interval sequence <−1, −1, −1>, which David Lewin identifies as the "Seufzer" or sighing motive (he also shows that it appears multiple times both at beginning and end of this song in different, and often conflicting, rhythmic contexts).[18] The simultaneous expansion of the motive, meanwhile, is vertical, and comes from the lowest line descending by leap rather than half-step, <−1, −6, −4>, allowing Schoenberg to enlarge the harmonies registrally from minor thirds, <3>, to the 3-12 <4, 4> and 3-5 <5, 6> mentioned above. Finally, notice that the "Seufzer" motive also expands and contracts dynamically, with its *crescendo* under the first two minor thirds and *diminuendo* under 3-12 and 3-5.

As the pianist breaks away from doubling the singer, we begin to hear offsets between its phrasing and that of the voice, the "skew" that Lewin describes in his article.[19] Therefore, my examples will sometimes repeat piano phrases from the end of one example to the beginning of the next, as in Example 3.2, the setting of the poem's second line.

Here, mm. 2b–3a's "Seufzer" motive with its expanding accompaniment (carried over from Example 3.1 to Example 3.2) repeats verbatim in mm. 3b–4a, then is followed in the piano accompaniment in mm. 4b–5a by what could be understood as an expansion – in multiple musical realms – of the repeating sigh motive. Measure 4b–5a's phrase extends the range of what preceded it, stretching from E5 down to B♭3, eighteen half-steps, where "Seufzer" had spanned B♭4 to A♭3, only fourteen. Rhythmically, the third phrase in Example 3.2 can also be understood as an expansion in two ways:

[18] Lewin, "A Way into Schoenberg's Opus 15, Number 7," 4–5, 9–13.    [19] Ibid., 4–5, 9.

Example 3.2  Schoenberg, "Angst und Hoffen," Op. 15, No. 7, mm. 2b–5a. Used by permission of Belmont Music Publishers and Universal Edition

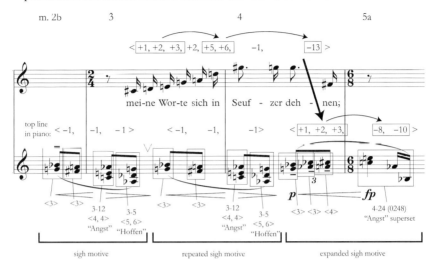

the two-eighth-note pickup of "Seufzer" becomes an eighth-note triplet (with tenuto marks on all three notes, stretching them), and the material after the downbeat expands from two eighths in 2/4 to a quarter and two sixteenths in 6/8. (The latter expansion pertains to increasing the number of attacks, not lengthening the overall duration, however, as the quarter note in 2/4 and the dotted quarter in 6/8 retain the same duration.) Dynamically, "Seufzer's" simple *crescendo* and *diminuendo* transforms into a *crescendo* to an *fp*, probably the easiest of these expansions to hear. Finally, one can perceive a harmonic expansion (among the unordered pitch intervals and set classes) from the progression <3>, <3>, 3-12 as <4, 4>, to the progression <3>, <3>, **<4>**, 4-**24** (3-12's superset).

The piano alone in Example 3.2, therefore, paints a picture for us as listeners of sighs growing longer and/or more intense, which will continue to be a principal element for the remainder of the song. But the third phrase of the piano in this example also echoes the singer's second line, "meine Worte sich in Seufzer dehnen," producing a kind of text-painting that is quite common in Schoenberg's atonal music and that will be encountered multiple times in this book – the intervals, pitches, and rhythms actually stand in for the main character; that is, they are subjected to the same experiences as he is.[20] In this case, the rhythms in the vocal phrase stretch

---

[20] Lewin recognizes this unique approach to text-painting as it applies to a later passage in the song: mm. 12–16. As he puts it: "the song *as a whole*, with its continual exhaustion of

out from sixteenths to dotted eighths right at that place where the text progresses from "Worte" to "Seufzer": the sighs are rhythmic expansions of the words. Furthermore, the vocal phrase in mm. 3–4, signifying "my words," expands musically into the piano phrase in mm. 4b–5a (which, as we have discussed already, emits a "sigh" that extends its predecessors). The expansion from vocal phrase to piano phrase takes several forms. Consider first the ordered pitch interval sequence of the voice part in mm. 3–4, <+1, +2, +3, +2, +5, +6, –1, –13>, and that of the piano's top line in mm. 4b–5a, <+1, +2, +3, –8, –10>. Though the piano extension has fewer intervals (and a shorter overall duration), it does expand the voice's succession in some ways – both successions start with the same intervals, <+1, +2, +3>, but the voice grows its intervals more incrementally, progressing to <+5, +6> and then to –13, while the piano seems to open up much more quickly with –8 and –10 coming directly after the opening three intervals. Both voice and piano end with precipitous descents; the voice's, on "Seufzer dehnen," falls –14 from G♯5 to F♯4, while the piano plunges further, –18, from E5 to B♭3 a half-measure later. Finally, there is the *fp* on E5 at the high point of the piano's phrase, which reproduces with increased intensity whatever accent the singer might give to her high G♯5 on the downbeat of m. 4, an articulative and dynamic "expansion."

Example 3.3 reproduces Schoenberg's setting of the third line of text, accompanied by more expanding sighs. The voice in line 3 projects an interval succession that begins similarly to line 2 and ends like line 1: after its opening <+1, +2, –3> it shrinks to smaller intervals while approaching a sixteenth-note quadruplet, <+1, –1, –1>, jumps +7, and finally plunges –11 in longer note values: quarter, eighth. Just like line 1, the overall pattern has an incremental interval expansion through m. 5, contracts intervallically and rhythmically in m. 6a, and then the intervals and rhythms widen again suddenly in m. 6b. An argument could be made that the narrower intervals and quicker rhythms represent "impetuosity" and the wider intervals and stretched rhythms "longing," but it seems more important to me that line 3 continues the same alternation between expansion and contraction that the first two lines had.

Meanwhile, the piano accompaniment in Example 3.3 continues to stretch its sighs both out and up, before cutting the third one off prior to its high point. Measures 4b–5a had projected the incremental interval expansion <+1, +2, +3, –8, –10> in its top line, the incremental harmonic

energy, and its quantum leap past measure 14 in that respect, also manifests the phenomenon described in line 2 exactly and literally: the singer's words extend (past m. 14) and expand into sighing." See "A Way into Schoenberg's Opus 15, Number 7," 4–5.

Example 3.3  Schoenberg, "Angst und Hoffen," Op. 15, No. 7, mm. 4b–6. Used by permission of Belmont Music Publishers and Universal Edition

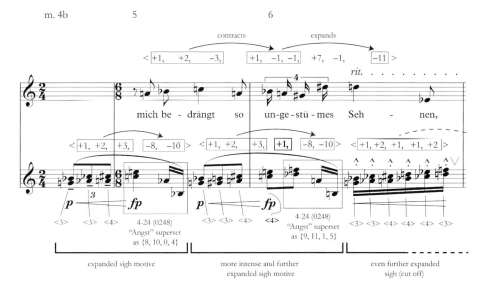

expansion <3>, <3>, <4>, 4-24 (superset of the "Angst" chord 3-12), an arched contour with a gradual ascent and quicker descent, and the dynamic shape *p* < *fp*. All these features led us to interpret it as a more protracted, intense "sigh" than the original "Seufzer" motive in mm. 2b–3a. What follows in mm. 5b–6a is an even more forceful version of the same gesture, created by inserting a second eighth note after the downbeat of m. 6. This has the effect of elongating the interval succession a step further to <+1, +2, +3, +1, −8, −10> and the harmonic succession to <3>, <3>, <4>, <4>, 4-24. Most noticeably, it raises the peak of the second arch beyond E5 (in m. 5a) to F5 (in m. 6a), and transposes the arch's descent up a half-step.[21] Then in m. 6b, the piano fashions what starts out as an even more lengthy version of the same sighing gesture: the top line drags out the <+1, +2> of previous phrases to <+1, +2, +1, +1, +2>, and the harmonic succession increases the

---

[21]  Robert Falck also recognizes the two piano phrases in mm. 4b–6a as starting at the same point and rising incrementally further "to C-E in measure 5; a half-step higher to D♭-F in measure 6." See Falck, "'Fear and Hope'," 96–97. And David Lewin also emphasizes the piano's high points E5 and F5 in his analysis, but for a different reason: he sees them as "correcting" the voice's D♭-E♭-F♭ in mm. 1–2 to D♭-E♭-F. (The pitch class F♭ is problematic because it prevents pitch symmetry in the Angst and Hoffen chords.) See "A Way into Schoenberg's Opus 15, Number 7," 18–20. I will show later why I also consider the long-range melodic D♭-E♭-F that completes itself in m. 6 as important, as a "middleground" vertical expansion of mm. 1–2's voice line.

alternation of minor thirds and major thirds that began the previous phrases to no less than six thirds. Not only that, but a *ritardando* stretches out the first part of this third arch durationally. It seems for a moment as though the piano might reach even further beyond the F5 high point it had attained in m. 6a, as part of a third, even more exaggerated, sighing gesture. But instead, this third sigh is cut off at the barline after m. 6, and after a short pause gives way to alternating "Angst" and "Hoffen" chords in m. 7.

Example 3.4 illustrates the fourth and fifth lines of the poem, ushered in by the alternating fear and hope chords, 3-12 and 3-5, in m. 7. As I mentioned above, these are not the original voicings of 3-12 and 3-5 from m. 1; instead 3-12 is presented as <B4, E♭5, G5> with unordered pitch intervals <4, 4> and 3-5 as <A4, D5, A♭5> with intervals <5, 6>. At the same time, a return to the song's original set classes with something close to their original rhythm suggests, together with the new tempo marking "Langsamer," the beginning of a new section, and most previous analysts have placed the beginning of the song's B section at m. 7.[22] From the standpoint of the song's basic image, however, the listener can interpret mm. 7–8 as interrupting m. 6's longer, stretched-out sigh with an "impetuous" return of alternating feelings of fear and hope.

The voice in line 4, singing "that I pay no mind to rest or sleep," narrows its registral compass overall from the previous lines, but still creates a clear arch form in its ordered pitch interval sizes, expanding out to the descending tritone and then constricting again: <+1, +2, +1, –2, +4, **–6**, +4, –2, +1>. (In Example 3.4 and subsequent examples, interval expansions will be represented by *crescendo* marks, contractions by *diminuendos*, to save space.) The piano accompanying line 4 begins with the alternation between 3-12 <B4, E♭5, G5> and 3-5 <A4, D5, A♭5> described above, following that in m. 8 with a second 3-12, which, surprisingly, moves to 3-4 (015) as <D♭4, F4, C5> instead of 3-5. The resulting succession Angst–Hoffen–Angst–???? seems to prepare for mm. 9–11a's almost-exclusive emphasis on arpeggiated and chordal forms of the Hoffen chord by creating an expectation for it.

Meanwhile, the top line of the piano in mm. 7–8, which adopts the rhythm and contour given to the voice in m. 1 – descending leaps in the rhythm of a quarter tied to a sixteenth followed by another sixteenth – produces an interval succession with intervals wider than the voice's in mm. 7–8 (signifying wild careening back and forth between fear and hope, maybe), but which still produces something like an arch: the intervals highlighted by the slurs (indicated in bold on Example 3.4)

[22] Lewin divides the song into "Sections 1–3" at mm. 1, 7, and 14, p. 3; Falck refers to a "middle section" from mm. 7–13, p. 98.

Example 3.4 Schoenberg, "Angst und Hoffen," Op. 15, No. 7, mm. 7–11a. Used by permission of Belmont Music Publishers and Universal Edition

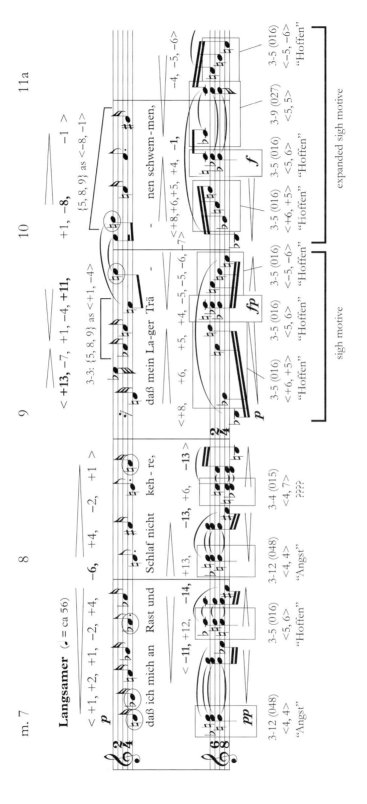

progress from −11 to −14, then take a step back to −13. The main components of the basic image, alternation between fear and hope, expanding, and contracting, are all in play at the B section's beginning.

As the B section progresses into line 5, the expanding and contracting continue, but the alternation between 3-12 and 3-5 ceases for a few measures, to focus our attention squarely on 3-5. The pianist in mm. 9–11a returns to playing short phrases that ascend and descend; arches that still can be comprehended as sighs growing longer (and slower, given the tempo change in m. 7). This outward expansion will culminate in the setting of line 6, but already during line 5 we hear additions that stretch the phrase. Measure 9's piano arch consists (with the exception of its first note, B♭3) almost entirely of arpeggiated and vertical forms of 3-5, the "Hoffen" chord, after m. 8's surprise turn away from that chord. The run up to the arch's peak (with a *crescendo*) has the ordered pitch intervals <+6, +5>, the *fp* vertical at the climax is <5, 6>, and the descent afterward (with a *decrescendo*) consists of <−5, −6>, all three of them Viennese Trichord voicings of 3-5. Mm. 10–11a extend the same pattern out horizontally by adding two elements: an A♭5 after the A5 melodic peak, forming set class 3-9 (027), the perfect fourth chord; and a durational expansion of that 3-9 to eighth-plus-sixteenth, extending the whole phrase by a quarter note from the previous phrase. As it turns out, this longer, slower sigh will be extended even further by the accompaniment to line 6, a 2½-measure descent, *diminuendo*, and gradual narrowing of intervals.

One aspect of mm. 9 and 10–11a that creates an interesting foil to the arch contours I just described is the ordered pitch-interval succession of the piano's top line (given just above the piano's pitches in mm. 9–11a). It grows incrementally smaller (constricting itself) as the register and dynamics both expand, <+8, +6, +5, +4> (the inclusion of +8 explains the B♭3s on the downbeats of mm. 9 and 10). As the two arches descend registrally and soften dynamically, the interval succession in m. 9 expands <−5, −5, −6, −7>, as does the one in m. 11a <−1, −4, −5, −6>. As the piece progresses, *Beklemmung* and *Dehnung* occur at the same time.

The voice in mm. 9–11a, setting the poem's fifth line, "that my bed is soaked with tears," contrasts the relatively circumspect contour of line 4 (which had not leapt any distance greater than a tritone) with a series including some much wider jumps, <+**13**, −7, +1, −4, +**11**, +1, −**8**, −1>. It makes sense here to speak of an expansion of interval size from one vocal phrase to the subsequent one, but there is also a sense in which expansion occurs within line 5 itself. The same unordered pitch-class set, {5, 8, 9}, appears twice in this line, as <A♭4, A4, F4> in the middle of m. 9 and <F5, A4, G♯4> in most of m. 10 (both of these successions are bracketed in Example 3.4). The pitch-class identity between these trichords is audible enough, but the second of them is stretched out intervallically with respect to the first: <+1, –4> becomes <–8, –1>, reinforcing the general tendency to expand intervals in line 5.

The wide jumps in the voice in mm. 9–11a also contribute to emphasizing the pitch classes that appear in the highest register, E♭5, E5, and F5, and David Lewin takes advantage of this emphasis to propose a longer-range process of expansion upward over the first ten measures of the song. He suggests that the upper voice of mm. 1–2's compound melody, <D5, E♭5, F♭5> (see again the bottom half of Example 3.1), needs correcting to <D5, E♭5, F5>, because the F♭, in its prior appearance as F♭4 on the second quarter note of m. 1, disrupts what would have been perfect vertical symmetry around B♭4 in the first two "Angst" and "Hoffen" chords (if F♭4 had been F4). The correction occurs first in the piano at m. 6's second eighth note (see Example 3.3), an F5 (approached by E5) at that place where we had discussed the extra eighth note pushing the top line of the piano up by half-step, extending and intensifying the sigh that had come before. The motion D4–E♭4–F♭4, the original line an octave lower, then sounds under the words "daß ich mich an Rast" of the fourth line in m. 7, but the F♭4 corrects itself to F4 at the end of the line under "kehre" in m. 8. Finally, the F5 appears in the proper octave in the voice for the first time just after the downbeat of m. 10, again approached by E5. Lewin explains these middleground progressions in terms of correcting a mistake, but I believe they could also be understood as large-scale expansions of the interval succession <+1, +1> to <+1, +2>, hidden repetitions of some of the more local expansions and contractions we have already detailed.[23]

Example 3.5 begins by reproducing mm. 10–11a in the piano from the previous example, Example 3.4. I do this because these measures, which I had characterized already as a sigh extended durationally by one quarter note, can also be joined up to mm. 11b–13a to form a sighing gesture with an even longer tail. After all, the *diminuendo* and registral descent from the high point of m. 10b does continue for 2½ more measures, though there is a break in the slur at the second sixteenth of m. 11. The ordered pitch-interval succession of the whole elongated sigh, mm. 10–13a, appears above the notes of the piano part in Example 3.5, and at the bottom of the page a graph showing the progression in size of its unordered pitch intervals. The overall motion is toward smaller and smaller pitch intervals, with a couple of rises during

---

[23] Lewin, "A Way into Schoenberg's Opus 15, Number 7," 18–21.

Example 3.5 Schoenberg, "Angst und Hoffen," Op. 15, No. 7, mm. 10–14a. Used by permission of Belmont Music Publishers and Universal Edition

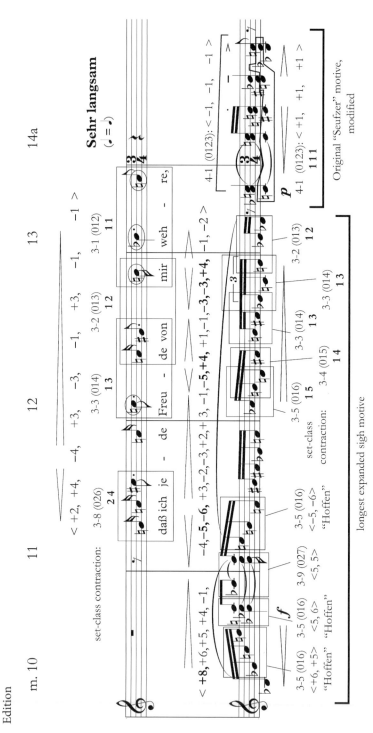
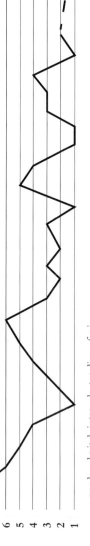

the course of the contraction (indicated in bold in the ordered pitch-interval string). At the same time, the set classes after m. 12 participate in their own contraction, starting at 3-5 (016) and progressing incrementally through 3-4 (015), 3-3 (014), and 3-2 (013) on their way to the descending and ascending chromatic scales in the piano's top and bottom/middle lines in mm. 13b–14a, whose contiguous subsets all belong to set class 3-1 (012). This brings to mind the incremental set-class expansions and contractions of the Op. 11 Piano Pieces that we discussed in Chapters 1 and 2 – an interesting connection, when we remember that Op. 11 was begun almost a year after this song.

The voice projects line 6 of the text over this long downward motion, *diminuendo*, and interval contraction in the piano, "that I repel every joy from me." The singer's ordered pitch interval sequence, given directly above her notation in Example 3.5, expands briefly, <+2, +4, –4>, followed by a longer contraction, imitating the pattern in the accompaniment, but with smaller intervals (nothing larger than four half-steps). The voice, like the piano, also contains a set-class contraction, beginning with 3-8 (026), another set class Op. 15 shares with Op. 11, and shrinking through 3-3 and 3-2, to end at 3-1 as <B4, Bb4, A4>, three of the same four pitches as the piano's descending chromatic scale at mm. 13b–14a. (If we hook the voice's last three pitches up to the preceding C5 on the downbeat of m. 12, however, we have a prediction of the complete pitch content of the piano in mm. 13b–14a.)

I have just described how the descending chromatic scale in the piano in mm. 13b–14a culminates the processes of interval and set-class contraction that immediately precede it. But it is also an important motive for the whole song: the return of Lewin's "Seufzer" motive, which was originally given in mm. 2b–3a and 3b–4a as <–1, –1, –1>. (Return to Example 3.2.) "Seufzer," in its original form, had been the starting point for the ever-longer sighs that constitute every measure of the piano part save mm. 7 and 8. Circling back to this motivic source, and the song's second major tempo change, to "Sehr langsam," signals the beginning of a third major section, including the setting of the seventh and last line and the codetta. This section, mm. 13b–19, is portrayed in Example 3.6.

One could designate mm. 13b–19 as a return of the A section (mm. 1–6), but in fact the piano presents the two main motivic components of A in *reverse* order, with several important changes. For those reasons, I have labeled the section A′. In mm. 13b–14a, "Seufzer" does not sound at its original pitch level, <Bb4, A4, Ab4, G4>, but is transposed up a step to <C5, B4, Bb4, A4> (originally the pitch content of m. 2's top line in the

Example 3.6 Schoenberg, "Angst und Hoffen," Op. 15, No. 7, mm. 13b–19. Used by permission of Belmont Music Publishers and Universal Edition

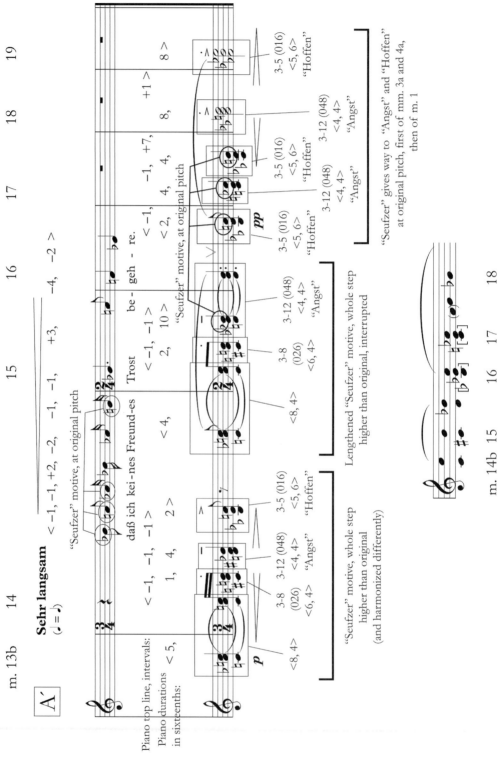

piano).[24] The motive's harmonization is also different from the original, for the first two verticals: the two minor thirds of m. 2b change to major thirds A♭4-C5 and G4-B4 in 13b–14a, and add a third voice on the bottom, <C4, C♯4>, beginning a wedge pattern that contracts to the end of the motive, <C5, B4, B♭4, A4> on top and <C4, C♯4, D4, E♭3> on the bottom.[25] But this inward wedge pattern is different from the original "Seufzer": what had been straight eighth notes (or <2, 2, 2, 2> as a duration succession in sixteenths) now becomes stretched out, irregularly, to <5, 1, 4, 2> in sixteenths. (The durations of the piano verticals are given directly above that instrument's notation in Example 3.6, and the ordered pitch intervals of the piano's top line above those.) Together with the slowing in tempo at this point, the A′ section's first sigh motive certainly undergoes *Dehnung* durationally. But its pitches are also *beklemmt* (literally pinched in) by the wedge, and it ends with an alternation of "Angst" and "Hoffen" chords. Again, the image inspired by lines 1 and 2 comes to the fore, and the sighs (that expand in one realm and constrict in another) lead to the alternation of fear and hope, as they did in mm. 2b–3a and 3b–4a. At the end of the song, however, the beginning's progression from emphasizing the alternation of fear and hope toward focusing on sighs is reversed: the lengthening sighs give way to alternating fear and hope.

This reversal of the basic image happens chiefly in the piano part. From the last eighth of m. 14 to m. 16a, we hear the first three chords of mm. 13b–14a's sigh, with the same inward wedge, and a drastically expanded duration succession (<5, 1, 4> in sixteenths stretches out to <4, 2, 10>). Then, after reaching the "Angst" chord and holding it for ten sixteenths,

---

[24] Lewin comments on how m. 13b–14a's statement of the "Seufzer" motive recalls both the four eighth notes of m. 2's top line and the motive spanning mm. 2b–3a, reminding the listener of how the motive was "skewed" against itself and creating rhythmic tension. He also discusses the identity between the voice's middleground <C5, B4, B♭4, A4> in mm. 12–13 and the "Seufzer" motive in 13b–14a, claiming that the rhythmic tensions that open the third section of the piece in m. 14 are "initiated and controlled by the voice." See "A Way into Schoenberg's Opus 15, Number 7," 9–13.

[25] This wedge is different from the one David Lewin discusses at length on pp. 14–16 of "A Way into Schoenberg's Opus 15, Number 7." His top voice is <A♭4, G4, F♯4, (F4)> and the bottom voice is the same as mine <C4, C♯4, D4, E♭4>. The F4 does not actually sound on the second eighth of beat 2 in m. 14, which together with the added B♭3, justifies starting the inward wedge over from the beginning on m. 14's last eighth (according to him). One advantage to Lewin's wedge is that its top line during the second attempt incorporates many of the notes of the voice, including its F4 and E♭4 in m. 16, which he claims converge on the E4 in the middle of the first quarter of m. 17. But he does not associate the two inward wedges with constricting sighs, nor does he interpret the "disruptive" B♭3 at the end of the first wedge as returning the song's image from sighs to alternating fear and hope.

the piano surprises us: it cuts off the phrase with a caret. The "Hoffen" chord at the expected pitch level does appear directly afterward, but as a pickup to the next phrase, mm. 17–19. To me, this gesture has the effect of turning listeners' attention away from repeated four-chord sighs that expand durationally while contracting their pitches, and setting us up to expect something else. What happens to the wedge between the outer voices of the piano in mm. 14b–18 confirms this, I believe: the bottom of Example 3.6 shows that it is first obscured by extra bass notes B♭3 and C4 in mm. 16b–17a (just as the first wedge had been obscured by B♭3 in m. 14), and then one of its notes, F4, goes missing on the second quarter of m. 17. It does complete itself, however, in the G♭4 of m. 18.

What is the reason for abandoning the inward wedge in m. 17? The extra C4 and the missing F4 are both necessary to recreate the "Angst" and "Hoffen" chords in the forms they had taken as the last two chords in the original "Seufzer" motives in mm. 3a and 4a, <**C4**, E4, A♭4> and <A♭3, D♭4, G4>. This is one reason the listener's attention begins to turn from expanding and contracting sigh motives back toward the alternation of "Angst" and "Hoffen," as the piece gives us the strong sense that it is returning toward its beginning. The phrasing also de-emphasizes "Seufzer" in favor of "Angst" and "Hoffen" here. The piano's top line of mm. 15b–17 actually does provide the "Seufzer" motive at original pitch and with extended durations, <B♭4, A4, A♭4, G4> and <10, 2, 4, 4> in sixteenths (circled and labeled above the notation in Example 3.6). But, because of the phrase break in the middle of m. 16, the listener is unlikely to notice the original "Seufzer"; rather, his or her attention will be propelled forward to the "Angst" and "Hoffen" chords of m. 17.

The voice's setting of line 7 in mm. 14–16 also participates in turning our attention away from the sigh motive. Its ordered pitch-interval succession increases slightly, from unordered pitch intervals 1 and 2 at the beginning to <+3, –4, –2> at the end. But in context, it seems more interesting to describe the voice in m. 14 as an ornamented version of the original "Seufzer" motive: <B♭4, A4, A♭4, (B♭4, A♭4), G4>. This sets up the expectation for an unornamented "Seufzer" at original pitch, since, as we have already seen, the piano is repeating "Seufzer" a step higher in the surrounding measures. But when the motive does appear at original pitch in the piano in mm. 15b–17, it is obscured by the phrase break after its first note. After m. 15, the descending chromatic motion in the voice begins to break apart and eventually leads to a whole step, F4–E♭4, as the piano takes over and leads us back toward alternating fear and hope.

I mentioned above that the return in m. 17 of "Angst" and "Hoffen" in the forms they had taken in mm. 3a and 4a gives us as listeners the sense that the piece is circling back around to its beginning. That sense is certainly confirmed by mm. 18 and 19, a final cadence consisting of "Angst" and "Hoffen," 3-12 and 3-5, with exactly the same pitches as m. 1, but longer durations (to represent the idea that the alternation between fear and hope has finally slowed to a near halt). The return of the song's original chords at the final cadence also has the effect of neutralizing any sense of either functional tonality or centric tonality, I think. As I already mentioned, the G♭4 at the bottom of the "Angst" chord in m. 18 could be heard as the focal point of the inward wedge between the outer voices starting on the last eighth of m. 14 (refer again to the bottom of Example 3.6). But that wedge looks and sounds nothing like a contrapuntal structure in functional tonality – almost every one of its intervals save the octave at the beginning and unison at the end is dissonant (the minor sixth from D4 to B♭4 is the exception), and its beginning and ending points C4, C5, and G♭4 create tritones, not perfect fifths or fourths. It would be impossible to argue for something like a Schenkerian linear progression here. Even if we wanted to claim that there is a centric emphasis on G♭ in this passage, we would have to deal with the facts that the G♭ is harmonized with an augmented triad, a symmetrical chord that does not effectively define it as a root, and that the G♭ chord is not the final chord: the piece ends on the "Hoffen" chord, a neighbor to the G♭ chord, in m. 19. It makes better sense to understand these measures as the close of an atonal song whose chord and interval progressions, as well as its rhythms, can be justified as projections of its basic image.

Now, I am not the only one to comment on the song's tendency to circle around to its beginning at its end. David Lewin suggests a way to understand this circularity as text-painting of line 7: the main character seeks solace from no friend, but wants something more from one – the beloved.[26] This very statement about seeking solace brings him around to remembering exactly what he was fearing and hoping, starting a new cycle of fear and hope. I too understand the song as circular, but prefer to interpret it in a more general way (not as text-painting of individual lines, but as a portrayal of only the first two lines in its basic image). In my reading, the constant, unrelenting alternation of fear and hope constricts the main character and brings on sighs that continually expand his words throughout the song, but that never leads him to a new place mentally – there is no progress, no happy ending. Rather, the song ends where it begins, and could probably continue circling

---

[26] Lewin, "A Way into Schoenberg's Op. 15, Number 7," 4.

forever. Therefore, this song's basic image is not compatible with what I understand as "musical idea": it has opposition, to be sure, but no synthesis. Other songs in Op. 15, however, do have images that are more compatible with the problem–elaboration–solution paradigm; including the one we will explore next, Song No. 11.

## "Als wir hinter dem beblümten Tore," Op. 15, No. 11[27]

I mentioned at the beginning of this chapter that Song No. 11 is one of those songs in Op. 15 for which we have no dated first draft, only undated fair copies.[28] Thus it is unclear exactly when the song was written between March 1908 and spring 1909. It could have been composed together with No. 7 in the first wave of songs, somewhere in the middle of the cycle's gestation period, or near the end. Bryan Simms speculates that the first drafts of Songs 9–12 may have occupied their own *Sammelhandschrift*, which is now lost and could have been written around the same time as the last two existing collections for Op. 15, *Sammelhandschriften* Nos. 22 and 23 (September 1908 and February 1909).[29] If that is indeed the case, it puts the composition of Song 11 closer to the end of the cycle, and that seems to be in line with the argument I am about to put forward – the basic image for this song is more complex than that for Song No. 7; it has more layers of meaning. But in the end, it is impossible to pinpoint exactly when "Als wir hinter" appeared.

What do I mean by saying that there are more layers of meaning in Song 11? This is one of many poems Schoenberg would set during his composing career that itself can be understood in terms of a problem or conflict of some sort, which is elaborated through the poem and resolved at or near the end, enabling the basic image that one might draw from the poem to do "double duty" as a musical idea. The text of the song appears below, with a translation by Robert Erich Wolf:[30]

---

[27] The following essay on Op. 15, No. 11 reworks part of an older publication by me: "The Musical Idea and the Basic Image in an Atonal Song and Recitation of Arnold Schoenberg," *Gamut* 2/1 (2009): 223–66.

[28] The fair copies and other materials can be found on the Schönberg Center site at www.schoenberg.at/compositions/werke_einzelansicht.php?werke_id=134&herkunft=allewerke.

[29] Simms, *The Atonal Music of Arnold Schoenberg*, pp. 48–49.

[30] Wolf's translation comes from the liner notes to Arnold Schoenberg, *Pierrot lunaire, Op. 21, The Book of the Hanging Gardens, Op. 15*, with Jan DeGaetani, mezzo-soprano, The Contemporary Chamber Ensemble, Arthur Weisberg, conductor, and Gilbert Kalish, piano, © 1990 by Elektra Nonesuch, Elektra Nonesuch 9-79237-2, compact disc.

| | |
|---|---|
| Als wir hinter dem beblümten tore | When hidden behind the flowergrown gate |
| Endlich nur das eigne hauchen spürten | at last alone and breath to breath, |
| Warden uns erdachte seligkeiten? | was our felicity quite what we dreamed? |
| Ich erinnere daß wie schwache rohre | I remember now that like quivering reeds |
| Beide stumm zu beben wir begannen | silently we both began to tremble |
| Wenn wir leis nur an uns rührten | when our bodies only brushed together |
| Und daß unsre augen rannen – | and that our eyes brimmed over – |
| So verbliebest du mir lang zu seiten. | You remained like that for long by my side. |

In my account of the whole cycle's text on pp. 113–14, I placed this song right after the climax (which may have involved a sexual union of some sort, or not); namely, at the beginning of the affair's gradual decline. As we begin Song 11, George's young dream-king is (in the absence or presence of his gender-unspecific beloved) trying to recall whether their sexual union was real or only imagined (and in exactly what way was it blissful?), but he is unable to do so in a conclusive way. He calls up remembered sensations of "feeling only our own breathing" and "trembling as our bodies lightly touched together," and in the last line he remembers enough to make a somewhat more definite statement – "You remained like that for long by my side." (Though more definite, it seems to fall short of a complete or explicit description of their sexual activity. But it could represent a more explicit thought.)

On pp. 114–15, I went on to make a proposal about how Schoenberg could have interpreted this text: in terms of a heterosexual marriage relationship that was once "blissful" in some sense, but was destroyed through an extramarital affair. In this reading, the betrayed husband tries desperately to bring to mind specific sensations from a sexual encounter he once had with his wife, but other, stronger images associated with the betrayal crowd in and prevent him from doing so. At the end, however, he is able to capture a faint, partial memory of his past marital union.

Characterizing Schoenberg's interpretation of "Als wir hinter dem beblümten Tore" this way enables me to explain its music as depictive text-painting – similar to what we have already seen in "Angst und Hoffen," with its unrelenting alternation of 3-12 and 3-5 and its contraction and expansion of pitches, intervals, and rhythms. Just like the earlier song, the musical elements of Song 11 stand in for the characters in the poem, the two Babylonian dream-lovers or (if you will) the betrayed husband and unfaithful wife. This time, the main "actors" are two pairs of set classes, 4-17 (0347)/4-18 (0147), and 4-4 (0125)/4-5 (0126). These pairs of sets are presented in such a way that trichord subsets common to the two members of each pair, such as 3-11 (037), 3-3 (014), 3-1 (012), and 3-4 (015), are first highlighted within their own parent tetrachords, then realized as actual overlappings between their supersets, then "broken off" so that they appear without their parent tetrachords, and finally – at the song's end – realized as overlappings once more.[31] The passage in Song 11 where two tetrachords literally overlap in a common trichord (mm. 8–9) can be thought of as an "ideal state" that is, in turn, contradicted by the common trichords appearing alone (without their tetrachord supersets) in mm. 11–12 (the "opposition" or "problem"), striven toward through a long process (in mm. 13–20) in which common trichords are highlighted within non-overlapping tetrachords as common pitch-class sets and interval successions, and finally reasserted as overlaps in mm. 21–23 (the first part of the process constitutes the song's "elaboration," and its culmination the song's "solution"). At the same time, a rhythmic process unfolds by which several dislocations between grouping and meter that had appeared in the opening measures are "solved" in the closing measures.

Both subset overlappings and rhythmic processes follow the basic image suggested earlier, which could be summarized as faint, clouded memories of two bodies lightly brushing together, perhaps uniting sexually at some point, followed by a more definite image of their union at the end of the song. At the same time, both pitch and rhythmic processes contribute to a framework within which problems are presented, elaborated, and eventually solved – a musical idea. Finally, both basic image and musical idea point the way to interpreting this song, like Song No. 7, as a ternary form with an altered return: (Introduction) A B A'. After the piano introduction, mm. 1–7, the A section includes that music where two tetrachords overlap in a common trichord for the first time, mm. 8–9, and the aftermath, mm. 10–12, where the union between tetrachords disappears and is brought into question. Mm. 13–17, those measures where the music begins to move back in the direction of its ideal state, constitute the B section; and mm. 18–24, which bring back motives and chords from A as well as the piano introduction in a different order from the original, make up the A' section.[32]

---

[31] These same four set classes are also acknowledged by David Lewin as principal agents in Song 11, in "Toward the Analysis of a Schoenberg Song (Op. 15, No. XI)," *Perspectives of New Music* 12/1–2 (1973–74): 43–86. Lewin recognizes 4-4 and 4-5 as a pair, calling them the "N" and "X" chords, and constructing much of his analysis around their repetitions at various transposition levels and chromatic voice-leadings that those repetitions embed. He calls 4-17 "T" (for major/minor triad) and 4-18 "the magic chord," but for the most part he speaks about their development through the song as separate entities, not as a pair. He does not place the same weight in his analysis on common trichords between the two pairs of tetrachords, and how the common trichords are represented, as I do.

[32] David Lewin's diagram of the song's form differs from mine at one point: he advocates for a two-part form with each part divided into two subsections. The piano introduction

A score of mm. 1–7, the piano introduction, is provided in Example 3.7a. The opening measures of the introduction present the four set classes mentioned above, 4-17 and 4-5 horizontally in mm. 1 and 2a, and their respective "partners," 4-18 and 4-4, vertically in mm. 2b and 3. Each of these pairs demonstrates both pitch-class similarity ($R_p$) and interval similarity ($R_1$ or $R_2$) according to Allen Forte's *The Structure of Atonal Music* (see Example 3.7b). Set classes 4-17 and 4-18 are in the $R_2$ relation (four corresponding entries in their interval vectors are identical); in addition, these set classes can be represented by pitch-class sets with common trichords (the defining characteristic for $R_p$) in a number of ways, two of which are shown on Example 3.7b. These common trichords all belong to set classes 3-11 (037) and 3-3 (014). Likewise, 4-4 and 4-5 are in the $R_1$ relation (four interval vector entries in common, the other two exchange positions); and they exhibit the $R_p$ relation in a number of ways – all of which form set classes 3-1 (012) and 3-4 (015).[33]

As "Als wir hinter" works out its musical idea, it uses the $R_p$ relations – the possible common trichordal subsets – to portray the basic image. In mm. 1–7, common trichords between 4-17 and 4-18 are emphasized contextually within their parent tetrachords, but not as common pitch classes. For example, 3-11 (037) stands out as the first three pitch classes of 4-17, <B♭, D♭, F>, in mm. 0–1, and also as the top three pitch classes of 4-18, <B, E, G♯>, in mm. 2b–3 (the common subsets are shaded in the example and their $R_p$ relation is indicated using arrows). When 4-17 returns in mm. 4 and 5, the 3-11 subset {F, A, C} separates itself rhythmically from the remaining pitch class, G♯. All of these highlighted 3-11s would form what Forte calls "weakly represented" $R_p$ relations between their parent

in mm. 1–7 forms his first subsection, and the first and second vocal phrases together (mm. 8–10 and 11–12) the second subsection. The third vocal phrase (mm. 13–19) constitutes its own subsection, and the fourth vocal phrase (mm. 20–24) makes up the final subsection. I prefer to begin my last section at m. 18 rather than Lewin's vocal phrase boundary, m. 20, because motivic material from the A section and introduction begins to return, rearranged, at m. 18.

Though his form is different, Lewin does agree with me on what he calls the narrative functions of certain sections of the song. He also characterizes mm. 1–7 as introductory, mm. 11–12 as "setting the problem of the narrative," and mm. 13–19 as carrying out the action of the poem, which he characterizes as the singer trying to remember details of the lovers' tryst. Thus his analysis also grows out of a framework that features a problem and its elaboration (consisting of attempts to solve it). Where he differs from me, as we will see, is that he does not interpret the song's final measures as a solution. See "Toward the Analysis of a Schoenberg Song," 43–45.

[33] See Forte, *The Structure of Atonal Music*, pp. 46–49, for a more detailed description of his interval and pitch-class similarity relations.

Example 3.7a Schoenberg, "Als wir hinter dem beblümten Tore," Op. 15, No. 11, mm. 1–7, piano introduction. Copyright © 1914, 1941 by Universal Edition AG Vienna, UE 5338. All rights reserved. Used by permission of Belmont Music Publishers and Universal Edition

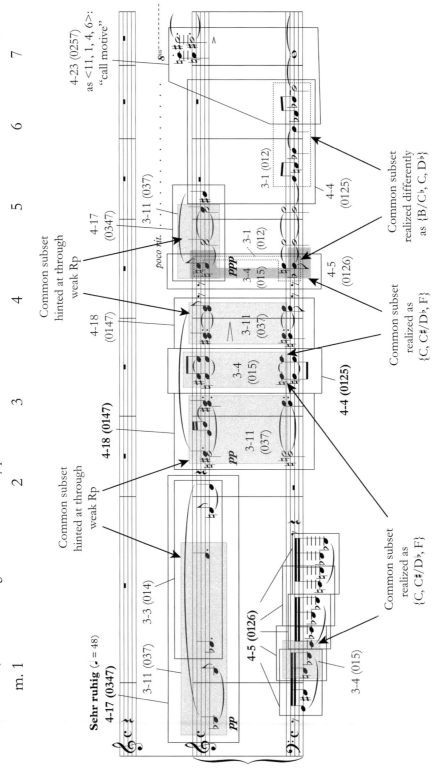

Example 3.7b  Interval-class and pitch-class similarities between 4-17 and 4-18, and 4-4 and 4-5

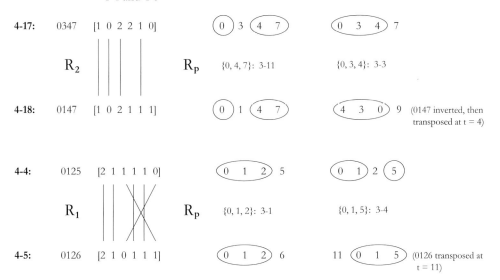

4-17s and 4-18s; that is, the common trichords are not common in the sense that the same *pitch classes* recur, but only in that they belong to a common *set class*. Meanwhile, 3-4 (015), one of the common subsets between 4-5 and 4-4, does occur twice as common pitch classes, in the form {C, C♯/D♭, F}: from the first three sixteenth notes in the piano left hand in m. 1 to the top three pitches of the second chord of m. 3, and from that trichord to the one formed by the bass and top two pitches of the second chord in m. 4 (shaded darker to make it easier to see). None of these common trichords cause an overlapping of their parent tetrachords, however, and by the time we reach mm. 5–6, the 4-4 projected over most of those two measures retains a new subset of three pitch classes with its predecessor set class 4-5 in m. 4: {B/C♭, C, D♭}, highlighted in the example by dotted boxes.[34] This new subset belongs to set class 3-1 (012). Between the 4-4 and 4-5 trichords in mm. 1–7, then, there are two strongly represented $R_p$ relations of one kind followed by a strongly represented $R_p$ of another kind.

With the entry of the voice in m. 8 comes the most obvious manifestation of pitch-class similarity we have yet heard (see Example 3.8, which illustrates the A section of the song).

[34]  Even though set class 4-4 in mm. 5–6 is spread out over two measures, I do not think of it as hierarchically superior to the other more-compact chords in the passage. It also is a "surface" phenomenon in my reckoning of the song. Later (mm. 14–15) I will speak of pitch successions that I consider to be at the "middleground" level, that have other, ornamental pitches interleaved between the "structural" ones.

Example 3.8 Schoenberg, "Als wir hinter dem beblümten Tore," Op. 15, No. 11, mm. 8–12, section A. Used by permission of Belmont Music Publishers and Universal Edition

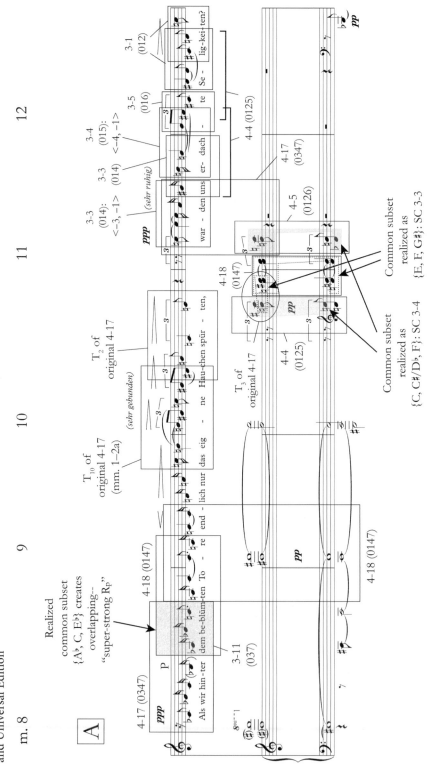

The first vocal phrase, "Als wir hinter den beblümten Tore," overlaps members of set classes 4-17 and 4-18 in three pitch classes (if the B♭ on "-ter" can be interpreted as a passing tone, which it does indeed resemble in its melodic function, if not its harmonic context).[35] The overlapping pitch classes are <A♭, E♭, C>, forming the common trichord 3-11. Here, then, $R_p$ is not only strongly represented but also facilitates an actual *intersection* between 4-17 and 4-18 – that is, what was hinted at or partially realized in mm. 1–7, through the weak and strong representations of common trichords, comes to fruition in mm. 8 and 9 (we might call it a "super-strong" $R_p$). This depicts quite well, I think, the text's image of two bodies standing apart yet full of desire for one another and then coming together in a distantly remembered sexual union. The tetrachords of each pair "stand apart" temporally in the introduction, while their common trichords "desire each other" by being highlighted as prominent subsets and sounding alike first as set classes, then as identical pitch-class sets. Then in the A section, two of the same tetrachords do unite, overlapping in one of their common trichords.

The passage immediately following mm. 8 and 9 seems to step back gradually from this super-strong $R_p$ relationship between 4-17 and 4-18. All four of the tetrachords we have been discussing appear within a short span, from the end of m. 9 to the beginning of m. 11: 4-17 twice in the voice on "das eigne Hauchen spürten" ("feeling [only] our own breath"), then, in relatively rapid succession as verticals, 4-4, 4-18, and 4-5 in mm. 10b and 11a. During the first two of these verticals, the right hand of the piano forms another member of 4-17.

The 4-17s in the voice at mm. 9 and 10 are transpositions of the original right-hand piano motive from mm. 1 and 2 at t = 10 and t = 2 (in pitch-class space), and the subsequent piano 4-17 in m. 10 is a transposition at t = 3. Joseph Straus has suggested that the tendency of these transpositions to "echo the opening gesture in a slightly off-center way" represents the main character's inability to remember clearly what happened during his tryst, an insight that fits well with the notion of stepping back from an intimate union.[36] At the same time, the piano's verticals in mm. 10 and 11 step back from what had been accomplished in the voice two bars earlier in a different way: the common trichords are no longer explicitly realized as

---

[35] David Lewin also interprets it as such; see "Toward the Analysis of a Schoenberg Song," 57–58.

[36] Joseph N. Straus, *Introduction to Post-Tonal Theory*, 3rd edn (Upper Saddle River, NJ: Pearson Prentice-Hall, 2004), p. 69.

overlappings. However, both pairs still demonstrate a strong $R_p$ relation, so we have not gone all the way back to the merely suggestive connections between 4-17 and 4-18 found in mm. 1–2. The 4-17 in the piano at m. 10b, and the 4-18 on the last beat of that same measure tied into m. 11, share three pitch classes, {E, F, G♯}, forming set class 3-3 (highlighted by dotted boxes); and the 4-4 vertical in m. 10b shares three pitch classes {C, C♯/D♭, F} (set class 3-4) with the 4-5 in m. 11a (highlighted by grey shading). Notice that the particular pitch-class set held in common between 4-17 and 4-18 here highlights the *other* common trichord from that emphasized in mm. 1–2 and 8–9 (here it is 3-3, before it was 3-11). It seems like the song is already beginning to pose its "problem" by asking how can 4-17 and 4-18, as well as 4-4 and 4-5, have common elements with one another? It hints at (but does not yet realize) a number of possible solutions.

The question in the poem's third line – "warden uns erdachte Seligkeiten?" – inspires yet another step away from the intimate union of mm. 8 and 9. Where the singer expresses uncertainty about whether their bliss was real or imagined, references to all but two of the four parent tetrachords disappear; 4-4 does occur twice, and 4-17 once. The set classes that seem more salient in mm. 11 and 12, however, made so by changes in melodic contour, are the trichords that had been n-1 common subsets in the earlier music; they now appear not as links, but on their own as part of what Schoenberg would call a "liquidation" process.[37] "Warden uns" yields 3-3, "erdach" presents 3-4 (expressed as <–4, –1>, an interval expansion from the previous trichord <–3, –1>), and the two sets are linked by <G♯, B, G>, another member of 3-3. After this, the focus turns to interval classes 1 and 2 during "Seligkeiten?," yielding two forms of set class 3-1, which had originally been a link between 4-4 and 4-5, but does not function as such here. I believe that the liquidation from parent tetrachords to common trichords only in mm. 11–12, together with the reduction in texture to the voice alone and the lowering of dynamics to *ppp*, portrays the main character's losing track of his memories of the blissful union in mm. 8–9, creating the song's principal problem.

The next five measures, mm. 13–17, shown in Example 3.9, what I have labeled the B section, depict a valiant attempt to regain some of those memories, marked by a drastic increase of rhythmic activity.

David Lewin, in his detailed, insightful account of "Als wir hinter," has described the singer's and pianist's function in these bars as (among other

---

[37] Schoenberg defines, describes, and gives examples of "liquidation" in *Fundamentals of Musical Composition*, 2nd edn, ed. Gerald Strang and Leonard Stein (London: Faber & Faber, 1970), pp. 58–59 and 63.

Example 3.9 Schoenberg, "Als wir hinter dem beblümten Tore," Op. 15, No. 11, mm. 13–17, section B. Used by permission of Belmont Music Publishers and Universal Edition

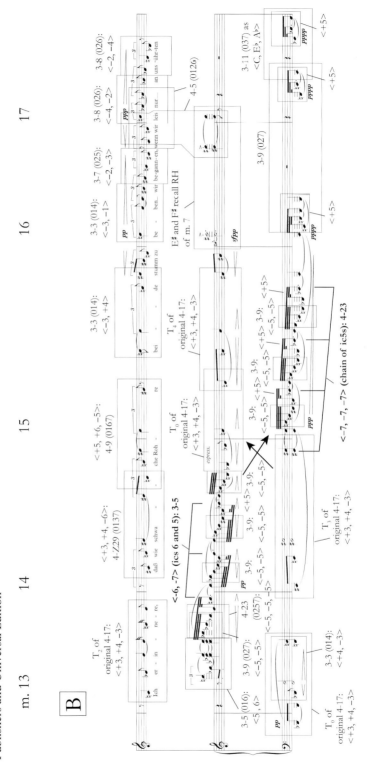

things) building excitement through increasing rhythmic diminution, ascending repetition, and interval expansion of the 4-17 motive that opened the song.[38] The piano left hand leads the way with the song's opening interval succession <+3, +4, –3> starting on B♭1 (two octaves lower than its original pitch), repeats that interval motive on C♯2 in m. 14, then pulls it up to the right hand and presents rhythmically diminuted forms on B♭3 and D4 that overlap with one another as well as the preceding form; all of this creates a *stretto* that gradually picks up speed through the employment of ever shorter durations. (It is interesting that when <+3, +4, –3> transfers up to the right hand at the end of m. 14, what had been mm. 13–14's right-hand material is pushed down into the left hand. This does not create invertible counterpoint in the sense that vertical intervals are complemented, as the motives line up differently in m. 15 from the way they had in m. 14 – but it does create what might be called a "motive exchange." Later I will say more about the function of the "countermelody" with which <+3, +4, –3> exchanges hands.)

The singer begins building excitement a bit more slowly – she has to be nudged by the pianist. She starts her first <+3, +4, –3> a quarter note later in m. 13, and on pitch class C rather than B♭, which suggests that the main character she portrays still cannot remember his tryst (or marital union) all that clearly. Her second attempt at the motive, in m. 14, starts on C♯ (as does the pianist's) and this time only a triplet eighth note late, so she is beginning to "get it" and pick up speed. But she is also representing the young king starting to lose control, in his excitement at remembering how their bodies silently trembled like reeds; so her motive, which begins m. 14, expands to <+3, +4, –6>, and the next one, which follows fast and furiously on the D4 in m. 14, expands even further to <+5, +6, –5>. By the time she gets halfway into m. 15, she breathlessly (but still quietly) cries out a fragment, <–3, +4>, which is the retrograde inversion of the original's last three notes (and a member of set class 3-3, one of the common trichords uniting 4-17 and 4-18). Then, in m. 16, her growing excitement subsides in the registral and contour domains (as does that of the piano, more obviously, in the rhythmic domain), although the motivic strategy remains the same – that is, interval expansion. "Beben wir" returns to the same specific pitches as "warden uns" in m. 11, <C5, A4, G♯4>, signifying a return to a questioning attitude. The singer then expands (and reverses) the <–3, –1> of that set to

[38] Lewin, "Toward the Analysis of a Schoenberg Song," 62–69. Lewin's account inspired much of my language in the following paragraphs about the pianist "nudging" the singer to remember, and her responding with increasing excitement by rhythmically diminuting the <+3, +4, –3> motive and expanding its intervals.

<-2, -3> on "begannen," and afterwards there are further expansions to
<-4, -2> and <-2, -4> on "leis nur an uns rührten," which begin to evoke the
even, steady progression of the whole-tone scale.

What comes through to my ear, starting at m. 16, is a sense of quiet and
relaxation brought about by combining interval expansion in the voice and
a descending contour together with a decrease in rhythmic activity in the
piano. David Lewin, on the other hand, has characterized the same music as
"frustration over the singer's forgetting the question (of mm. 11 and 12),"
and he makes a convincing argument based on the piano's sudden rhythmic
inactivity and the motivic liquidation of mm. 11–12's question in mm. 16
and 17, not to mention the melodic stasis and overall descent in the voice
(coming as it does after a pronounced upward chromatic drive in the
preceding measures).[39] But I would counter by arguing that a sudden lapse
into inactivity and stasis, and the sense that a directional motion has been cut
off, can signify (instead of frustration) a state in which the main character
ceases striving for an answer to his question (at m. 16), only to have that
answer gradually slip into his mind after he quiets down (mm. 17–23). This
reading seems to fit better my view of what happens at and after m. 18.

Before discussing that music, it remains for me to explore the other
contrapuntal strand in mm. 13–17: the countermelody of the piano right
hand in mm. 13–14 and left hand in mm. 15–17. The countermelody begins
in m. 13 with a vertical pitch-interval profile that we have encountered
multiple times already in previous analyses. Reckoned as a chord from the
bottom up, the countermelody <A6, B♭5, E♭6> in m. 13 yields unordered
pitch intervals <5, 6>: yet another Viennese Trichord, a member of set class
3-5 (016). The pianist then immediately contracts this <5, 6> chord to
a horizontal <-5, -5> by lowering A6 to A♭6,[40] and adds another -5 to
create a perfect-fourth chord, belonging to set class 4-23 (0257). That set
class, its subset 3-9 (027) represented by two perfect fourths or fifths in
succession, and interval class 5 in general begin to dominate the countermelody thereafter. Set class 3-9 as <-5, -5> appears repeatedly as
the second, third, and fourth notes of every group of four thirty-second
notes, and it is often followed immediately by an ascending perfect fourth
<+5>. But interval class 5 also leaves its mark on the middleground that is
ornamented by all these 3-9s and perfect fourths. Observe that the pitches
at the end of each slurred five-note group, <B5, F5, B♭4> in mm. 13b–14

[39] Lewin, "Toward the Analysis of a Schoenberg Song," 68.
[40] The <5, 6> chord and subsequent <-5, -5> just described may be a subtle reference
to m. 10 of "Angst und Hoffen," which set the description of the "bed soaked with tears."
Their pitches are identical to the earlier passage's pitches, one octave higher.

and E♯3/F3–B♭2–E♭2–A♭1 in mm. 14–15, are (with the exception of the first B5–F5), connected by descending perfect fifths <-7>. (These pitches are highlighted with brackets in Example 3.9.) Moreover, the descending tritone and perfect fifth <-6, -7> between the middleground notes in mm. 13-14 create set class 3-5, and the three descending perfect fifths between the middleground notes <-7, -7, -7> in mm. 14–15 create 4-23; as a result, mm. 13–15 project a "hidden repetition" of the set-class progression in the right hand of m. 13. After the rhythmic action subsides in m. 16, the interval-class 5s continue to be just as salient, now represented by the ascending <+5>s that had ended each slurred group. D1–G1 in m. 16 leads to G1–C2 in m. 17, which projects set class 3-9 one last time; then we hear E♭2–A♭2, which forms 3-11 with the last pitch (C2) of the preceding perfect fourth, a foreshadowing at the same pitch classes of the overlap to come in mm. 21–22, and a recall of mm. 8-9's climactic overlapping.

Now, after my detailed description of the importance of 4-23, 3-9, and interval class 5 in mm. 13–17, the reader may wonder just what significance these elements have within the song as a whole, as 4-23 is not one of the four parent tetrachords that generate the piece. We hear 4-23 for the first time in the piano introduction, mm. 6–7, where it is prominently displayed as two ascending whole steps a (compound) perfect fourth apart. (Refer again to Example 3.7a for mm. 6–7.) This initial 4-23 had functioned as a kind of "call" to the singer to remember and produce the 4-17 and 4-18 "bodies" intersecting in 3-11, which she did in mm. 8–9. When 4-23 and its subset 3-9 are developed extensively in mm. 13–17, it seems to call even more insistently for a return to the music that accompanied the words "Als wir hinter dem beblümten Tore," a return of A section material, which I believe represents the intimate union the main character is trying to remember.[41] My association of mm. 13–17 with mm. 6–7 is strengthened considerably by specific pitch-class references to the earlier measures in the piano's right hand in mm. 16–17: pitch classes E–F♯ in m. 7 have changed to E♯–F♯ in mm. 16–17, and they are placed an octave lower, but many other characteristics are the same (especially contour and articulation).

The expected music of "Als wir hinter dem beblümten Tore" does not appear immediately in m. 18, however, which is the main reason I have labeled mm. 18–24 as A′ (there is a change of order in A′s components). Before this song comes back around to the voice's starting point, it ties up

---

[41] Lewin also interprets mm. 6–7's "call motive" as a cue to the singer, and connects it to the perfect fourth chords after m. 13. He does not interpret the music of mm. 13–17 as calling for a return to mm. 8–9 specifically, however. See "Toward the Analysis of a Schoenberg Song," 54–55.

Example 3.10 Schoenberg, "Als wir hinter dem beblümten Tore," Op. 15, No. 11, mm. 18–24, section A'. Used by permission of Belmont Music Publishers and Universal Edition

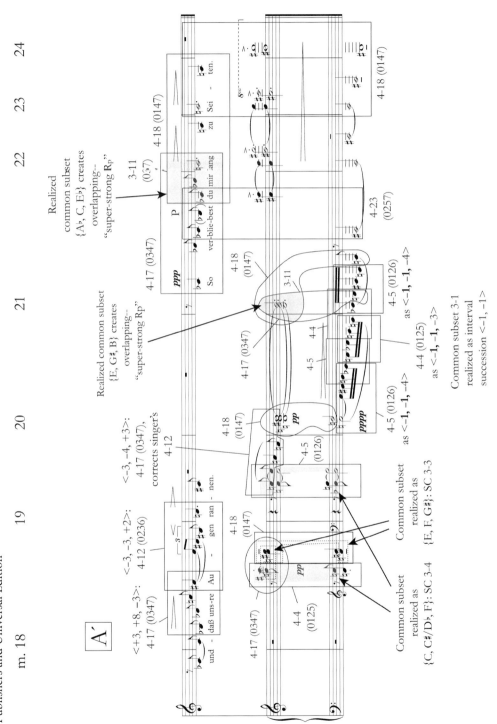

several "loose ends" of pitch and rhythm by repeating material from later in A and from the piano introduction with certain adjustments. This process, with the return of the music from mm. 8–9 at its end in mm. 21–23, constitutes the solution of the song's problem, and the completion of its musical idea. All this is portrayed in Example 3.10.

The voice in mm. 18 and 19 puts forward two variations of the original pitch-interval motive of m. 1 (<+3, +4, –3>), and neither is quite right. The first starts correctly on B♭3 and moves the requisite +3 to D♭4, but then jumps +8 to A4, and falls –3 to F♯4. The second variation starts to invert m. 1's motive, but ends up contracting its intervals to <–3, –3, +2>, forming set class 4-12 (0236), before the voice drops <–1> to C♯4 on the second eighth note of m. 19, beat 2 to double the bass of the piano chord. But, over that same chord, the piano right hand corrects the singer, producing the true pitch-interval inversion of the opening motive, <–3, –4, +3>.[42] At the point where it corrects the singer in mm. 19–20, the piano had already begun the process of returning the song step-by-step to the circumstances of mm. 8 and 9. The three chords that had appeared in mm. 10 and 11 return in mm. 18 and 19, strongly representing the common trichords 3-4 between 4-4 and 4-5, and 3-3 between 4-17 and 4-18. This trend continues in the left hand of m. 20, a pitch and rhythmic variation of the opening measures of the piano introduction, where the common trichord 3-1 between 4-5 and 4-4 is not strongly represented as a set of pitch classes, but its ordered pitch-interval succession <–1, –1> (in bold) is clearly shown to be a link between the <–1, –1, –4> of 4-5 and the <–1, –1, –3> of 4-4. At the same time, because the pianist's right hand sustains the <B3, E4, G♯4> (originally from m. 2) in mm. 20 and 21, letting the descending 4-4s and 4-5s play against it, we hear that 3-11 is common to both 4-17, formed when G appears in the bass, and 4-18, formed when F appears in the bass. (See my marked enclosures in m. 21a of the piano part.) This 3-11 creates what I have called a "super-strongly represented" $R_p$ relation between 4-17 and 4-18: not only do its members appear as the same three pitch classes, {E, G♯, B}, but they actually create an overlapping of tetrachords. Still, the segments creating 4-17 and 4-18 are not presented as saliently in mm. 20–21 as they were in mm. 8–9 (or will be in mm. 21–23).

All the revelations of common trichords just described prepare the listener for the ultimate common trichord: the 3-11 intersection <A♭3, E♭4, C4> between 4-17 and 4-18 in mm. 21–23. Notice that this intersection, which had set the relatively insignificant syllables "dem beblüm"

---

[42] Lewin characterizes the interaction between the voice and piano in mm. 18–20 in the same terms; see "Towards the Analysis of a Schoenberg Song," 69–71.

in m. 8, now sets "du mir lang," the three words that most directly signify the two lovers or husband/wife in some sort of physical contact for a long time. Mcasures 21–23 signify, to me, a definite image illustrating what the tryst or union was like – what the singer has been striving for, ever since m. 11.

   This passage, mm. 18–24, also ties up a number of rhythmic loose ends. From reviewing Examples 3.7a, 3.8, and 3.9, the reader can see that until the end of the song, significant motives rarely enter on the downbeat. The opening right-hand 4-17 <+3, +4, –3> enters on a quarter-note pickup to m. 1, and the left hand's 4-5 arrives one eighth note later (still before the notated beat). The first 4-18 chord comes in on the third beat of m. 2. The singer enters for the first time one sixteenth note after the downbeat of m. 8. And the beginning of the B section features the piano anticipating the downbeat of m. 13 by an eighth note, and the singer coming in an eighth note after that same downbeat. In general, there is confusion through most of the song about the relationship between the important rhythmic shapes of the piece and the underlying meter.

   The song begins its process of dispelling that confusion in mm. 16 and 17, where the singer accents (through melodic contour and *crescendo*) two consecutive downbeats (see again the end of Example 3.9). The piano helps with an accented E♯ in the right hand on the downbeat of m. 16, followed in m. 17 by ascending fourths in the low bass, on the second and fourth beats (the "back beats," so to speak). The singer's D emphasizes the downbeat of m. 19 (in Example 3.10) with a slight swell on "**ran**nen." All of these downbeat emphases set the stage for what happens in mm. 20–21. Not only does the 4-18 of m. 2's third beat come back squarely on the downbeat of m. 20, but it then gives way on the third beat of m. 20 to a metrically corrected version of the descending bass line from the opening of the piece. Now, each group of four starts *on* the beat, rather than an eighth note before as they had in m. 1.

   Thus, in the few measures leading up to and including the return of the singer's music from mm. 8–9 in mm. 21–23, we hear several solutions to the song's original problems of dislocation between rhythm and meter (mm. 16–21), reminders that 4-4 and 4-5 have two common trichord subsets, 3-4 and 3-1 (mm. 18–21), and two super-strong realizations of the common 3-11 (as an overlap) between 4-17 and 4-18 – initially, with less salient segments in mm. 20–21, then with the more obvious over-lapping of mm. 8–9 on "du mir lang" in mm. 21 and 22. These processes lead me to hear all of mm. 16–24 as resolving problems created earlier in the song, marking Op. 15, No. 11 as a complete idea involving problems, elaborations, and solutions. The idea lines up with the text's basic image:

two bodies brushing together, coming apart, striving to come back together, and then staying together more permanently, as well as the parallel image of a memory (of the two bodies together) coming into the main character's mind, then disappearing, then returning again.

My account of the eleventh song of Op. 15 has said nothing about tonality or tonal references, and I should justify that. It is true that certain pitch classes do stand out from the texture, like the B♭ that begins the piano introduction as well as the B section in m. 13, the A♭ at the bottom of the important <A♭3, E♭4, C4> motives in m. 8 and mm. 21–22, and the C♯/D♭ that serves as a bass note in mm. 5–9 as well as at the end, mm. 22–24. Possibly an analyst might even suggest a vi–V–I progression in D♭ in the background of this song, in a similar way to Steve Larson's approach to Song No. 2. But I was discouraged from that sort of inquiry by the same issues I encountered in all of the pieces we have analyzed thus far: most importantly, it is impossible to find a traditional *Urlinie* for the contrapuntal structure that would include the hypothetical vi–V–I, and the basic chords of this structure have dissonant additions and are missing crucial elements. The "tonic" C♯ in mm. 8–9 and again at piece's end, mm. 21–24, for example, has no third E♯ or fifth G♯, only a fourth, F♯. Song No. 11 meets my criteria for atonality, as I defined them at the beginning of this book.[43] (One could, I suppose, point to the return of the song's opening motive on B♭1 at mm. 12b–13, two octaves below its original appearance in mm. 0–1, as using functional tonality briefly in a larger atonal context as a text-painting device, to represent the notion of "remembering." But this single return to B♭ seems to me much less pronounced than Schoenberg's often-repeated use of D2 as a "tonic" arrival point in *Erwartung*: what I will call the earliest instance of using brief tonal references for expressive purposes in the next chapter.)

The "basic image," on the other hand, does serve as a useful framework for connecting many of the pitch, intervallic, and rhythmic details of both Songs No. 7 and No. 11. And it will continue to be an important analytic tool throughout the remainder of this book. But in the next chapter, I also want to focus on another approach to text-painting that certainly was

---

[43] David Lewin takes up the issue of tonality in Op. 15, No. 11, in a long footnote (number 10). He also focuses on B♭ and D♭/C♯, but interprets the D♭/C♯ as a dominant, which leads to F♯ (in second inversion) in the final measures. In the end, though, he concludes (like me) that such an interpretation makes it difficult to account for many of the important elements and relationships of the song as anything more than dissonant additions, and he chooses (like me) to give priority to the patterns formed by (all of) the intervals and chords themselves. See "Toward the Analysis of a Schoenberg Song," 71–74.

traditional in Schoenberg's culture, that manifested itself in the named motives in "Angst und Hoffen" ("Angst," "Hoffen," "Seufzer"), and that he seems to have favored for his stage works written in the atonal and twelve-tone styles. I am referring, of course, to the use of leitmotives, and we will explore how they – both as specific intervallic and rhythmic shapes, and also generalized as set-class motives – contribute to large-scale coherence in a work that many scholars believe has little or no motivic coherence: *Erwartung*, Op. 17.

# 4   *Erwartung*, Op. 17

*A Leitmotivic Opera and a "Cumulative Setting," Atomized*

In Chapter 2, I considered the international controversy surrounding Op. 11, No. 3 – between English-speaking authors who understand that piano piece as ushering in Schoenberg's "intuitive aesthetic," characterized by the utter lack of clear form and thematic and motivic repetition, and German-speaking authors who hear in it various kinds of motivic and harmonic networks. Op. 17, the monodrama *Erwartung*, written right after Op. 11, No. 3 in late August to early September 1909, has been the subject of a similar controversy, which does not fall along geographic lines to the same extent. On the one hand, there are scholars, both English- and German-speaking, who understand it to be the high point of Schoenberg's "intuitive" period, the work in which his drive toward non-repetition of themes and motives reached its climax, in a texture that resembles a stream of consciousness. Joseph Auner, in the article that coined the term "intuitive aesthetic," describes *Erwartung* in this way:

> In *Erwartung* and other works of the period such as the Six Little Piano Pieces, Op. 19, and *Herzgewächse*, Op. 20, unvaried motivic or thematic repetition, a traditional approach to form, and imitative counterpoint are carefully avoided.[1]

Auner is certainly correct as regards "traditional form": *Erwartung* has more in common with the Op. 15 songs that build themselves around visual images than with the abbreviated sonata-rondo or three-part forms of Op. 11, Nos. 1 and 2. (Schoenberg would return to the practice of repeating larger sections in 1912 in his next opera, *Die glückliche Hand*, as Auner shows clearly in his study of the sketches for that work.[2]) But I will show that motivic repetition is as important to the monodrama as it is to Schoenberg's earlier music. Ethan Haimo is even stronger in his assertion about the lack of motivic repetition:

> On 27 August 1909 . . . Schoenberg launched into an opera (the monodrama, *Erwartung*, Op. 17), during the entire course of which (other than immediate repetitions) there was not a single recurring theme or motive.[3]

---

[1]   Auner, "Schoenberg's Aesthetic Transformations," 123.   [2]   Ibid., 109–24.
[3]   Haimo, *Schoenberg's Transformation of Musical Language*, p. 348.

Finally, Bryan Simms, with respect to the form, comments on how it is made up of "a series of disjunct and contrasting sections whose character mimics the rapidly changing emotional states of the woman."[4]

On the other side of the controversy, H. H. Stuckenschmidt, in his biography of Schoenberg, described a handful of motivic and harmonic networks in the piece, chief among them the one based on the pitch-class succession <D, F, C♯>, which he considered to be "almost a leitmotive."[5] Theodor W. Adorno in his *Philosophy of New Music* (1949) was the first to make the claim that *Erwartung* includes quotations from Schoenberg's earlier song "Am Wegrand," Op. 6, No. 6 (1905), near the end in mm. 401–02 and 411–13 (Adorno explains the quotations as Schoenberg's portrayal of the "collective loneliness" inherent in modern society).[6] Numerous others since then have described and illustrated networks through the piece that grow out of those quotations, or out of other important elements in *Erwartung* itself. Herbert H. Buchanan illustrates a small handful of places in the monodrama where Schoenberg clearly borrows the primary theme, its countermelody, and transitional elements from the Op. 6 song (we will consider these quotations in more detail later), and claims that there are a multitude of other such borrowings, some of which are not as obvious as those he illustrates.[7] Alan Lessem describes a more extensive network of motives derived from the "Am Wegrand" quotation, including some of the same ones I will discuss below. Lessem groups his motives into three categories and assigns leitmotivic significance to the categories; there are motives associated with the "memory and anticipation of love," those representing the "anxiety of guilt," and finally those portraying "intimations of death." Though his leitmotivic categories address some of the same topics as mine, his correspondences between the type of motive and what the category represents are different.[8] Jan Maegaard, with his habitual extreme thoroughness, traces an extensive and exhaustive network of ordered pitch-interval successions, contours, unordered pitch sets, and unordered pitch-class sets that have their origin, in part, in the materials borrowed from "Am Wegrand."[9] Most recently, Kathryn Whitney has traced connections between the voice's setting

[4] Simms, *The Atonal Music of Arnold Schoenberg*, p. 96.

[5] Stuckenschmidt, *Schoenberg: His Life, World, and Work*, p. 121.

[6] Theodor W. Adorno, *Philosophy of New Music*, trans., ed. and with an introduction by Robert Hullot-Kentor (Minneapolis: University of Minnesota Press, 2006), pp. 40–41.

[7] Herbert H. Buchanan, "A Key to Schoenberg's *Erwartung* (op. 17)," *Journal of the American Musicological Society* 20/3 (Autumn 1967): 434–49.

[8] Alan Lessem, *Music and Text in the Works of Arnold Schoenberg* (Ann Arbor: UMI Research Press, 1979), pp. 66–95.

[9] Maegaard, *Studien zur Entwicklung des dodekaphonen Satzes*, II, pp. 312–437.

of "Tausend Menschen ziehen vorüber" in mm. 411–412 (which counter-points with the primary theme from "Am Wegrand" in the bass), the bassoon and oboe *Hauptstimmen* in mm. 1–2, and several vocal phrases and *Hauptstimmen* in the first scene. Whitney's correspondences consist of unordered pitch-class sets and unordered pitch-interval successions, as well as trichord set-classes (thus taking the final step toward abstraction). She divides the trichords into "primary" (set classes 3-1, 3-2, 3-3) and "secondary" (3-4 through 3-12) groups, anticipating the division of set classes into groups by leitmotivic topic that I will attempt in this chapter.[10]

My contribution to this discussion, then, similar to what I did for Op. 11, No. 3, will be to show that *Erwartung* is characterized not only by motivic networks, but also by clear motivic processes that span the entire piece and give it large-scale coherence. I start from the assertions others such as Simms and Maegaard have made, that Schoenberg's music follows the progression of Marie Pappenheim's text unusually closely.[11] Indeed, the first (and nearly the only existing) sketches that he made for the mono-drama consist of margin notes to Pappenheim's handwritten libretto. An example of such a sketch is shown in Example 4.1, remarkably similar to the final version of the passage in mm. 245–46 where the woman exclaims "Wie kannst du tot sein?" ("How can you be dead?").[12]

It seems as though the composer jotted down the musical phrase on the right as an immediate, direct reaction to the corresponding text on the left. Because of Schoenberg's apparent concern to make the music follow the progress of the text as closely as possible, the first place to look for a large-scale pattern of some kind is in Pappenheim's libretto (as revised by Schoenberg and the author in collaboration). Although the text does shift topics and moods quickly and rather erratically on its surface, causing numerous scholars to compare it to a patient's responses during

---

[10] Kathryn Whitney, "Schoenberg's 'Single Second of Maximum Spiritual Excitement': Compression and Expansion in 'Erwartung,' Op. 17," *Journal of Music Theory* 47/1 (Spring, 2003): 155–214. An even more recent analytical investigation of the opera, in a doctoral dissertation by Russell C. Knight ("Operand Set Theory and Schoenberg's *Erwartung*, Op. 17," University of California at Santa Barbara, 2008), suggests the possibility of understanding it as disconnected and fragmentary in pitch-class space, but unified through longer-range networks in interval-vector space, through the use of "non-subset operands." These are interval vectors of smaller set classes that add up to form the vectors of larger, "reference" sets.

[11] Simms, *The Atonal Music of Arnold Schoenberg*, pp. 96–97; Maegaard, *Studien zur Entwicklung*, II, pp. 315–16.

[12] The larger sketch page from which this excerpt is taken may be found at the Schönberg Center website at www.schoenberg.at/compositions/manuskripte.php?werke_id=472&id_quelle=1400&image=T80_15_2416.jpg&groesse=100&aktion=einzelbild&bild_id=16.

Example 4.1  Excerpt from Schoenberg's marginal sketches on Marie
Pappenheim's handwritten libretto (MS 2416, Arnold Schönberg Center). Used by
permission of Belmont Music Publishers

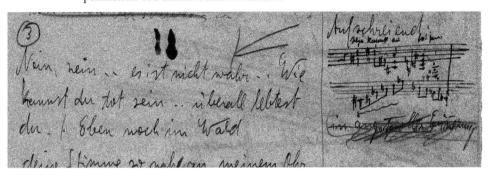

psychoanalysis, it still follows an overall framework. Maegaard has characterized both libretto and piece as splitting into two parts: the woman's search
for her lover (up to the general pause in m. 158), and her reaction after she
finds his body.[13] I would go further, to characterize the large arc of the story
as two gradual processes of emergence: 1) the "expectation" or anticipation
of, and resistance against, some indistinct threat, which gradually takes
definite shape as the lover's dead body – the climax of this first process
occurs at m. 153, as she finally acknowledges "Das ist er!" (It is he!); 2) the
anticipation of, resistance against, and emerging realization of the unavoidable fact that he is indeed dead, and she is doomed to a life of solitude
without him, an epitome of the "collective loneliness" that Adorno claimed
to be the essence of *Erwartung*. This second process reaches its culmination
at mm. 411–413 with the words "Tausend Menschen ziehen vorüber, aber
ich erkenne dich nicht" ("A thousand people pass by, but I don't recognize
you").[14] The text "Tausend Menschen ziehen vorüber" is lifted directly (by
Pappenheim, perhaps unintentionally) from John Henry Mackay's text for
Schoenberg's Op. 6 song "Am Wegrand," but, in addition, the topic of
Mackay's entire poem, involving someone waiting by the side of the road
for a lover who never comes, fits the situation at the second climax of
*Erwartung* perfectly. Both reasons apparently inspired Schoenberg to
quote the aforementioned passages from his earlier song, and to base
much of the monodrama's texture on wide-ranging variations of them.

---

[13]  Maegaard, *Studien zur Entwicklung*, II, p. 315.
[14]  Lessem calls this second climax "the moment (m. 411) when the woman must finally
recognize her lover's death and the hopelessness of her quest." See *Music and Text in the
Works of Schoenberg*, p. 75.

The double emergence of, first, the lover's dead body and then the irreversible certainty of the woman's lonely future does qualify, I think, as an extended "basic image," and my analyses in this chapter will show how this image controls pitch, rhythm, and orchestration at key points in the piece, similarly to the basic images in Chapter 3, but in a more drawn-out and complex way. Since *Erwartung* is a work for the stage, however, it is also useful to compare it with techniques Schoenberg used in other works of a similar kind. Particularly the symphonic poem *Pelleas und Melisande*, also based on a staged work and written only six years before *Erwartung*, provides important musical models for portraying emergence. *Pelleas* is a thoroughly leitmotivic work, and Michael Cherlin has shown that its "Fate" motive portrays gradual materialization by repeating itself more and more insistently in the bass line at the beginning of the piece, and sudden, unexpected, catastrophic materialization by moving up into the higher register at a loud dynamic. The leitmotive representing Mélisande's "Death Drive" (as Cherlin calls it) portrays gradual emergence by adding notes incrementally as it repeats itself.[15] All these musical processes carry over into *Erwartung*, and, as I will show, others are added to them to express the gradual and unavoidable materialization of those things that are dreaded. Not only that, but the second leitmotive, "Death Drive," is intervallically identical to *Erwartung*'s quotation of the main melody from "Am Wegrand," once several ornamental notes are removed. The three melodies are given in Example 4.2.

The middleground do–me–sol–ti (using movable-do) is projected in "Death Drive" in C♯ minor, and in "Am Wegrand" in D minor. In *Erwartung*, this same motive is the central one that portrays both emergences: it gradually materializes as do–me–ti in D minor (Stuckenschmidt's "almost-leitmotive") in and before mm. 151–53, and as do–me–sol–ti with neighbor notes in mm. 411–412a (as illustrated in Example 4.2). Whether this gradual emerging motive by itself enables us to describe *Erwartung* as a "D minor piece" in any sense is questionable.[16] But it is certain that a sense of D minor emerges tentatively in mm. 151–53, and more distinctly in mm. 411–12, if only for a few measures, and the pitch D2 and pitch class D appear prominently many times leading up to those two arrivals. This is why I think we can understand this "intuitive" opera of 1909 as the first piece in which Schoenberg makes use of functional tonality as an occasional text-painting device, after abandoning it

---

[15] Michael Cherlin, *Schoenberg's Musical Imagination* (Cambridge: Cambridge University Press, 2007), pp. 95–98 and 147.

[16] Herbert H. Buchanan makes the argument for such a key attribution in "A Key to Schoenberg's *Erwartung*," 436.

Example 4.2  Comparison of the "Death Drive" leitmotive in *Pelleas und
Melisande*, the voice's entrance in "Am Wegrand," mm. 3–4, and Schoenberg's
quotation of "Am Wegrand" in the bass line of *Erwartung*, mm. 411–12a.
Copyright © 1912, 1920 by Universal Edition AG Vienna, UE 3371. "Am
Wegrand," Op. 6, No. 6. Copyright © 1907 by Dreililien Verlag. *Erwartung*, Op. 17.
Copyright © 1916, 1950 by Universal Edition AG Vienna, UE 13612. All rights
reserved. Used by permission of Belmont Music Publishers, Universal Edition, and
Dreililien Verlag, Richard Birnbach, Berlin

*Pelleas und Melisande*, starting 1 measure after rehearsal 50: "Death Drive"

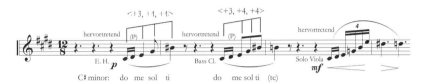

"Am Wegrand," mm. 3–4

*Erwartung*, mm. 411–12a

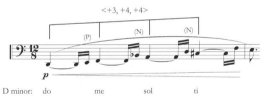

a year earlier as a large-structural one.[17] This technique of using tonal
fragments for expressive purposes will continue to develop until the end of
Schoenberg's middle period.

---

[17] Cherlin makes a claim for "spectres of tonality" appearing earlier than Op. 17, in his
reference to Thomas Christensen's essay on Op. 11, No. 1 and its motivic antecedents in
Wagner's *Tristan und Isolde* (Christensen, "Schoenberg's Opus 11, No. 1: A Parody of
Pitch Cells from *Tristan*," *Journal of the Arnold Schoenberg Institute* 10/1 (June 1987):
38–44). But, as I suggested in Chapter 1, the ordered pitch-class successions that
Schoenberg borrowed from the opening of the *Tristan* prelude, according to
Christensen, are removed from their original harmonic contexts, so that I cannot accept
them as specters of tonal *function*, though they are interesting and convincing from the
motivic standpoint. Cherlin cites Christensen's article in "Schoenberg and *Das
Unheimliche*: Spectres of Tonality," 362–63.

Before considering in more detail how the double emergence of <D, F, C♯> and <D, F, A, C♯> is worked out and accounts for a surprisingly large amount of *Erwartung's* texture, with detailed "snapshots" taken from different parts of the monodrama, I will remark that Schoenberg's technique seems uncannily similar to the motivic procedure that Charles Ives was using at around the same time. J. Peter Burkholder has called Ives's approach to building a quotation up gradually from fragments of itself "cumulative setting." Ives typically applies it to eighteenth- and nineteenth-century American hymn tunes, taking short phrases from them at the beginning, altering their rhythms, and transposing them to various keys, but accumulating larger and larger segments until he reaches the entire hymn tune in nearly correct rhythm at the end. He typically does this both with the principal hymn tune and a countermelody, which often is realized in its complete form first.[18] Schoenberg's approach seems to be a similar process applied to much smaller elements; as we will see, he begins with groups of two or three notes, first stated as set class 3-3 and unordered pitch class collection {1, 2, 5}, then materializing into the ordered pitch intervals <+3, +8>, and after 400 measures he builds up to just the one phrase from "Am Wegrand," together with its one-phrase countermelody (also taken from the Op. 6 song). Thus I would characterize Schoenberg's procedure in *Erwartung* as an "atomized cumulative setting." This is not to say that either composer had any influence on the other, but it is interesting that their thoughts apparently ran along similar lines.

### *Erwartung*, mm. 1–6 (opening)

I will now describe several passages from the monodrama in detail, in an attempt to show how the gradual revelations of first the succession <D, F, C♯> and then the three quotations from Op. 6, No. 6 work themselves out over the span of the piece. This approach will of course have the disadvantage of passing over dozens of measures that are not included in my chosen passages: the reader should understand that similar motivic and harmonic procedures are at work there as well, toward the same ends. The opening of *Erwartung* is illustrated in Examples 4.3a and b. These six measures introduce more-or-less specific versions of all three elements that the monodrama borrows from "Am Wegrand," and fill out the remainder of the texture with four families of set classes that correspond to and portray different emotions expressed in the text and staging directions. Two of these families relate directly to the quoted "Am Wegrand" material, the

---

[18] J. Peter Burkholder, *All Made of Tunes: Charles Ives and the Uses of Musical Borrowing* (New Haven and London: Yale University Press, 1995), pp. 137–266.

Example 4.3a Schoenberg, *Erwartung*, mm. 1–3. Used by permission of Belmont Music Publishers, Universal Edition, and Dreililien Verlag, Richard Birnbach, Berlin

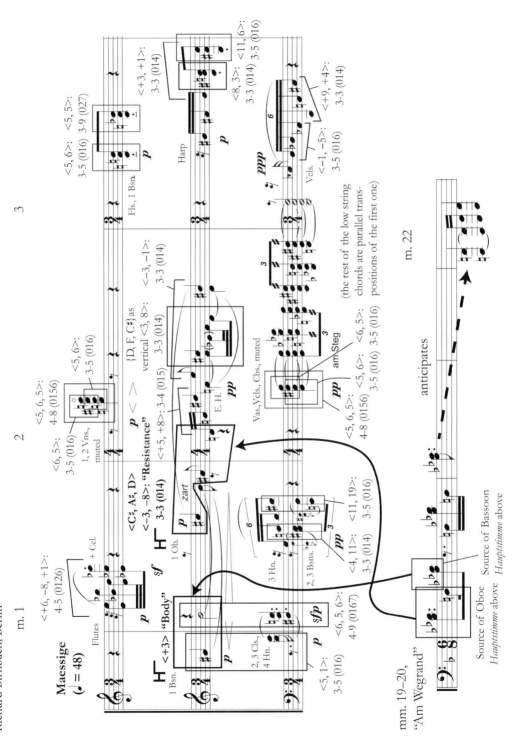

others do not (but one of them features an unordered pitch-interval stack common to many of the pieces we have studied thus far).

In Example 4.3a, the first three measures, H. H. Buchanan shows us that the *Hauptstimmen* in the 1st bassoon and 1st oboe that come to the fore among the initial sounds of *Erwartung* are borrowed directly from a transitional passage in "Am Wegrand," mm. 19–20.[19] (These borrowings are indicated in Example 4.3a with boxes and crossed arrows from the score of the song to the score of the opera.) The bassoon in the pickup measure and m. 1 of the monodrama takes the A♭3 and C♭4 on the third eighth note of m. 19 of the song, raises them an octave, and respells them as <G♯4, B4>, while the oboe in mm. 1b–2 follows it with a quotation of the three pitches that had originally come first in m. 19, B♭3 and D♭4 followed by D3. The oboe raises these pitches an octave and respells them, stating C♯5 before A♯4, and then descends eight half-steps to D4, in a similar way to the first three notes of m. 19.

The reproduction of the original "Am Wegrand" transitional passage at the bottom left corner of Example 4.3a is followed by two blank measures indicating its distance from the downbeat of m. 22 in the song. This makes clear the context of mm. 19–20 in "Am Wegrand": these measures transition to, and anticipate (*erwarten*), the return of the song's opening melody (from mm. 3–4 in the voice) in the bass line of the piano at m. 22. Since that returning melody, both in the song and in the monodrama, signifies the singer's final realization that she will die a lonely woman, the transitional material in mm. 19–20 of the song, *and* its counterpart in mm. 1–2 of the monodrama, can be understood as signifying the expectation of her inevitable fate.

But, of course, there is one important difference between the song and the monodrama: in "Am Wegrand," only two measures intervene between m. 19 and m. 22, perhaps a few seconds at a fast tempo (Schoenberg marks the song "Bewegt"). In *Erwartung*, there is a much longer stretch of 408 measures from mm. 1–2 to a more literal quotation of the transitional material in m. 410b, followed immediately by the entry of the main melody from "Am Wegrand" in the bass at m. 411. One wonders if this difference is what Schoenberg was referring to when he claimed that *Erwartung* "represent[ed] in slow motion everything that occurs during a single second of maximum spiritual excitement, stretching it out to half an hour."[20] Could the two measures 20 and 21 of "Am Wegrand" be what he intended to stretch out? In any case, our focus will be on how anticipation is drawn out through the gradual, incremental materialization of the components of mm. 22–24 of the song within those 408 measures of the opera.

---

[19] Buchanan, "A Key to Schoenberg's *Erwartung*," pp. 440–41.

[20] Schoenberg, "New Music: My Music" (c. 1930), in *Style and Idea*, p. 105.

Both the bassoon and oboe *Hauptstimmen* serve to represent elements of the drama, as well as beginning the long process of anticipation; they are leitmotivic in the usual sense. The bassoon's <G♯, B> forms an ascending minor third, pitch interval +3, which is the first element of <+3, +8>, the pitch-interval succession associated with Stuckenschmidt's central motive <D, F, C♯>. Stuckenschmidt calls this interval and pitch succession "almost leitmotivic" without telling us what it signifies. Since it takes over the texture with its incessant repeats in mm. 152–54, those measures in which the woman finally recognizes the dead body of her lover after numerous measures of almost discovering it (this passage will be discussed in more detail in Example 4.7), I will call it the "Body" motive and claim that its gradual emergence represents her slow but inevitable discovery of his corpse, the main motivic process of the monodrama's first part.

There is another intimation of the Body motive in m. 2b, created by the solo oboe together with the English horn: while the oboe sustains C♯5, the English horn descends from F4 to D4, with a decorative lower neighbor E♭4. The Body motive's pitches are presented mostly simultaneously here, but in the correct registral order, from the bottom up. In addition, two prominent pitch-interval successions approximate the Body motive's <+3, +8> in mm. 1–3: the solo oboe in m. 2a plays <+5, +8>, and the 'cellos in m. 3 end their flourish with <+9, +4>. Finally, one of the harp chords that sound immediately before the voice makes its entry on the pickup to m. 4 projects the unordered pitch-interval stack <8, 3>, if only briefly. All of these ought to be heard as vague suggestions of the increasingly intense development of "Body," <+3, +8>, that will come 150 measures later.

The oboe's three notes in mm. 1b–2, <C♯5, A♯4, D4>, while quoting m. 19 of "Am Wegrand" as discussed above, at the same time constitute a second leitmotive that repeats and varies itself throughout *Erwartung*, and as it does, it gradually picks up the connotation of the woman pushing back against the fear that the inevitable discovery of her lover's body creates in her. The text phrases that it sets in later music contribute to this motive's sense of meaning (generally having to do with her reproaches to herself to keep looking for him and, later, her refusals to admit that he is actually dead). Not only that, but the motive, which I will call "Resistance," literally contradicts the "Body" motive by inverting it: its ordered pitch interval sequence is <−3, −8>. In the measures to come we will see a number of descending successions combining −3 or −4 with −7, −8 or −9, with the smaller interval usually preceding the larger one: these should be understood as developments of the Resistance motive. (Jan Maegaard's detailed study of *Erwartung* points out several instances of what he calls the "defense" motive in the voice during the second part of the monodrama: the first three give prominence to Resistance as either a foreground or middleground element, while setting texts that begin with "Nein, nein".)[21]

Example 4.3b, which contains mm. 4–6 of *Erwartung*, introduces a third leitmotive that will continue to repeat and develop throughout the opera. It also can be understood as having its ultimate source in "Am Wegrand," but in this case the connection seems more tenuous than the ones we discussed above, at least initially. The voice's initial entry in mm. 3b–4 of *Erwartung*, "Hier hinein?" ("In here?"), creates the pitch-interval succession <–2, +1>, which as the boxes and leftmost curved arrow in Example 4.3b show, inverts the succession <+2, –1> formed by the third, fourth, and fifth notes of the voice in "Am Wegrand" mm. 22–24, part of the countermelody that accompanies the return of the song's motto in the bass. (Or, it could also be heard as a retrograde of the second, third, and fourth notes of this countermelody.) Even though the exact intervallic profile of "Fear," <–2, +1>, is not found in mm. 22–23 of "Am Wegrand," only variations, the immediately following segment of the song's countermelody, <C♯5, D5, E♭5, E5, F5>, carries over *at pitch* into m. 5 of the opera, beginning with the flute and solo viola (second staff of Example 4.3b) and carried on by the first two pitches of the voice. This seems to confirm the connection between the introduction of the "Fear" motive in mm. 3b–4 of the opera and its source in the song. In mm. 22–24 of "Am Wegrand," the soloist is singing the text "Sehnsucht erfüllt die Bezirke des Lebens" ("Longing fills the regions of my life"), an expression of the same sort of "collective loneliness" the woman in *Erwartung* fears and is trying to avoid. For this reason, and because this motive will usually associate in the coming measures with texts that represent the woman's fear response to being startled, I will call it the "Fear" motive.[22]

After its introduction by the voice, Fear appears immediately at the beginning of the first clarinet's flourish in m. 4, now retrograded to form <–1, +2>. It then overlaps itself three times in m. 5, at the beginning of the voice's phrase "Wie silbern die Stämme schimmern … wie Birken!" ("How silvery the tree trunks shimmer … like birches!"). "Wie silbern die Stäm-" is set by <+1, –2>, a retrograde inversion of the voice's initial Fear motive, interlocking with <–2, +1>, a transposition, and another <+1, –2>.

[21] Maegaard, *Studien zur Entwicklung des dodekaphonen Satzes*, II, p. 317.

[22] "Fear's" motivic importance has been recognized by others, most notably Alban Berg, who circled it in his copy of the piano reduction of *Erwartung* and marked it "Frage" (Question). Kathryn Whitney explores various analytic interpretations of Berg's markings in "Schoenberg's 'Single Second of Maximum Spiritual Excitement'," 187–203.

Example 4.3b Schoenberg, *Erwartung*, mm. 4–6. Used by permission of Belmont Music Publishers, Universal Edition, and Dreililien Verlag, Richard Birnbach, Berlin

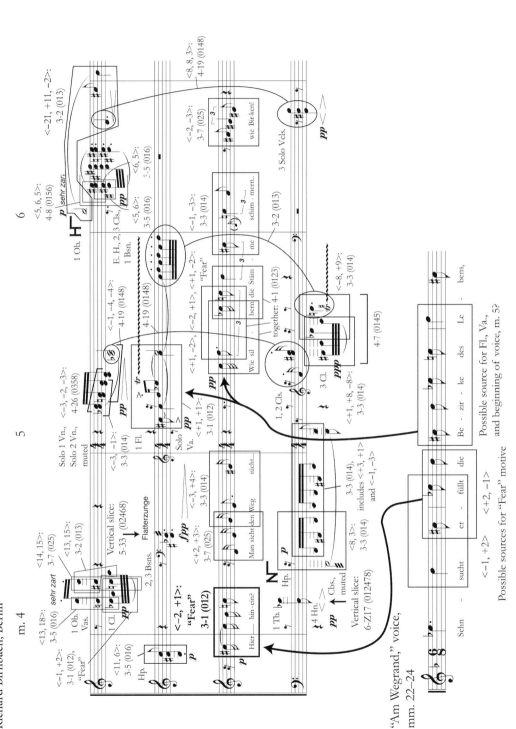

This RI-chain of Fear motives gives way first to <–1, –3> in mm. 5b–6a, a member of the same set class, 3-3, as the Body motive, and finally reaches a less dissonant set in m. 6b, a subset of the diatonic and pentatonic scales, <–2, –3>, 3-7 (025). One could interpret the progression from chromatic Fear variations (set classes 3-1) toward a diatonic subset (3-7) as representing the woman trying to calm her nerves through admiring her natural surroundings. There are other places in the music to come where progressions from chromatic to diatonic set-classes portray her attempts to reassure herself, some of which we will consider in detail.

The shift that my analysis has just made from focusing on pitch-interval successions to describing the progressions of set classes leads naturally into a discussion of the parts of *Erwartung*'s opening musical fabric we have not yet explored, those accompanimental voices (and in some cases, parts of main voices) that do not project the pitch-interval leitmotives discussed above. These other components of *Erwartung* should not be explained away as "intuitive" or improvisatory. In almost every case, the other parts of the texture in mm. 1–6 consist of members of four families of set classes – two of them relate closely to the Body and Fear motives, but the third and fourth do not relate directly to any leitmotive that appears in the opening measures. The third family builds itself around a three-note sonority (or vertical stack of two unordered pitch intervals) that we have encountered repeatedly in our analyses of Opp. 11 and 15 in earlier chapters – the Viennese Trichord, <5, 6> or <6, 5>, belonging to set class 3-5 (016). The fourth contains subsets of the pentatonic or diatonic scales, represented in mm. 1–6 by set class 3-7 (025).

By "families" of set-classes I mean groups that are related primarily through inclusion relations – subsets and supersets of one another. The first of these builds itself around the set class 3-3 (014) that contains the Body motive. In Examples 4.3a and b, we hear several examples of that set class created by interval stacks or successions that are not related to <+3, +8> in any other way; some examples are the <4, 11> in horn and bassoons in m. 1b, the voice's <–3, +4> in m. 4b on "den Weg nicht," and the <–1, –3> in the voice in mm. 5b–6 we mentioned previously at the top of this page. Another trichordal member of the "Body" family is the set class created by the oboe's <+5, +8> in m. 2a, set class 3-4 (015). Finally, set class 3-2 (013), which appears between the 3rd clarinet and solo viola at the end of m. 5, and frequently in later music, often appears interlocked with 3-3 and 3-4 and can be understood as part of the same family.

Both 3-3 and 3-4 are subsets of set class 4-19 (0148), the set class projected by the middleground notes of the "Am Wegrand" main melody, <D, F, A, C♯> or do–me–sol–ti, illustrated in Examples 4.2b and c.

At *Erwartung's* opening, 4-19 begins to come to the fore in mm. 5 and 6: the violin and clarinet sonority on the third beat of m. 5 (top and bottom staves of my reduction), the second solo violin line on the second and third beats of m. 5 that leads into that sonority <–1, –4, –4>, and the 'cello and oboe sonority on the third beat of m. 6 all belong to 4-19. Another tetrachord that includes both 3-3 and 3-4 is 4-7 (0145), which appears in the third clarinet in m. 5b as an overlapping of 3-3 with itself.

Members of the 3-3/3-4/4-7/4-19 family (which will add other, larger sets as the monodrama continues) often represent the lover's dead body directly: a good example is 4-19 in the horns portraying the vanishing lover in the last measure of *Erwartung*, as he disappears under streams of whole-tone and chromatic segments in the remainder of the orchestra (look forward to Example 4.14 for this passage). But these set classes also typically occur when the text refers to darkness in general, as in the latter half of m. 4. As the woman sings "Man sieht den Weg nicht" ("One cannot see the path"), her set-class content "darkens" from a diatonic subset, 3-7 (025), to 3-3 (014), reinforced by a different transposition of 3-3 in the basses and harp. (This set-class succession will be reversed by the following statement about the tree trunks shimmering like birches in mm. 5–6 that we discussed on pp. 162–64, which has a lightening effect: 3-3 back to 3-7.) Perhaps the fact that the dead body is portrayed in the first half of the libretto as an indistinct dark object (in mm. 143–45, the woman mistakes it for the "shadow of a bench") enables Schoenberg to use the same group of set classes for both the dead lover and darkness in general.

The second family of set classes builds itself around the "Fear" motive and its set class 3-1 (012). In Example 4.3b, this family is only in the beginning stages of its development: other than the statements of Fear in mm. 4 and 5 remarked on already, set class 3-1 appears as the chromatic ascent in m. 5a between the viola and flute that quotes m. 23 of "Am Wegrand" at pitch, and the voice's interlocking Fear motives in m. 5b together form set class 4-1 (0123). As the monodrama progresses, we will encounter continually larger subsets of the chromatic scale, until finally the entire scale emerges at *Erwartung's* final cadence (seemingly representing the triumph of fear and loneliness over the woman's hope that her lover might return).

The third family of set classes, the one built around the Viennese Trichord and its set class, 3-5 (016), accounts for most of the vertical sonorities in the opening measures of *Erwartung*. In mm. 1–3, for example, most of the quiet outbursts of orchestral color that accompany the two *Hauptstimmen* in bassoon and oboe are either statements of the Viennese Trichord <5, 6> or <6, 5>, vertical overlappings of them to form <5, 6, 5>, set class 4-8 (0156), or <6, 5, 6>, set class 4-9 (0167), or members of 3-5 that are not Viennese Trichords (e.g., <11, 6> in the woodwinds and harp at the end of m. 3).

Though it is not directly related to a pitch-interval leitmotive like the two families just discussed, the 3-5 family's presence throughout *Erwartung* consistently occurs at places in the text where something startles the woman. Typically, the orchestra produces members of the 3-5 family (to represent the object or thought that startles her), and the woman responds in fear with members of the 3-1 family, or sometimes in defense, with "Resistance." In fact, one could describe the interplay between the accompanying voices and the two *Hauptstimmen* in Example 4.3a in terms of objects that startle the woman and her reactions. The initial pitch-interval stacks of the piece are <5, 1> (a member of 3-5) and <6, 5, 6>, set class 4-9 (0167), created by the clarinets and horn "harmonizing" the intimation of the Body motive in the bassoon. Immediately after, the flutes emit a quickly flashing motive that belongs to 4-5 (0126), a superset of 3-5, and the horn and bassoons add another brief outburst that ends on <11, 19>, again 3-5. The oboe (standing in for the woman) responds to all these 3-5 sets and supersets and the bassoon's suggestion of "Body" with "Resistance" in mm. 1b–2a, but not long after, the violins sound <5, 6, 5> (SC 4-8) for a brief quarter note, and the low strings pick that same sonority up and present it in parallel motion for the rest of m. 2, finishing on the downbeat of m. 3 – more startling noises. As the woodwinds and harp in the treble and the 'cellos in the bass take over in m. 3, both groups begin with versions of 3-5, the Viennese Trichord <5, 6> in the woodwinds and the pitch-interval succession <–1, –5> in the 'cellos. After moving to the <8, 3> 3-3 chord we commented on in our discussion of the Body motive, the harp then ends on <11, 6>, another 3-5 sonority, to which the woman responds immediately with her Fear motive in mm. 3b–4.

The final family of set classes that appears in the opening six measures of *Erwartung* consists of subsets of the diatonic and pentatonic scales. As we saw in Example 4.3b with the progression from 3-7 (025) to 3-3 (014) on the text "Man sieht den Weg nicht" and from 4-1 and 3-3 back to 3-7 on "Wie silbern die Stämme schimmern . . . wie Birken!," diatonic or pentatonic subsets typically signify periods of relative relaxation, places where the woman is able to reassure and recollect herself for a moment before the next startling experience or thought. As *Erwartung* progresses, larger diatonic subsets will also be called on to play similar roles.

My explanation of the orchestral accompanying voices in terms of families of motives and set classes related by inclusion that portray characters or emotions in the text takes a different direction from many other approaches to Schoenberg's atonal music, and certainly diverges substantially from those who would claim that "not a single motive repeats in *Erwartung*." But a remarkably similar approach is at the core of Janet Schmalfeldt's analysis of the opera *Wozzeck* by Schoenberg's student, Alban Berg.[23] Schmalfeldt presents one family of set classes, many of them containing or contained within one another, that represent various aspects of Wozzeck as character: 4-19 (0148) and 5-30 (01468) for his poverty and desperation, 5-26 (02458) for his suspicion of Marie's infidelity, 6-34 (013579) for his reaction to the psychological and physical abuse he suffers from the Captain, Doctor, and Drum Major, and 8-24 (0124568T) as a cadential set class, which summarizes and brings all these topics together. (Interestingly, the first and most important member of this family, Wozzeck's primary leitmotive 4-19, shares its set class with one of the main tetrachords associated with *Erwartung's* Body motive.) She then discusses a second family of set classes, many of them tetrachords, which have common subsets as well as supersets, and claims that they together represent Marie as character and her various emotions and conditions.

If Schmalfeldt's "set-class as leitmotive" approach enables her to explain *Wozzeck's* harmonic language as motivated by the dramatic design and progression (and I believe that it does), then perhaps a similar approach can help us interpret a work by Berg's teacher and mentor that seems to have served as a model for the younger composer. After all, we know that Berg was heavily involved in proofreading *Erwartung* between 1909 and 1915 (just before and as he began working on *Wozzeck*),[24] and we have already mentioned (p. 162, fn 22) that he owned a copy of the piano reduction in which he carefully marked and labeled many of the leitmotives and significant sonorities. Why would networks and processes involving leitmotivic set classes, similar to those in *Wozzeck*, not be active in a piece that served as its model?

## Measures 18b–38 (end of Scene 1)

I have chosen a relatively large chunk of Scene 1 extending into the first few notes of Scene 2 for my second excerpt. These measures illustrate well the incremental growth of the "Body" motive, from fleeting suggestions of its intervals or pitch classes to a full-fledged statement of both ordered pitch

[23] Janet Schmalfeldt, *Berg's Wozzeck: Harmonic Language and Dramatic Design* (New Haven: Yale University Press, 1983), chs. 3 and 4.
[24] Jessica Payette, "Seismographic Screams: *Erwartung's* Reverberations through Twentieth-Century Culture" (PhD dissertation, Stanford University, 2008), p. 113.

intervals <+3, +8> and pitch classes <D, F, C♯>, in the basses and timpani at m. 38. As "Body" gradually takes shape and grows more prominent, it interacts in interesting and consistent ways with the "Resistance" and "Fear" motives and the four families of set classes described in the previous paragraphs. Typically "Body," vertical 3-5 sets and supersets (which connote something startling), or both, will enter the texture suddenly and will immediately call forth either "Fear" or "Resistance" as a response. The text in the last twenty measures of Scene 1 motivates such sequences. It is given below (my translation):

> Oh, still the cricket with its love song . . . Don't speak . . . it is so sweet beside you . . . the moon is in the twilight . . .
> You coward, won't you look for him? . . . then die here . . .
> How threatening the silence is . . . the moon is full of horror . . . can IT see in there? . . .
> I am alone . . . in the gloomy shadows . . . I want to sing, then he will hear me . . .

The first appearance of the Body motive in this excerpt (see Example 4.4a) is buried in the middle of the woman's phrase about the cricket's love song ("ihrem Lie-"), not as salient as some of the later occurrences of it in this passage will be.

This <+3, +8> represented by the pitch classes <F♯, A, F>, a member of set class 3-3 (014), is surrounded in the orchestra by set classes 3-3, 3-4 (015), and 4-7 (0145), members of the associated family (again, representing the lover's dead body and darkness). The one exception is the cricket call in the celesta, which projects 4-1 (0123), part of the Fear motive's family. As she sings about the crickets, her thoughts begin to stray toward him, bringing on fear. In m. 19, after a few set classes from the "Body" group at the beginning of the measure in the higher strings (4-12, a superset of 3-3, and 5-22, a superset of 4-19), and two diatonic tetrachords in the lower strings, the last triplet eighth note of beat 2 yields the unordered pitch-interval stack <6, 5, 5> in the 'cellos and basses, set class 4-16, a startling sonority since it contains 3-5 <6, 5> as its lowest three pitches. Above it one solo 'cello quietly emits <+2, –1>, the pitch inversion of the original Fear motive. Not long after, in mm. 19b–20a, the woman, telling her lover not to speak (though she hasn't found him yet), sings a variation of the Fear motive, <+1, –2>, the retrograde of the preceding 'cello utterance. The thought of her lover back in m. 18 while the crickets were singing startles her in m. 19a, and she responds in fear in mm. 19b–20. The same motivic gesture repeats in m. 20, again signifying a fear response to something startling: the contrabassoon, bass clarinet, and trombones

Example 4.4a  Schoenberg, *Erwartung*, mm. 18b–20. Used by permission of Belmont Music Publishers and Universal Edition

m. 18b

19

20

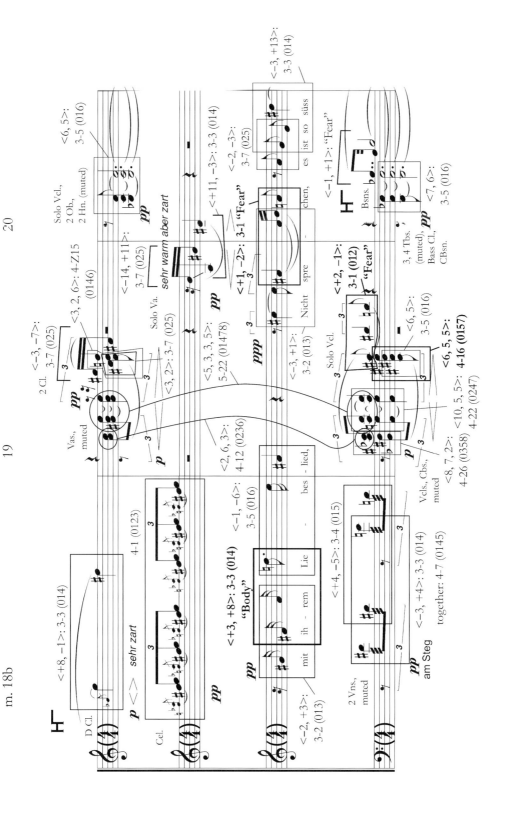

play one 3-5 <7, 6> in the lower register, accompanied by another 3-5 <6, 5> in the middle register in the 'cello, oboe, and horn, beginning on the second eighth note of beat 1. Almost immediately after, the bassoons reply with <−1, +1>, which can be understood as a varied "Fear" motive in this context.[25]

The following passage, illustrated in Example 4.4b, continues to feature "startling" verticals that state 3-5 as <5, 6> or <6, 5> (basses in m. 21) or contain 3-5 as part of a larger set (the 4-Z29 (0137) in the solo violin and high woodwinds in the same measure), while the singer works with melodic segments belonging to 3-5, 3-3, and 4-19.

As she sings about the moon in the twilight in m. 22, the bass clarinet, at an ominous *pianissimo* dynamic, begins to repeat D2 and F2 in an ostinato, then touches briefly on C♯3 as it swells to *ff* and the bassoons join it. For the first time, we hear the Body motive at the correct pitch-class level, increasing in prominence at the very bottom of the texture, but not yet broken off from the rest of the line as a salient fragment, nor yet in its final ordering as <D, F, C♯>.

Though she had reacted to previous intimations of the Body motive and 3-5 verticals with the Fear motive, in m. 23 the woman practically screams "Resistance" on her words "Feig bist du" ("You coward!"). This leitmotive is at exactly the same pitch level as the oboe's initial statement of it in mm. 1b–2a, and nearly the same rhythm (quarter–sixteenth–sixteenth in m. 23, quarter–eighth–sixteenth in mm. 1b–2). Its reversal of <+3, +8> to <−3, −8> has little effect on the surrounding orchestral texture, however, which continues to depend on verticals consisting of either the 3-5 subset <6> (in the 'cellos and basses) or 3-5 itself and its superset 4-18 (in the trumpet, oboe, and horn). And, all these verticals are grouped together under rising pitch-interval sequences, <+5, +4> in the low strings, and <+4, +11> in the trumpet, the top voice of the upper instruments. Though these intervals do not exactly match the <+3, +8> of Body, still the prominence of so many ascending, marked three-note figures in m. 23 attests to the motive's continued presence (and *his* continued presence, both in her mind and in the woods out there somewhere). A closer relative of the Body motive, <+9, +4>, then appears later in the measure as part of her phrase "willst ihn nicht suchen" ("won't you look for him?").

---

[25] In his analysis of the piano reduction of *Erwartung*, Berg grouped <−2, +2> in m. 28, in a dotted rhythm quite similar to m. 20's bassoon motive, together with <−2, +1>, in the motivic family he called "Frage" (the same family I am calling "Fear"). Apparently, for him, the Fear (or Frage) motive could descend and ascend by the same interval. See Whitney, "Schoenberg's 'Single Second of Maximum Spiritual Excitement'," 189.

Example 4.4b  Schoenberg, *Erwartung*, mm. 21–23. Used by permission of Belmont Music Publishers and Universal Edition

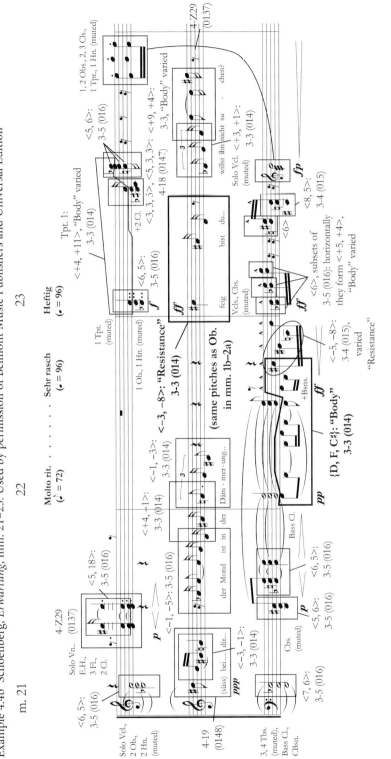

Earlier, I commented on the strong possibility that *Erwartung* was a model for Alban Berg as he composed *Wozzeck*, since both operas use short leitmotives as well as families of set classes with leitmotivic significance to project the progression of the drama. In this light, Schoenberg's loud thirty-second-note figure in the violins and violas that serves as pickup notes into m. 24 is quite fascinating (see Example 4.4c).

Its pitches <G♯4, E4, A3, C4> form ordered pitch intervals <–4, –7, +3> and set class 4-19, the identical interval succession and set class to *Wozzeck*'s motto, which that opera's principal character introduces in Act I, scene 1 with the words "Wir arme Leut!" ("we poor people"). Not only that, but "Wir arme Leut," as the excerpt from m. 136 of *Wozzeck* below Example 4.4c shows, consists of three shorter notes approaching a longer note, the same rhythmic contour as Schoenberg's motive in mm. 23b–24a. Whether Schoenberg's motive in *Erwartung* served as the model for "Wir arme Leut" or not, its function in its immediate context seems totally different: in *Erwartung* it acts as a weaker variation, an echo, of the "Resistance" motive that had appeared at m. 23: even though it matches the *fortissimo* dynamic of its predecessor, its quicker note values cause it to be less distinct. It descends <–4, –7>, varying Resistance's <–3, –8>, but then turns back up again, ending with <+3>, the first interval of Body. The voice responds to the thirty-second-note figure with a further variation, <–11, –3, +1>, on her words "So stirb doch hier" ("Then die here"), softer in dynamic than the violin figure, longer in note values, but with the same melodic contour, and also sharing the rhythmic contour of three shorter durations (sixteenths) serving as pickups into a longer one (quarter). The overall effect in mm. 23–24 is of a strong statement, "Feig bist du," followed by two echoes of it that are progressively less confident as fearful thoughts of the dead lover continue on, represented by set classes 4-19, 3-4, and 3-2.

In mm. 24 and 25, the woman turns back toward the woods (according to the accompanying stage direction in m. 25), and the orchestra depicts this using two ostinati, one in the flutes in their middle register and another in the low strings. The 'cello and bass ostinato alternates trichords from all four of the families we introduced earlier: two related to the Body motive and darkness (3-3, 3-4), startling sets (3-5s, one voiced as <7, 6>), the Fear trichord 3-1 voiced as <1, 1>, and diatonic subsets like 3-7 (025) and 3-8 (026). This portrays darkness, startling objects, fear, and reassurance continuing indefinitely in a kind of cycle, a summary of what had just happened in the previous measures by the alternation of Body motives and 3-3 and 3-5 (and their supersets) with the woman's fear and resistance responses. The flutes, meanwhile, with assistance from oboe and clarinet

Example 4.4c Schoenberg, *Erwartung*, mm. 23–26. Used by permission of Belmont Music Publishers and Universal Edition

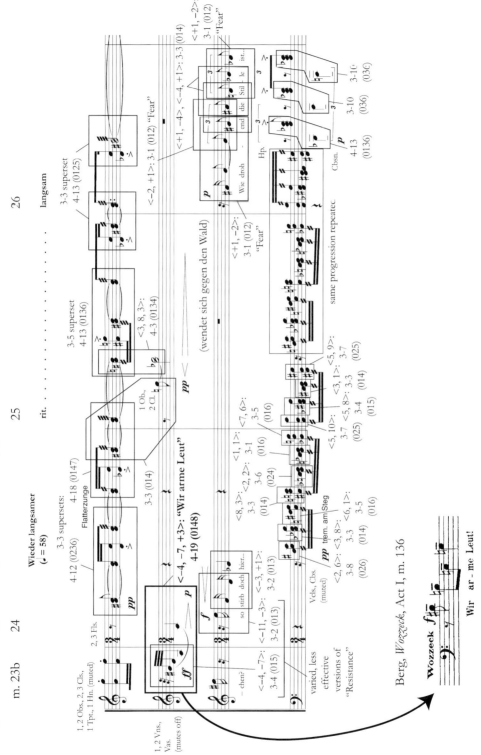

in m. 25, present a rhythmic ostinato whose intervals expand out from B4–above–G♯4 and contract back into it. The flute ostinato alternates tetrachords belonging to the 3-3 and 3-5 families, confirming objects that startle the woman and thoughts of her lover as the main elements that characterize the surrounding forest.

When she sings again in m. 26 on the words "Wie drohend die Stille ist" ("how threatening the silence is"), it is not surprising that her musical material consists of yet another fear response to what had come immediately before. Now she overlaps a number of 3-1 set classes in what would have been an RI-chain, had two members of 3-3 on "die Stille" not intruded. After a number of 3-3 and 3-5 supersets in the orchestra at the beginning of m. 27 (shown in Example 4.4d), her next phrase, "Der Mond ist voll Entsetzen" ("the moon is full of horror"), begins <+1, −3> to form set class 3-2, then on the key words "full of horror" she sings an ascending <+8, +3> motive, which has to this point usually been associated with the lover's dead body.

But this particular Body motive, <D4, A♯4, C♯5>, also reverses, at exact pitch and in its general rhythmic contour (two short notes progressing to a longer one), the strong "Resistance" motive she had sung four measures before. (Compare Example 4.4d with Example 4.4b.) This particular horrific thought of his dead body undoes the burst of confidence she had expressed in m. 23, and its effect is portrayed well by the high screeching piccolo *Hauptstimme* sounding just before it in m. 27, <+1>, and the three-octave piccolo and celesta *Hauptstimme*, <−2, +2>, immediately following it. Though its intervals are not exactly the same, Alban Berg grouped the latter motive together with the voice's initial Fear motive in mm. 3b–4 by labeling them both "Frage," and so I will identify the piccolo/celesta motive in m. 28 as an instance of "Fear," as well as the piccolo in the measure preceding.[26] Meanwhile, the surrounding harmonies in mm. 27b–28 include some 3-3 supersets and a prominent (and startling) 3-5 in the D clarinet line that plunges down beneath the piccolo's first entry – but the majority of the chords in m. 28 are members of set class 4-27 (0258), voiced as half-diminished seventh chords. Perhaps these diatonic elements signify reassurance, or maybe they are there to provide a bit of old-fashioned tonal tension.

In m. 29, 3-3, 3-5, and their supersets begin to dominate the texture again. The voices marked as *Hauptstimmen* by Schoenberg project 3-3 in the horn as <+3, +1, −1>, reminiscent of several of the voice's figures in the preceding measures, and 3-5 as <−5, −6> in the bass clarinet, a recall of the

---

[26] Whitney, "Schoenberg's 'Single Second of Maximum Spiritual Excitement'," 189.

Example 4.4d  Schoenberg, *Erwartung*, mm. 27–29. Used by permission of Belmont Music Publishers and Universal Edition

m. 27

28

29

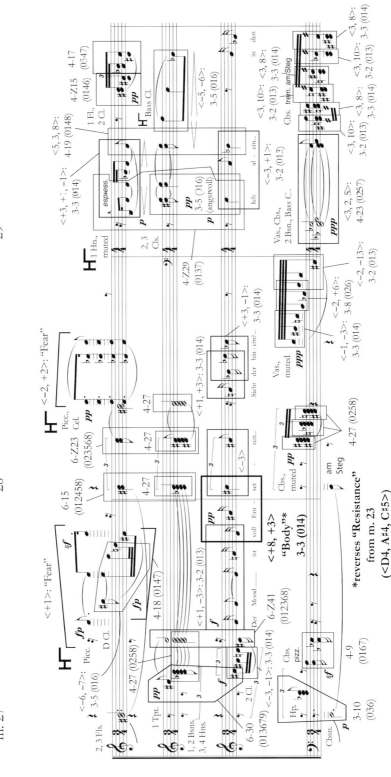

Viennese Trichord that has served throughout the first scene as a sign for something startling. The voice, meanwhile, sings the words "Ich allein" ("I am alone") to a <–3, +1> motive creating set class 3-2. The set class evokes darkness and the looming dead body, but also her fear: the contour is a close relative of the Fear motive's <–2, +1>. Indeed, Berg marked "Ich allein" in his piano reduction of *Erwartung* as a member of his "Frage" group, which I have been equating to my Fear motive.[27]

A series of 3-2 and 3-3 chords in the basses leads into the woman's continuation of her line, "in den dumpfen Schatten" ("in the gloomy shadows") in the following measure. Note that the 3-3 chords in the series are projected as <3, 8>s, evoking the lover's body again. These gloomy shadows give rise to more dark 3-2 and 3-3 sets in the voice itself (see Example 4.4e), ordered pitch-interval successions <–4, +1>, <–3, +1>, and <+1, –3>, and call forth another ostinato, in the solo viola, clarinet, contrabassoon, and harp this time, that goes on for the next five measures. Berg marked this ostinato in his piano reduction with the words "Schattenbleibsel des Waldes" ("fleeting woodland shadows"), and my interpretation of it seems to explain and justify his marking.[28] The set classes formed in the ostinato from m. 30 all the way through to m. 34 alternate members of the 3-3 and 3-4 superset family such as 4-7 (0145), 4-19 (0148), and 4-20 (0158) with supersets of 3-5 such as 4-5 (0126), 4-8 (0156), 4-9 (0167), and 4-16 (0157). Set class 4-Z15 (0146), which includes both 3-3 and 3-5, also appears. As we have seen, the 3-3/3-4 group connotes darkness (as well as the dead body), while the 3-5 supersets typically evoke images of something frightening. Both kinds of images fit well within the overall context of shadows in the woods.

Above the ostinato, a counterpoint consisting of four strands begins with the pickup notes to m. 31 in the solo clarinet, which is answered in turn at the beginning of m. 31 by the muted second violins playing an accompanimental figuration, the voice declaring "Ich will singen . . . denn hört er mich" ("I want to sing . . . then he will hear me"), and lastly a muted solo violin in its upper register at the end of m. 31. These four continue together through the second beat of measure 32, when the singer drops out. The other three voices continue for one more measure, joined in m. 33 by the solo tuba. Then the solo violin and second violins drop out, leaving the clarinet to play a duet with the tuba over the "woodland shadow" ostinato. Each strand stands in for some aspect of the drama at this point: the clarinet and solo violin portray the woman's singing voice (by continuing on after she states "I want to sing"), and the second violin figures represent

---

[27] Ibid., 189.     [28] Ibid., 188.

Example 4.4e  Schoenberg, *Erwartung*, mm. 29b–32. Used by permission of Belmont Music Publishers and Universal Edition

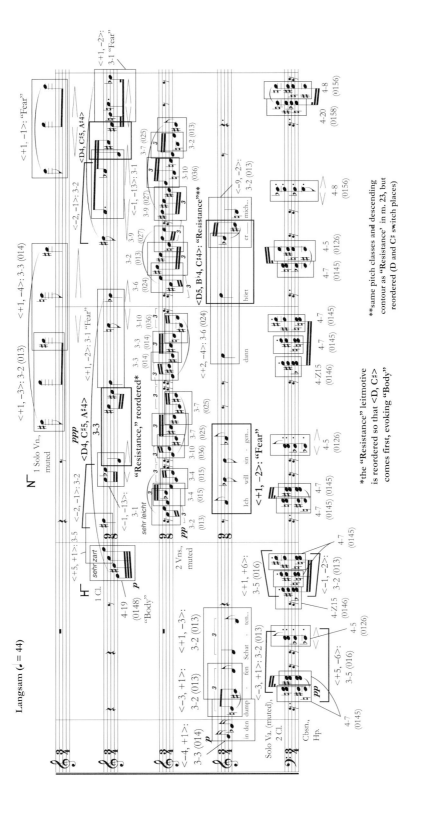

her fluctuating between dark thoughts of his body and confidence. The tuba, I believe, represents his voice calling back to her (in her imagination). Let us investigate how the leitmotives and leitmotivic set classes embedded within the four lines, as well as register and instrumentation, enable each contrapuntal strand to play its dramatic role.

First, the singer. She tells us she wants to sing using <+1, −2>, a variation of the original Fear motive – suggesting that her resolve at this point is rather timid. As she continues ("then he will hear me"), her words "hört er" produce a varied Resistance motive with its middle note spelled enharmonically and the pitch classes of its first and last notes reversed, <D5, B♭4, C♯4> rather than <C♯5, A♯4, D4>. (The descending melodic contour is the same as before, as is the rhythmic contour: the first note is longer, the last two notes shorter.) Since this Resistance motive is varied, since it is not set off rhythmically as was the one back at m. 23 ("Feig bist du"), and because it is at a *p* dynamic rather than *f*, it seems more uncertain than its predecessor.

The two lines that represent the woman's singing voice also reflect her uncertainty. The solo clarinet begins its first phrase with an upward arpeggiation of set class 4-19, evoking the lover's dead body. As it progresses, it reorders Resistance to <D4, C♯5, A♯4> on the second beat of m. 31: an important move because it places <D4, C♯5>, the first and third pitch classes of Body, together at Resistance's beginning, neutralizing its ability to invert Body's intervals and transforming Resistance into yet another premonition of the dead body. (This reordering also looks forward to the appearance of the transitional music from mm. 19–20 of "Am Wegrand," in the same way as a passage in m. 231 that will be discussed later in connection with Example 4.11.) The motivic reminder of the possibility that he may be dead calls forth another Fear motive immediately, on the third beat of m. 31, <+1, −2>. The clarinet then repeats the same motivic sequence (and, indeed, the same pitches from F♯5 through B♭4) in m. 32. The solo violin line, meanwhile, begins with a phrase that overlaps 3-2 and 3-3 sets in mm. 31–32b, suggesting the surrounding darkness and intimations of the dead body, but in m. 32b the violin emits <+1, −1>, which as we have seen, can be understood as a variation of the Fear motive (like the <−1, +1> in the bassoons at m. 20). Both solo instruments progress from darkness and the Body motive to the Fear motive in mm. 31–32.

The three principal strands in the counterpoint above the "woodland shadows" ostinato are joined by a second violin line in mm. 31–33 that initially seems to function merely as an accompanimental figuration. But even this part has leitmotivic significance: note that the groups of trichords that combine to form the two phrases of the second violin part on the first two dotted-quarter beats of m. 31 alternate between the family associated with the Body motive and darkness (3-2, 3-4), and diatonic sets that signify the momentary illusion of reassurance and normalcy (3-7 (025), 3-10 (036)). As the second violins continue, the phrases start to mix Body trichords with diatonic trichords, oscillating more quickly: 3-3, 3-3, 3-10 on the third beat of m. 31; then 3-6, 3-2, 3-9 followed by 3-9, 3-10, 3-7, 3-2 in m. 32. Finally, in m. 33 as the second violins shift to pizzicato and are doubled by the flutes, the balance shifts to trichords associated with the Body motive: 3-2, 3-3, 3-4, and 3-12 (048), a subset of 4-19, before they fall silent (refer to Example 4.4f). In m. 33, then, the woman's hope for a more positive outcome, a reunion with her living lover, seems to dissipate under the weight of all the trichords related to his dead body.

The reason for this turn toward darker set classes, I think, is the entrance of the solo tuba in m. 33. I suggested above that the tuba represents his voice singing back to her in her imagination – but the initial motive he sings communicates anything but a reassuring message. It is <+8, +3> as <C♯2, A2, C3>, a close relative of the motive that represents his dead body. This constitutes yet another step in the gradual, incremental emergence of Body through the whole first scene, which will assume its final shape as <D, F, C♯> and <+3, +8> in a few measures (m. 38), and take over the texture later at mm. 153–55. As would be expected, the clarinet responds to the tuba's entrance in mm. 33–34a with several trichords that fall into the "Fear" category, first <–11, +10>, a registral variation of <+1, –2>, then a member of set class 3-1, and finally <+1, –2> itself. At the end of m. 34, the clarinet completes its line with <–2, +1>, the same intervals as the original Fear motive in mm. 3b–4. The tuba, after its statement of Body, reinforces the clarinet's expression of her fearful thoughts by playing <+1, –2> in m. 34 (echoing the clarinet's <+1, –2> played immediately before). It then moves on to <+13, +1>, another member of set class 3-1.

The last three measures of the first scene, mm. 35–37, portrayed by Examples 4.4f and g, create a large *crescendo* and accelerando pointing toward m. 38, the opera's first motivic climax at the onset of Scene II.

This passage consists of three main strands: the continuation of the series of vertical tetrachords that had represented "woodland shadows," now brought up into higher registers (woodwinds and first violins) and made more prominent, the continuing solo tuba line, and a new line played by half of the viola section that gradually comes to the fore and leads motivically into the culminating statement of Body in the basses and timpani at m. 38. I will explore each of these components in turn.

Example 4.4f Schoenberg, *Erwartung*, mm. 33–35. Used by permission of Belmont Music Publishers and Universal Edition

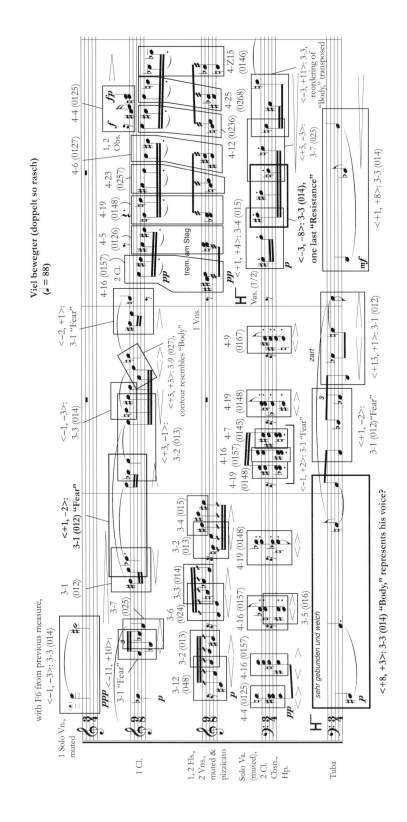

In m. 35, the second clarinet and first violins quietly play a series of descending vertical tetrachords that recall many of the set classes characteristic of the preceding "woodland shadows" music: alternating between supersets of 3-5 like 4-16 (0157), 4-5 (0126), and 4-6 (0127), supersets of 3-3 and 3-4 like 4-19 (0148), 4-12 (0236), and 4-Z15 (0146), and diatonic sets like 4-23 (0257) and 4-25 (0268). As before, this could be interpreted as a rapid cycling of emotions from fear to gloominess to hope and back again. At the end of the measure, the oboes join this group at a much louder dynamic with their statement of set class 4-4 (0125), a 3-3 superset. The series of verticals continues in m. 36 with a different ensemble (see Example 4.4g), consisting of half the viola section on top, the oboes in the middle, and the clarinets on the bottom. They begin with 4-4, a superset of the Body motive that includes 3-3, <8, 3>, as its top three notes, then turn back to diatonic sets again: 4-14 (0237) and 4-20 (0158).

But this diatonic respite is short-lived. In m. 37, horns and trombones take over, returning the verticals to the middle and lower registers, and enlarging them to five- and six-note sets: 5-21 (01458), a superset of 3-3 and 4-19, 5-Z18 (01457), a superset of 3-3 and 4-7, and 6-Z6 (012567), a superset of 3-5. This turn toward sets from the Body and "startling" families continues in the upper register with piccolo, high bassoons, and horns: 5-29 (01368), which contains 3-5 <6, 5> as its bottom three notes, and 5-Z18 again. Then the strings take over at the end of m. 37 with a series of 4-19 chords descending chromatically, narrowing the focus to relatives of the Body motive, just before the motive itself appears powerfully in m. 38 to end the scene.

The solo tuba in mm. 33–34 had presented <+8, +3>, a close relative of the Body motive, and several trichords from the Fear family directly afterward as a reaction to that motive. After m. 35, it comes to the fore dynamically on <+1, +8>, another premonition of Body's <+3, +8> that starts on the same pitch, D2, and belongs to the same set class, 3-3. It then plays, *forte*, three trichords all belonging to set class 3-5, the last of them taking the form of an arpeggiated Viennese Trichord, <+5, +6>.

The tuba's expression of startling, frightening thoughts having to do with the presence of the lover's dead body gets reinforcement from the remaining strand in the counterpoint, the lower half of the viola section, which plays from mm. 35–36, joined by the rest of the violas in m. 37. Not only does this line consist almost entirely of trichords from the Body family, 3-4, 3-3, and 3-2, but it also contains five rising three-note motives that incrementally grow closer to "Body's" <+3, +8>, and (near the beginning) a single Resistance motive that seems to be swallowed up by the others. The viola line's first rising motive in m. 35 is <+1, +4>, a member of

Example 4.4g Schoenberg, *Erwartung*, mm. 36–38. Used by permission of Belmont Music Publishers and Universal Edition

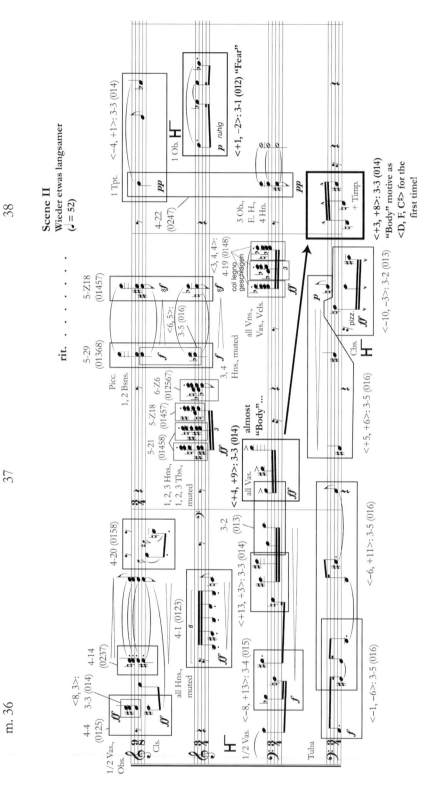

set class 3-4 that ends on the final pitch class C♯ of "Body." It immediately calls forth what seems to portray the woman's last attempt at resistance, <–3, –8> as <C♯4, A♯3, D3> (one octave below the original Resistance motive in mm. 1b–2 and "Feig bist du" in m. 23). But at the end of the same measure, we hear another three-note motive that reorders "Body," <–3, +11>, also therefore a member of set class 3-3. A similar motive follows on first and second beats of m. 36, <–8, +13>, creating 3-4, leading directly into a rising three-note figure, <+13, +3>, belonging to 3-3 again. On the downbeat of m. 37, as the two halves of the viola section join, they play, *fortissimo* and accented, <+4, +9> (again 3-3), which should be heard in this context as almost but not quite <+3, +8>. Finally, as a culminating gesture, the basses, joined by the timpani on their second note, play the Body motive <+3, +8> as <D2, F2, C♯3> for the first time in the opera, *fortissimo* and accented. Predictably, the oboe responds to it with a fear motive to usher in the second scene of *Erwartung*.

With all the rich motivic detail we have just described through twenty measures of music, the directed progression of Body motives from m. 18 toward their ultimate goal in m. 38 may have been obscured. Thus it would be useful to review this sequence of three-note figures separately from the Fear and Resistance motives and the motivic families of set classes. Example 4.5 lists them in chronological order.

We begin with m. 18b's statement of the intervals of the motive, <+3, +8>, without their eventual pitch classes, and m. 22's statement of its pitches {D2, F2, C♯3} without their eventual order and pitch-interval succession. These two near-approaches to the dead body from different directions then give way to two instances that reverse the intervals of the motive, <+8, +3>, m. 28 on "voll Entsetzen" ("full of horror") and m. 33 where the tuba portrays his imagined voice. These take a step away from the ultimate realization of "Body's" final version, but still anticipate it. Then, in mm. 35–38, we hear, in the tuba, violas, and basses, a sequence of seven three-note motives that incrementally take on the characteristics of that final version, as they gradually grow louder and louder. The tuba begins in m. 35 with <+1, +8>, a member of 3-3 that begins on D2 and ends with <+8>. The lower half of the viola section answers with <+1, +4>, changing the set class to 3-4, but returns to 3-3 as <–3, +11> two beats later. They expand those intervals to <–8, +13> in m. 36, forming 3-4 again, but on the pickup to the third beat of that measure they lock in to presenting motive variations that stay within set class 3-3 and gradually shrink their intervals as they approach the ultimate version of "Body." <+13, +3> in m. 36 leads inexorably to <+4, +9> played accented by all the violas in m. 37, and

Example 4.5 Schoenberg, *Erwartung*, the gradual emergence of the "Body" motive in mm. 18–38

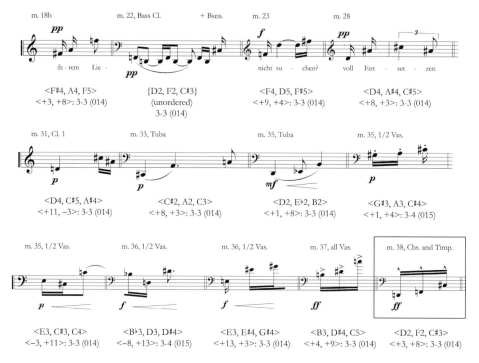

finally <+3, +8> and <D2, F2, C♯3> emerge at m. 38 in basses and timpani, as the culmination of the long motivic process.

## Measures 146–53 (Scene 4, just preceding the grand pause)

Still, within m. 38 we have heard only a single iteration of "Body," and its leitmotivic connection with the lover's dead body is less than obvious – there are no mentions of the body in the vicinity of m. 38's motive. "Body" becomes more salient and its significance becomes much clearer in the following measures, leading to a second climactic point at mm. 146–53, which we will study in detail below. In the intervening measures between m. 38 and m. 145, the "Body" motive appears prominently twice, at mm. 80 and 84 near the end of Scene 2, and its association with the dead body is strengthened considerably by the texts it sets there. Example 4.6 shows m. 80 followed by mm. 84–85.

In the first passage, the trombones play <+3, +8> and <+8, +3> loudly, the Body motive overlapping with a variation of itself, as the woman sings <–3, –11, +3>, an expanded and weakened form of "Resistance," on the words

Example 4.6 Schoenberg, *Erwartung*, mm. 80, 84–85. Used by permission of Belmont Music Publishers and Universal Edition

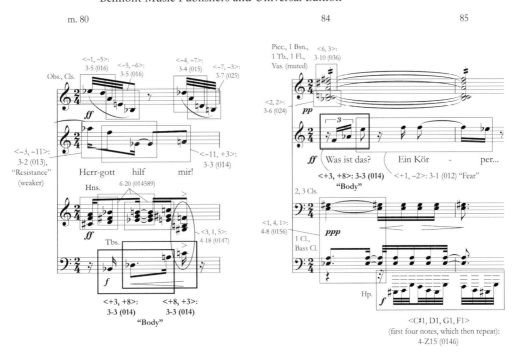

"Herr Gott, hilf mir!" ("Lord God, help me!"). Here the Body motive rises up from the bass and terrifies her, and the reason it does so becomes clear not long after, in mm. 84–85. There, she sings "Body" itself on her words "Was ist das?" ("What is that?"), then continues with <+1, –2>, a variation of "Fear," on "Ein Körper" ("A body"). Here, for the first time, Pappenheim's text mentions his dead body, as it answers the woman's question "What is that?" that had been set musically by <+3, +8>. The Body motive is thus connected with the looming "that" that she is being drawn toward, despite her best efforts to avoid it. The next step in the process of association would be to set words that refer to the body directly with <+3, +8>, which will happen in m. 153.

Example 4.7 portrays m. 153's motivic climax, and the gradual buildup to it in the preceding seven measures. It begins in m. 146 with a prominent <+3, +7> outburst in the bass clarinet and bassoons, its second pitch interval one half-step smaller than the final version of the "Body" motive (see Example 4.7a).

This first link in what will become a chain of Body motive variations could signify the "that" she is singing about when she exclaims: "No, that's not the shadow of the bench!" As she makes her exclamation, the set classes she sings stay mostly within the families associated with the body and with

Example 4.7a  Schoenberg, *Erwartung*, mm. 146–48. Used by permission of Belmont Music Publishers and Universal Edition

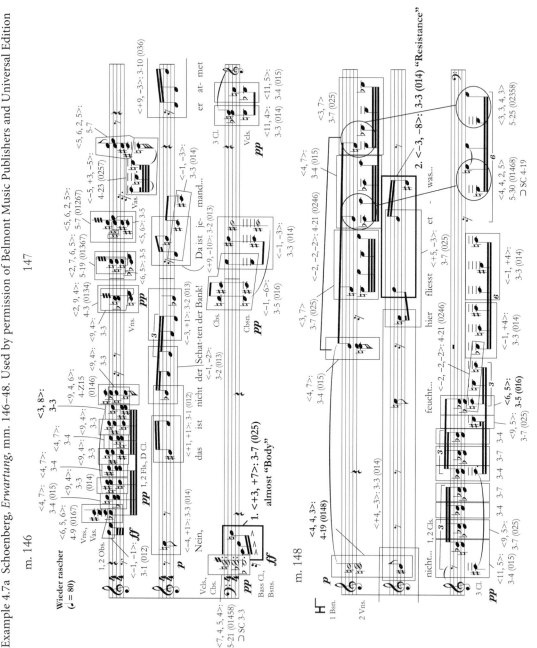

fear: 3-3, 3-2, and 3-1. The orchestral instruments surrounding her do likewise: the low strings sustain 5-21 (01458), a pentachord that contains 3-3 multiple times, while the high woodwinds alternate 3-3 and 3-4, after a *fortissimo* overlap of Viennese Trichords <6, 5, 6> in the violins, violas, and oboes on the second beat of the measure, no doubt put there to shock her and the listener. Near the end of this series of trichords, 3-3 appears as <3, 8>, perhaps a veiled allusion to the dead lover's body she is just now stumbling upon.

The music's dependence on 3-3, 3-5, and their supersets continues into m. 147 as the woman recognizes that "there is someone ... he does not breathe." The tremolo chords in the violins on the first two beats of m. 147 particularly, 5-19 (01367) and 5-7 (01267), with their embedded Viennese Trichords (boxed in the example), portray the startling nature of her discovery. Not long after, several diatonic subsets work themselves into the musical fabric: 4-23 (0257) in the violas on the pickups to the third beat of m. 147; 3-10 (036) in the voice on "er atmet nicht" ("He does not breathe"); 3-7 (025), which alternates with 3-4 in the clarinets in the first half of m. 148 and the bassoon and second violins in the second half; and 4-21 (0246), which migrates from the third clarinet to the bassoon in an imitative texture. These diatonic elements could signify her trying to recover from her shock and steady herself: in m. 148 she encounters his flowing blood and in m. 149 tries to explain it away as coming from her own hands. (Or, alternatively, the <–2, –2, –2> motives could be heard as whole-tone subsets that signify blood flowing downward.) The second motive in the chain leading up to Body's emergence in mm. 152–53, on the words "fliesst etwas" ("something flows here"), is <–3, –8> in m. 149, a half-step higher than the "Resistance" motives of mm. 1b–2 and m. 23, suggesting even more strongly that she is trying to reassure herself.

But in mm. 147 and 148, sets associated with "Body" and with the startling Viennese Trichord continue to infest different places in the texture: including a prominent 4-19 (0148) chord on "nicht" beginning m. 148, and a 3-5 as <6, 5> in the clarinets accompanying her word "feucht" ("damp") on the second eighth note of beat 2 in that measure. These continual reminders that his dead body is somewhere in the vicinity (and getting ever closer) persist through m. 149, together with the 3-1 set class signifying "Fear" and a couple of diatonic sets. All this leads to mm. 150–53, a four-measure tempo, rhythmic, textural, and dynamic buildup that culminates in the moment where she recognizes his dead body for the first time (refer to Example 4.7b).

It begins in m. 150 with the woman singing a number of rising motives that start with <+3>, but join it to a second interval that is too large for

Example 4.7b  Schoenberg, *Erwartung*, mm. 149–51. Used by permission of Belmont Music Publishers and Universal Edition

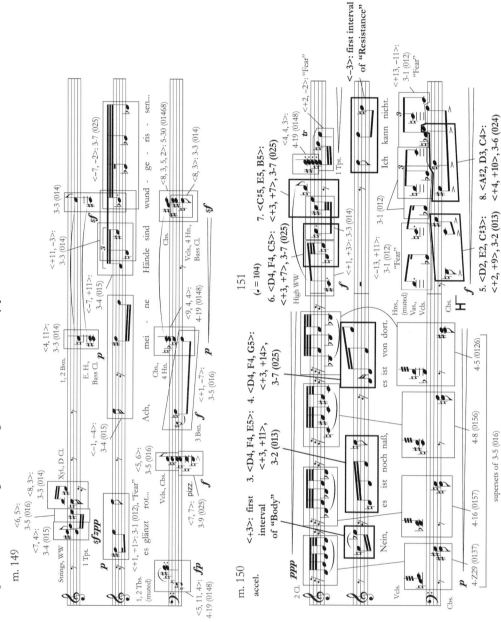

"Body." "Nein" is set by <+3>, "es ist noch naß" ("it is still wet") by <+3, +11>, and "es ist von dort" ("it comes from there") by <+3, +14>. Note that the second and third phrases, numbers 3 and 4 in our chain of variations of "Body," begin <D4, F4>: the same pitch classes as the motive in m. 38, to which it will return to stay in m. 152. This is the first time the soloist herself has approached the Body motive as a distinct short phrase (it was always in the middle of a longer phrase in the previous music), but in her growing excitement she progressively overshoots the third note. In m. 151, the high woodwinds seem to correct her, returning the motive to the form it had taken in m. 146, <+3, +7>, to produce numbers 6 and 7 in our motivic chain. (Number 6 again uses <D4, F4> as the first two notes of the motive, then No. 7 transposes No. 6 up eleven half-steps.) Meanwhile, the basses in m. 151, in numbers 5 and 8 of the chain, imitate the woman's wild interval expansions, <+2, +9> and <+4, +10>.

The rest of the musical texture in mm. 150–51 contributes to the buildup of tension through using set classes that are supersets of 3-5 and 3-3. The second clarinet, 'cellos, and basses play four tetrachords on the four beats of m. 150 that are all supersets of 3-5: 4-Z29 (0137), 4-16 (0157), 4-8 (0156), and 4-5 (0126). Many of them contain prominent perfect fourths or tritones, though the two intervals are not stacked above one another in Viennese Trichord style. In the following measure, the focus turns toward 3-3 and its superset 4-19 in the woodwinds (together with the set classes 3-7 formed by "Body" motive variations 6 and 7), as well as chromatic trichords signifying "Fear" in the horns, violas, and 'cellos, and a <+2, –2> motive in the trumpet that also evokes fear. As all these "Body" and "Fear" sets combine to fill up the orchestral texture in m. 151, the woman responds by singing <–3>, <D5, B5>, on "Ich kann nicht" ("I can't"). This short outburst can be understood as an incomplete repetition of the "Resistance" motive she sang back in m. 148 on "fliesst etwas," <D5, B5, D♯4> – incomplete precisely because her resistance is breaking down.

The culminating step in the motivic progression traced by Example 4.7 occurs already in m. 152, as the basses, bass clarinet, and bassoons play <+3, +8> as <D3, F3, C♯4> twice, motives 9 and 10 in our chain (see Example 4.7c).

Now that it has finally been attained in its complete form, the "Body" motive gains in volume as the 'cellos are added in m. 153, and shortens its duration from eighths to sixteenths, repeating ever more quickly and insistently (motives 11, 13, 14, and 15). The rest of the orchestra, also growing to a full *tutti* in mm. 152–53, relies on supersets of 3-3 such as 4-19 (0148) and 5-21 (01458) in the high woodwinds and 5-Z18 (01457) in the trumpets and trombones (which enter in m. 153). The horns form another

Example 4.7c  Schoenberg, *Erwartung*, mm. 152–53. Used by permission of Belmont Music Publishers and Universal Edition

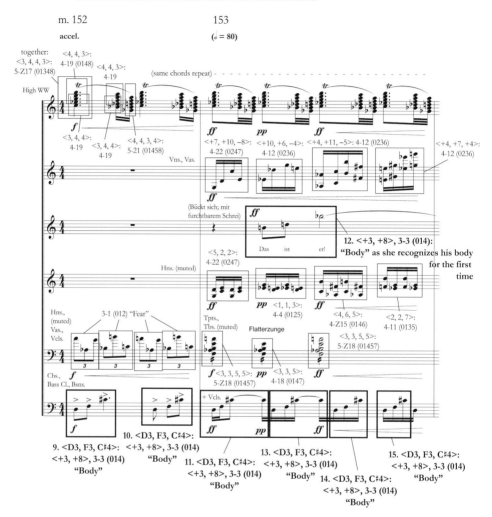

strand of the texture in m. 153, playing diatonic sets 4-22 (0247) and 4-11 (0135), but also "Body" supersets 4-4 (0125) and 4-Z15 (0146). The violins and violas enter in the same measure, also producing a mix of "Body" supersets and diatonic sets.

Motivically, the orchestra is signaling to the woman (and to the listener) that her lover's dead body is *right there*, with its ever-more insistent <D3, F3, C♯4> repetitions and proliferation of set classes that include 3-3 and 3-4 as subsets. And the increase in tempo, dynamics, and orchestral texture clearly signifies an escalation in excitement and tension, as his body finally emerges from the darkness and becomes clearly visible to her. Her response is portrayed leitmotivically: she sings (or rather screams, as Schoenberg indicates in the performance notes) "Das ist er!" ("It is he!") on <+3, +8>, *fortissimo*. She transposes the "Body" motive to a different pitch-class level, <B4, D5, B♭5>, which could possibly signify her unwillingness to accept his death. In any case, she sings <+3, +8> as a distinct phrase for the first time in the opera in m. 153, on words that describe her initial recognition of his body – so that I believe we are justified in claiming that the gradual, incremental emergence of <D, F, C♯> and <+3, +8> as a significant motive through the opera's first 153 measures parallels and metaphorically represents her gradual, incremental discovery of his dead body. And the <D, F, C♯> motive in mm. 152–53 itself, though it is surrounded by so much music that cancels it out tonally, through its incessant repetition begins to draw a connection between D centricity and the woman's realization of her loss that will bear its final fruit at m. 411.

## The Second Main Part of *Erwartung*: mm. 158–426

After the woman discovers her lover's body, the second stage in the large narrative arch that spans *Erwartung* is where she begins to come to terms with the fact that he is no longer alive, which means that she must face a lifetime of loneliness, even in the midst of the crowd (Adorno's "collective loneliness"). As I sketched out at the beginning of the chapter, her full realization of that awful fact is represented by the final stage of the cumulative setting, Schoenberg's quotations from "Am Wegrand" in measures 410–11. Between m. 158 (the grand pause following her discovery of his body) and m. 410 there are more than 250 measures where she addresses him directly as if he were alive, sometimes with great affection and sentimentality, other times in jealous anger. This music, as we shall see, continues to use the "Body" and "Resistance" motives in response to one another to portray her encounters with his body and her protestations that he "cannot be dead." But slowly she comes to the realization that he is no longer there with her, and as she does, the motives begin to transform gradually from <+3, +8>, the bottom two and top notes of a minor–major seventh chord, into <+3, +4, +4>, the full arpeggiation of that chord (m. 245), and then take on passing tones and neighbors (in m. 401), finally completing the bass voice of the "Am Wegrand" quotation at the original pitch (starting on D and thus signifying D minor) in m. 411. Since <+3, +4, +4> projects 4-19 as its set class, the frequent chordal presentations of that set class throughout these measures can also be understood as looking forward to "Am Wegrand's" arrival.

Example 4.8 Schoenberg, *Erwartung*, "Body" and "Resistance" motives in mm. 173–84. Used by permission of Belmont Music Publishers and Universal Edition

m. 173, Bass Cl.

m. 173b:  Es ist noch da.
m. 174:  Herr Gott in Himmel...
mm. 174b–75:  Es ist lebendig...
Es hat Haut...  Augen, Haar...
seine Augen...

mm. 176b–77

mm.178–79:  Du--- Du---
m. 180:  bist du es...
mm. 181–82:  Ich habe dich so lang gesucht..
m. 183:  im Wald und...

m. 184

(wants him to be alive:
"Do you hear me?")

It will be necessary for me to skim over most of the leitmotive sequences in mm. 158–426, but I want to describe three passages in more detail; mm. 227–30, mm. 243–45, and a longer passage leading up to and away from m. 411's climax, mm. 398–413. I will also give a detailed description of the components of the final measure, m. 426. In the long span between m. 158 and m. 227, there are two instances of "Body" breaking in to the orchestral texture, followed first by text and motives sung by the woman that acknowledge his body, then by one or more "Resistance" motives in the voice, setting text that pushes back in some way against the notion that he might be dead. The first instance is at mm. 173–84, and these measures' principal motives and text in German are given in Example 4.8. The bass clarinet enters softly, then swells quickly to *forte* in m. 173 with "Body," <+3, +8>, at its ultimate pitch-class level, <D, F, C♯>. In response, the woman sings "It [the body] is still there . . . Lord God

Example 4.9 Schoenberg, *Erwartung*, "Body" and "Resistance" motives in mm. 195–205. Used by permission of Belmont Music Publishers and Universal Edition

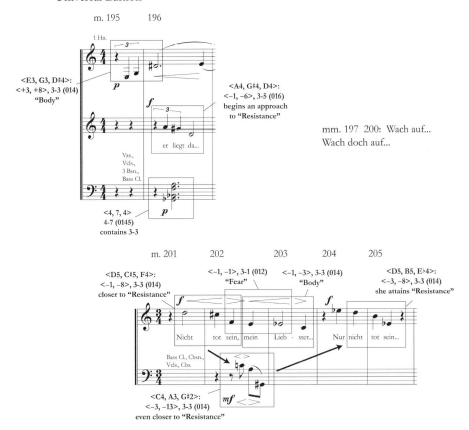

in Heaven . . . It is alive . . . it has skin, eyes, hair . . . his eyes . . . it has his mouth." As she bends down to look at his face and recognizes his mouth, she repeats the bass clarinet's "Body" motive a perfect fifth higher, <A4, C4, G#5>, signifying perhaps that she is aware of his body but is not fully convinced yet that he is dead (otherwise, she would sing "Body" at the correct pitch-class level). An address to him follows: "You . . . You . . . is it you? . . . I sought you so for so long . . . in the woods and . . . " She then breaks off suddenly to ask "Do you hear me?" On this text, which expresses her hope (mixed with doubt) that he still may be alive and able to hear, she sings "Resistance," <–3, –8> on <G, E, A♭>.

A remarkably similar sequence happens eleven measures later, illustrated by Example 4.9. This time it is the solo horn that breaks into the texture in m. 195, directing the woman's and the audience's attention back toward his body after she has been calling for help in previous measures, with its statement of "Body" on <E3, G3, D♯4>.

She responds immediately with a descending motive on "He lies there," not the <–3, –8> of "Resistance" but <–1, –6>, creating set class 3-5, which could represent her shock at seeing him dead, but also begins a chain of descending three-note motives that culminates in "Resistance." (The accompanying instruments sustain a 4-7 (0145) chord, another member of the family of set classes that share "Body" as a subset.) After a few measures where she pleads with him to wake up, she begins to protest loudly against his death in m. 201: "Don't be dead, my darling . . . just don't be dead." She sings both iterations of the key words "Nicht tot sein" to motives that gradually transform themselves into "Resistance," expressing her protests motivically. First we hear <–1, –8> in mm. 201–02, which shares its second interval and its set class with the goal motive, and then (after she passes through a descending line that touches on "Fear" and "Body" set classes) the motive itself appears in mm. 204–05, <–3, –8>. Between the woman's almost-"Resistance" motive on the first "Nicht tot sein" and her full realization of it on the second, a line appears in the low strings and woodwinds in m. 202 that approaches "Resistance" from a different direction: playing the first interval correctly but expanding the second, <–3, –13>, to form another member of set class 3-3. Maybe this brief interjection could be understood as encouraging her to find "Resistance," which she does two measures later.

## Measures 227–30 (Midway through Scene 4)

My first detailed analysis from the second part of *Erwartung* reveals a motivic and set-class sequence very much like the two just described, but denser – to the point that the "Body" and "Resistance" motives in this sequence, together with their variations and associated set classes, fill up almost all of the texture. The text here addresses the dead lover as if he were alive, describing parts of his body in close contact with hers: "The sun shines on us . . . your hands rest on me . . . your kisses . . . you are mine . . . You!" She revels in her close contact with his body, but soon begins to push back with increasing intensity against the idea that he is dead as the passage nears its end in a dynamic climax at mm. 229–30.

Example 4.10 shows that in mm. 227 and 228, "Body" motives can be found in some of the higher parts, the upper woodwinds, as well as the lowest, trombones and tuba. The oboes and clarinets on beats 3 and 4 of m. 227 play thirty-second-note runs in groups of four notes; the first one ends with <+8, +3>, "Body's" intervals reversed, followed immediately by <+3, +8> itself in the last three notes of the second. The thirty-second-note

Example 4.10 Schoenberg, *Erwartung*, mm. 227–30. Used by permission of Belmont Music Publishers and Universal Edition

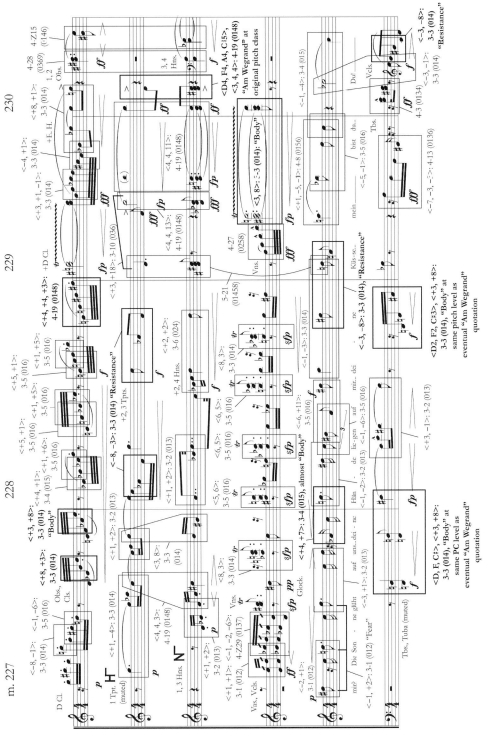

runs then continue in m. 228 by turning toward overlapping figures belonging to set class 3-5 on the first three beats, which could signify the woman being startled by the appearance of his body (this is what "Body" followed by 3-5 has represented before). On the last beat of m. 228, a thirty-second-note run appears, <+4, +4, +3>, belonging to set class 4-19. This final thirty-second-note interval sequence not only attains the same set class as the main notes of the upcoming "Am Wegrand" quotation, 4-19 (the quotation's main pitch classes are <D, F, A, C♯>), but also produces the same ordered pitch intervals in reverse. Before much longer (m. 245), we will hear motives in the bass with the intervals <+3, +4, +4>, preparing us for "Am Wegrand" itself in m. 411.

As the woodwinds proceed from <+3, +8> to set class 3-5 to <+4, +4, +3>, the lowest instruments in the texture, the trombones and tuba, play two iterations of "Body," both of them on the same pitch classes and the second of them at the same pitch level, <D2, F2, C♯3>, the motive will ultimately take as part of "Am Wegrand." The first trombone/tuba "Body" in m. 227 is in quarters and eighths, the second at the end of m. 228 in sixteenths, so they can be heard, together with an overall increase in dynamics, as ratcheting up the tension as m. 227 passes into m. 228. Perhaps in response, as she had done before, the woman sings an approximation of "Body" on the words "deine Hände," <+4, +7>, set class 3-4, with two sixteenths leading to a dotted eighth, above the first trombone/tuba motive. But she will begin to push back against the "Body" motive a measure later.

The harmonic content of Example 4.10 also proceeds generally along the same path from set classes and unordered pitch-interval stacks that project the intervals of "Body" to those that signify something frightening, and eventually to a pitch collection that adumbrates m. 411's "Am Wegrand" quotation. In mm. 227 and 228, the high strings and high brass present stacks of unordered pitch intervals that can be heard as beginning such a sequence – the strings as simultaneities, the brass as vertical slices of a two-voice counterpoint between trumpets and horns. The violins and violas start with <8, 3> on the fourth beat of m. 227, then on the four quarter note beats of m. 228 they play <5, 6>, <6, 5>, <6, 5>, and <8, 3> again. Like the clarinets and oboes playing in the same measures, they move from an interval stack associated with 3-3 and "Body" to those associated with 3-5, particularly Viennese Trichords. Unlike the woodwinds, however, the high strings return to <8, 3> again at the end of m. 228, and in mm. 229–30, they sustain <3, 8>, the vertical image of "Body," for most of a measure.

The trumpets and horns, meanwhile, create two interval stacks between their contrapuntal voices that evoke "Am Wegrand" and "Body" in m. 227, <4, 4, 3> on the third beat and <3, 8> on the second eighth note of the fourth beat. Their motivic material in m. 228 signifies something different and will be discussed below, but in the latter half of m. 229 and first part of m. 230 they return to three massive chords, all of which project set class 4-19, having the intervals <4, 4, 13>, <4, 4, 11>, and <3, 4, 4>. The last of these is notable in that it consists of the pitch classes <D, F, A, C♯> reckoned up from the bottom, and is thus a foreshadowing at the same pitch classes of the "Am Wegrand" quotation to come 180 measures later.

While most of the orchestra is preoccupied with "Body" as motive and interval stack, which leads to Viennese Trichords and melodic presentations of 3-5, and finally the loud premonition of "Am Wegrand" in the trumpets and horns, the woman (after briefly going along with the rest at the end of m. 227) begins to resist motivically at the end of m. 228. She is motivated, by two increasingly insistent (i.e., louder and slower) statements of <−8, −3> <E5, A♭4, F4> in the trumpets in m. 228, to sing <−3, −8>, "Resistance" itself, on her words "deine Küsse." After that, she loses a little of her resolve, as indicated by her <−5, −1> 3-5 descent on "mein bist du" at the end of m. 229, not to mention the low brass figure accompanying that descent that starts with <−7, −3>, falling short of the <−8, −3> motive by a half-step. But at the end of the passage, just as the dynamic climax of Example 4.10 is beginning to subside, the 'cellos beneath her "Du!" emit one more clear <−3, −8>, preparing her for another address to him in the following measures. The general motivic profile of mm. 227–30, similar to numerous other passages we have studied (and others we have not), begins with the sudden entrance of "Body" motives, and moves on from them to startling Viennese Trichords and other sets belonging to 3-5, ending with "Resistance" motives.

## Measures 231 and 243–46 (Midway through Scene 4)

These passages warrant detailed description and illustration as places where the "Resistance" and "Body" motives begin to take on characteristics of the eventual "Am Wegrand" quotations, not just the bass line from m. 22 of the song quoted at m. 411 of the opera, but also the transitional material from mm. 19–20 of the song, which also will be quoted in more complete form at m. 410 of the opera. We hear a premonition of the transitional material first, in the voice at m. 231 (illustrated in Example 4.11).

The woman's <D4, C♯5, A♯4> on "an, Liebster," part of her plea "but look at me, beloved," is a reordering of the exact pitches from the oboe's original "Resistance" motive back in mm. 1b–2 of *Erwartung*. "Resistance," of course, seems like an appropriate leitmotive to portray her desperate hope that he is still alive. But the *specific* reordering that takes place in m. 231 transforms

Example 4.11 Transformation of "Resistance" into a premonition of the transitional music from "Am Wegrand." Used by permission of Belmont Music Publishers, Universal Edition, and Dreililien Verlag, Richard Birnbach, Berlin

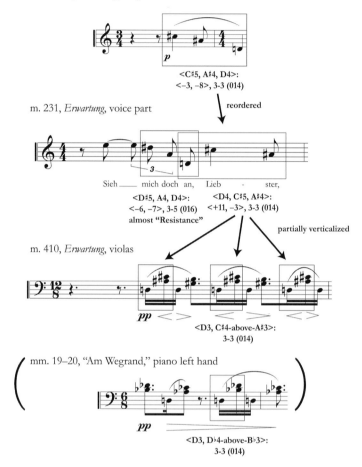

"Resistance" into a premonition of the coming "Am Wegrand" transitional music, signifying the anticipation of her life without him, as the arrows from the second excerpt of Example 4.11 to the third excerpt show. When the voice jumps +11 from D4 to C♯5 and follows it immediately with A♯4, it looks forward to the violas' repeated leaps from D3 to C♯4 with A♯3 underneath in m. 410, which in turn evoke the piano's leaps from D3 to D♭4 with B♭3 underneath in the same rhythm in m. 19 of the song.

The transformation we have just discussed of "Resistance" into a premonition of the impending "Am Wegrand" transitional music could be dismissed, I suppose, as picking a few repetitions of the same pitches and

pitch classes out of the surrounding texture to prove a motivic point – a case
of the analyst finding and isolating exactly those things he needs to find in
this dense chromatic setting. But what makes it more convincing is that
a similar process of transformation, from the "Body" motive <+3, +8> into
something closer to the quotation of the "Am Wegrand" bass line at m. 411,
comes only fourteen measures later, at m. 245. All of measures 243–46, and
excerpts from mm. 401–02 and 411 that show further stages in this second
process of transformation, are given in Examples 4.12a, b, and c.

The passage begins with the woman's loud protest: "Nein, nein, es ist
nicht wahr ... " ("No, no, it isn't true ..."). "Nein, nein" is set by +3, the
opening interval of "Body," but "es ist nicht" tries one more time to
counteract it with a variation of "Resistance," <–8, –3>. The orchestral
accompaniment, however, seems to project her growing realization that it
*is* true, through the set classes it projects. The first large chord in m. 243 has
no trace of the family of set classes related to "Body": both the full sonority,
7-31 (0134679), and its subsets, 5-10 (01346) in the strings, 4-28 (0369) in
the oboes, English horn, and trumpets, and 3-10 (036) in the horns,
strongly evoke the octatonic collection instead. But the second chord
in m. 243 and third on the downbeat of m. 244 increasingly display
prominent subsets that belong to the "Body" family, particularly 4-19
(0148). The second chord as a whole belongs to set-class 7-21 (0124589),
which includes 4-19 multiple times as a subset, and one of those 4-19s sits
atop the large chord in the oboes, English horn, trumpets, and violas as
<B♭4, D♭5, F5, A5>, with unordered pitch intervals <3, 4, 4>, a voicing
which adumbrates the coming <+3, +4, +4> of the "Am Wegrand" bass
line. The third chord also belongs to 7-21 as a whole, and contains two
prominent 4-19s as its top four {4, 5, 8, 0} and bottom four {5, 6, 9, 1} pitch
classes. Schoenberg again voices the top tetrachord in a way that resembles
"Am Wegrand": this time the C is doubled at the top to yield <3, 4, 4, 8>.

At the end of m. 244, a woodwind chord and horn line lead into mm.
245–46, the passage we discussed near the beginning of the chapter, that
Schoenberg sketched into Marie Pappenheim's handwritten libretto
to represent musically (and motivically, I believe) the woman fighting back
against her growing certainty that her lover is dead. (Look again at
Example 4.1 for Schoenberg's sketch.) The chord and line in m. 244
are also of some interest; the chord belongs to SC 3-4 (015), one of the set
classes we have associated with "Body," and the horns overlap three SC 3-5s,
<–1, –5, –6, –1>, leading into <–1, –3>, a member of 3-3. The same trichord
sequence, 3-5 to 3-3, will be heard again with some of the same intervals in
the voice at mm. 401–02, as a counterpoint to those measures' preview of the
"Am Wegrand" bass line. (See Example 4.12b for an illustration.)

Example 4.12a  Schoenberg, *Erwartung*, mm. 243–46. Used by permission of Belmont Music Publishers and Universal Edition

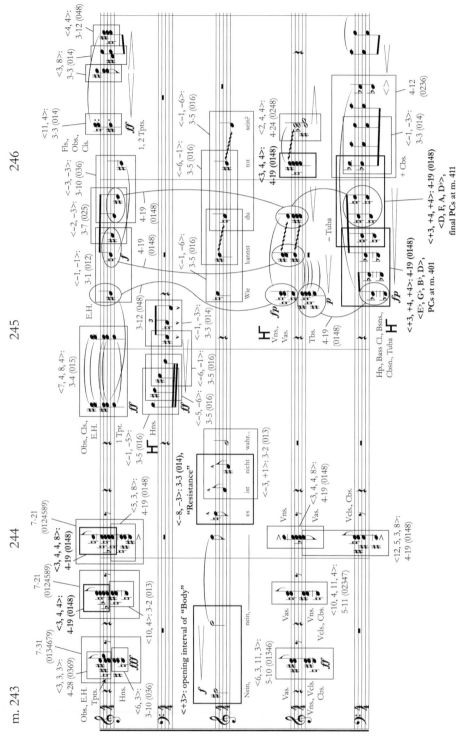

Example 4.12b  Schoenberg, *Erwartung*, mm. 401–02, voice and *Hauptstimme*.
Used by permission of Belmont Music Publishers and Universal Edition

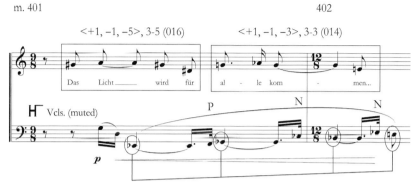

<+3, +4, +4> as <E♭2, G♭2, B♭2, D3>, 4-19 (0148)
Buchanan talks about this as a "premonition" of m. 411

Schoenberg's final version of "Wie kannst du tot sein?" ("How can you be dead?") is almost completely identical to the original sketch I reproduced back in Example 4.1. The sole difference (not counting enharmonic equivalents and octave doublings) is that the A♮ octaves in the bass line on the last eighth of m. 245 were originally written as A♭s in the sketch. This change did have significant consequences – it transformed the bass line of mm. 245–46 into overlapping <+3, +4, +4> tetrachords, the first one <E♭, G♭, B♭, D>, the second <D, F, A, D♭>. These 4-19 arpeggiations can be understood as premonitions of the two places in *Erwartung* where the bass line of "Am Wegrand" emerges out of the texture: the first, in mm. 401–02 in the 'cellos starting on E♭, portrayed in Example 4.12b, the second, in the low woodwinds starting on D, mm. 411–12, portrayed in Example 4.12c. (Herbert Buchanan has already discussed how mm. 401–02 are themselves an anticipation of mm. 411–12.[29]) These later passages simply add passing and neighbor notes (marked in the examples) to each <+3, +4, +4> to create the quotations from "Am Wegrand." In effect, the bass line under "Wie kannst du tot sein" back in mm. 245–46, together with the <3, 4, 4> chords that immediately precede it, constitutes an intermediate stage in the cumulative process that began with the gradual materialization of <D, F, C♯> in the opera's first part and will complete itself with m. 411's quotation.

The chords that accompany this rising premonition of the "Am Wegrand" quotation in the bass and "Wie kannst du tot sein" in the voice are also not without significance. The second beat of m. 245,

[29] Buchanan, "A Key to Schoenberg's *Erwartung*," 434–35.

Example 4.12c  Schoenberg, *Erwartung*, mm. 411–12a, *Hauptstimme* only. Used by permission of Belmont Music Publishers and Universal Edition

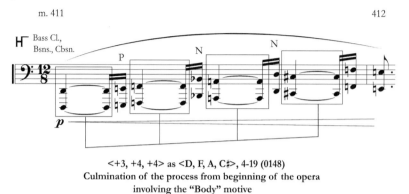

<+3, +4, +4> as <D, F, A, C♯>, 4-19 (0148)
Culmination of the process from beginning of the opera
involving the "Body" motive

"Wie," begins the progression with {0, 4, 8} in all the higher voices: high strings, English horn, and voice – set class 3-12, a subset of the chord associated with "Body," 4-19 (0148). On the same beat, the trombones together with the bass instruments sound 4-19 itself. On the following beat, "kannst," taking both eighth notes of the English horn with the quarter note in the high strings and voice yields {11, 3, 6, 7}, the full 4-19 chord. The string/English horn/voice chord on "du," when combined with <F, A> in the bass, creates yet another 4-19. Finally, the Body chord appears one last time on "tot" on the downbeat of m. 246 in the high strings and voice alone. Not just the set class 4-19, but also the specific voicing of this chord is important. Its unordered pitch intervals in the high strings read <3, 4, 4>, which we have already identified as a step in the direction of the ordered pitch interval sequence <+3, +4, +4>, the middleground of the "Am Wegrand" bass. The "tot" chord provides yet another association between the lover's *dead* body and the motive <+3, +8>, as that motive is in the process of transforming itself into <+3, +4, +4>. The flutes, oboes, clarinets, and trumpets in the latter part of m. 246 then echo many of the trichord types that have just been played, 3-3, 3-3, 3-3, and 3-12, under a falling contour similar to that of "Wie kannst du tot sein."

## Measures 398–413, Near the End of Scene 4

Again, we need to fly over about 150 measures to conserve space in this exhaustive discussion of *Erwartung*. But we can characterize the measures between m. 246 and m. 398, I think, as continuing to contribute to the process of transforming the Body motive <+3, +8> into the bass line from

"Am Wegrand"; with 4-19, <3, 4, 4>, and <+3, +4, +4> as intermediate stages. The "Resistance" motive <−3, −8> also shows up in the voice in mm. 279, 320–21, and 328, to push back against the overall motivic trend. These measures are places where the woman is reproaching her lover about the "other woman" (as if he were alive) or pleading with him to show some sign of life. But from time to time, we hear unyielding reminders of the fact that he is dead: <3, 8> as a pungent vertical in the oboes and high strings in m. 284; "Body" with the intervals reversed, <+8, +3>, in oboes and clarinets in m. 306–07, just before she asks: "why did they kill you?"; a 4-19 chord in the strings under the first note of the woman's "Resistance" motive in m. 320; and <D, F, C♯> in the trombones in m. 330 with surrounding 4-19 chords in the high woodwinds, trumpets, and horns.

However, it is at m. 398 where the soloist and orchestra embark on a buildup to a climax in mm. 411–13 that is comparable to the one we described at mm. 146–53 (in the discussion of Example 4.7). Comparable in the sense that the motives and chords reach the goal they have been striving toward since the opera's beginning, the quotation of the "Am Wegrand" bass line at the words "Tausend Menschen ziehen vorüber," and also comparable in its increase in texture – but very different in the sense that there is no dynamic buildup: "Am Wegrand's" bass comes in at m. 411 at *p*. Example 4.13 illustrates the whole passage, and its text is translated (by me) below:

> And all the colors of the world . . . broke forth from your eyes . . .
> Light will come for everyone . . . but me, alone, in my night?
> Morning separates us . . . always morning . . .
> you kissed me so deeply at parting . . .
> Again another eternal day of waiting . . .
> Oh . . . but you won't wake up any more . . .
> A thousand people pass by . . . but I don't recognize you . . .

The beginning of the buildup can be seen in Example 4.13a. Not every chord and motive in mm. 398–99 is associated with the lover's dead body, but there are several prominent ones that remind the woman and the listener of the present state of things, as well as other motives and chords that anticipate what is about to happen (her loss of contact with him altogether).

The passage begins with a horn and trumpet chord that projects <3, 4, 4> and set class 4-19, the vertical equivalent of the expected <+3, +4, +4> motive to come later. (In m. 398, the first and third horns and first and second trumpets stagger their entrances, with each pair creating a small dynamic swell. Later in the measure, the first and second flutes take the place of the trumpets, continuing an alternation of tone colors that

Example 4.13a  Schoenberg, *Erwartung*, mm. 398b–99. Used by permission of Belmont Music Publishers and Universal Edition

399

m. 398b

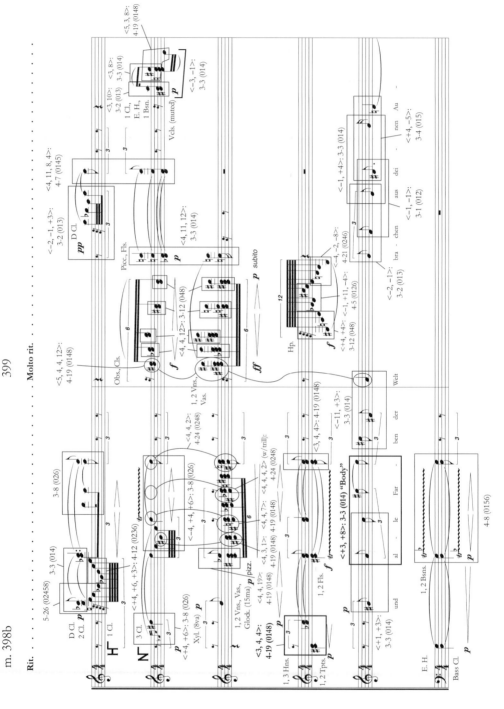

is somewhat reminiscent of the third movement of Schoenberg's Five Pieces, Op. 16, which was written in June 1909, two months before he started work on *Erwartung*. One wonders if the woman's word "Farben" (colors), which is also the title of Op. 16, No. 3, could have motivated this allusion to the earlier piece.) Together with the trumpets, the third clarinet enters on the second eighth note of beat 2's triplet to form <+4, +6>, expanding the bottom intervals <3, 4> from the previous chord and forming the set class 3-8 (026). This little whole-tone trichord seems incidental in its present context, but it is, in fact, a harbinger of a wave of larger whole-tone segments that will increase in size and frequency gradu ally in the following measures and flood the texture after m. 412. The woman responds to these opening sonorities by singing <+3, +8>, the Body motive, on "alle Farben" (all the colors), while the 4-19 <3, 4, 4> chord sustains and changes from trumpets and horns to flutes and horns to create a number of colors, as noted above. The violins and violas enter on the third and fourth beats of m. 398 with a series of augmented triads (set class 3-12) in parallel motion. With the xylophone and third clarinet *Nebenstimme*, the high strings form three verticals belonging to set class 4-19, representing the presence of his dead body, but the last two verticals between third clarinet and strings create set classes 4-24 (0248) instead, another harbinger of the whole-tone music to come.

In m. 399, the whole-tone segments fade from view momentarily, as the previous measure's slowing in tempo is intensified. But other chords and combinations from the previous measures carry through. The first sound we hear is the voice's A4 on "Welt," followed immediately by an augmented triad {D, F♯, A♯} in the high strings and woodwinds, together forming set class 4-19 yet again. Out of that Body chord grows another series of augmented triads in parallel motion on the remainder of the first beat, leading to set class 3-3 on the second beat. The voice responds in the last three beats of m. 399 with trichords that represent the body and her fear: 3-2, 3-1, 3-3, 3-4; while above her in the woodwinds we hear a group of set classes associated with the dead body, supersets and close relatives of 3-3, together with 3-3 as <3, 8> itself (the final eighth note in clarinet, English horn, and bassoon) and 4-19, formed when the 'cello resolves down to E4 under the <3, 8> chord. While she sings of colors breaking forth from his eyes, the orchestra continues to remind us that no light is shining from them at this moment.

But, as the tempo slows to a crawl in m. 400, all these Body motives and chords are supplanted again by a sustained whole-tone chord – now grown into a pentachord, 5-33 (02468), which enters on the second beat (see Example 4.13b).

Example 4.13b  Schoenberg, *Erwartung*, mm. 400–02a. Used by permission of Belmont Music Publishers and Universal Edition

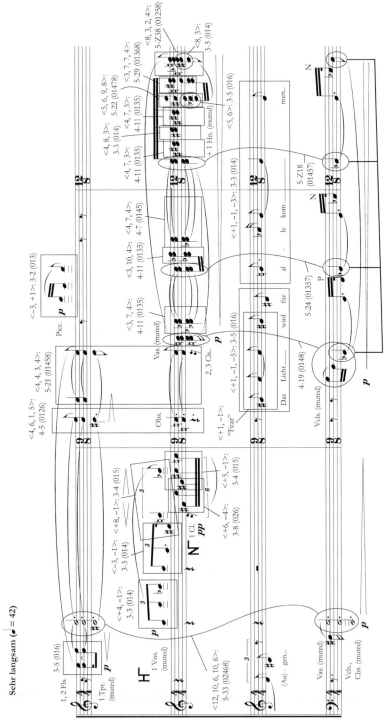

<+3, +4, +4> as <E♭2, G♭2, B♭2, D3>, 4-19 (0148),
"Am Wegrand" bass line a half step higher

This third chord progression from Body trichords and tetrachords to whole-tone subsets, which like the previous ones signifies her imminent realization that she will never see him alive again, seems to call forth two crucial developments in mm. 401–02a. The first is found in Pappenheim's text, which reads in English "The light will come for everyone." This can of course be interpreted to mean the rising of the sun, which is beginning to happen at this point in the scene. But it has an additional meaning, I think – at this point "the light turns on" for the woman, who begins to realize that she is going to be alone forever. The evidence for my second interpretation is leitmotivic: as she sings these words, Schoenberg places most of the bass line from m. 22 of "Am Wegrand," transposed a half-step higher to E♭, beneath her in the 'cellos (as H. H. Buchanan was the first to point out).[30] If the appearance of the complete "Am Wegrand" bass line on D ten measures later signifies her full realization of her lonely fate (and I believe that it does; after all, it *is* followed immediately by the words "I don't recognize you"), then this preview on E♭ certainly must indicate her growing intimations of it. But the 'cello line in mm. 401–02a also can be understood as a culminating point for much of the music in the 400 measures preceding. It fills in <+3, +4, +4> with passing tones and neighboring tones in a way that enables it to serve as a consummation of all the appearances of 3-3, <3, 8>, <+3, +8>, 4-19, <3, 4, 4>, and <+3, +4, +4> that preceded it, especially that one at m. 245 under the words "How can you be dead?" that we discussed in Example 4.12a, <E♭, G♭, B♭, D>. It also links all of them to the full appearance of "Am Wegrand" on D that will come at m. 411.

The voice part and accompanying orchestral parts during mm. 401–02a reinforce the function of this partial "Am Wegrand" bass line; that is, they portray the presence of the dead body while simultaneously sending the message that it is about to disappear. Supersets of Body sets 4-19 and 3-3 such as 5-21 (01458), 5-22 (01478), 5-Z18 (01457), and 5-Z38 (01258) are scattered through these measures. Set class 4-19 itself makes an appearance, as the first chord in the four-part viola and clarinet stream that accompanies the 'cellos, {2, 7, 11}, together with the pcs <7, 2, 3> initiating the 'cello line. And 3-3 is formed by the last notes of the voice part, <–1, –3>. But many of the other motives and chords in this passage move beyond the family of set classes associated with the Body motive: the stream of viola and clarinet chords includes no less than four instances of 4-11 (0135), a chord that can be described as "whole-tone plus 1," and thus serves as a bridge to more whole-tone subsets in the following measures. And the voice includes two <+1, –1> "Fear" motives, the first of which opens out into <+1, –1, –5>,

[30] Buchanan, "A Key to Schoenberg's *Erwartung*," 434–35.

a member of set class 3-5. This music still seems to be setting us up for an eventual move away from 4-19, 3-3, and the dead lover they represent, while it creates a culminating point for all the Body motives and sets that have occurred.

The following passage, mm. 402b–04, portrayed on the top half of Example 4.13c, sets the words "but me, alone, in my night?," the woman's complaint that true light can never come for her if he is no longer alive.

It again follows the same sequence that we have seen several times already in Example 4.13: prominent references to Body sets and motives, followed not long after by whole-tone subsets. Her "ich allein" in m. 402b is set by 3-3 as <–1, +4>, and immediately after we hear 3-3, <8, 3>, as a chord in the harp (the timpani and basses below the harp's chord project a set class 3-10, and this combination of the two trichord set classes in close proximity may be a reference forward to m. 410 and its quotation of m. 19 from "Am Wegrand," which we will discuss in more detail below). "In meiner Nacht?" is set by an octave-displaced "Fear" motive, <+1, +11>, and the musical representative of that thing she fears quickly follows, again in the harp: 4-19 as <4, 4, 3>. After a pause to allow her question to linger in the air for a bit, the orchestra answers her in m. 404 with two <+3> motives in first violins and second clarinet, together forming 4-3 (0134), a superset of 3-3, overlapping with a rendition of 4-19 in the clarinet and muted trombones. But as the measure progresses, these Body sets give way, first to 4-21 (0246) in the trombones and finally to 4-24 (0248) in the trombones, timpani, and harp. The orchestra's answer, that 3-3 and 4-19 must indeed be supplanted by whole-tone segments, is their affirmation that even the presence of his dead body is about to be swept away in a rush of people passing by, and she is doomed to enter an eternity of loneliness.

Before that moment, however, she still has a few things to say. As she begins to reminisce about them always being separated by the morning, and the last time he kissed her goodbye, she and the orchestra manage to produce a few more references to him. The pickup to m. 405 and its downbeat combine her A♯4 on "Der Mor-" with B3 and D4 in the English horn and second clarinet, again forming 3-3 as <3, 8>. Not long after, on the second half of beat 2 and beginning of beat 3, all four voices in the texture form consecutive 4-19 chords on the word "trennt" (separate). But immediately after, as though reacting to that word, the Body sets disappear from the vertical dimension for 1½ measures, and are replaced by a variety of other set classes, some of them supersets of Body sets (like the 5-Z18 (01457) on the second half of beat 3), but many of them more distantly related, such as 4-Z29 (0137), 4-27 (0258), and 4-25 (0268). (Note that these more distant sets are either whole-tone or "whole tone plus 1.")

Example 4.13c  Schoenberg, *Erwartung*, mm. 402b–07. Used by permission of Belmont Music Publishers and Universal Edition

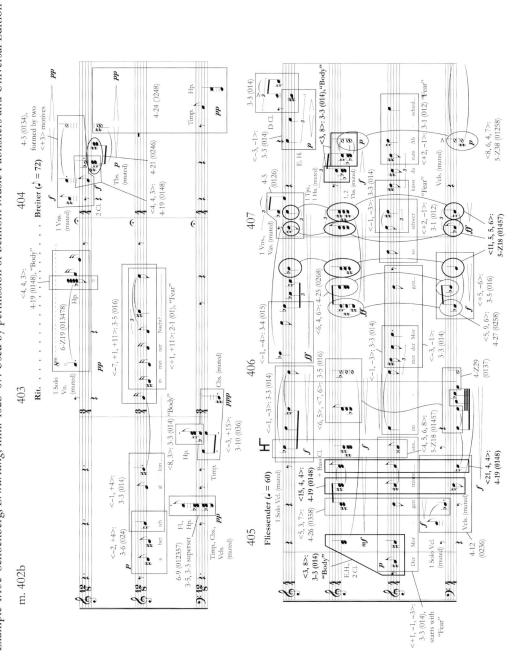

On the last beat of m. 406 and in m. 407, the "Body" supersets begin to dominate the vertical texture again – three 5-Z18s in a rising half-step arrangement in the solo 'cello, 'cellos, bass clarinet, English horn, and 2nd clarinet, followed by 3-3 as <3, 8> itself twice, in the brasses, played *f*. The second of these <3, 8>s sustains into the third beat of the measure, where the 'cellos add two notes to it to form 5-Z38, another superset of 3-3 that is 5-Z18's Z-relation.

While the orchestra abandons and comes back to set classes associated with the lover's dead body, the woman repeats the same intervallic motive, <–1, –3>, three times at higher pitch levels, as well as singing a close relative, <–3, –1>, on "-mer der Morgen." All of these motives belong to set class 3-3, and could signify her obsessive desire to hold on to him or thoughts of him, though she knows she will have to be separated eventually. (<–1, –3> and <–3, –1> will be prominent in her voicing of "Tausend Menschen ziehen vorüber" in m. 411 as the low woodwinds make the separation final by sounding the full "Am Wegrand" quotation beneath her.) The solo 'cello *Hauptstimme* beginning on the second half of beat 3 in m. 405 echoes her, then varies her motive slightly: <–1, –3>, <–1, –4>. And the English horn follows with another echo of <–3, –1> at the end of m. 407. By this time, however, the woman has progressed to singing "Fear" motives, <+2, –1> on "so schwer" ("how deeply") and the same succession on "zum Abschied" (at parting). Her resolve to hold on to him seems to be giving way to fear that they are about to be separated.

Example 4.13d portrays mm. 408–09a, which set her words "Wieder ein ewiger Tag des Wartens" ("Again another eternal day of waiting") – this is her final expression of hope that daybreak will begin another cycle of waiting for him during the day and being reunited at night, as it had so many times before.

Forward motion seems to stop here, as the tempo slows and the orchestra sustains a single chord, 5-28 (02368), another almost whole-tone set, while the woman sings mostly <+1, –1> motives, surrounding them by set classes 3-3 and 3-5. Since whole-tone-related sets have signified moving away from or on beyond the dead lover in recent measures (and will do so even more strongly in the following measures), I would claim that the musical setting suggests that the cycle is about to be broken, and she is reacting to that probability primarily with fear. Indeed, her next words in mm. 409b–10a show that she finally gets it: "Oh . . . You won't wake up anymore." This phrase is sung to <–1, –3> at the beginning and overlapping Fear motives at the end, <–1, +2, –1>, as though her connection to him is being snuffed out, making her afraid for her future. The chord progression beneath her in the orchestra communicates the same message:

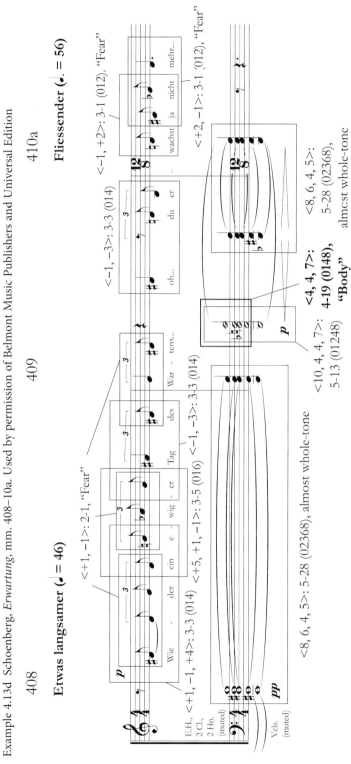

Example 4.13d  Schoenberg, *Erwartung*, mm. 408–10a. Used by permission of Belmont Music Publishers and Universal Edition

two chords, the first 5-13 (01248), whose 4-19 subset is clearly displayed as the top four notes, giving way to 5-28, the almost whole-tone set again. Yet again, the four-note chord that signifies his body appears and then vanishes.

Her final realization that he will not wake up anymore leads directly to mm. 410b–12a, illustrated in Example 4.13e.

Adorno, Buchanan, and others have characterized this specific passage as central or climactic for the opera as a whole, and my own account of *Erwartung* has tried to show that the text, set-class progressions, and particularly the motivic sequences of the piece all point forward to this moment – they are all "anticipations" of it.[31] The entire text of *Erwartung* looks forward to mm. 410–13 in the sense that these measures set the line from "Am Wegrand" (in English), "A thousand people pass by, but I don't recognize you." This articulates Adorno's "collective loneliness," utter loneliness in the midst of the crowd, which is the final consequence led up to in stages by the woman's discovery of his body and, later, her gradual loss of hope that he might still be alive. She has been alternating between anticipating and pushing back against her arrival at mm. 410–12 for the entire opera, but all the time she has been inexorably drawn toward this point.

The motivic path toward mm. 410–12, as we have characterized it already, begins with <+3>, the opera's first interval in the bassoon, and progresses through the appearance of {C♯, D, F} as an unordered set, to <D, F, C♯> as an ordered set, to the multiple repetitions of <D, F, C♯> that overwhelm the texture at mm. 146–52, to which the woman responds with a transposition of the same motive, <+3, +8>, on "Das ist er!" In the second part of the piece, <D, F, C♯> or <+3, +8> adds a fourth element to become <E♭, G♭, B♭, D> and <D, F, A, C♯> at m. 246, then adds passing and neighboring tones to produce <E♭, F, G♭, C♭, B♭, E♭, D> in the rhythm of "Am Wegrand's" bass line at mm. 401–02, and finally, here in mm. 411–12, grows to <**D**, E, **F**, B♭, **A**, D, **C♯**, F>, the full "Am Wegrand" quotation at its original transposition on D. All along the path of this cumulative setting, the various stages are reinforced with vertical unordered pitch-interval stacks corresponding to them such as <3, 8> and <3, 4, 4>, and with their set classes, 3-3 and 4-19.

---

[31] Adorno: "*Erwartung* contains a musical quotation that accompanies the words 'thousands of people march past.' Schoenberg borrowed the quotation from an earlier tonal song whose theme and counterpoint are embedded with the greatest artistry in the freely moving vocal texture without breaching the atonality" (*Philosophy of New Music*, p. 40). And Buchanan adds, "further, the borrowed music can be viewed profitably as both source *and summary* of a significant amount of the musical material which creates the coherent structure of Op. 17" ("A Key to Schoenberg's *Erwartung*," 434; italics mine). Buchanan also refers to m. 411 as "the start of the final climax of the work" (ibid., 437).

Example 4.13e Schoenberg, *Erwartung*, mm. 410b–12a. Used by permission of Belmont Music Publishers and Universal Edition

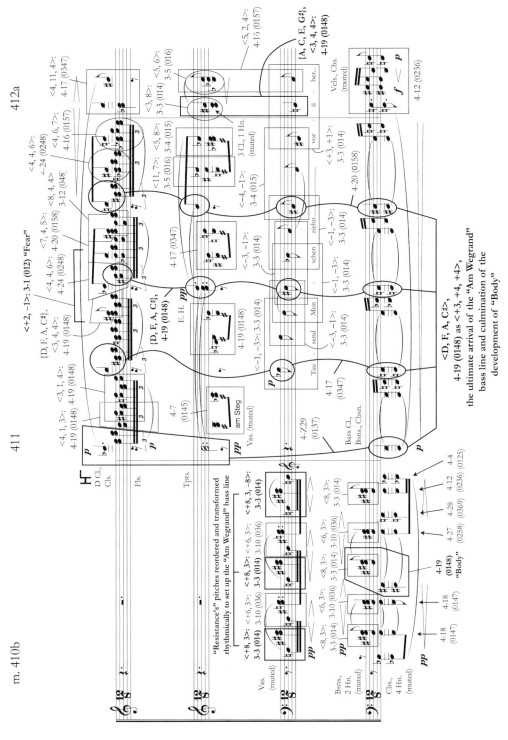

But before we get to m. 411's climax, there is one last stage in the buildup to it to describe: the last half of m. 410. As I mentioned back on p. 160 (in connection with Example 4.3a), this music, particularly the viola figure (which is doubled by bassoons and horn), is a quotation of the piano right hand from mm. 19–20 of the song "Am Wegrand." In the song, it was a transition leading to the return of the main theme in the piano's bass line at m. 22. I also commented in that earlier discussion (following H. H. Buchanan) that the bassoon and oboe *Hauptstimmen* in mm. 1–2 of *Erwartung*, <G♯4, B4> and <C♯5, A♯4, D4>, are presentiments or anticipations of this transition, that m. 410b can be understood as a more complete version of it that sets up for the bass line from "Am Wegrand" in m. 411, and that the 408 measures in between, most of *Erwartung*, can be interpreted as Schoenberg "stretching out" the "single second" of anticipation between mm. 19 and 22 of the song to a "half hour" (as he claimed).

But our study of some of the intervening music between m. 2 and m. 410 has revealed another aspect of this final rendition of the transition, beyond the fact that it is more complete. Namely, it reverses the direction of <C♯5, A♯4, D4>, m. 2's "Resistance" motive, from downward to upward: D3, rising to A♯3 and C♯4 as a vertical. We had discussed one place in the previous measures where "Resistance" was reordered in a similar way and thus neutralized, at m. 231 (return to Example 4.11). There, the woman's <D4, C♯5, A♯4> on "Sieh mich doch an, Liebster" ("Look at me, beloved") had twisted the descent of the original motive to a mostly ascending contour. The violas in m. 410b do the same, quoting the pitch classes of the Resistance motive and changing their contour to ascending, but now also take the further step of clothing them in the rhythm of the "Am Wegrand" transition. This portrays not only the neutralization of her resistance (she has just acknowledged his death in mm. 409b–10a), but also signals the imminence of the long-expected "Am Wegrand" bass, with all its connotations of eternal separation and loneliness. (In addition, the descending chromatic line in the contrabasses and 4th horn that is added to the transitional material at m. 410 causes the progression to touch on set class 4-19, {D, F♯, A♯, C♯}, right at that place where the bass line pauses on F♯ momentarily, and then to turn away from 4-19 to other set classes – a more subtle hint of what is about to come.)

Measures 411–13 portray first the certainty and finality of the lover's death, and then the reality of the woman's separation from him, with two musical gestures – represented by Examples 4.13e and 4.13f. In Example 4.13e we encounter the "Am Wegrand" bass in its final and most complete version,[32] transposed to begin on D, so that its cumulative identity as a larger, more decorated version of all the previous <D, F, A, C♯> and <D, F, C♯> Body motives is utterly clear. As the earlier versions of the motive had represented first her discovery of his body, and later the increasing certainty of his death, now this final, most complete version of it (in bass clarinet, bassoons, and contrabassoon) portrays the moment where the realization of her fate descends on her with crushing finality. Together with the "Am Wegrand" bass, Schoenberg also quotes the original vocal counterpoint to the bass line from mm. 22–23 of the song, in the clarinet *Hauptstimme* at the top of the texture (the upward-stemmed notes on the top staff of my reduction). In the song, this melody had set the words "Sehnsucht erfüllt die Bezirke des Lebens" ("Longing fills the regions of my life"), so its quotation at this point in the opera reinforces the sense of "collective loneliness." It consists mostly of three-note chromatic ascents and descents, members of set class 3-1, and includes <+2, –1> as a segment, so (as I suggested earlier) we may be able to hear it as a culmination of all the "Fear" motives in previous measures: but its connection with them is not as obvious as that between the "Am Wegrand" bass and the Body motives.

In addition, since the counterpoint in the clarinets comes from the original song, it reinforces the D minor sound of the "Am Wegrand" quotation in the bass. The F4 and A4 sustained in the trumpets and D5 in the English horn during the first three dotted quarter beats of m. 411 also contribute to a vague but unmistakable sense of tonic in D minor, which dissipates again before the end of the measure – as we will see, it gives way to segments of the odd whole-tone collection, $WT_1$. As I mentioned earlier, this signifies, I think, the first clear instance in Schoenberg's music of a functionally tonal segment appearing within an atonal context for text-painting reasons; that is, D minor represents the finality of the lover's death.

The voice creates a third contrapuntal strand in mm. 411–12a, her setting of "Tausend Menschen ziehen vorüber." This is *not* a quoted melody, but unique to *Erwartung* – it begins with a complete octave

---

[32] It should be pointed out that this "final and most complete version of the *Am Wegrand* bass" in *Erwartung* corresponds to the pitch-class sequence of the voice at the song's beginning (mm. 3–4), <D, E, F, B♭, A, D, C♯, F>, rather than the form it takes in the bass line of the piano in mm. 22–23, which is <D, E, F, B♭, A, E♭, D>. In a sense, then, *Erwartung*'s quotation actually combines elements of both passages in "Am Wegrand": the specific pitch-class succession of mm. 3–4 with the bass register and octave doubling of mm. 22–23.

from the hexatonic scale, <–1, –3, –1, –3, –1, –3>, before taking a different path at the end of the word "ziehen." Since m. 411 is the point at which the woman begins to resign herself to her fate, it is tempting to interpret <–1, –3> and <–3, –1> as another leitmotive, which we might call "Resignation." To be sure, both interval patterns were prevalent in the immediately preceding music of Example 4.13c, especially mm. 405–07, as the woman was preparing for this final separation. But the "Resignation" motive, though it is just as widespread in the opera as Body, Fear, or Resistance, does not seem to appear with the same text associations as consistently, until these final measures – so its leitmotivic influence is local, at best.

The harmonies in mm. 411–12a, including vertical slices of the whole texture from top to bottom (highlighted with bold circles and connecting lines) as well as smaller segments, reinforce the emergence in the bass line of <D, F, A, C♯> with members of its set class, 4-19 (0148). But, at the same time, they also set the listener up for the second stage of this climactic passage, in which the lover's body begins to disappear. There is a prominent {D, F, A, C♯} chord on the third dotted quarter beat of m. 411 (excluding the clarinets' E♭6); and 4-19 also appears as {A, C, E, G♯} in the English horn, 3rd clarinet, 1st horn, and voice at the end of the phrase (downbeat of m. 412). Several individual strands of the texture also create the same tetrachord: the flutes twice within the first dotted quarter beat of m. 411, and the flutes as {D, F, A, C♯} and violas as {E♭, G, A♭, B} within the second beat of the same measure. In addition, all the <–1, –3> and <–3, –1> motives in the voice we spoke of earlier belong to set class 3-3 (014), the subset of 4-19 that is most closely tied to his dead body. But most of the sets formed by the individual strands we are considering do not belong to 4-19 or 3-3; there is a sense in m. 411 that the harmonic repertoire is beginning to move beyond portrayals of the lover's body. The existence of two members of set class 4-24 (0248) created between the flute strand and the clarinet line clarifies this sense of moving beyond – the first of these, on the third beat of m. 411, comes directly after an instance of set class 4-19, setting up the by-now familiar progression of 4-19 to a whole-tone subset, which has already associated and will associate itself with depictions of her contact with him being broken off.

This connection between whole-tone subsets taking over the texture and the idea of final separation becomes absolutely unmistakable in the following passage, mm. 412b–13a, portrayed in Example 4.13f. She sings "Ich erkenne dich nicht" ("I don't recognize you"), and at that exact point where she jumps to high E♭5 on "ken" on the third beat of m. 412, the harmonic repertoire transforms itself. The 2nd violins and violas had played 4-19 as a tremolo on the third eighth of the second beat of m. 412, but with the

Example 4.13f Schoenberg, *Erwartung*, mm. 412b–13. Used by permission of Belmont Music Publishers and Universal Edition

m. 412b

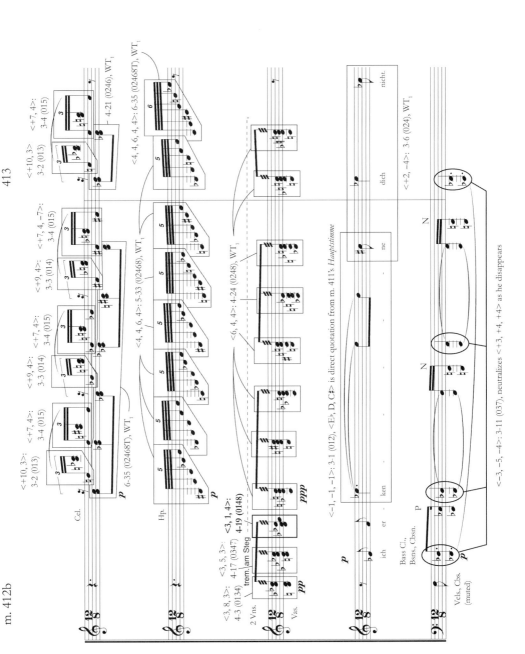

third beat they switch to parallel 4-24 chords that continue for the rest of the passage. At that same point, the harp enters with a series of arpeggios, all belonging to set-class 5-33 (02468). And, at that same point, the left hand of the celesta begins two descending whole-tone scales separated by a major third. All three strands of the texture consist of odd pitch-classes only, so a single whole-tone collection, $WT_1$, is being projected through much of this passage. As if in response, the woman's phrase ends with pitch classes <1, 3, 11>, merging into the same odd whole-tone collection, forming set class 3-6 (024).

The other strands in the texture of Example 4.13f either express the notion of final separation in a different way or seem to push back against it. The bass line, still in the low woodwinds, neutralizes the <+3, +4, +4> that had immediately come before it with <−3, −5, −4>, a descending B♭ minor triad with neighboring and passing tones. Both the descent and the change to a diatonic sound world contradict the preceding "Body" motive, further reinforcing the overall sense that his presence is vanishing in this passage. The one strand of the texture that is not either whole-tone or diatonic is the right hand of the celesta. It varies the transitional material from m. 410b, creating trichords that have been associated with his dead body: 3-2, 3-4, and two instances of 3-3. One could understand the celesta's right hand as a last-ditch effort to hold on to some musical material that evokes the dead lover, as the whole-tone collection begins to wash over the texture.

## Measure 426 (final measure of the opera)

The idea that whole-tone (and other) collections are washing over the texture, like a tidal wave, erasing any trace of the dead lover (or even his memory), is even more strongly communicated by the opera's last gesture, m. 426, illustrated in Example 4.14. This measure consists almost entirely of whole-tone chords in parallel motion up or down through the chromatic scale. The planed chords finally break out to cover almost the whole texture here, after a number of less successful attempts between mm. 413 and 425. Examples of whole-tone chords moving chromatically, or in parallel motion, or both, in parts of the texture (not illustrated here, consult the score) include the horns and trumpets at m. 416, the flutes and clarinets at m. 417, the horns, viola, and 'cellos at m. 423, the high woodwinds at m. 424, and the clarinets and bassoons at the end of m. 425, which lead directly into the parallel strands that begin Example 4.14. As if in response to all these planed whole-tone chords, the voice in mm. 424–25, after singing 3-3 as <−3, −1, +4>, perhaps representing a last lingering memory of him, on "Oh, bist du da" ("Oh, there you are"), follows it immediately with the whole-tone subset 3-8 as <+2, –6> on "Ich suchte" ("I was look-ing"), her final words, which do not seem to be directed to her dead lover anymore.

In Example 4.14, each of the twelve strands of the texture in the opera's final measure is given its own staff, to highlight what kinds of chords are being planed and through what kinds of parallel motion they project themselves. As I suggested above, almost the whole texture consists of whole-tone chords in parallel chromatic motion. From the top of Example 4.14 down, the flutes, D clarinet, and piccolos plane 5-33 (02468) up chromatically, while the clarinets do likewise with 3-12 (048). The 1st and 2nd violins subject 4-24 (0248) as <2, 4, 4> to upward chromatic parallel motion, as do the oboes to 4-24 as the pitch-interval inversion <4, 4, 2>. In the middle of the example, the celesta plays a chromatic run from C4 to C8. The bassoons, like the clarinets, plane 3-12 up chromatically (and the two strands together form an upward chromatic planing of the full whole-tone collection, 6-35 (02468T), until they break apart rhythmically on the third beat). The violas and 'cellos plane 3-12 (048) as <4, 4, 4> upward chromatically. And, finally, one strand subjects a whole-tone subset to *downward* chromatic planing: the trom-bones and tuba, which do this to 5-33 (02468).

But not every strand of m. 426 involves chromatic planing of whole-tone chords. Two of the other strands reinforce the whole-tone sound of the measure by projecting it horizontally rather than vertically. The harp has a whole-tone glissando through the $WT_0$ scale up from D1 to D7, and the bass clarinet, contrabasses, and contrabassoon plane a major third and doubled octave <4, 8> downward through the whole-tone 0 scale, up to the last eighth note of the measure, where they break into rhythmically distinct $WT_0$ fragments.

The only strand left to describe is the held fluttertongue chords in the trumpets and horns. The trumpets seem to follow the rest of the orchestra in m. 426; their chord is 3-12 as <4, 4>, matching the verticals in the clarinet and bassoon strands. But the horns play something different – which is at least partially hidden by virtue of being in the same rhythm with and close in register to the trumpets, but perhaps distinguishable because of the different timbre. They play 4-19, softly, as <3, 4, 4>, the pitch-interval stack that has been established throughout the opera as a representative for the lover's dead body. *Erwartung*'s last measure seems to me to be the most graphic way possible to portray the final disappearance of the lover and his memory amidst the noise and tumult of the "thousand people passing by." Understanding its final cadence this way invites, one more time, a comparison with Berg's opera *Wozzeck* – in which the final cadence

Example 4.14 Schoenberg, *Erwartung*, m. 426 (final measure). Used by permission of Belmont Music Publishers and Universal Edition

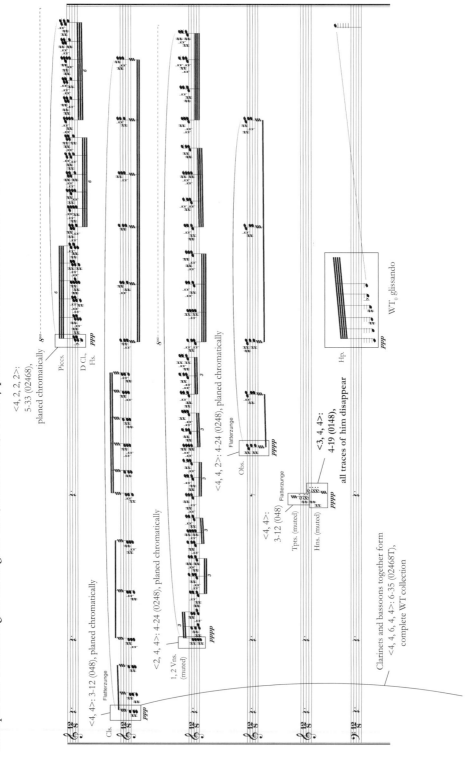

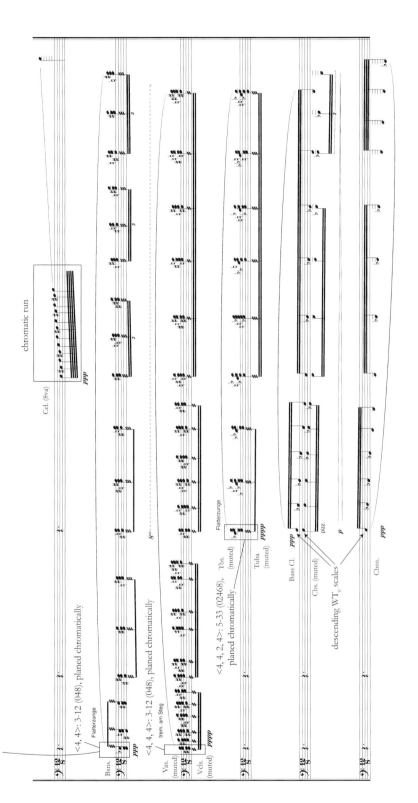

222222222222 Op. 17

subsumes the "Marie's Lullaby" leitmotive gradually under an aimless-sounding ostinato, to represent Marie's child losing contact with his mother (and, like *Erwartung*'s woman, being doomed to a life of "collective loneliness").[33]

With our consideration of the final measure, our long, detailed treatment of *Erwartung* has come to an end. What motivated all the detail, particularly my steadfast attempts to identify nearly every motive and chord as some repetition or variation of a leitmotive or leitmotivic set-class, was my conception of this chapter as an extended argument against the conventional wisdom (among at least half of the scholars who write about this work) that claims "there is not a single recurring theme or motive." Rather than understanding *Erwartung* as the climactic point of a short period in Schoenberg's career where he abandoned thematic and motivic work, it seems more useful to me to comprehend it as an important step forward in Schoenberg's development of the leitmotivic opera or symphonic poem. It is certainly true that neither *Erwartung*'s text nor its music has repetitions or variations of large sections that would allow us to label them with letters on a form chart: still, its text *does* contain a teleological narrative that divides into two large stages, the gradual revelation of the lover's dead body and the woman's even more gradual realization that she will be alone forever. Schoenberg artfully portrays these processes, and the efforts of the woman to push back against them, using motives, stacks of unordered pitch intervals, and set classes – the "expressionist sonorities" and "impressionist themes" that Berg discovered in his study of the work.[34] These elements are different from leitmotives in Schoenberg's earlier works (such as *Pelleas und Melisande*) on account of their brevity (generally two, three, or four notes; one, two, or three intervals) and abstract nature (the use of set classes as leitmotives). They portray gradual revelation or realization by participating in a "cumulative setting" of material from Schoenberg's song "Am Wegrand," which would have served as a clear sign for "collective loneliness" for those who knew (or know) the song's text.

Finally, the quotation from "Am Wegrand" itself, the endpoint of the cumulative setting, includes enough evidence from supporting voices to hear it as a momentary prolongation of the tonic triad in D minor. This

---

[33] Janet Schmalfeldt describes the passage this way: "as the Lullaby tune now merges with the final cadential harmony, references to Marie lose their identity as they become absorbed within the broader domain of that harmony." See *Berg's Wozzeck: Harmonic Language and Dramatic Design*, p. 208.

[34] Whitney discusses these in "Schoenberg's 'Single Second of Maximum Spiritual Excitement'," 156.

marks probably the first time that functional tonality reappears in Schoenberg's music after it was abandoned in 1908, now acting not as the main device for producing long-range coherence, but as a brief expressive tool to represent the finality of the lover's death, one characteristic of the "Am Wegrand" leitmotive in its complete and final state.

Understanding it as an incremental step forward in the development of the leitmotivic opera, we can appreciate *Erwartung*'s role as an inspiration and model for Alban Berg as he wrote his own masterpiece in that genre, *Wozzeck*. Not only the reliance on impressionist themes (brief motives) and expressionist sonorities (set classes) to convey dramatic process is carried over into Berg's work, but also Berg seems to borrow from his teacher specific motives such as the motto, "Wir arme Leut," cadential gestures such as allowing a central motive to be subsumed by more nondescript-sounding material, and the use of tonal elements and passages for expressive and text-painting purposes.

The next pieces to examine in our tour of Schoenberg's atonal music involve a drastic scaling-down: from an opera of 426 measures to works of about ten measures each – the Op. 19 Little Piano Pieces. As we examine closely Nos. 2, 3, and 6 from that collection, however, we will find that, despite their diminutive size, they too are clear expressions of basic image, musical idea, or both.

# 5 Six Little Piano Pieces, Op. 19 (Nos. 2, 3, and 6)

## Musical Idea and Basic Image in Miniature

The six little pieces of Op. 19 were composed in winter and early summer of 1911; Schoenberg dated the first five as written on February 19 of that year, and the sixth on June 17. They came to life during one of his less-prolific periods as a composer. During the one and a half years following the completion of *Erwartung* in September 1909, he managed only to sketch two chamber orchestra miniatures and begin a third (in February 1910) and start a draft of the score of *Die Glückliche Hand* (in September 1910). The composition of *Die Glückliche Hand* would continue in fits and starts until its completion in November 1913;[1] the chamber orchestra pieces were never completed.

Bryan Simms attributes Schoenberg's dry spell to a "compositional crisis" brought on by his supposed decision in late 1909 to eliminate motivic development and traditional form in his music. In Simms's words, the end of 1909 and beginning of 1910 was

> the onset of a period during which the composer, by his own admission, felt that he had lost his way, stricken by such self-doubt and artistic confusion that few pieces were begun and even fewer completed. The style of the chamber orchestra pieces must be implicated in this crisis: their incompleteness is an indication that they represented a troubled time in Schoenberg's creative life. The composer often remarked that he could not compose unless inspired to do so, an observation that bears more on the atonal style than any other. It was just this inspiration that must have been undermined by a music – however ingenious and original – that was fragmented, radically abbreviated, and nondevelopmental. The early atonal period had been for Schoenberg a time of exuberant expansion of a new language, during which the composer was perpetually looking ahead for new and untried techniques. But in the elimination of motivic work, of which the extreme aphoristic style was a product, he seems to have overstepped, stumbling into an artistic quandary from which he would need thirteen years to extricate himself fully.[2]

---

[1] See the description accompanying the home page for *Die Glückliche Hand* in the Schönberg Center music manuscripts archive: http://archive.schoenberg.at/compositions/werke_einzelansicht.php?werke_id=474&herkunft=allewerke. See also Joseph Auner's description of the chronology of the piece in "Schoenberg's Aesthetic Transformations and the Evolution of Form in Die Glückliche Hand."

[2] Simms, *The Atonal Music of Arnold Schoenberg*, p. 84.

Ethan Haimo, likewise, characterizes the period of summer 1909 to February 1911 as Schoenberg venturing down an amotivic path that would eventually lead to a creative "dead end." And, like Simms, he understands the Op. 19 Piano Pieces as a first step out of the "artistic quandary" that Schoenberg had stumbled into.[3] For both of them, the *Sechs kleine Klavierstücke*, while still aphoristic in style, are characterized by the first stirrings of a revival: of motivic and thematic development and traditional notions of form.

Since I devoted much of Chapters 2 and 4 of this book to showing how Schoenberg never really abandoned "motivic working" or large-scale narratives that create coherence, even in works such as Op. 11, No. 3 or *Erwartung*, there are two questions I must answer to explain my conception of how Op. 19 fits into Schoenberg's overall development as a composer. First, if the compositional dry spell of late 1909–11 was not the result of Schoenberg stumbling into a creative blind alley (Op. 11, No. 3 and *Erwartung* are simply too good as pieces of music to bring on a creative blind alley!), then why *did* this almost two-year hiatus happen? Second, if Op. 19 does not mark the return of motivic development and large-scale narrative after their complete absence from Schoenberg's music for two years, then what accounts for the sense the listener has that these pieces are, indeed, somewhat more traditional-sounding from what came immediately before? I will answer both questions in turn.

Hans Heinz Stuckenschmidt, in his exhaustive, diary-like, biography of Schoenberg, carefully accounts for the composer's activities and life situations during the time period in question. Reading Stuckenschmidt, we learn that during 1910, the composer moved to a larger apartment in the Vienna suburbs, which made his financial situation difficult. His daughter Trudi was in school, and his wife Mathilde's health was poor. He had a growing number of private composition students, and was negotiating with Artur Bodansky in Mannheim for a premiere performance of *Erwartung* (a plan that did not come to fruition; the opera was first performed under Alexander von Zemlinsky in 1924). In March he took up a teaching position at the Vienna Music Academy, and finally, he had begun writing his first book, the *Harmonielehre* (whose first edition would be published in 1911), a massive study of traditional tonal harmony ending with an argument supporting his own innovations in that realm. In addition, there were parts to be copied and proofs to be corrected for a number of recently composed pieces, including the Op. 11 Piano Pieces,

[3] Haimo, *Schoenberg's Transformation*, pp. 350–51.

and the orchestration of a large portion of *Gurrelieder*.[4] Could it be, then, that the "compositional crisis" Simms speaks of had less to do with Schoenberg's creative dissatisfaction with his (supposedly) amotivic style, and more to do with financial and family pressures and an overload of teaching and book-writing duties as well as the mundane but necessary tasks a composer must complete to have his music published and performed?

Even if that is the case, though, there is still the unmistakable sense that the Op. 19 piano pieces do take a step back in the direction of traditional form and motivic development. My arguments in previous chapters should have convinced the reader that I would avoid characterizing this shift the way Simms and Haimo do, as a complete disappearance of motivic work-ing from late 1909 to 1911, with the first few "cracks in the façade" of amotivicism appearing in the Op. 19 pieces.[5] I have already described Op. 11, No. 3 in Chapter 2 as "full of motivic . . . repetition [and progression] on the levels of set class, unordered pitch-interval stack, and even ordered pitch-interval motive" (p. 109). And I claimed further that the motive progressions participate in a "large plan that involves the interaction of two processes": a process that explains set class 4-19 as created by pitch-interval motivic content, and the process of set-class expansion, which eventually overwhelms the explanatory process (p. 109). In Chapter 4, I showed how *Erwartung* uses motives, stacks of unordered pitch intervals, and set classes to portray a two-stage basic image representing the woman's discovery of her lover's dead body and her subsequent realization that she is condemned to a life of "collective loneliness." The leitmotivic elements "portray gradual revelation or realization by participating in a 'cumulative setting' of material from Schoenberg's song 'Am Wegrand'" (p. 222).

Though these two works from Schoenberg's 'intuitive period' are full of motives and motivic processes, one can certainly argue that many of their motivic elements are brief, of a relatively abstract nature, or both – making them less immediately graspable for the listener. The main motivic process in Op. 11, No. 3 is predicated on set-class expansion, a process that manifests itself to the hearer not so much as a literal expansion, but as a shift in interval content from more closed-sounding intervals (minor seconds and major sevenths) to more open-sounding ones (perfect fourths and fifths, and tritones). And the set classes that are expanded are mostly trichords: 3-2 to 3-3 to 3-4 to 3-5. The motives in *Erwartung*, while still small, are more concrete and immediate than those of the piano piece; for

---

[4] Stuckenschmidt, *Schoenberg: His Life, World, and Work*, pp. 128–44.
[5] Haimo, *Schoenberg's Transformation*, p. 351.

instance, the ordered pitch-interval succession <+3, +8> and the ordered pitch-class succession <D, F, C♯>. But the processes connecting them to each other and the eventual attainment of the "Am Wegrand" phrase are spread out over 411 measures. Between these statements of the "Body" motive, there are large stretches of intervening material: some of which connects to "Body" through easily heard interval transformations, some through more abstract set-class relations, along with projections of other motives as the constantly shifting text calls for them.

Compare these less-easily grasped procedures with the process of motivic development in Op. 19, No. 2. The central pitch dyad (B4-above-G4) is presented in a distinct rhythm (quarter rest, three eighths, two eighth rests, one eighth), and then both the same pitch dyad and the same rhythm repeat. After this, we immediately hear variations on these pitches and rhythms through the addition of closely related intervals (minor thirds, mainly) and by varying the rhythmic motto of three eighths, adding other durations to it, and shifting its position in the meter. Or consider Op. 19, No. 6, where the same two trichords repeat at the same pitch and durational distance, and then again at a smaller distance before adding a third chord, a transposition of the second. After two measures of contrasting material, the initial pair of chords returns, again at pitch. In these pieces, not only the motivic elements themselves but also their processes of development are quickly recognizable by the "naked ear," as it were – little or no study of the score is required to comprehend these motivic networks and processes, unlike those in Op. 11, No. 3 and *Erwartung*. Part of the reason for the more immediate comprehensibility of Op. 19 is the fact that these pieces are so short – there is much less room for motivic material that does not relate closely and directly to the main process. And another part is that these motivic processes are contained within miniature versions of recognizable tonal forms.

Now, I would not go so far as to admit that the motives and processes I described in Op. 11, No. 3 and *Erwartung* are *completely* hidden to the "naked ear." I believe they do indeed influence the listener's comprehension of the piece in subtle ways, the ultimate justification for me to describe them in such detail in Chapters 2 and 4. For example, my analysis of Op. 11, No. 3 was intended to help us understand why it is that one sensitive, knowledgeable listener would say this about the piece: "one is constantly struck by the feeling that a given passage sounds vaguely like things we have heard before."[6] But with Op. 19, the feelings are much less vague, much easier to describe on first hearing – Schoenberg did indeed take

---

[6] Haimo, *Schoenberg's Transformation*, p. 344.

a step back toward bringing his motivic processes closer to the audible musical surface. If he was suffering through a "compositional crisis" from late 1909 to 1911, it was not brought on by the complete absence of motives and motivic relations from his music. If anything, he may have been taking time off to figure out how to make the developmental processes he had been perfecting more immediately graspable.

However, the principal topic of my book is not to compare Op. 19 with the music that immediately preceded it, as interesting and important as that comparison may be. My main purpose is to demonstrate a line of continuity between Op. 15, Op. 11, Nos. 1 and 2, the "intuitive" music, the Six Little Pieces themselves, and the music that followed, particularly Op. 21, *Pierrot lunaire*. This continuity stems from the consistent use of the large-scale narratives we have been discussing from the beginning of the book: the problem, elaboration, and solution of the musical idea, and (in music with text) the use of a visual image abstracted from the text to control pitch and rhythm. The "intuitive" pieces we discussed did indeed express large-scale narratives like these, with some interesting twists. As we saw, Op. 11, No. 3 created and elaborated the conflict associated with a musical idea, but instead of resolution, it simply allowed one conflicting process to overwhelm the other. And *Erwartung*'s large-scale coherence could be understood in terms of a visual image which takes a half hour to unfold: the lover's dead body gradually emerging from the darkness, followed by the woman's similarly emerging realization that she will die alone. The movements of Op. 19 we will study in detail also embellish musical idea and basic image in different ways: in one case (Op. 19, No. 3) by providing a *negative* version of the musical idea after the preceding piece's more conventional idea narrative, in another (Op. 19, No. 6) by combining an unresolved conflict (the first two parts of a musical idea) with a visual and aural image of Schoenberg lamenting Mahler's death and at the same time trying to reach up to the tonal perfection of his mentor, but being turned back and falling into the depths of despair, atonality, or both.

## Op. 19, No. 2

Perhaps no other piece in all of Schoenberg's *oeuvre* has attracted as much analytical and critical commentary as these nine measures. There have been conventional tonal analyses with altered Roman numerals (Hicken), quasi-Schenkerian analyses in which the last chord is a composite of tonic and dominant chords (Travis), reductive analyses based on redefining the traditional distinctions between chordal and voice-leading intervals

(Väisälä and Lewandowski), and reductive analyses that ignore those distinctions completely, and depend instead on contextual salience (Lerdahl).[7] Many of these analyses have an important feature in common: they portray Op. 19, No. 2 as somehow culminating in its final chord.

In 1963, a few years before his introduction of the mature version of pitch-class set theory, Allen Forte produced an analysis of the second little piece that treated the opening, repeating B4-above-G4, as a "reference set," grouped the other pitch classes of the chromatic collection according to their associations with one or both pitch classes, and then described the last five measures as a succession of these groups. A few years later, Deborah Stein took Forte's assertion that the repeating G-B is a point of reference, and built from it a different reading of the piece that explains the remaining pitches as motions by step or third from the reference point, with register transfer. And Marion Guck responded to Stein with another reading that highlighted the various horizontal and vertical symmetries in the piece. Another, later, analysis by Jonathan Dunsby and Arnold Whittall sought to incorporate all of Op. 19, No. 2 within a vertically symmetrical framework.[8]

Finally, a third group of published analyses is most interesting to me, because in different ways their authors create narratives that span the second piece from beginning to end, and involve conflict that is elaborated and then resolved. But none of them explicitly recognize the analytical stories they have proposed as expressions of "musical idea." Both Thomas DeLio and Edgar Warren Williams characterize the piece in terms of the major third (first represented by G-B) coming into conflict with the minor third, nearly being supplanted by it (at m. 6b), but eventually over-coming and subsuming it in the final chord (m. 9b). Matthew Greenbaum creates a strikingly similar narrative, expanding the conflict between thirds

[7] Kenneth Hicken, "Tonal Organization in Schoenberg's Six Little Piano Pieces, Op. 19," *Canadian University Music Review* 1 (1980): 130–46; Roy Travis, "Directed Motion in Schoenberg and Webern," *Perspectives of New Music* 4/2 (Spring–Summer 1966): 85–89; Väisälä, "Concepts of Harmony and Prolongation in Schoenberg's Op. 19/2"; Stephan Lewandowski, "'A Far Higher Power,' Gedanken zu ideengeschichtlichen Vorgängermodellen der Pitch-Class Set Theory," *Tijdschrift voor Muziektheorie* 15/3 (2010): 190–210; and Fred Lerdahl, "Atonal Prolongational Structure," *Contemporary Music Review* 4 (1989): 65–87.

[8] Allen Forte, "Context and Continuity in an Atonal Work," *Perspectives of New Music* 1/2 (Spring 1963): 72–82; Deborah Stein, "Schoenberg's Opus 19, No. 2: Voice-Leading and Overall Structure in an Atonal Work," *In Theory Only* 2/7 (October 1976): 27–43; Marion Guck, "*A noir – à miroir*: Past Senses Reverses Nests (A Priori?)," *In Theory Only* 2/10 (January 1977): 29–34; Jonathan Dunsby and Arnold Whittall, *Music Analysis in Theory and Practice* (New Haven: Yale University Press, 1988), pp. 125–26.

out to the augmented and diminished triads (an elaboration). In contrast, Charles Morrison describes the central conflict of the piece as a rhythmic one: a syncopated rhythm on the third and fourth beats of the piece's 4/4 meter, eighth–quarter–eighth, is at first unable to "resolve" onto the following downbeat, and then is shifted to other parts of the meter and projected onto other duration levels (elaboration, again). In m. 6, the syncopated figure on beats 1 and 2 is able to resolve onto a strong beat, beat 3 – but without involving the central dyad G-B, something Morrison understands as falling short of a true resolution. But at the end in m. 9, the syncopated rhythm on beats 1 and 2 resolves into beat 3 again, this time including the central G-B as a component, bringing the piece to a convincing resolution at its close.[9]

My analysis of the second Little Piano Piece, then, will follow the outline that DeLio, Williams, Greenbaum, and Morrison have set out – but recognizing the piece explicitly as a manifestation of what Schoenberg would call musical idea. Like them, I will also show that the opening measures present an opposition and elaborate it, leading to a climax (of conflict) in m. 6. The conflict is then resolved convincingly in the final measure. I want to base my narrative on different elements from theirs, however – the various transformations and extensions of the opening three-note rhythmic motive ♩♪, and the large pitch-class collections that the piece passes through during those transformations and extensions: transpositions of the hexatonic, octatonic, and whole-tone. (My focus on tracking large pitch-class collections is modeled on approaches by Arthur Berger and Pieter van den Toorn, among others, originally devised for Stravinsky's music.[10]) In this way, I can account for patterns created by specific pitch classes, not just interval- or set classes, within my analysis while limiting myself to contiguous segments of the piece (thus avoiding some of the questionable segmentations of my predecessors).

The use of collection labels such as HEX, OCT, WT, and DIA in my analysis of Op. 19, No. 2 should not be understood as detracting in any way

[9] Thomas DeLio, "Language and Form in an Early Atonal Composition: Schoenberg's Op. 19/2," *Indiana Theory Review* 15/2 (Fall 1994): 17–40; Edgar Warren Williams Jr., "A View of Schoenberg's Op. 19, No. 2," *College Music Symposium* 25 (1985): 144–51; Matthew Greenbaum, "Dialectic in Miniature: Arnold Schoenberg's Sechs Kleine Klavierstücke Op. 19," *Ex Tempore* 14/2 (Spring–Summer 2009): 51–52; and Charles Morrison, "Syncopation as Motive in Schoenberg's Op. 19, Nos. 2, 3 and 4," *Music Analysis* 11/1 (1992): 85–90.

[10] See Berger, "Problems of Pitch Organization in Stravinsky," *Perspectives of New Music* 2/1 (1963): 11–42; van den Toorn, *The Music of Igor Stravinsky* (New Haven: Yale University Press, 1983).

from this piece's atonal or "chromatic" quality (likewise for pieces 3 and 6). Schoenberg's way of using these collections is not to sustain single ones for longer periods of time (as Stravinsky would), but instead he combines them with different transpositions of themselves and with each other at a considerably faster rate, often overlapping them with one another. In this way, the "high rate of pitch-class circulation" Dmitri Tymoczko uses to characterize Schoenberg's music remains an important feature (see footnote 40 on pp. 35–36 for a discussion of Tymoczko's concept). For that reason, it makes less sense to determine a central pitch or pitch class within every collection or even most of them, as one might do in a Stravinsky analysis – though I *will* consider it useful to assign tonics to certain diatonic collections, to show how traditional tonal function reappears in this music as an expressive device. But the main reason I label pitch-class collections is to show how their succession creates shapes that resemble "musical idea" and "basic image."

A number of the previous published analyses split Op. 19, No. 2 into three sections: mm. 1–3, the last eighth of m. 3 to first eighth of m. 7, and the second eighth of m. 7 to m. 9.[11] Since all three sections start with the B4-above-G4 dyad and then continue from it in different ways, I will refer to them as A1, A2, and A3. These section labels evoke traditional formal practices – particularly, the baroque and classical binary and ternary forms in which each section begins with a statement of the opening motive or theme. (In these older models, the first section typically presents the motto in the tonic, the second section begins with a dominant transposition, and the third section (if it exists) recapitulates the motto in the tonic; in Op. 19/2, there is no transposition.) But at the same time, Op. 19, No. 2's section labels also recall my form chart of Op. 11, No. 3 in Chapter 2 (pp. 82–83). In that "intuitive" piece, the seemingly unrelated individual sections A through S were gathered together under three large groupings, A1, A2, and A3, because of "interval patterns, textures, rhythms and contours" in sections F and L that "strongly recall the opening five measures, Section A." Again, as was the case with motivic development, in the realm of musical form we have a situation where the "intuitive" piece alludes to a traditional pattern in a more tenuous and vague manner (sections F and L had some of the same unordered pitch-interval and set-class elements and successions, as well as some of the same contours and textures, as A, but never exactly the same pitches), and the Op. 19 piece presents the same pattern in a clearer, more immediately grasped manner (each section begins with the same B4-above-G4 dyad, either repeated, staccato, or both).

---

[11] See, for example, Fred Lerdahl's "grouping structure" in his first analysis of Op. 19, No. 2, Figure 10 on p. 80 of "Atonal Prolongational Structure."

Example 5.1 Schoenberg, Little Piano Piece Op. 19, No. 2, mm. 1–3, section A1.
Copyright © 1913, 1940 by Universal Edition AG Vienna, UE 5069. All rights
reserved. Used by permission of Belmont Music Publishers and Universal Edition

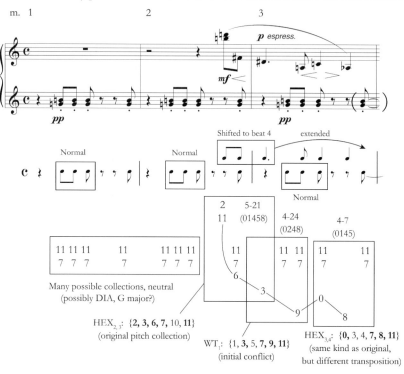

Section A1 of the second Little Piano Piece is illustrated in Example 5.1:
the score on top, a representation of the two-part rhythmic counterpoint
on the middle level, and a pitch-class map, showing the collections to
which each boxed pitch-class set belongs, on the bottom.

The rhythmic level shows that in mm. 1–2, the motto ♫ ♪ (boxed)
appears twice in its initial, normal context: three staccato eighths on
the second and third beats following a quarter rest on the first beat. But
on the fourth beat of m. 2, a second contrapuntal voice starts to vary the
rhythmic motto – shifting it metrically from the second beat to the fourth
beat, and placing it under a slur. These adjustments give rise to an extended
legato rhythmic pattern that grows out of the motto in m. 3, symbolized by
a curved arrow pointing to the right. Meanwhile, the original contrapuntal
strand presents the motto a third time in its original metrical position,
increasing the complexity of the texture.

The pitch-class map also reflects the sense in which mm. 1–3 introduce
a norm and then throw it out of alignment. The B4-above-G4 dyad alone

in mm. 1–2 is relatively neutral regarding which larger pitch collection it represents: we might posit a major scale on G, but that is essentially "guesswork" – a conclusion made in the absence of other evidence.[12] As the first rhythmic transformation appears at the end of m. 2 and beginning of m. 3, it forms a larger collection including both contrapuntal voices, {2, 3, 6, 7, 11}, set-class 5-21 (01458). This is one pitch-class short of the entire hexatonic collection at the specific pitch-class level {2, 3, 6, 7, 10, 11}. (From here on, I will refer to it, using Joseph Straus's nomenclature, as $HEX_{2,3}$.)[13] As the piece progresses, $HEX_{2,3}$ will eventually come to be understood as the "original" or "home" collection, but at this point, it is one of multiple possibilities. (As I pointed out at the beginning of Chapter 1 on p. 2, the hexatonic scale and collection, 6-20 (014589), is one of Schoenberg's favorite atonal pitch elements, since it can be generated by alternating half-steps and minor thirds, and contains multiple half-step-major third subsets.)

At the beginning of m. 3, the point where shifted and original versions of the rhythmic motto together begin to make the texture more complicated, the pitch-class set {3, 7, 9, 11}, 4-24 (0248), emerges. This tetrachord is a subset of a different kind of collection, the "odd" whole-tone scale (which will be referred to as WT1). Here we have the piece's initial pitch conflict, which could be represented in the form of a question: to which larger collection does B4-above-G4, {7, 11}, properly belong, $HEX_{2,3}$ or $WT_1$ (or does it belong to the major scale on G)? The last part of m. 3 answers, provisionally: it suggests a hexatonic home for the G–B dyad, enclosing {7, 11} in {7, 8, 11, 0}, set class 4-7 (0145). But this 4-7 is not part of the *original* hexatonic collection; instead, it belongs to $HEX_{3,4}$, {0, 3, 4, 7, 8, 11}. In the pitch-class realm, as well as the rhythmic one, mm. 1–3 present a norm ($HEX_{2,3}$) and challenge it with $WT_1$, after

---

[12] This situation in the opening measures may remind the reader of Schoenberg's well-known definition of musical idea:

> Every tone which is added to a beginning tone makes the meaning of that tone doubtful. If, for instance, G follows after C, the ear may not be sure whether this expresses C major or G major, or even F major or E minor; and the addition of other tones may or may not clarify this problem. In this manner there is produced a state of unrest, of imbalance, which grows throughout most of the piece, and is enforced further by similar functions of the rhythm.

> (Schoenberg, "New Music, Outmoded Music, Style and Idea" (1946), in *Style and Idea*, pp. 122–23.)

[13] Joseph N. Straus, *Introduction to Post-Tonal Theory*, 4th edn (New York: Norton, 2016), p. 257.

which the music attempts to return to the norm but cannot quite get all the way back ($HEX_{3,4}$).[14]

A different, more extensive, challenge to the norm that leads to a climax is portrayed in Example 5.2, which provides the score, rhythmic counterpoint, and pitch-class map for Section A2. This section begins right away with a variation to the ♩ ♪ rhythmic motto – mm. 3b–4a doubles its first note to a quarter in duration, tying it over the barline from m. 3 to m. 4, another new metrical location for the beginning of the motto. The third eighth note of the same rhythmic motto (on beat 2) slurs to another eighth note, creating a short extension. Together with these more extensive rhythmic adjustments, the motto undergoes a small pitch adjustment. Its third eighth note moves up from B4-above-G4 to E♭5-above-C5, falling back to G-B during the added eighth note of the slurred extension, creating a pitch extension to accompany the rhythmic one. The resulting tetrachord, {7, 11, 0, 3}, set class 4-19 (0148), is a subset of $HEX_{3,4}$, the same collection that had ended Section A1. The carrying-over of $HEX_{3,4}$ from the previous section provides a starting point for more wide-ranging variations in the following measures.

In m. 5, these more extensive variations begin, based on elements first introduced in m. 4. The last two dyads of m. 4's extended motive, C-E♭ slurred back to G-B, repeat beginning on the downbeat of m. 5 in the left hand, and an accented sixteenth-note trichord sounds above the C-E♭. The pitch-class map shows that m. 5's downbeat sonority forms {10, 0, 3, 4, 6}, set-class 5-28 (02368) – a subset of an octatonic collection, specifically $OCT_{0,1}$. Here we have another, different kind of competitor with $HEX_{2,3}$ for the status of "home" collection of the piece, elaborating the conflict that was initiated by $WT_1$ back in m. 3. In the rhythmic counterpoint (middle level of

[14] An analysis of Op. 19, No. 2 that I have not mentioned yet, by Elaine Barkin, captures – using her unique brand of "analytic poetry" – the way in which the A1 section presents its norm, throws it out of alignment by means of a second contrapuntal line, and tries to return to it but cannot get all the way back. Barkin represents the normal pitch and rhythmic state of mm. 1–2 using the text "blinking blips winking wips," and the second contrapuntal line in mm. 2b–3 with a totally different text in a different font, "downswooping undersong," portraying not only its contour but its role as something new that upsets the equilibrium. Entwined with "downswooping undersong," the continuation of the first contrapuntal line in m. 3 is set by the words "wipping wink," showing that even though the pitches and rhythm are the same as mm. 1–2, this music is not quite able to return to the original state: either that found in m. 1, or the one found on the fourth beat of m. 2 and first beat of m. 3 (i.e., the "home" transposition of the hexatonic collection). See Barkin, "(a song of ing)," *In Theory Only* 6/1 (1981): 40. Claire Boge provides a helpful introduction to Barkin's work and uses it as an inspiration for her own analysis of Op. 19, No. 2 in "Poetic Analysis as Part of Analysis Pedagogy," *In Theory Only* 12/3–4 (1992): 47–67.

Example 5.2  Schoenberg, Little Piano Piece Op. 19, No. 2, mm. 3b–7a, section A2.
Used by permission of Belmont Music Publishers and Universal Edition

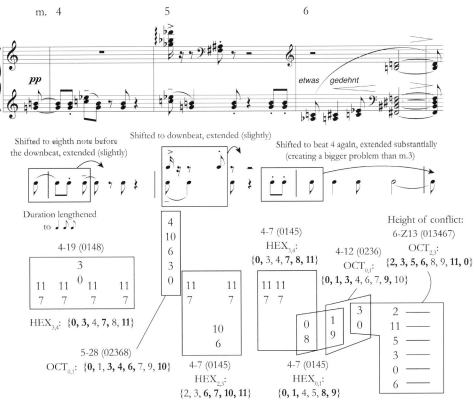

Example 5.2), the octatonic intrusion marks the onset of another ♩ ♪ motive:
since greater emphasis is placed on the first note of this motto by texture and
articulation, the conflicting pitch material is highlighted even more.

After the downbeat, the remainder of the first half of m. 5 is taken up by
the rhythmic motto I have just mentioned and its extension by one eighth
note. Measure 5a, though it is not able to recapture all of the original motto
after the octatonic outbreak on its downbeat, does manage to recall the
repeated B4-above-G4 in the left hand twice, and adds to it another dyad,
A♯3-above-F♯3, forming the tetrachord {6, 7, 10, 11}, set class 4-7 (0145).
This particular chord refers to HEX$_{2,3}$, meaning that the piece's original
large collection also returns, for the first time since mm. 2b–3. We can hear
this moment, perhaps, as putting the piece's pitch structure back in order
before a more serious conflict emerges in mm. 5b and 6.

The more serious conflict begins at the end of m. 5, where a metrical shift
of the ♩ ♪ rhythmic motto to begin on beat 4 is followed by its extension

through m. 6, almost exactly the same rhythmic pattern as we found
in mm. 2b and 3 (creating something like an "end rhyme" for sections
A1 and A2). But the pitch material presented in mm. 5b and 6 is very
different from mm. 2b–3. It begins innocently enough, with the tetrachord
$\{7, 8, 11, 0\}$ created by the rhythmic motto itself, the same set class 4-7
(0145) we had heard at the end of Section A1, in fact, the same specific
pitches, again projecting $HEX_{3,4}$. If the listener continues to group pairs of
dyads together, the next in the chain is $\{8, 9, 0, 1\}$, another transposition of
4-7 that stays within the hexatonic orbit: this time, $HEX_{0,1}$. But from then
on, the hexatonic collection gives way to the same challenger that had
threatened it back in m. 5. $\{9, 0, 1, 3\}$ projects SC 4-12 (0236), a subset of
$OCT_{0,1}$, followed by a six-note chord, $\{11, 0, 2, 3, 5, 6\}$, or SC 6-Z13
(013467), containing all but two notes of $OCT_{2,3}$. The six-note chord
through which the $OCT_{2,3}$ collection wrests control from hexatonic is
emphasized strongly by a *crescendo* into it, Schoenberg's marking *etwas
gedehnt* ("stretched somewhat") and its sheer length: a half-note tied into
an eighth, the longest duration heard thus far. No wonder commentators
on the piece point to the last half of m. 6 as "the climactic moment of the
composition" (DeLio), a "minor-third coup" (Williams), or a "sullying
Crunch" (Barkin).[15] This is the greatest distance that the piece will travel
from its home hexatonic collection, the outer limit of its centrifugal
motion. Indeed, only a single pitch class of the original dyad remains, PC
11, and it is placed an octave lower than usual.

The work of section A3 according to the musical idea model, then,
would be to enable $HEX_{2,3}$ to reassert its control over the piece
after m. 6's octatonic "coup," preferably as a superset of the initial
G-B dyad (which would round the piece off). It does exactly that, but not
before a further challenge from an already-established competitor. The A3
section is illustrated in Example 5.3. Measures 7–8 return to a ***pp*** dynamic,
presenting a stream of fragmentary staccato notes that could be heard
as containing two retrogrades ♪ ♫ of the basic rhythmic motto. In both,
the first eighth sets itself off from the second two by being part of the
descending bass line, while the second and third eighths repeat the central
B4-above-G4 dyad, which returns here after being absent since m. 5. Both
iterations of the retrograde rhythmic motto move its starting point to new
places in the meter: the first to beat 3, the second to the second eighth of
beat 3 (indicated as "3+" in the example).

---

[15] DeLio, "Language and Form in an Early Atonal Composition," 28; Williams, "A View of
Schoenberg's Opus 19, No. 2," 150; Barkin, "(a song of ing)," 40.

Example 5.3 Schoenberg, Little Piano Piece Op. 19, No. 2, mm. 7–9, section A3.
Used by permission of Belmont Music Publishers and Universal Edition

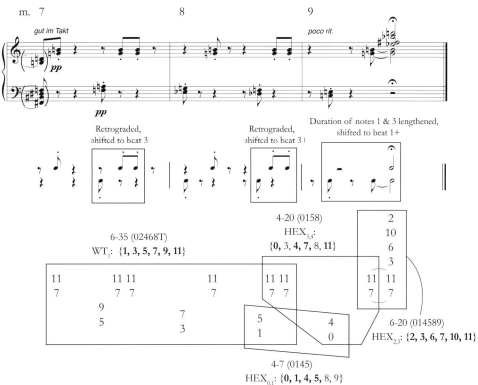

In the pitch-class map, mm. 7–8 are taken up mostly with the complete appearance of one of HEX$_{2,3}$'s two main competitors for "home" collection status: the odd whole-tone scale, which had only partially raised its head in m. 3 as $\{3, 7, 9, 11\}$ – just as in mm. 5–6, a conflict suggested previously is now being elaborated. The listener might wonder at this point whether the whole-tone scale will stage a "coup" similar to that of the octatonic collection in m. 6b, especially because of the prominent whole-step descent (doubled in major thirds) in the left hand in mm. 7–8. The piece averts its final challenge to the hegemony of the hexatonic collection at m. 9, however, with the double resolution by *half-*step from F3-above-D♭3 to E3-above-C3. These last two left-hand dyads form $\{0, 1, 4, 5\}$, set class 4-7, a contiguous subset of the HEX$_{0,1}$ collection. But, even with the return of HEX$_{0,1}$, we have not come all the way "home" quite yet.[16] The bass

---

[16] This is a very different way of explaining the sense of "arrival" that occurs in m. 9 from the strategy of Roy Travis, who asserts that C3 progresses from the repeated G4s of the first eight measures in the conventional, functionally tonal, way; that is, dominant to tonic. But

C-E both follows and precedes iterations of the central G4-B4 dyad, creating {11, 0, 4, 7}, SC 4-20 (0158), a member of HEX$_{3,4}$. Then, on the final held chord that G and B tie into, Schoenberg finally presents all of HEX$_{2,3}$: {2, 3, 6, 7, 10, 11}. The full hexatonic collection at the specific transposition suggested back in mm. 2b–3 regains control at the final cadence, and even encloses the central G-B dyad, as if it were saying to the odd whole-tone scale: "This dyad (and piece) is mine, not yours." There is even a hidden, stretched-out, reference to the basic rhythmic motto at this final resolution: two eighth notes on the afterbeats of beats 1 and 2, followed by the sustained chord on beat 3.

My detailed tour through Op. 19, No. 2 has shown that Schoenberg has not only made traditional procedures of motivic development and musical form more immediately hearable in this piece (once more, I strongly believe that such procedures also existed in the "intuitive" music, but were often hidden beneath the surface), but he has also manifested the problem, elaboration, and solution of the musical idea in a crystal-clear manner. At least four previous scholars seem to recognize the presence of "idea" through the use of language evoking it, like "minor-third coup" (for m. 6) or "fully resolved" (DeLio's description of m. 9).[17] But I hopefully have demonstrated that paying attention to variations of the rhythmic motto, and to the pitch-class collections that the piece travels through as it varies and extends that motto, enables us to hear the idea most clearly.

## Op. 19, No. 3

The next piece in the collection has an interesting relationship to its predecessor – if we pay attention again to large pitch-class collections that contain the various segments of Piece No. 3, we hear what could be described as a "photographic negative" of the musical idea just presented in No. 2. In the final section of Piece No. 3, the HEX$_{3,4}$ collection {0, 3, 4, 7, 8, 11} takes control of the texture in m. 7, but two of its notes, PCS 3 and 7, isolate themselves in m. 8, and suggest E♭ major for a few beats, before the piece moves in a different diatonic direction, cadencing on a diatonic subset with B♭ as its bass. (This reverses the order of hexatonic and non-hexatonic collections from section A3 of the second piece, which had

my approach does give me the advantage of explaining most of the voices of the chord in m. 9b as part of the "goal" collection, rather than as altered and/or added tones. See Travis, "Directed Motion in Schoenberg and Webern," 86.

[17] DeLio, "Language and Form in an Early Atonal Composition," 21.

sustained the odd whole-tone scale for two measures before resolving to HEX$_{2,3}$ around the pedal G-B.)

The suggestion of E♭ major just before the cadence is only one of several passages that briefly veer into functional tonality – as we will see, there is an even stronger reference to D♭ major in mm. 2b–4a. Because of such moments, no doubt, the articles I have found devoted solely to analysis of Op. 19, No. 3 both emphasize strongly its tonal aspects. In 1971, H. H. Stuckenschmidt produced a short analysis where he claimed that the piece ought to be understood as bitonal: B♭ minor with lowered seventh A♭ in the bass, and a succession of tonal chords and keys in the upper voices. (He was no doubt inspired to do so by the two dynamic layers in mm. 1–4; right hand *f*, left hand *pp*.) A few years later (1982), Alex Lubet produced a modified Schenkerian graph that asserted an *Ursatz* in E♭ major spanning the piece. Lubet admitted the presence of numerous pitches that contradict this fundamental structure, but said of them (p. 17): "the precise non-tonal pitch content is not important ... they could be sensitively altered without lessening the value of the work."[18] As we have seen before with tonal analyses of Schoenberg's middle-period music, these two scholars disagree regarding the operative tonality, which calls the effectiveness of their tonal attributions into question. I believe the problem with both Stuckenschmidt's and Lubet's analyses has to do with trying to assign a *single* overarching tonality to the entire piece, where Schoenberg's aesthetic seems to have been impelling him to create a conflict between tonal and non-tonal by placing passages of both kinds one after another. Thus, as I already suggested above, my analytic strategy will be different from theirs: I want to characterize the piece in terms of different collections that succeed one another and contradict one another, in accordance with the musical idea's conflict and elaboration. In certain places where the diatonic collection has the upper hand, for instance D♭ major in mm. 2b–4a, I will attempt to create a middleground Schenkerian graph to show exactly where the functionally harmonic arrangement of the diatonic scale comes into effect, and where it breaks down. But to construct a single *Ursatz* spanning the whole nine measures would seem to go against the whole point of the piece. Tonality in Op. 19, No. 3, as it did in *Erwartung*, serves as a brief expressive device, not as the guarantor of long-range coherence.

---

[18] H. H. Stuckenschmidt, "Opus 19, Nummer 3: Eine Schönberg-Analyse," *Orbis musicae* 1/ 1 (Summer 1971): 88–90; Alex Lubet, "Vestiges of Tonality in a Work of Arnold Schoenberg," *Indiana Theory Review* 5/3 (Spring 1982): 11–21.

Both Stuckenschmidt and Lubet identify Op. 19, No. 3 as a binary form with the two main sections being mm. 1–4 and 5-9.[19] I would prefer to read it as rounded binary, with the B section entering at m. 5, and the ½ A at m. 7. The "rounding" effect in mm. 7–9 is created by those measures focusing in on the same conflict between hexatonic and diatonic that had held the stage in mm. 1–4, after the B section had moved away from hexatonic toward octatonic. Section A, the opening four measures, can be found in Example 5.4. From the rhythmic counterpoint and pitch-class map, we see that the opening measure combines different rhythms, four in total, and overlaps pitch-class sets from three different kinds of collection. The opening chord {11, 1, 2, 6}, set class 4-14 (0237), is a diatonic subset, and without any further information could be interpreted as a first inversion tonic chord in B minor with an added 2nd. But as the F♯ resolves to G and the bass brings in B♭ and E♭, the collection grows to {1, 2, 3, 6, 7, 10, 11}. If we leave off the C♯ on top, the remaining notes create a hexatonic collection, specifically $HEX_{2,3}$, the same transposition that ended Piece No. 2 as its triumphant victor. I believe that the $HEX_{2,3}$ at Piece No. 2's cadence and the one that seems to emerge in the lower voices at the beginning of Piece No. 3 are an audible link between the two pieces, one that may cause the listener to anticipate that the third piece will continue the harmonic logic of its predecessor.

The hexatonic attributions continue in the second half of m. 1, as the right hand *crescendos* into PCS 0 and 4, and the left hand plays <5, 8> below them. These four notes create PC set 4-19 (0148), a member of $HEX_{0,1}$. But if the listener attends instead to the bass notes that we have heard so far, <10, 3, 5, 8>, which is not hard to do since their **pp** dynamic sets them off from the rest of the texture, another diatonic tetrachord comes to the fore: 4-23 (0257). This could be heard (and even sung!) as do-fa-sol-te in B♭ Aeolian, as Stuckenschmidt would have us do; or as sol-do-re-fa in E♭ major, as Lubet would have us do. But I will suggest a different key attribution because of where the bass line is headed in mm. 2–3: la-re-mi-sol in D♭ major. Measure 1 ends with a pickup to the four-note chord on the downbeat of m. 2 – pickup and chord together form {7, 8, 10, 11, 2} or 5-16 (01347), a subset of the $OCT_{1,2}$ collection.

So far, my description of the opening measure and downbeat of m. 2 has characterized it as different tonalities and symmetrical collections jostling with each other for preeminence, an interpretation that is consonant with my reading of Op. 19, No. 2, and describes the listening experience well (for me). What I have not emphasized in my description yet was that all of m. 1 and the downbeat of m. 2 participates in a large *crescendo* (in the right

---

[19] Lubet, "Vestiges of Tonality," 15, Stuckenschmidt, "Opus 19, Nummer 3," 89.

hand) to the second beat of m. 2, which is further emphasized by means of an accent. The rhythmic counterpoint also draws our attention to that same second beat – as Charles Morrison has already shown, in m. 1 there is a latent syncopated rhythm, ♩ ♩ ♩, that is suggested by both the bass line (voice no. 4 in m. 1's rhythmic counterpoint) and the tenor line (voice no. 3). That same rhythm is then brought to the surface in the right hand of m. 2, and the more salient syncopation in turn highlights beat 2 of that measure. Neither the suggested syncopation in m. 1 nor the realized one in m. 2 resolves onto a downbeat in the following measure.[20] The collection that appears on the accented beat in m. 2, the peak of the *crescendo*, is {5, 6, 9, 10, 1}, SC 5-21, a member of $HEX_{1,2}$. This could suggest, then, near the middle of section A, that hexatonic will prove to be the dominant collection once again in the third piece (represented in the musical score part of Example 5.4 by the exclamation "HEX!!" between the staves).

But conflicting information presents itself already with the third beat of m. 2. PC 0 in the bass under the sustained right hand produces {5, 6, 9, 10, 0, 1}, 6-Z19 (013478), a hexachord that was a favorite of Schoenberg's, but not completely hexatonic (the adjacent ordered pc intervals of its prime form are 1, 2, 1, 3, 1). And the fourth beat connects with the downbeat of m. 3 to create the collection {0, 1, 3, 5, 6, 8}, set-class 6-Z25. Like the opening chord, this is again a diatonic subset, but rather than projecting B minor, it encompasses every note of the D♭ major scale save B♭. Its D♭ major quality is especially enhanced by the bass line, which starts at do and proceeds up the scale to mi (the fact that the bass line is still at a softer dynamic than the upper chords gives the D♭ the quality of a partially hidden root of the chord, but a root nonetheless). Thus, even though I argued against the usefulness of Roman numerals for Schoenberg's atonal music (specifically in Op. 11, No. 1) in Chapter 1, in this particular case they illustrate quite well the momentary D♭ major feel of mm. 2b–3. The chord from beat 4 of m. 2 through the downbeat of m 3 would be I add4 with a major 7th.

Roman-numeral analysis is also possible for the next two beats, beats 2 and 3 of m. 3. Below the score in Example 5.4, I indicated them as an inverted major VI chord with flatted fifth and raised seventh (the flatted fifth F♭ is respelled as E and can be found in the bass), and a root-position major II chord with an added 4th and major 7th, similar to the I chord back in m. 2. If the reader is skeptical about these Roman-numeral attributions (no doubt, many will be), I invite him or her to reimagine mm. 2b–4 as the recomposed progression in Example 5.5a (playing both Schoenberg's and my versions at the piano), and ask him- or herself whether my progression leads to its final D♭

---

[20] Morrison, "Syncopation as Motive in Schoenberg's Op. 19," 82.

Example 5.5a  Schoenberg, Little Piano Piece Op. 19, No. 3, mm. 2b–4 reimagined as a tonal progression

chord convincingly. The first three chords of my recomposition are more-or-less the same as Schoenberg's, though I put the second chord in root position.

But, of course, Schoenberg did not present the final two chords of Example 5.5a in anything like the form I gave them. The A♭2 does indeed appear in the bass on the last eighth of m. 3, but it is surrounded not by the pitches of the dominant seventh, instead by {8, 9, 10, 11, 0}, SC 5-1, a chromatic subset. (Contiguous subsets of the chromatic scale will be represented as "CHROM" on my pitch-class maps.) And that low A♭, rather than yielding to D♭ on the downbeat of m. 4, instead sustains into the downbeat, and then is followed by PCs 4, 0, and 10, the first of which seems to take us out of the realm of D♭ major. Meanwhile, a D♭ triad does appear in the upper voices on the downbeat of m. 4, but the expected major tonic triad alters itself to an augmented one, changing the nascent tonal progression's resolution to another forward-pointing sonority. The situation is pictured well by Example 5.5b, a Schenkerian analysis of mm. 2b–4 as they actually appear. (The purpose of this graph, just like the graphs of Op. 2, No. 2 in Chapter 1, is to show to what extent, and in which voices, a traditional contrapuntal structure appears to draw our ears toward D♭, and also how that structure disappears.)

In my graph, most everything is explainable as functionally tonal outer voices with added dissonances in the inner voices (a situation remarkably similar to my analysis of "Jesus bettelt" in Chapter 1) until we reach the last three eighth notes in the tenor voice of m. 3. Those notes are placed in a bracket and given a question mark, because, as I mentioned above, they surround A♭ with a chromatic subset, 5-1, rather than a dominant seventh chord. And the final three bass notes of m. 4 get a similar treatment: the first two of them add PCS 4 and 0 to the augmented triad on the downbeat of m. 4, PCS {1, 5, 9}, and the PC 8 in the bass sustaining into m. 4. All together, these replace the failed functional progression in D♭ with {0, 1, 4, 5, 8, 9}, $HEX_{0,1}$. The last bass note, PC 10, expands the set-class out to 7-21 (0124589).

Example 5.5b  Schoenberg, Little Piano Piece Op. 19, No. 3, Schenkerian graph of mm. 2b–4

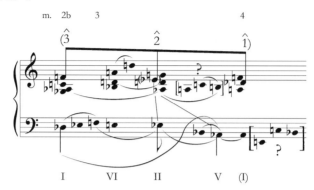

To summarize, the A section of Op. 19, No. 3 presents a conflict between collections: in which diatonic, hexatonic, and octatonic jostle with each other for preeminence in mm. 1–2a, then hexatonic seems to have the upper hand on the second beat of m. 2, only to be supplanted by D♭ major for four beats, followed by hexatonic taking back control again at the cadence in m. 4. The middle section, B, is shown in Example 5.6.

The score shows that this two-measure phrase grows out of the same B4-above-G4 dyad that began the second piece, but it soon gives way to a mixture of collections in the same way that the B minor add 2 chord had in section A. M. 5 produces two members of set class 4-4, {6, 7, 8, 11} spanning beat 2 in both hands, and {9, 0, 1, 2} on the first eighth of beat 4. These represent the chromatic collection. Meanwhile, the chords on the first eighth of beat 3 and the downbeat of m. 6 are both members of set class 5-19 (01367). The first of these 5-19s belongs to $OCT_{0,1}$ and the second to $OCT_{2,3}$. Another segment of $OCT_{2,3}$ can be found in the right hand spanning beat 4, {0, 2, 5, 11} or set class 4-13 (0136). Finally, two other passages besides the opening G-B dyad suggest diatonic readings. First is the bass line in m. 5, which could be heard as sol-ti-do in D♭ major, the most prominent diatonic element in the preceding A section. In addition, the right hand spanning beat 3 produces {9, 11, 3, 4} or set class 4-16, belonging to the E major scale.

The opening of B uses the same strategy as the beginning of A: different kinds of collection jostle with each other for the listener's attention. And like A, the latter part of B then narrows down to presenting one collection after another. But unlike A, the hexatonic collection is completely absent from the succession in m. 6. As I mentioned already, the right-hand 4-13 on beat 4 of m. 5 and the 5-19 chord on the downbeat of m. 6 are both subsets of $OCT_{2,3}$. Together, they form {8, 9, 11, 0, 2, 3, 5}, a member of set-class 7-31 (0134679), the only seven-note octatonic set class, thus a clear sign of the

Example 5.6  Schoenberg, Little Piano Piece Op. 19, No. 3, mm. 5–6, section B.
Used by permission of Belmont Music Publishers and Universal Edition

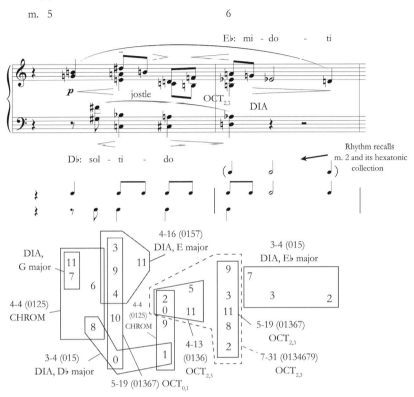

octatonic quality of the passage. After $OCT_{2,3}$ takes over the texture in mm.
5b and 6a, the final three notes of the phrase form {2, 3, 7}, set class 3-4 (015),
which belongs to the E♭ major scale. The absence of the hexatonic collection
from mm. 5 and 6 creates a similar situation to the A2 section in Piece No. 2,
where octatonic came to the forefront and hexatonic was temporarily overcome by it. It is at least possible that Piece No. 3 is here setting up a strong
expectation for the hexatonic collection to return and take control of the
texture at the final cadence, just as it had in the previous piece. The return of
the syncopated rhythm ♩♩ ♩ in m. 6, which had highlighted $HEX_{1,2}$ when it
appeared back in m. 2, only strengthens this sense of anticipation.

But the ½ A section turns out in a different way; it is illustrated in
Example 5.7.

The pitch-class map shows that this section indeed begins with a full
hexatonic collection – $HEX_{3,4}$, which spans measure 7. But this strong
assertion of HEX, unlike the one in Piece No. 2, does not bring the piece to
a convincing close, tying up its loose ends. (Morrison has pointed out

Example 5.7  Schoenberg, Little Piano Piece Op. 19, No. 3, mm. 7–9, section ½ A.
Used by permission of Belmont Music Publishers and Universal Edition

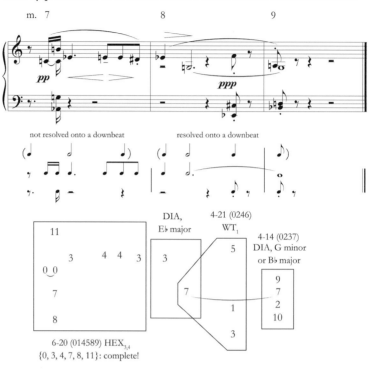

that m. 7 contains yet another unresolved ♩♩ ♩ syncopation, which also contributes to this sense of incompletion.[21]) Instead, pitch classes 3 and 7 continue into m. 8, sounding by themselves for three beats, and allowing the ear to wander from the $HEX_{3,4}$ sound world to that of the E♭ major tonic triad. The effect is reminiscent of the last section of Piece No. 2, where G4-B4, {7, 11}, were surrounded first by members of the odd whole-tone scale in mm. 7–8, then found their proper home in $HEX_{2,3}$ in m. 9. But here in Piece No. 3, the sustained pedal point is drawn away from a hexatonic collection to a major one, creating a diametrically opposed situation to Piece No. 2's cadence. And, as the rest of the pitch-class map shows, E♭ major is not the final resting point: the fourth beat of m. 8 surrounds PCS 3 and 7 with 1 and 5, creating a momentary segment of the odd whole-tone scale, 4-21 (0246). The final chord in m. 9 is, as others have noted, a transposition down a major third from the initial chord; also set class 4-14 (0237), perhaps suggesting a G minor add 2 chord in first inversion, or

---

[21]  Ibid., 84.

Example 5.8  Progressions of collections in Schoenberg, Op. 19, Nos. 2 and 3

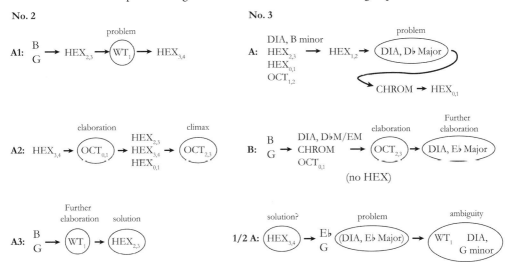

possibly a root-position B♭ triad with added 6th and major 7th. Whatever the tonal attribution, it seems clear that the ½ A section can be characterized as moving from hexatonic to diatonic, then from whole tone to an ambiguous diatonic cadence, though the final cadence does finally resolve the ♩♩ ♩ syncopation onto a downbeat at m. 9.

As I mentioned in my introduction to Piece No. 3, keeping track of the large collections that this piece passes through, as we have just done, reveals a design that parallels that of Piece No. 2 in certain places, but on the whole can be understood as a negative image of the second piece's musical idea. My next example, 5.8, provides a chart that abstracts the progressions of collections from both pieces, lining up their corresponding sections horizontally.

We can see from the example that the A1 section of Op. 19, No. 2 and the A section of Op. 19, No. 3 follow similar patterns, both presenting the "home" collection, $HEX_{2,3}$, at or near the beginning, introducing a conflict near the end of the section ($WT_1$ in piece 2, D♭ major in piece 3), and allowing hexatonic to return at section's end (but in a different transposition from $HEX_{2,3}$). The A section of Piece No. 3 differs in that it starts from a complex of collections, instead of the simple G-B dyad of the second piece. Nevertheless, both introductory sections present the problem, the first stage of the musical idea.

The two middle sections, A2 in Piece No. 2 and B in Piece No. 3, present a prominent octatonic collection, in both cases $OCT_{2,3}$, as an elaboration or climax of the conflict with the home hexatonic collection. Again, the third piece is different in that the $OCT_{2,3}$ emerges out of a complex of collections (like that of the same piece's A section). But the main difference between the second and third pieces is that the hexatonic collection does not sound at all in the middle section of the latter, so that the sense of the home collection being obscured is even stronger. Finally, it is in the third section where Op. 19, No. 3 most clearly seems to offer a "photographic negative" of its predecessor – in the second piece, $HEX_{2,3}$ had appeared at the closing cadence after a final challenge from $WT_1$, to take ownership of the G-B ostinato away from the whole-tone collection and claim the piece for itself. But in Op. 19, No. 3, $HEX_{3,4}$ *opens* the third section, then is supplanted by E♭ major, which takes ownership of E♭ and G away from *it* – a reversal of the second piece's solution. The ambiguity continues into the final cadence, as E♭ major is followed by $WT_1$ and a tonal chord that could belong to either G minor or B♭ major.

## Op. 19, No. 6

Though we will continue to track the progress of hexatonic, diatonic, and other collections through the final piece of Op. 19, it is important at the outset to set it apart from the other two with respect to its large-scale pattern. Op. 19, No. 6, as many have remarked, is Schoenberg's depiction of his friend and benefactor Gustav Mahler's funeral in May 1911, and as such it not only presents an (unresolved) musical idea, but, even more importantly, also portrays a visual and aural image associated with what had to have been a devastating experience for the composer, as a person and as a musician. This visual and aural image represents not only Schoenberg's grief at Mahler's death, but also what appears to be his regret at being ordered by the "Supreme Commander" onto a "harder road" than the one Mahler walked (even though this book maintains the position throughout that there was, and is, no inherent musical reason for regret at Schoenberg's turn to atonality).[22] We can put the sixth piece in the "basic image" category, therefore. In a way, it also presents some of the functions of sonata form, in an extremely abbreviated manner.

Similar to Op. 19, No. 2, Piece No. 6 has been a favorite target for scholars, and there are published analyses putting forth a wide variety of perspectives – sometimes, more than one perspective from the same author. In a book chapter, David Lewin approaches the piece from a rhythmic viewpoint – identifying places in mm. 1–6 where the same duration between attack points occurs more than once, creating "peaks,"

---

[22] Arnold Schoenberg, "On revient toujours" (1948), in *Style and Idea*, p. 109.

and suggesting the effect of such patterns on the sense of meter.[23] Two more Lewin articles use isographic networks of transformations between different kinds of nodal elements (such as individual pitch classes, pitch-class groups, and transformations themselves) to illustrate a number of similar and recursive pitch-class structures throughout piece No. 6.[24] Allen Forte visited the piece twice, once in his early article "Context and Continuity" to comment on the balance of its final measure in its associations with G4 and B4, and a second time in *The Structure of Atonal Music* to illustrate the value of constructing a "Kh table" to pinpoint its "reciprocal complement relations," pairs of complement-related set classes that form subsets and supersets between them.[25]

Other authors argue for tonal readings of the piece. Hugo Leichtentritt claims that its principal melody "is written in pure and simple E major," and explains most of the important chords as either functional in that key or as half-step voice leadings from E major tonic triads. Kenneth Hicken, in a way similar to his Op. 19, No. 2 analysis mentioned above, creates a Roman-numeral progression, with substantial numbers of added notes, beginning in C major and ending with a bitonal construction melding D major and A♭ major.[26] Hicken and Leichtentritt attribute the same music to different keys (as was the case with the tonal analyses of Op. 19, No. 3), which indicates to me, again, that it may not be advisable to subject the whole piece to a single tonality or even a single modulation from one to two other keys. I will show in the next few pages that Piece No. 6 does indeed reach up toward E major for a brief moment, a crucial feature of both its musical idea and its basic image, but that moment is juxtaposed with (and conflicts with) other collections that are diatonic but non-functional, as well as whole-tone and hexatonic segments. The effect of conflict between functional diatonic and other kinds of collections is similar to what we heard in Op. 19, No. 3.

[23]  David Lewin, "Some Investigations into Foreground Rhythmic and Metric Patterning," in *Music Theory: Special Topics*, ed. Richmond Browne (New York: Academic Press, 1981), pp. 110–17.

[24]  Lewin, "Transformational Techniques in Atonal and Other Music Theories," *Perspectives of New Music* 21/1–2 (Autumn 1982–Summer 1983): 335–48; idem, "Klumpenhouwer Networks and Some Isographies that Involve Them," *Music Theory Spectrum* 12/1 (Spring 1990): 83–87.

[25]  Allen Forte, "Context and Continuity in an Atonal Work," 81–82; idem, *The Structure of Atonal Music*, pp. 96–100.

[26]  Hugo Leichtentritt, *Musical Form* (Cambridge, MA: Harvard University Press, 1951), pp. 444–45; Kenneth Hicken, "Tonal Organization in Schoenberg's Six Little Piano Pieces," 136–46.

Finally, as was the case with Op. 19, No. 2, there are numerous analyses of the sixth piece that create chronological narratives that span it. Some of them interpret the succession of musical elements in terms of a program, and others allow the musical narrative to stand for itself. In the second category, Jonathan Dunsby and Arnold Whittall, like Lewin and Forte, present multiple accounts from different perspectives (which, however, invariably describe the entire piece from beginning to end). They focus successively on functional tonal relations, vertically symmetrical interval patterns, aggregate completion, pitch-class set content, and "motive," which is considered first from a wide perspective including pitch, intervallic, rhythmic, and dynamic features, and then more narrowly, limited to relations between groups of pitch classes.[27] Robert Cogan and Pozzi Escot trace the progression of harmonic and melodic "fields" through the piece, showing that the melodic fields continually push downward in register while the harmonic ones descend, then pull themselves back up to the original register at the end. And Elaine Barkin devotes one of her analytic poems, "Play it AS it Lays," to the piece, as well as a slightly more technical reading in a separate publication. Barkin's analyses bring into relief a variety of important pitch-class features, such as the fact that the sonority in m. 8 contains trichords of all twelve types, or the emphasis on the wholetone collection at mm. 5b–6. She combines these with detailed descriptions of the tactile sensations of performing the piece.[28]

The analyses of the sixth Little Piano Piece that extrapolate a program of some sort from the circumstances under which Schoenberg composed it agree that the opening pair of chords that repeat twice in mm. 2–6 and return in m. 9 represent tolling bells at Mahler's funeral. Likewise, the melodic intrusions in mm. 3b–4, 5b–6, 7, 8, and at the end of 9 are generally understood as either human or divine utterances responding to the bells and to Mahler's death. But within those limits, authors attempt a variety of hermeneutic approaches. Eric McKee interprets the "bell" chords as signifying Mahler's death, identifying the composer by means of the typical "mildly dissonant" diatonic sonorities of his music. The melodic insertions at mm. 3b–4 and 5b–6, because of their association

---

[27] Dunsby and Whittall, *Music Analysis in Theory and Practice*, pp. 116–20, 126–30, 140–41, and 158–61.

[28] Robert Cogan and Pozzi Escot, *Sonic Design* (Englewood Cliffs, NJ: Prentice-Hall, 1976), pp. 49–59; Elaine Barkin, "Play it AS it Lays," *Perspectives of New Music* 17/2 (Spring–Summer 1979): 17–24; eadem, Untitled essay (on Schoenberg's Op. 19, No. 6), *In Theory Only* 4/8 (February–March 1979): 18–26. As was the case with "(a song of ing)," Claire Boge provides a helpful introduction to Barkin's Op. 19/6 analyses in "Poetic Analysis as Part of Analysis Pedagogy."

with the key of E major, historically understood as a key of "spirituality," portray the divine presence that surrounds Mahler (registrally, from above as well as below). The isolated single line at m. 7 stands for Mahler's voice (and, by extension, Schoenberg's own voice) calling out to God for salvation, and the sonority of m. 8 is God's affirmative response, binding together previous elements of the piece and experience under the protection of the E major and minor collections. Finally, m. 9 marks Mahler's final expiration with its descent to A♭.[29]

This more positive reading of the piece is contrasted by those of Albrecht von Massow and David Lewin, who see in it a portrayal of Mahler's death from Schoenberg's perspective only, and von Massow takes that interpretation one step further by allowing Mahler's death to serve as a metaphor for the death of tonality (in Schoenberg's music, at least). Massow understands the two bell chords of mm. 1–2 as signifying two different musical styles: the first, a tonal sonority in a higher register, represents the ideal of tonal music as composed by Mahler, while the second, quartal, sonority in a lower register represents the darker reality of Schoenberg's atonal music. The melodic insertions throughout the piece then are heard as Schoenberg's expressions of pain and frustration at no longer being able to reach Mahler's tonal ideal (the first one, with its ascent to high E that is then turned back to D♯, fits von Massow's reading particularly well).[30] As for Lewin, he limits his suggestions about the program of Piece No. 6 to a single footnote in his article on "Transformational Techniques," but in that limited space he sketches out an interpretation that has the first six measures setting the stage (again, with tolling bells at Mahler's funeral) for Schoenberg's ruminations on Mahler in the remainder of the piece. M. 7 in particular contains a quote from the beginning of the first movement of Beethoven's Eroica Symphony, D–C♯–D–E♭, possibly alluding to Schoenberg's view of Mahler as a hero (or, alternatively, a reminiscence of Mahler conducting the piece).[31]

My own reading of the piece is closest to von Massow's, since I want to interpret it as a visual and aural image that at the same time manifests an unresolved musical idea. The aural image consists of the two "bells" that serve as metaphors for Mahler's tonality and Schoenberg's failing attempts to imitate it, as von Massow suggested, though I prefer to read the second, quartal, bell as another diatonic entity that cancels out the tonal aspirations

---

[29] Eric McKee, "On the Death of Mahler: Schoenberg's Op. 19, No. 6," *Theory and Practice* 30 (2005): 121–51.

[30] Albrecht von Massow, "Abschied und Neuorientierung – Schönbergs Klavierstück op. 19, 6," *Archiv für Musikwissenschaft* 50/2 (1993): 187–95.

[31] David Lewin, "Transformational Techniques in Atonal and Other Music Theories," p. 369, fn16.

of the first bell, rather than an inherently atonal sound. The melodic interpolations then represent Schoenberg's frustrated attempts to follow Mahler's path that lead ultimately to quiet, low-register despair. These begin with an attempt to reach up to E major in mm. 3b–4 but being turned back, followed by, in turn and in successively lower registers, a $WT_0$ utterance in mm. 5b–6, a $HEX_{2,3}$ trichord utterance in m. 7, a summary of all that has gone before in m. 8 (including quartal, whole-tone, and hexatonic components), and a final cadence that restates the still-unresolved problem, followed by a despairing $WT_0$ drop into the piece's lowest register. The overall descending contour of the melodic insertions that Cogan and Escot remarked on serve as a visual image of Schoenberg reaching up in the direction of tonality, being pushed back down, and then falling further from his goal, finally abandoning it.

Most previous analyses lay out the form of the piece as varied repetition of the two opening chords in mm. 1–6, contrasting music in mm. 7–8, and a return to the original material in m. 9 – McKee's description of it as A A B A is representative.[32] My form chart, Example 5.9, tweaks this usual ternary model just a little, to show that Op. 19, no. 6's form, surprisingly, parallels (and looks forward to?) a later, much longer piece, the Piano Piece Op. 33a.

In my book on Schoenberg's twelve-tone music I described Op. 33a as a sonata with two variations on the first theme, a shorter *cantabile* second theme, a development that fragments and recombines material from the exposition, and a substantially truncated recapitulation.[33] In Op. 19, No. 6 the same functions appear in miniature: mm. 2b–4a and 4b–6 can be heard as variations of mm. 0–2a, m. 7 creates a "tenderly expressed" contrast in terms of pitch structure as well as texture, m. 8 fragments and recombines material from all four of the sections preceding it, and finally m. 9 brings back small segments, echoes, one might say, of both mm. 1–6 and m. 7. I am not claiming that Op. 19, No. 6 "is" a sonata movement in any sense: the very nature of its program prevents it from making use of the key relationships that define sonata form, or anything corresponding to them. But I find it interesting that its sections fulfill some of the functions of the parts of a sonata form, and in the correct order – again, this seems to be part of Schoenberg's attempt in the Op. 19 collection to make his musical forms more immediate and easy to grasp than the forms of the "intuitive" pieces, like *Erwartung* or Op. 11, No. 3, that preceded it. The miniature sonata form could also be a way to memorialize Mahler.

---

[32]  McKee, "On the Death of Mahler," 123.

[33]  Boss, *Schoenberg's Twelve-Tone Music: Symmetry and the Musical Idea*, ch. 5.

Example 5.9  Schoenberg, Little Piano Piece Op. 19, No. 6, form chart

| Measures | 0–2a | 2b–4a | 4b–6 | 7 | 8 | 9 |
|---|---|---|---|---|---|---|
| Section | **A** | **A1** | **A2** | **B** | **C** | **A3** |
| Sonata equivalent | exposition first theme | 1st variation | 2nd variation | second theme | development | recapitulation |
| Stages of the musical idea and aural/ visual images | *Problem presented:* Mahler's tonality (1st chord in RH) is neutralized by Schoenberg's quartal chord in LH | *Problem repeated and elaborated:* the RH chord attempts to resolve up as V7 to EM, but is turned back down to D♯6 | *Problem repeated again and elaborated further:* through the upward continuation of the LH chord's T5 cycle by a third chord in the RH in m. 5b, and through a $WT_0$ subset in the LH in mm. 5b-6, taking us down further from the EM "ideal" | A personal, "tender," response from Schoenberg, reviewing the fall from EM functionality in sections A1 and A2, and adding a characteristic "atonal" $HEX_{2,3}$ subset, continuing the motion down and away from E major | Fragments of all the A and B sections are recombined in new ways: a $WT_0$ chord, a quartal chord, a hexatonic subset, and E -D♯ (representing the failed attempt to reach E major) | Brief, truncated echoes of both 1st and 2nd themes; 1st theme's problem is unchanged except for closer durational distance between the chords. 2nd theme fragment disappears into the piece's lowest register |

The bottom row on Example 5.9 summarizes the stages of the unresolved musical idea in each section, as well as those of the piece's visual and aural images. I will elaborate these different stages now, as I describe each section in more detail. Example 5.10 illustrates the A and A1 sections, mm. 0–4a.

The A section in mm. 0–2a introduces the piece's signature "bell chords," 3-7 (025) and 3-9 (027). These are both diatonic subsets, of the E major and C major collections respectively, so von Massow's claim that the first represents tonality and the second atonality seems a little too strong. However, the first chord does include three notes of the dominant $\frac{4}{2}$ chord in E major (it lacks only the leading tone D♯), so it could be heard as having a more pronounced functional-tonal tendency than the second, a perfect fourth chord on the fifth scale degree of C major. Whether the second chord is atonal or tonal in itself, von Massow is correct in saying that it "paralyzes the tonal effect of the first chord": it neutralizes the incomplete E major V7's tendency to resolve by countering with three notes that are non-diatonic in that key.[34] Together, the two chords produce 6-Z12 (012467), a chromatic subset that does not pull toward any tonic. In this way, the piece's main problem is

---

[34] Von Massow, "Abscheid und Neuorientierung," 189.

Example 5.10 Schoenberg, Little Piano Piece Op. 19, No. 6, mm. 0–5a, sections A and A1.

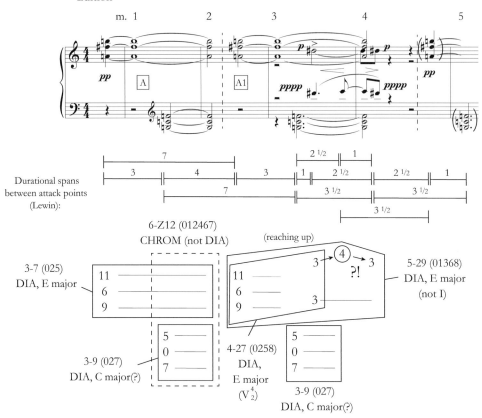

introduced – the right-hand bell creates an urge to resolve in E major that the left-hand bell denies. We could say that Schoenberg is thwarted here in his attempt to follow in the footsteps of Mahler, the tonal composer.

The A1 section, mm. 2b–4a, elaborates this problem and at the same time introduces the piece's main visual image, of Schoenberg reaching up toward the tonic in E major, but being denied and then sinking back down. The bell chords repeat at the same distance, three quarter notes, but on the second half note of m. 3, the upper register intensifies the urge of the first chord {B, F♯, A} to resolve as $V_2^4$ by adding the missing leading tone D♯ to it – in two octaves. The upper D♯6 then climbs quietly (starting **pppp**) to E6, which seems momentarily to provide its tonal resolution: except that the right-hand chord does not change from $V_2^4$ underneath (even the D♯5 sustains), the problematic {G, C, F} is still hanging on in the left hand, and the E6 lasts only one quarter before falling back down to D♯6. The pitch-class set analysis in Example 5.10 represents the attempted resolution with an upward arrow between {3, 6, 9, 11} and the desired {4}, and the denial of that resolution with a downward arrow and the symbols "?!".[35]

Meanwhile, a rhythmic feature of mm. 3–4 also contributes to the strong sense of unfulfilled expectation: as David Lewin describes, there is a change in the most common durations between attack points.[36] Up until the second quarter of m. 3, all the durations between attacks were three, four, or seven quarters long. Since they both appear twice (they "peak" in Lewin's termi-nology), the durations of 3 and 7 quarters are most salient and define a meter that could be described as 3/4 with rubato (lengthening) in mm. 1b–2a. But with the second quarter of m. 3, other distances begin to replace 3 and 7 as standard: particularly 2½ and 3½ quarters, which each appear three times as inter-attack durations between the second quarter of m. 3 and the downbeat of m. 5 (the score and durational graph of Example 5.10 both extend into the beginning of section A2, m. 5, to show this). Thus, at the same time the pitches in the upper register attempt to resolve in E major and are turned back, the rhythms also express the sense of breaking an estab-lished pattern and denying an expectation. Here is another good example of "similar functions of the rhythm" reinforcing the stage of the musical idea – in this case, elaboration of the problem – expressed by the pitches.[37]

In Section A2, mm. 4b–6, shown in Example 5.11, the problem is elaborated even further. (In Jonathan Dunsby and Arnold Whittall's first motivic analysis of Op. 19, No. 6, they also refer to mm. 2b–4a as A1 and 4b–6 as A2; and describe them respectively as "varied repeat of A" and "modified repeat of A1," depicting the incremental elaboration of these sections in a similar way to what I do.)[38]

In mm. 4b–5, the right-hand bell chord's tendency to resolve as V$^4_2$ to E is cut back to what it was able to do in section A (sustain itself briefly without a leading tone), and the left-hand quartal chord is given more license to develop in *its* own unique way, through transpositions up and down by its main adjacent interval, the perfect fourth. The collection {0, 5, 7} leaps up one perfect fourth to {5, 10, 0} on the second half note of m. 5, and then

---

[35] A number of features in my account of mm. 3b–4; my reading of D♯5 and D♯6 as completing V$^4_2$ in E major, of E6 as momentarily resolving that dominant, and of {G, C, F} as contradicting the E major attribution, line up not only with Albrecht von Massow's reading, but with Elaine Barkin's "archaic" interpretation, posited in her untitled essay on Op. 19/6, 25.

[36] Lewin, "Some Investigations into Foreground Rhythmic and Metric Patterning."

[37] Schoenberg, "New Music, Outmoded Music, Style and Idea," p. 123.

[38] Jonathan Dunsby and Arnold Whittall, *Music Analysis in Theory and Practice*, p. 159.

Example 5.11  Schoenberg, Little Piano Piece Op. 19, No. 6, mm. 4b–6, section A2. Used by permission of Belmont Music Publishers and Universal Edition

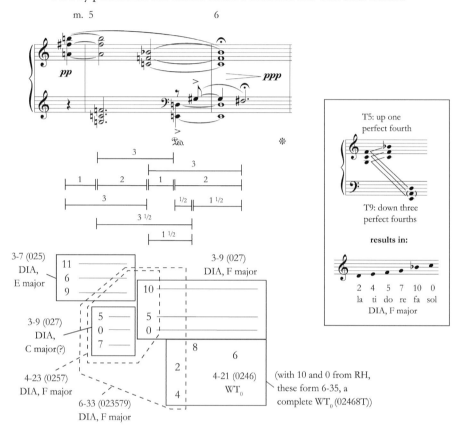

down to {2, 4} on the fourth quarter note, which can be heard as an incomplete {9, 2, 4}; that is, a T9 transposition, or down three perfect fourths in pitch space. (A schematic focusing on these transpositions can be found in the sidebar at the right side of Example 5.11.) Von Massow and Lewin both call attention to an ongoing pattern of T5 transpositions in the piece that begins at this point, and von Massow refers to it as "extending into an atonal harmonic space."[39] But what results from the T5 transpositions up and down are actually more diatonic subsets; 4-23 (0257) when {5, 10, 0} is added to {0, 5, 7}, and the diatonic hexachord 6-33 (023579) when PCS 2 and 4 are added. It would be more accurate to refer to this music as

---

[39]  Von Massow, "Abschied und Neuorientierung," 190. Lewin mentions the importance of T5 transpositions that "extend chains of fourths up and down" in "Transformational Techniques in Atonal and Other Music Theories," 342.

extending into an F major collection, where the tonic is not emphasized. Nevertheless, von Massow rightly recognizes that the way the left-hand bell chord develops in Op. 19, No. 6 is very different from the way the right-hand bell chord had tried to continue itself – into non-functional diatonicism (commonly called pandiatonicism) rather than functional tonality. This constitutes a step away from (as well as registrally down from) mm. 3–4's attempt to reach up to tonic in E major.

The D3-above-E2 dyad on the fourth quarter of m. 5 then initiates a further step away, the first time in this piece that the music in one or the other register, upper or lower, has ventured away from diatonicism. (There had been chromaticism *between* the registers and hands of the pianist from the piece's beginning.) E2 and D3 continue into an accented G♯3 that falls, appoggiatura-like, into an F♯3 at the section's end. These four pitch classes produce set class 4-21(0246), a contiguous subset of $WT_0$, the first time the whole-tone collection appears in Piece No. 6. And, since the pianist is directed to press the sustain pedal down on the fourth quarter of m. 5, these four notes mingle with the sustained right-hand notes of mm. 5b–6. Two of those right-hand notes, PCS 10 and 0, combine with {2, 4, 6, 8} to fill out the entire $WT_0$ collection, and the single odd note, the sustained F4, cannot completely overcome the general whole-tone quality of the passage.

Thus both the bell chords and the melodic insertion in section A2 move further away from, and further down from, the piece's early attempt at resolution up to E major – the bell chords into pandiatonicism and the melodic insertion into a low-register whole-tone realm. Rhythmically, the same effect of moving away from or contradicting an expected outcome is projected by the durations between attack points, similar to what we heard in section A1. M. 4b and the first part of m. 5 contain mostly durations in whole quarters, with an emphasis on the 3-quarter unit that began the piece (and can be heard as its standard). But right at that point where G♯3 turns the pitch-class content from quartal into whole tone, the second eighth of beat 4 in m. 5, the inter-attack durations turn mostly into fractions, ½, 1½, and 3½, the last of which also served as one of the main conflicting durations in section A1. The accent mark on the G♯3 could signify its role as a turning point in both the pitch and the rhythmic realms.

Example 5.12 illustrates both the B and C sections, the main contrasting sections of Op. 19, No. 6. (Again, Dunsby and Whittall in their earlier analysis assign these sections the same formal labels as I do, and their descriptions emphasize the contrasting nature of B and the idea that C brings together various elements from previous music.)[40]

---

[40] Dunsby and Whittall, *Music Analysis in Theory and Practice*, p. 159.

Example 5.12 Schoenberg, Little Piano Piece Op. 19, No. 6, mm. 7–8, sections B and C. Used by permission of Belmont Music Publishers and Universal Edition

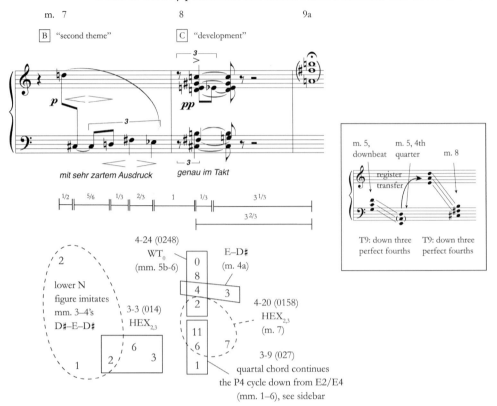

The B section, m. 7, creates contrast with mm. 1–6 in quite a few ways. The bells disappear and the texture reduces to a single line "with very tender expression," which has caused interpreters to understand m. 7 as a human response to the bells, either Mahler's voice praying audibly (McKee) or Schoenberg's ruminations (Lewin and von Massow).[41] The durations between attacks, because of the triplet in the second half of the measure, mostly shift from multiples of quarters or eighths to divisions of the quarter note into thirds and sixths (which continue on into section C). And finally, the pitch-class collection that comes to the fore, if we read C♯3 as a lower neighbor note, is {2, 3, 6}, set class 3-3 (014), a subset of HEX$_{2,3}$. Though this set and large collection are both favorites of Schoenberg (HEX$_{2,3}$ was

[41] McKee, "On the Death of Mahler," 138–40; Lewin, "Transformational Techniques," p. 369, fn 16; von Massow, "Abschied und Neuorientierung," 192.

the "victorious" collection at the final cadence of Op. 19, No. 2), this is their initial appearance in the sixth piece. On the other hand, one feature of m. 7 that connects it to the preceding music is the <D5, C♯3, D3> motive at the beginning. Von Massow explains this lower-neighbor figure as an inversion of the D♯6–E6–D♯6 upper neighbor in mm. 3–4.[42]

My preference, different from previous readings, is to hear m. 7 as a *cantabile* "second theme" in which Schoenberg responds vocally (not just in his mind) to the musical circumstances of mm. 1–6, expressing, first, his sorrow over Mahler's passing and second, his frustration at his inability to follow in Mahler's footsteps as a tonal composer – which to him are two sides of the same coin. He reviews his failed attempt to reach up to E major and his subsequent fall into pandiatonicism and whole-tone territory in the precipitous descent from D5 to C♯3 and the subsequent passage in $HEX_{2,3}$, which, like $WT_0$, is a more dissonant collection located far below the desired E major. Even more than $WT_0$, $HEX_{2,3}$ is a collection that has been defined as native to Schoenberg, associated with "home," earlier in Op. 19 (in the second piece) – so that this fall from tonality is portrayed as falling into a style more appropriate for him.

If m. 7, section B, can be heard as a drastically reduced *cantabile* theme where Schoenberg reviews his plight in a tender song, then m. 8, section C, which takes fragments from all of the previous sections and combines them in new ways, can be understood as an even more severely attenuated development section. The pitch-class map at the bottom center of Example 5.12 identifies the various chords and bits of melody that refer to previous music: m. 8's right-hand chord, {0, 2, 4, 8}, 4-24 (0248), recalls the $WT_0$ music that had ended section A2 in mm. 5b–6. The first left-hand chord, {11, 1, 6} or 3-9 (027), meanwhile, is voiced as yet another perfect fourth chord. Given as <C♯3, F♯3, B3> from bottom to top, this chord is a T9 transposition from the <E2, (A2), D3> chord on the fourth quarter of m. 5. This means that, if we imagine a two-octave register transfer up in pitch space following that m. 5 fourth-quarter chord to <E4, (A4), D5>, <C♯3, F♯3, B3> could be understood as another transposition down three perfect fourths from it, just as the original <E2, (A2), D3> had been a transposition down three perfect fourths from <G3, C4, F4> on the downbeat of m. 5. (The two transpositions down and imagined register transfer are shown as a totality in the sidebar at the right of Example 5.12.) In this way, the extension of the second bell chord by T5 transpositions into pandiatonic territory remarked on earlier continues into chromatic territory, and the new installment <C♯, F♯, B> in m. 8 can be understood – if

---

[42] Von Massow, "Abschied und Neuorientierung," 192.

one ignores the register transfer in between the two T9 transpositions – as continuing the downward trajectory of m. 5.

Finally, the two melodic dyads, one in the right hand, one in the left, also allude to earlier moments in Piece No. 6. The right-hand melody, <E4, E♭4>, has been recognized by other scholars as a reminiscence (in a lower register) of the failed attempt to reach E major in mm. 3–4, <E6, D♯6>.[43] The left-hand dyad, <F♯3, G3>, can be combined with the two sustained pitches directly above it to yield {11, 2, 6, 7}, set class 4-20 (0158), a subset of HEX$_{2,3}$ and thus a reference to m. 7. In summary, different chords and melodic dyads of m. 8 recall the second bell chord in mm. 1–2 and its T5 transpositions in mm. 5–6, the failed attempt to reach E in mm. 3–4, the descent into whole-tone territory in mm. 5b–6, and the corresponding fall into HEX$_{2,3}$ in m. 7. The "development" measure, as we would expect, reviews most everything that has gone before.[44]

But Schoenberg's tender lament and his following review of the circumstances of mm. 1–6 have no effect on his situation. Mahler is still dead, and Schoenberg is still prevented from taking up his mantle as tonal composer by the "harder road" onto which God has ordered him. M. 9 therefore returns the two bell chords just as they appeared in mm. 0–1, followed by a two-note descent into the lowest register yet occupied by Op. 19, No. 6. This final section, A3, appears in Example 5.13. Note that it brings back not only the chords but also some of the inter-attack durations of mm. 0–3a, particularly the 3-quarter duration that had begun the piece as its standard. But the bell chords themselves are now only separated by a single quarter note; which, with the dynamic drop to ***ppp*** (from ***pp*** at the piece's beginning), gives me the impression that a reduced version of the opening music is intended, an echo of it, if you will. In a similar way, the eighth-note descent on the fourth quarter brings back, also at a reduced dynamic, the opening descent of the *cantabile* theme in m. 7. In this way, quiet, brief echoes of both first and second themes are presented by way of recapitulation. This is very different from the usual recapitulation practice in sonata form; but reduced

[43] Von Massow, "Abschied und Neuorientierung," 192. Eric McKee also connects the alto <E4, E♭4> in m. 8 with the high <D♯6, E6, D♯6> in mm. 3b–4, but in his interpretation, these motives do not represent Schoenberg's failure to reach E major; they are both signs for God. See McKee, "On the Death of Mahler," 138–40.

[44] It is interesting in this connection to point out that Elaine Barkin in "Play it AS it Lays" represents m. 8 by a box containing the word "INTERLOCK," surrounded by the words "He's got the whole world in his hands." Barkin in her explanatory essay claims that this refers to the inclusion of all twelve types of trichord in m. 8, but it could also be interpreted as m. 8 bringing together and summarizing the "world" of Op. 19/6's chords, melodies, and transposition processes. See Barkin, untitled essay on Schoenberg's Op. 19, No. 6, 23, and Boge, "Poetic Analysis as Part of Analysis Pedagogy," 49 and 55.

Example 5.13  Schoenberg, Little Piano Piece Op. 19, No. 6, m. 9, section A3. Used by permission of Belmont Music Publishers and Universal Edition

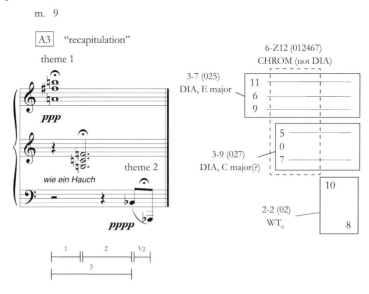

recapitulations were a feature of Schoenberg's earlier music (e.g., the truncated sonata-rondo in Op. 11, No. 1, which we discussed in Chapter 1) and would be a feature of his later music as well (Op. 33a).

The reader may have noticed, however, that what I am calling the recap of the second theme on the fourth quarter of m. 9 does not repeat the initial falling interval of m. 7 exactly. (Perhaps for that reason, Jonathan Dunsby and Arnold Whittall seek other sources for the final descending interval of what they also call A3: the outside notes of the piece's initial chord, or the G♯/F♯ descent in m. 6.)[45] M. 7 had begun with ordered pitch interval –25, resulting from the register transfer of the lower neighbor D-C♯, whereas the final descent in m. 9 produces –14 using pitch classes 10 and 8. This small difference enables the final gesture to recall another part of the piece in addition to m. 7's second theme: the descent into $WT_0$ territory in mm. 5b–6. The pitch-class content over m. 9 thus serves as a final reminder of the piece's trajectory – this measure moves down from $V_2^4$ in E major to 6-Z12, a chromatic subset, on the second beat with the addition of {G3, C4, F4}, and then finally places an emphasis on two $WT_0$ notes at the bottom of its descent on the fourth beat.

In this way, the last measure leaves us with clear reminders of the visual and aural images that characterize Op. 19, No. 6, as well as its incomplete

---

[45] Dunsby and Whittall, *Music Analysis in Theory and Practice*, p. 159.

musical idea. The aural image consists of two bells tolling at Mahler's funeral, with Schoenberg lamenting his friend's death in between the bell sounds, through melodic outbursts of various kinds, some painful, some tender. The visual image adds to this picture, helping us to understand a second reason Schoenberg is lamenting: we see him (represented by the pitches in mm. 3b–4) reaching up to resolve in E major, to follow in Mahler's footsteps as a tonal composer, but his compulsion toward originality and the modern pushes him back down into chromaticism, pandiatonicism, whole-tone music, and his favorite hexatonic collection. (My argument throughout this chapter and in previous ones has been that his progression into atonality and into and out of the "intuitive" period was in itself no reason for sorrow; at every stage in his development as a composer, he produced well-ordered and beautiful music. But Op. 19, No. 6 does seem to portray Schoenberg's movement down and away from tonality as worthy of lament, whether appropriate or not.) Finally, both the aural and the visual images present a problem in section A and elaborate it in sections A1, A2, B, and C, but never resolve it, creating the incomplete musical idea.

The use of diatonic, whole-tone, and hexatonic collections to manifest Op. 19, No. 6's idea and aural/visual images ties this piece stylistically to its predecessors, Nos. 2 and 3. It is particularly interesting to me that the technique of juxtaposing segments that are functionally diatonic for a brief moment with those based on symmetrical collections appears both in Piece No. 3 (which contains passages in Db and Eb major) and No. 6 (which has E major at its high point). Piece No. 2, on the other hand, was more dependent on alternating symmetrical collections with one another to project its musical idea, though it did begin with a vague reference to G major. Functional tonality plays a role in these little pieces, to be sure: but *not* as the guarantor of large-scale coherence. The momentary tonal passages (as I have argued throughout this book) ought to be understood as smaller components of an atonal whole, expressive tools used at appropriate times to create part of the all-embracing image or idea, in cooperation with the miniature version of a standard musical form, and the clear and concise presentation of motivic processes in pitch and rhythm. We will find that techniques similar to these continue in the next collection of pieces we will consider, the recitations of *Pierrot lunaire*. In *Pierrot*, the emphasis shifts to projecting visual images abstracted from the text more consistently (very much like the images we discussed from Op. 15 in Chapter 3). But in all of the pieces we will analyze, juxtaposed whole-tone, hexatonic, octatonic, and even functional-diatonic collections play a crucial role in manifesting the basic image.

# 6  *Pierrot lunaire*, Op. 21, Nos. 1, 14, and 21

## *Basic Image at the Apex of Its Development*

A number of Schoenberg biographers give essentially the same account of the circumstances surrounding the genesis of *Pierrot lunaire* in 1912. Steuermann, Dunsby, Simms, and Kurth, among others, tell us that Albert Giraud, a Belgian poet, had published a collection of fifty *rondels* in French under that title in 1884.[1] This set portrayed various escapades of both the old Italian *commedia dell'arte* character Pierrot and his nine-teenth-century French incarnation as a "decadent *fin-de-siècle* dandy,"[2] as an allegory for Giraud's own return to the Parnassian poetic ideal after flirting with more modern trends such as Symbolism and Decadence.

In 1892, Otto Erich Hartleben translated Giraud's poems into German, obscuring the rhyme scheme and meter (some of the very qualities that marked Giraud's poems as Parnassian), but at the same time using more vivid and colorful language, as well as alliteration and consonance, to depict and sometimes enhance the images within each melodrama. A number of critics, Susan Youens chief among them, consider Hartleben's translations to be a vast improvement over Giraud, because he "breaks up the even flow of Giraud's flat and preternaturally calm recitation with fragmented phrases, exclamations, and questions, much more vivid language expressive of stronger feelings."[3] On the other hand, Robert Vilain and Roger Marsh express a clear preference for Giraud's originals, because the original language gives a clearer picture of the aesthetic context that surrounded Giraud himself, something very different from the expressionist aesthetic that motivated Hartleben.[4] Vilain argues

---

[1] Eduard Steuermann, "*Pierrot Lunaire* in Retrospect," *Journal of the Arnold Schoenberg Institute* 2/1 (October 1977): 49–51; Jonathan Dunsby, *Schoenberg: Pierrot lunaire* (Cambridge: Cambridge University Press, 1992), pp. 21–27; Simms, *The Atonal Music of Arnold Schoenberg*, pp. 119–39; and Richard Kurth, "*Pierrot lunaire*: Persona, Voice, and the Fabric of Allusion," in *The Cambridge Companion to Schoenberg*, ed. Jennifer Shaw and Joseph Auner (Cambridge: Cambridge University Press, 2010), pp. 120–34.

[2] Kurth, "*Pierrot lunaire*," *Cambridge Companion to Schoenberg*, p. 120.

[3] Susan Youens, "Excavating an Allegory: The Texts of *Pierrot Lunaire*," *Journal of the Arnold Schoenberg Institute* 8/2 (1984): 104.

[4] Robert Vilain, "*Pierrot Lunaire*: Cyclic Coherence in Giraud and Schoenberg," in *Pierrot Lunaire: Giraud/Hartleben/Schoenberg*, ed. Mark Delaere and Jan Herman (Louvain: Peeters, 2014), pp. 127–44; Roger Marsh, "'A Multicolored Alphabet': Rediscovering Albert Giraud's *Pierrot Lunaire*," *Twentieth-Century Music* 4/1: 97–121.

that Hartleben removed or obscured images and references in Giraud's French that were necessary to accomplish the original purpose of the poetry – to describe the poet's venture into Symbolism and Decadence and his shrinking back (or his attempt to synthesize various aspects of Symbolism, but not Decadence, with the Parnassian style). An illustrative example is Giraud's first line in one of the poems Schoenberg did not set, "Mendiante de Têtes." It reads "Un panier rouge empli de son" ("a red basket filled with *sounds*"), referring to the basket a guillotine thrusts toward the severed head of the condemned one, hoping to catch its scream but getting only silence. Vilain understands this as an allegorical description of the sounds of Symbolist poetry, cut off from their "body," that is, their form and substance. But Hartleben obscures the reference by changing the first line to "Ihren schmutzig roten Korb" ("Her dirty red basket"), explaining several lines later that the guillotine holds out her red basket like a poor woman begging for severed *heads*, not sounds ("Sprich, was willst Du? – Köpfe! Köpfe!").[5]

Regardless of which version of *Pierrot lunaire* was the superior one, Schoenberg was introduced to the Hartleben translations early in 1912. The actress Albertine Zehme had been touring Germany in 1910 and 1911, reciting selections from Hartleben's *Pierrot lunaire* with musical accompaniments by Otto Vrieslander, a student of Heinrich Schenker and a composer of rather conventional late Romantic *Lieder*. As Eduard Steuermann (Schoenberg's pianist for the premiere of *Pierrot*) tells it, "[Vrieslander's] music was obviously not strong enough, and someone advised her to approach Schoenberg, who was also considered 'bizarre' [like the poetry], to say the least."[6] So, Zehme's agent, Emil Gutmann, went to Schoenberg in January 1912 to give him a copy of the 1911 edition of Hartleben's translation of the fifty poems and offer 1000 marks for the composition of a cycle of recitations taken from them, and Schoenberg responded favorably, for artistic as well as financial reasons. As he put it in his diary entry of January 28:

> Have read the preface, looked at the poems, am enthusiastic. A marvelous idea, quite right for me. Would do it even without a fee.[7]

The little phrase "quite right for me" indicates that Schoenberg was somehow aware of a parallel between the tale Giraud tells of a poet stepping too close to the edge of Decadence and then shrinking back, and his own

---

[5] Vilain, "*Pierrot Lunaire*: Cyclic Coherence," pp. 134–35.
[6] Steuermann, "*Pierrot Lunaire* in Retrospect," 49.
[7] Stuckenschmidt, *Schoenberg: His Life, World and Work*, p. 195.

experience as a composer intoxicated by the modern spirit. He again suggested his awareness of his kinship with Giraud and Pierrot a few years later, in a dedication he wrote to his friend and brother-in-law Alexander Zemlinsky on a copy of *Pierrot* that he gave him for Christmas in 1916. I reproduce Bryan Simms's translation here, with a few small additions and changes in brackets. One of my changes replaces Simms's noun "fools" with the German original, for a reason that I will explain below.[8]

> [Dear friend, my most heartfelt wishes for Christmas 1916.] It is banal to say that we are all [such] moonstruck [Wursteln]; what the poet means is that we are trying our best to wipe off the imaginary moon spots from our clothing at the same time that we worship our crosses. Let us be thankful that we have our wounds: with them we have something that helps us to place a low value on [material things]. From the scorn for our wounds comes our scorn for our enemies and our power to sacrifice our lives to a moonbeam. One could easily get emotional by thinking about the Pierrot poetry. But for the cuckoo is anything more important than the price of grain? [Many greetings, your Arnold Schoenberg.]

Schoenberg suggests that he, Zemlinsky, and other modern artists could be described as "Wursteln," even if it would be banal to do so. This is a reference to the character Hanswurst, the Viennese cousin of the French Pierrot. Schoenberg seems to be saying that his path as a creative artist, like Giraud's, is well represented by the misadventures of Hanswurst/Pierrot, going on to explain that he too has been led astray into modern music by the same intoxicating moonlight, so that his artistic creations also have become crosses that earn him wounds: punishments that come from not being able to communicate to his audience.[9]

   Schoenberg's selection and ordering of twenty-one poems from Giraud's collection also reflects his awareness of his kinship with Giraud. The eventual order, which went through at least one revision before he settled on it in July 1912, falls into three large sections of seven poems each that resembles Giraud's tri-partite division of the full 50 poems in many respects. Example 6.1 lists Giraud's order next to the one Schoenberg finally agreed on in summer 1912, with general descriptions of the content

---

[8]  Simms, The *Atonal Music of Arnold Schoenberg*, p. 126. The original German of the dedication can be found in Reinhold Brinkmann, "The Fool as Paradigm: Schoenberg's *Pierrot lunaire* and the Modern Artist," in *Schoenberg and Kandinsky: An Historic Encounter* (Amsterdam: Harwood Academic, 1997), p. 146.

[9]  Brinkmann also emphasizes Schoenberg's use of Hanswurst to represent himself, as a parallel to Giraud's identification with Pierrot, in "The Fool as Paradigm," pp. 159–62.

Example 6.1  Parallels between Giraud's and Schoenberg's orderings of *Pierrot lunaire*

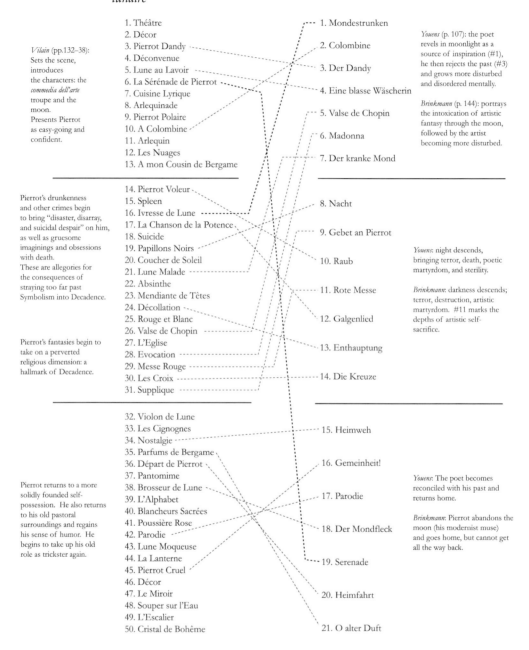

*Vilain* (pp.132–38): Sets the scene, introduces the characters: the *commedia dell'arte* troupe and the moon. Presents Pierrot as easy-going and confident.

1. Théâtre
2. Décor
3. Pierrot Dandy
4. Déconvenue
5. Lune au Lavoir
6. La Sérénade de Pierrot
7. Cuisine Lyrique
8. Arlequinade
9. Pierrot Polaire
10. A Colombine
11. Arlequin
12. Les Nuages
13. A mon Cousin de Bergame

Pierrot's drunkenness and other crimes begin to bring "disaster, disarray, and suicidal despair" on him, as well as gruesome imaginings and obsessions with death.
These are allegories for the consequences of straying too far past Symbolism into Decadence.

14. Pierrot Voleur
15. Spleen
16. Ivresse de Lune
17. La Chanson de la Potence
18. Suicide
19. Papillons Noirs
20. Coucher de Soleil
21. Lune Malade
22. Absinthe
23. Mendiante de Têtes
24. Décollation
25. Rouge et Blanc
26. Valse de Chopin

Pierrot's fantasies begin to take on a perverted religious dimension: a hallmark of Decadence.

27. L'Eglise
28. Evocation
29. Messe Rouge
30. Les Croix
31. Supplique

Pierrot returns to a more solidly founded self-possession. He also returns to his old pastoral surroundings and regains his sense of humor. He begins to take up his old role as trickster again.

32. Violon de Lune
33. Les Cignognes
34. Nostalgie
35. Parfums de Bergame
36. Départ de Pierrot
37. Pantomime
38. Brosseur de Lune
39. L'Alphabet
40. Blancheurs Sacrées
41. Poussière Rose
42. Parodie
43. Lune Moqueuse
44. La Lanterne
45. Pierrot Cruel
46. Décor
47. Le Miroir
48. Souper sur l'Eau
49. L'Escalier
50. Cristal de Bohême

1. Mondestrunken
2. Colombine
3. Der Dandy
4. Eine blasse Wäscherin
5. Valse de Chopin
6. Madonna
7. Der kranke Mond

8. Nacht
9. Gebet an Pierrot
10. Raub
11. Rote Messe
12. Galgenlied
13. Enthauptung
14. Die Kreuze

15. Heimweh
16. Gemeinheit!
17. Parodie
18. Der Mondfleck
19. Serenade
20. Heimfahrt
21. O alter Duft

*Youens* (p. 107): the poet revels in moonlight as a source of inspiration (#1), he then rejects the past (#3) and grows more disturbed and disordered mentally.

*Brinkmann* (p. 144): portrays the intoxication of artistic fantasy through the moon, followed by the artist becoming more disturbed.

*Youens*: night descends, bringing terror, death, poetic martyrdom, and sterility.

*Brinkmann*: darkness descends; terror, destruction, artistic martyrdom. #11 marks the depths of artistic self-sacrifice.

*Youens*: The poet becomes reconciled with his past and returns home.

*Brinkmann*: Pierrot abandons the moon (his modernist muse) and goes home, but cannot get all the way back.

of each of the three parts given by Robert Vilain (for Giraud) and Susan Youens and Reinhold Brinkmann (for Schoenberg).[10]

The left side of the example shows that Giraud's original set of fifty *rondels* divides into three main parts. Poems 1–13 set the stage and introduce the characters: Pierrot, the moon, Cassander, Harlequin, and Colombine. In this section, Pierrot appears as an easy-going, confident prankster – for example, the poem ("La Sérénade de Pierrot," No. 6) that Hartleben would paraphrase as "Serenade" and Schoenberg would set as No. 19 in his collection portrays him as gracefully "zebra-striping" Cassander's belly with his large bow. With poem No. 13, however, "A mon Cousin de Bergame," Giraud associates himself as author with Pierrot for the first time, and this brings on the second part, Poems 14–31. In this section, Pierrot's more serious offenses of drunkenness, larceny, and blasphemy lead to him either suffering or obsessively imagining frightening, gruesome images of death – being hung, smothered by giant black bloodsucking butterflies, decapitated by first the guillotine and then the crescent moon, and finally being crucified. Vilain explains that these should be understood as allegories for the fate of the poet who commits the crime of straying too far into Symbolist or Decadent styles; the smothering, strangling, or cutting off of the poet's voice, followed by artistic death. Poems 27–30, particularly, focus in on a hallmark of the Decadent style, the perversion of religious images, like offering one's own bloody heart as the Eucharist in poem No. 29, "Messe Rouge." Pierrot's (and the Decadent poet's) blasphemies lead inexorably to his real or imagined punishment in poem No. 30 at the hands of the ultimate religious image, the cross.[11]

Poem No. 31, "Supplique" (which Hartleben would translate as "Gebet an Pierrot"), in the larger context that Giraud provides for it, is not so much about Colombine lamenting the loss of her virginity to Pierrot (a meaning that some have ascribed to it in Schoenberg's cycle),[12] but rather the poet (as Pierrot) pleading with himself to leave behind all his gruesome Decadent fantasies and return to his fun-loving self. He then proceeds to do just that, in Giraud's third and final part, poems 32–50. Poems Nos. 34 and 35, "Nostalgie" and "Parfums de Bergame" ("Heimweh" and "O alter Duft" in Hartleben's translation), describe Pierrot's longing for Bergamo and his partners in the *commedia dell'arte*,

---

[10] Vilain, *Pierrot Lunaire*: Cyclic Coherence," pp. 132–38; Youens, "Excavating an Allegory," 107; Brinkmann, "The Fool as Paradigm," p. 144.

[11] Vilain, "*Pierrot Lunaire*: Cyclic Coherence," pp. 133–36.

[12] For example, Susan Youens in "Excavating an Allegory," 108.

and No. 36, "Départ de Pierrot" (which became "Heimfahrt"), portrays him beginning his journey home. In the following poems, we see Pierrot returning to his old tricks. He gives Cassander a beating in "Pantomime," poem No. 37, tries to go out in his evening dress but is prevented by a spot of moonlight, which he thinks is a stain in No. 38, "Brosseur de Lune" ("Der Mondfleck" in Hartleben's translation), and again tortures Cassander by drilling a hole into his wooden puppet head and smoking it like a pipe in No. 45, "Pierrot Cruel" (which became "Gemeinheit!"). Giraud closes the cycle in poem No. 50, "Cristal de Bohême," by again reminding his reader, "the one I love," that he has been using Pierrot to describe his own journey as a creative artist.

Susan Youens has called Schoenberg's reduction of Giraud's fifty poems to twenty-one "[imposing] a coherent structure" on a "deliberately(?) jumbled series of poems," "[excavating] from the larger source its principal 'idea' or 'concept,' liberating it from the unrelated images that cluster about and hide it from view."[13] Now, it may well be that cutting away twenty-nine poems enabled Schoenberg to tell his story more concisely, but it is important to point out here, again, that this story does not differ much if at all from Giraud's – it follows the same three-part structure with the same basic themes, as shown by the horizontal line divisions on the right side of Example 6.1, and the notes about the content of Schoenberg's three parts I culled from Youens and Brinkmann. Schoenberg's structure begins with an introduction to Pierrot, Colombine, and the moon in the first four melodramas, describes a few of Pierrot's crimes and a few more of his punishments (which now become an allegory for Schoenberg's venture into atonality and its consequences) in the last three melodramas of the first part and all of the second part, and finally portrays Pierrot/Schoenberg as returning home (to tonality, or at least trying to) and taking up his old role as trickster in the third part. How close Schoenberg's final arrangement comes to Giraud's original one can be seen from the dotted lines in the middle of my Example 6.1, which connect the Giraud poems that Schoenberg used on the left with their location in Schoenberg's ordering on the right. With two exceptions, every melodrama in Schoenberg's ordering remains in the same part to which it had belonged in Giraud's structure, or close to it. "Mondestrunken" moves up to the initial position in Schoenberg's first part from the original position of "Ivresse de Lune" at No. 16 in Giraud's second part. It seems that Schoenberg wanted to begin with the image of himself (which he mentioned in his note to Zemlinsky) as an artist being led astray into modernism by the influence of moonlight.

---

[13] Youens, "Excavating an Allegory," 95–96.

And Giraud's "La Sérénade de Pierrot," which had been in the first part, moves down into Schoenberg's third part at No. 19. Since the poem represents Pierrot as *commedia dell'arte* trickster (either playing on Cassander's belly with his bow, or on his wooden head in Hartleben's German), it seems appropriate for a third part that portrays Pierrot returning home and taking up his familiar role. In addition, three of Giraud's poems from the second part, Nos. 26, 28, and 21, do migrate up into the end of Schoenberg's first part as Nos. 5–7, "Valse de Chopin," "Madonna," and "Der kranke Mond." But I believe we can think of these as a transition from Schoenberg's brief introduction of some of the main characters in his first section to his description of the horrible punishments of the composer who dares to wander away from tonality in his second part.

Thus, Schoenberg tells essentially the same story as his predecessor Giraud, a three-part saga of the artist who strays too far into modern styles, suffers the consequences, and tries to return to his old way of doing things – but from the composer's viewpoint rather than the poet's. To explain how he uses music to accomplish his purpose, I will return to a concept I introduced in Chapter 1 of this book – the "basic image." In the first chapter (pp. 4–5), I defined basic image as "a visual and/or aural pattern summarizing the text of a vocal piece, which is translated into intervals and rhythms." As we saw in Chapters 3, 4, and 5, the use of visual and aural images to organize the pitches and rhythms of a piece manifests itself differently in the Op. 15 songs, *Erwartung* (where a two-part image of "emerging" stretches over more than 400 measures), and the Op. 19 piano pieces, particularly No. 6 with its image of Schoenberg reaching up toward Mahler's tonal ideal and being pushed back down. But it is in *Pierrot lunaire* where the "basic image" truly reaches the apex of its development. Indeed, it was in three melodramas from *Pierrot*, "Nacht," "Der Mondfleck," and "Parodie," that Kathryn Bailey first described what she called "structural imagery," an important predecessor to the concept I am discussing here.[14] Bailey showed that "Nacht" uses the basic image of swarms of giant black butterflies descending and bringing on darkness to motivate pitch, rhythm, the use and variation of canonic devices, texture, and instrumentation.[15] "Der Mondfleck's" main image is that of Pierrot

---

[14] Bailey, "Formal Organization and Structural Imagery in Schoenberg's *Pierrot lunaire*."

[15] I published my own analysis of "Nacht" as an illustration of basic image in 2009 in "The Musical Idea and the Basic Image in an Atonal Song and Recitation of Arnold Schoenberg," 248–62. My analysis described many of the same features as Bailey's, such as <+3, –4> butterfly motives chaining together and ornamenting one another in long descents, as well as the gradual disruptions in the melodrama's canonic material, but, in

trying to move forward while turning around to look at a spot of moonlight on the back of his dress coat. This gives rise to a strict canon in the string instruments, a looser imitative texture in the woodwinds, and a fugue in the piano, where the string and woodwind parts begin to mirror their previous pitches, intervals, and rhythms at the exact point where the text mentions turning around. The piano, however, continues to move forward. Finally, in "Parodie," the image of the moon mocking the old woman calls forth a series of canons with one voice imitating in inversion.

Bailey claims that such instances of "structural imagery" in these three melodramas are somewhat unique within *Pierrot lunaire*, limiting themselves to a few pieces that "exhibit the highest degree of structural organization." Like Ethan Haimo, she understands the full set of twenty-one melodramas as "a collection of dissimilar – one might even say contradictory – elements."[16] But I want to make the counterargument: that images abstracted from the text, one for each melodrama, can be thought of as *the* unifying feature in *Pierrot lunaire*. There is not enough room in a single chapter to show how these images work themselves out musically in each and every melodrama – but I can point to suggestions other authors have made along the same lines, such as Stephan Weytjens's analysis of "Eine blasse Wäscherin," where the image of a woven pale white sheet spread out over the meadow motivates the continual instrument crossings and the bland tone colors.[17] And the bulk of my chapter will be devoted to detailed and complete analyses of "Mondestrunken" and "Die Kreuze," and a less-complete analysis of "O alter Duft": one melodrama from each of Schoenberg's three parts, demonstrating how a visual image abstracted from the text gives rise to pitch, rhythm, texture, and timbre in each one.

Before moving on to my detailed analyses, however, I want to discuss the crucial question of *what* specific elements of the text give rise to the basic images in *Pierrot lunaire*. Certain authors who have written about text-painting in *Pierrot* have highlighted a statement Schoenberg made in his essay "The Relationship to the Text," written just before the composition of *Pierrot* in 1912. I mentioned the essay briefly in Chapter 3 (p. 117) to support my argument that the basic images of songs in Op. 15 are

---

addition, I suggested a *cause-and-effect* relationship between the increasing density of descending butterflies and the growing canonic disruptions, a metaphor for the creations of the poet/composer turning on him and smothering him (making it impossible for him to communicate artistically or canonically).

[16]  Bailey, "Formal Organization and Structural Imagery," 93; Ethan Haimo, "Schoenberg's *Pierrot Lunaire*: A Cycle?," in *Pierrot Lunaire: Giraud/Hartleben/Schoenberg*, pp. 145–55.

[17]  Stephan Weytjens, "Text as a Crutch in Schoenberg's *Pierrot Lunaire*?," in *Pierrot Lunaire: Giraud/Hartleben/Schoenberg*, p. 121.

abstractions from the first line or two of the poetry – but I did not consider the specific source of Schoenberg's inspiration that the quotation below describes:

> Inspired by the *sound* of the first words of the text, I had composed many of my songs straight through to the end without troubling myself in the slightest about the continuation of the poetic events, without even grasping them in the ecstasy of composing, and . . . only days later I thought of looking back to see just what was the real poetic content of my song. It then turned out, to my greatest astonishment, that I had never done greater justice to the poet than when, guided by my first direct contact with the *sound* of the beginning, I divined everything that obviously had to follow this first sound with inevitability.[18] (italics mine)

Richard Kurth, in two lucid and well-written book chapters about *Pierrot*, argues that Schoenberg "believed at this time that poetic language conveys meaning directly through its sensuous sounds (rather than through syntax, semantics, concepts)."[19] In other words, the basic image that controls musical processes is communicated to the composer by the poem through word sounds alone. Kurth goes so far as to identify Schoenberg as a "Cratylist," a follower of Plato's *Cratylus*; that is, one who seeks the essence of a word in the sounds of its vowels and consonants.[20] His argument actually seems reasonable when one considers the opening lines of "Nacht" – "Finstre, schwarze Riesenfalter (etc.)." All the swishing "fff," "sss," and "shhh" consonants that Hartleben introduced in his translation do indeed call up the image of a thick mass of black butterfly wings, and the progression from the bright-sounding "eee" in "Riesenfalter" to the darker "ah" in "Glanz" could be heard as a gradual, inexorable descent. Or, one might think of the beginning of a piece Kurth discusses briefly in "Pierrot's Cave"; that is, "Mondestrunken," where the regular repetition of similar phrases such as "Den Wein," "den man," and "der Mond," or the larger cycles caused by rhymes between words in similar line locations, such as "Augen" and "Wogen," suggest the regular motion of incoming and outgoing waves.[21]

Nevertheless, there are other scholars who are skeptical about whether Schoenberg could have really divined the poem's central image from word

---

[18] "The Relationship to the Text" (1912), in *Style and Idea*, p. 144.

[19] Richard Kurth, "Pierrot's Cave: Representation, Reverberation, Radiance," in *Schoenberg and Words: The Modernist Years*, ed. Charlotte M. Cross and Russell A. Berman (New York: Garland, 2000), pp. 203–41; and idem, "*Pierrot lunaire*: Persona, Voice, and the Fabric of Allusion." The quotation comes from the second edited collection, p. 124.

[20] Kurth, "Pierrot's Cave," pp. 216–26.    [21] Ibid., pp. 222–23.

sounds alone, without paying any attention to the meaning, either in the first few lines, or throughout the poem as a whole. Kathryn Bailey Puffett, in her "revisiting" of the 1977 article in which she introduced "structural imagery," expresses such incredulity:

> [Did Schoenberg] really believe that inculcating and sustaining the idea of his messianic status was more important than admitting to quite brilliant interpretations of someone else's poetic texts? I cannot believe that the obviously picturesque in "Nacht" and "Der Mondfleck" represents a miraculous coincidence that occurred during Schoenberg's "ecstasy of composing" on Giraud's [or Hartleben's] unread words. Perhaps upon reflection even Schoenberg found his pronouncement on words and music in *Der blaue Reiter* rather extreme and decided to read more closely in the future.[22]

It is my habit in such disputes to choose a middle path. As I did in my analyses of the Op. 15 songs in Chapter 3, I will take the basic images of "Mondestrunken," "Die Kreuze," and "O alter Duft" mostly from the first two lines of Hartleben's translations of the poems. Since every poem in Pierrot is a *rondel*, meaning that the first two lines repeat at the end of the second stanza, and a repetition of the first line is added on after the third stanza, the first two lines can be heard as a continual presence throughout the poem. However, I will be a little less insistent than Kurth that the basic image must come from the word *sounds* of the beginning alone, but rather will consider its semantic content, in addition to the sound. I read Schoenberg's statement in "The Relationship to the Text" as close to the truth, but incomplete: he seems to have been inspired by the sound *and meaning* of the first words of the text. In a few cases, I will show that he even occasionally reacts to and represents concepts in the text that appear after the first two lines.

### "Mondestrunken," No. 1

To enable myself to carry on detailed and more-or-less complete analyses of some of the individual melodramas in *Pierrot*, I will limit the number that I consider to three – one each from the three parts of Schoenberg's final ordering. These three poems encapsulate the themes of the three parts: "Mondestrunken" pictures the Decadent poet or modernist composer being intoxicated and led astray by waves of moonlight; "Die Kreuze" portrays the creations of that poet/composer as crosses on which he hangs silently (unable to communicate artistically), the punishment for writing under the influence of moonlight; and "O alter Duft" shows the artist

---

[22] Bailey Puffett, "Structural Imagery: 'Pierrot Lunaire' Revisited," 22.

returning back to his old home and way of life (but, as was the case with Schoenberg and tonal composition, not being able to get all the way back).

The text of "Mondestrunken," with my own English translation, is given below:

| | |
|---|---|
| Den Wein, den man mit Augen trinkt, | The wine, which one drinks with one's eyes, |
| Gießt nachts der Mond in Wogen nieder, | Pours down from the moon in waves at night, |
| Und eine Springflut überschwemmt | And a spring flood overflows |
| Den stillen Horizont. | The still horizon. |
| | |
| Gelüste, schauerlich und süß, | Longings, horrible and sweet, |
| Durchschwimmen ohne Zahl die Fluten! | Swim through the flood without number! |
| Den Wein, den man mit Augen trinkt, | The wine, which one drinks with one's eyes, |
| Gießt nachts der Mond in Wogen nieder. | Pours down from the moon in waves at night. |
| | |
| Der Dichter, den die Andacht treibt, | The poet, driven by his devotion, |
| Berauscht sich an dem heilgen Tranke, | Is intoxicated by the holy drink, |
| Gen Himmel wendet er verzückt | He turns his head ecstatically toward heaven |
| Das Haupt und taumeld saugt und schlürft er | And, staggering, he sucks up and slurps |
| Den Wein, den man mit Augen trinkt. | The wine, which one drinks with one's eyes. |

The basic image that the first two lines evoke has already been identified by several scholars, including Kurth, Cherlin, and Simms: waves of moonlight, going out and coming in, like waves at the seashore.[23] I will add one small refinement, based on lines 3 and 4: often one of the incoming waves comes in too far and creates a flood, leaving a pool of still water. This image motivates the pitch, pitch-class, rhythmic, and timbral content of the entire melodrama, so that all thirty-nine measures of it can be heard as "guided by Schoenberg's direct contact with the sound (and meaning) of the beginning." As for the form of "Mondestrunken," it follows the division of the poem into three stanzas, A B A′, with a lengthy retransition at the end of the B section that develops the piece's opening material in preparation for a varied return of that opening in m. 29.

Outward and inward wave motions begin the piece in mm. 1–4, represented in Example 6.2 by the score and a pitch-class map.

The high range of the piano, pizzicato in the violin, and $pp$ dynamic give the passage's timbre a sparkling quality that depicts waves of moonlight. The outgoing wave, the piano's augmented triad <8, 4, 0> and the violin's {6}, produces set class 4-24 (0248), a subset of the $WT_0$ collection. The incoming wave, which I define as such because it comes further and further in as the piece goes on, combines <2, 10, 1, 7> in the piano, set class

[23] Kurth, "*Pierrot lunaire*: Persona, Voice, and the Fabric of Allusion," p. 129; Michael Cherlin, "*Pierrot Lunaire* as Lunar Nexus," *Music Analysis* 31/2 (2012): 188; Simms, *The Atonal Music of Arnold Schoenberg*, p. 132.

Example 6.2 Schoenberg, "Mondestrunken," *Pierrot lunaire*, Op. 21, mm. 1–5a, beginning of section A. Copyright © 1914, 1941 by Universal Edition AG Vienna, UE 34806. All rights reserved. Used by permission of Belmont Music Publishers and Universal Edition

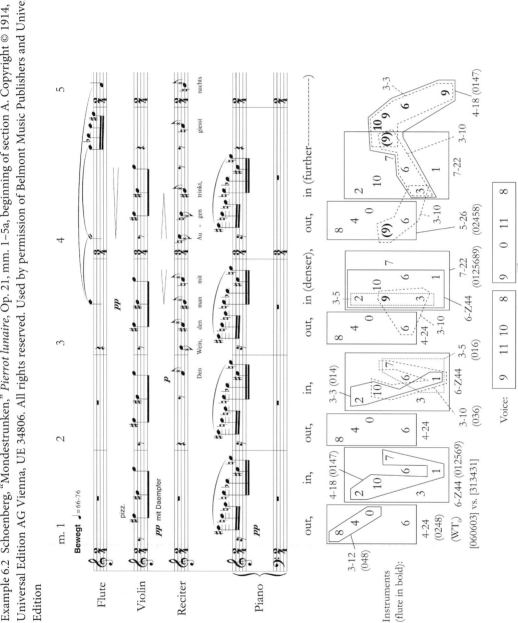

4-18 (0147), with <3, 6> in the violin to form set-class 6-Z44 (012569), Schoenberg's "signature" set. One of the reasons we can hear $WT_0$ and 6-Z44 as signifying waves moving in opposite directions is the marked contrast in their interval contents: [060603] for the whole-tone scale (all even intervals), [313431] for 6-Z44 (mostly odd intervals except for ic 4). The 6-Z44 and 4-18 also contain a number of subsets (illustrated in m. 2 of the pitch-class map) that will play important roles in the extended inward wave motions to come. The piano's 4-18 has two subsets, <2, 10, 1> forming 3-3 (014) and <10, 1, 7> forming the diminished triad 3-10 (036); and the piano and violin together yield {1, 6, 7} at the end of the measure, set class 3-5 (016).

Measure 1's progression repeats *verbatim* in the piano and violin in m. 2, but at the end of m. 2 the voice enters, and in m. 3b the flute enters with an A5 that sustains until the end of m. 4. The flute pedal changes the alternating pattern to 5-26 (02458) and 7-22 (0125689) after m. 3b. These larger sets do not have the same pronounced difference in interval content as 4-24 and 6-Z44; but some of the qualities of the original alternation are preserved by the multiplication of 6-Z44's characteristic subsets in 7-22. The added PC 9 produces a second set class 3-5, {2, 3, 9} on the second quarter of m. 3 between the flute, violin, and piano, a Viennese Trichord <6, 5>; further instances of 3-10, {3, 6, 9}, between the flute's 9 and the violin's {3, 6} through most of mm. 3 and 4; and a second version of 6-Z44 itself, {1, 2, 3, 6, 9, 10}, in mm. 3b and 4b. One could say that the incoming wave is gaining both textural and pitch-class set density in mm. 3–4, which leads to its first small influx in the last beat of m. 4 and first beat of m. 5. The piano and violin halt for a quarter note, and the flute continues with <9, 10, 9, 6, 9>, which itself creates 3-3, and yields 4-18 if we add it to the violin's {3, 6} in the middle of m. 4. In this way, the second part of the alternation is extended one quarter note by different members of the same set classes, 3-3, 3-10, and 4-18, that had been featured within 6-Z44 earlier – the incoming wave comes in a bit further.

The voice embarks on a different line of development from the instruments when it enters in m. 2. (To understand that development properly, however, we *do* need to treat the *Sprechstimme* as pitched, though the reciter is warned by Schoenberg in the preface to the first edition not to sustain the pitches for any longer than the briefest of moments.) The voice produces two related tetrachords on "Den Wein, den man" and "mit Augen trinkt": <+2, –1, –2>, forming 4-1 (0123); and its expansion <+3, –1, –3>, forming 4-3 (0134). David Lewin has referred to these as the "Wein" and "Augen" tetrachords, and proposes a relation between them that he demonstrates to be important for the continuation of the piece: "the motif of the chrom/octa tetrachords." Lewin defines this relation as "a progression whereby a chromatic tetrachord progresses to (or follows) an octatonic tetrachord with which it shares three common tones."[24] Here, I want to generalize Lewin's motif to a relation that connects any two tetrachords that have three common tones, not just 4-1 and 4-3; and in addition I will include those tetrachords whose prime forms or other transformations of them have three common tones, even if the pitch-class sets themselves do not. In other words, I understand the "Wein" and "Augen" tetrachords themselves as the manifestation of what Allen Forte calls a "strong Rp" relation (the two pitch-class sets themselves have three tones in common). As "Mondestrunken" continues, we hear numerous chains of tetrachords that connect through "weak Rp" – in these later instances, only the prime forms or other transformations have three notes in common, not the pitch-class sets themselves, but often the same three notes (or transpositions of them) are shared by most or all of the prime forms in the chain.[25] These chains, based loosely on the voice's relation that introduced "the wine that eyes drink" in mm. 2–4, portray waves of moonlight coming in further and further, eventually creating a flood.

The first chain of Rp-related tetrachords occurs already in mm. 5–6 in the piano's right hand, shown in Example 6.3a. In the pitch-class map beneath the score, now in straight lines for each instrument or voice for easier reading, one can see that after an initial trichord 3-2 (013), the next three groups of four in the piano RH (defined by grouping within the beat) yield set classes 4-4 (0125), 4-7 (0145), and 4-18 (0147).

These prime forms all contain some transposition of 3-3 (014) as an n-1 common subset: (125) in the first, (014) in the second and third, but none of the pitch-class collections themselves have more than two notes in common – meaning that the three tetrachords relate to one another through weak Rp. Now, Forte himself commented on how most tetrachord set classes relate to most others through weak Rp, with a few exceptions (4-18, for example, can have Rp with twenty-one of the other twenty-eight tetrachords). He claimed, further, that because of this surfeit of relations, the pitch-similarity relation should only be used in connection with interval-similarity measures.[26] But, in this instance, I find it interesting that the weak Rp relations between 4-4, 4-7, and 4-18 all involve the same set class, 3-3, which has just been played by the flute in the pickup notes to m. 5. In my hearing, the common 3-3 trichords, which are highlighted as larger

---

[24] David Lewin, "Some Notes on *Pierrot Lunaire*," in *Music Theory in Concept and Practice*, ed. James M. Baker, David W. Beach, and Jonathan W. Bernard (Rochester, NY: University of Rochester Press, 1997), pp. 439–40.

[25] Forte's introduction to the pitch-class similarity relations (Rp) can be found in *The Structure of Atonal Music*, pp. 46–50.

[26] Forte, *Structure of Atonal Music*, pp. 46–51.

Example 6.3a  Schoenberg, "Mondestrunken," *Pierrot lunaire*, Op. 21, mm. 4b–8a.
Used by permission of Belmont Music Publishers and Universal Edition

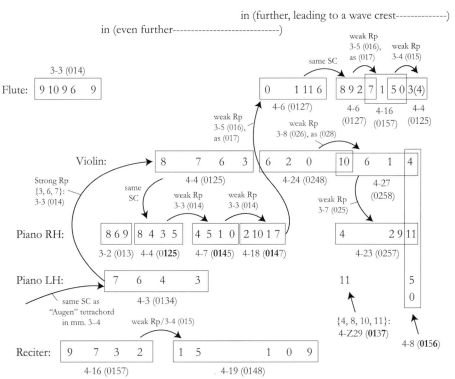

Example 6.3b  N-1 common pitch-class sets in piano RH, mm. 5–6 and in
flute, mm. 6–7

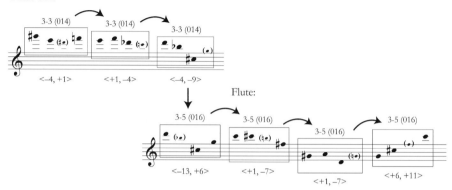

noteheads at the top of Example 6.3b, do form an audible link between the
three tetrachords in this passage, and also link them to the music that has
come just before.

Further, since the 4-18 ending this passage in the piano's right hand
in m. 6 is <2, 10, 1, 7>, the same pitch-class (and pitch) set that we have
been hearing in the right hand of the piano during incoming waves since
the beginning of the piece, it is easy to hear the whole chain of tetrachords
as an extended incoming wave.[27]

Closer inspection of the pitch-class map of Example 6.3a shows that the
entire texture of mm. 5–7 is filled with similar chains of tetrachords related
by either weak or strong Rp, or set-class identity. (A look at the score
confirms that these chains all descend in mm. 5–6, portraying the waves of
moonlight moving *down* (toward the poet) as well as in.) For example, the
left hand of the piano, <7, 6, 4, 3>, is imitated by the violin, <8, 7, 6, 3>,
forming a strong Rp through the common subset <7, 6, 3> – 3-3 again.
The set classes of these tetrachords are 4-3 (0134), the "Augen" tetrachord,
and 4-4 (0125), the starting point of the piano RH chain just described, so
maybe these two inner voices can be understood as a link between mm. 1–4
and the piano RH in m. 5. Meanwhile, the voice on "gießt nachts der Mond

27  J. Daniel Jenkins explains another way in which the piano right hand in mm. 5–6 extends
the alternating wave motion of m. 1: within the 3-2, 4-4, and 4-7 tetrachords the pitches
G♯6, E6, and C6 occur in the same order and register as they do in m. 1. The other notes of
those tetrachords could then be heard as ornamenting those three main notes. See
Jenkins, "Schoenberg's Concept of 'ruhende Bewegung'," *Theory and Practice* 34
(2009): 96–97.

in Wogen nieder" produces two tetrachords, <9, 7, 3, 2> or 4-16 (0157) and <1, 5, 1, 0, 9> or 4-19 (0148). These set classes have a weak Rp through 3-4 (015), a close relative of 3-3, which is manifested as {2, 3, 7} in the first set and {0, 1, 5} in the second.

At the end of m. 6, my pitch-class map shows the <2, 10, 1, 7> 4-18 in the piano right hand linking up with a series of tetrachords in the flute, which takes over the role of leading voice from the piano RH in mm. 6b–7 and creates another incoming wave that can be heard as overlapping with the previous one. The whole series consists of 4-18 (0147), 4-6 (0127), 4-6, 4-16 (0157), and 4-4 (0125). From the prime forms, it can be seen that the first four tetrachords either link through 3-5 (016) in its inverted form (017), or are the same set class. As I already did for the chain in the piano RH, the lower half of Example 6.3b highlights the common 3-5s in the piano and flute's chain with larger noteheads, suggesting how they form audible links from piano to flute, and from one tetrachord to the next in the flute. Finally, <7, 1, 5, 0>, 4-16, links to the last tetrachord in the flute chain, 4-4 <5, 0, 3, 4>, as a weak Rp relation through 3-4 (015).

At its beginning, the piano and flute's tetrachord chain descends, like all those that came before it. But as m. 7 begins, the flute suddenly turns upward, together with the violin in m. 7 (and the voice later in mm. 7b–8), in an explosive gesture. This eruption is made more sudden by a septuplet of sixteenths in the flute, as well as an abrupt dynamic increase to *ff* at the beginning of m. 7 and a *crescendo*, followed by subito *pp* at the end of the measure. If the descending tetrachord chains signify incoming waves of moonlight, as I have been arguing, then perhaps this loud but quickly dissipating ascent represents the flute's wave breaking as it rushes in. This cresting wave creates a pair of vertical set classes on the two beats of m. 7 that are of interest: both 4-Z29 (0137) and 4-8 (0156) are supersets of 3-5, the trichord that has just played such an important role as link in mm. 6–7.

The voice's ascent in mm. 7b–8a, reacting to this upward explosion, introduces the third and fourth lines of stanza 1, "and a spring flood overflows the still horizon," shown in Example 6.4. In mm. 7b–8, the principal downward wave motion returns to the piano, now represented by chains of tetrachords in both hands, in canon at the octave below and one sixteenth note later. In the right hand, the chain consists of 4-3 (0134), 4-13 (0136), 4-13, and 4-12 (0236), four sets that are related either by identity or weak Rp with a common set of 3-2 (013). The common set is found in the four prime forms either as (013) or its inversion (023). Just as 3-3 had done in mm. 4b–5, a statement of 3-2 immediately precedes this chain, <4, 5, 2> in the violin at the end of m. 7. In addition, the voice's upward trajectory that begins the section on "und eine Spring–," <0, 2, 10, 3>, contains a prominent 3-2 subset,

Example 6.4  Schoenberg, "Mondestrunken," *Pierrot lunaire*, Op. 21, mm. 7b–11a.
Used by permission of Belmont Music Publishers and Universal Edition

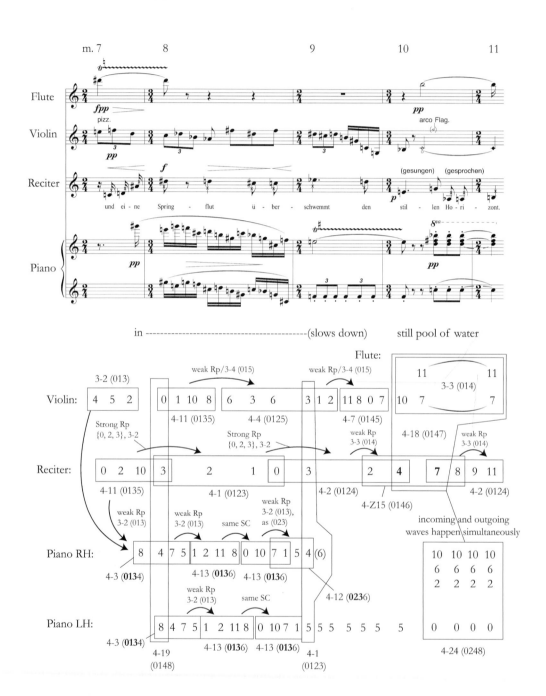

<0, 2, 3>. The piano left hand's *comes* is incomplete, but it does include the first three tetrachords 4-3, 4-13, and 4-13, and ends on the sequence <10, 7, 1>: calling to mind the motive that marked the ends of the incoming waves in mm. 1–4 and m. 6, <2, **10, 1, 7**>, and suggesting that another wave ending is about to come (at the end of m. 9).

As in mm. 5–6, the subsidiary voices in mm. 8–9 also form chains of tetrachords related by either strong or weak Rp. The violin after its initial 3-2, <4, 5, 2>, produces 4-11 (0135), 4-4 (0125), and finally 4-7 (0145), all connected by weak Rp with 3-4 (015) as a common subset. And the voice on "und eine Springflut überschwemmt den stil-" chains three tetrachords with Rp relations involving 3-2 again. This time, they are strong Rp relations via the pitch-class set {0, 2, 3}: <0, 10, 2, 3>, <3, 2, 1, 0>, and <0, 3, 2, 4>, forming set classes 4-11, 4-1, and 4-2. The continuation, "den stillen Horizont," chains 4-Z15 (0146) and 4-2 (0124) via a weak Rp involving 3-3 (014). The contours of all these chains descend, mostly, marking them as incoming waves, like those in the piano.

In m. 9, however, these cascades of incoming waves slow down, and in mm. 10 and 11, they stop altogether, leaving a still pool of water (as is often seen at the seashore when the tide goes out). This effect is at least partly due to the lengthening of note values in the piano in m. 9 and in all voices in the following measures. But Schoenberg also makes use of a harmonic device to portray the desired image quite effectively: he takes the alternating groups of set classes that had portrayed the outward and inward motion of waves in mm. 1–4, and sustains them simultaneously. In mm. 10–11, the flute and violin together prolong 3-3, {7, 10, 11}, and the addition of the sung (sustained in their own way) PCs 4 and 7 in the voice yields 4-18, both sets that had been associated with incoming waves. Underneath, the piano repeats 4-24 (0248) four times, the tetrachord that had signified outgoing waves at the beginning. It is difficult to imagine a more effective way to portray the cessation of wave motion and the resulting pool of still water.

So far, we have heard the following wave patterns in the first ten measures (refer back to the tops of the pitch-class maps in Exx. 6.2, 6.3a, and 6.4): out (for 1 quarter note), in (1 quarter), out (1), in (1), out (1), in (1), out (1), in (longer, for 3 quarters; mm. 4b–5), in (even longer, for 4 quarters; mm. 5–6a), in (longer still, for 4½ quarters; mm. 6b–8a, including the "breaking" part in m. 7), in but slowing down (now for 5¼ quarters; mm. 7b–9), still pool of water (mm. 10–11a). The constantly encroaching inward waves have indeed led to a spring flood, creating a convincing cadence at the end of the first stanza.

But the waves pick up again in the following instrumental transition between the first and second stanzas, mm. 11–18, portrayed in

Example 6.5 Schoenberg, "Mondestrunken," *Pierrot lunaire*, Op. 21, mm. 11–18, transition to section B. Used by permission of Belmont Music Publishers and Universal Edition

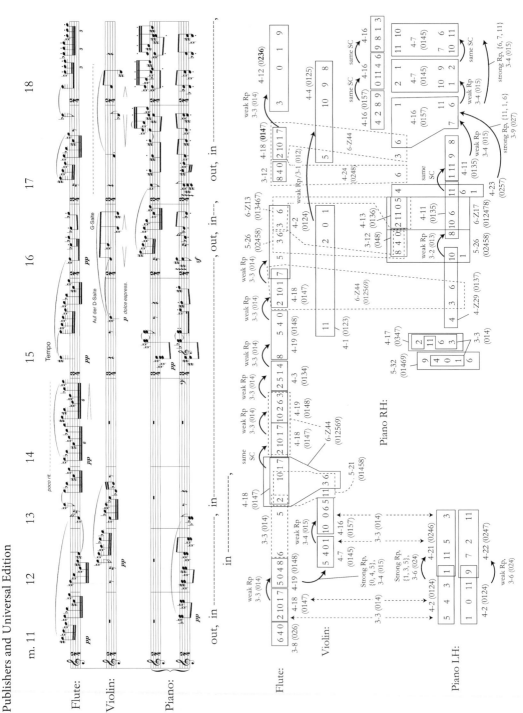

Example 6.5. The leading voice up to the downbeat of m. 16 is the flute, which creates a short outward wave and two longer inward waves, two chains of tetrachords linked mostly by weak Rp using 3-3 (014) as the common subset. The second of them is the longest chain we have heard yet, seven quarter notes. The first chain is preceded in m. 11a by <6, 4, 0>, set class 3-8 (026), another whole-tone 0 subset to portray outgoing wave motion. The incoming wave then links <2, 10, 1, 7>, SC 4-18 (0147) to <5, 0, 4, 8>, SC 4-19 (0148) through their common (014). Interestingly, the <2, 10, 1, 7> motive now *begins* the incoming wave in m. 11b rather than ending it, as it had the incoming waves earlier in the piece, and <2, 10, 1, 7> is followed by a tetrachord in m. 12a that includes the three notes {0, 4, 8} that had preceded it in the wave alternations at the beginning. Schoenberg is reversing the pitch-class successions and sets from the piece's opening measures, possibly to represent the confusion caused by the constant influx of moonlight.

After the flute plays <6, 5, 2> in longer note values (yet another member of set class 3-3), its second and longer chain of tetrachords begins in m. 13b. This particular inward wave again begins with <2, 10, 1, 7>, and the violin plays <3, 6> below it to reproduce the same six pitch classes that made up the incoming waves in mm. 1–3 (creating the same set class, 6-Z44). The 4-18 (0147) produced by <2, 10, 1, 7> then repeats in m. 14a, continuing on to 4-19 (0148), 4-3 (0134), 4-19 (0148), 4-18 (0147), and 4-2 (0124), all linked through weak Rp using (014) as common subset. Some notable features of this tetrachord chain are the duplication of the original "incoming wave" pitch classes in the first eight notes of m. 14, <2, 10, 1, 7> followed by <10, 2, 6, 3> – showing that 6-Z44 can be understood as linked 4-18 and 4-19 tetrachords, as well as <2, 10, 1, 7> in one voice and <3, 6> in another. In m. 15b, <2, 10, 1, 7> returns, this time functioning as an ending for the inward wave motion rather than a beginning, and is preceded by <8, 5, 4, 0>, which includes as a subset the original "outgoing wave" trichord <8, 4, 0>. The addition of PC 5 turns this quotation of the piece's original out–in alternation into two tetrachords linked by (014): functioning as part of a longer inward wave. Regular alternation gives way to constant inward motion, portraying the spring flood, it seems to me.

Set class 3-3 is not limited to serving as an n-1 common subset between successive melodic tetrachords in this passage, however. It occurs frequently as a vertical, both alone and as component of larger chords. In m. 11b, the two three-note chords created on the eighth-note beats between flute and piano are {1, 2, 5} and {0, 1, 4}, and other members of 3-3 appear as verticals on the last eighth of m. 12, {1, 2, 5}, and the first eighth of m. 13, {11, 0, 3}. Later, the two punctuating chords that begin m. 15 in the piano, 5-32 (01469) and 4-17 (0347), both contain 3-3 multiple times.

The subsidiary chains in mm. 11–13 in the violin and piano also connect in significant ways to their immediate context. The violin in mm. 12–13, imitating the flute's incoming wave a measure earlier, presents two tetrachords different from those in the flute, 4-7 (0145) and 4-16 (0157). These sets link to each other through weak Rp using 3-4 (015) as a common subset, a link that had been used nearly as much as 3-3 in the preceding ten measures. The violin's set classes also recur at the end of the passage (mm. 17b and 18) in the left hand of the piano in reverse order, 4-16 before 4-7, and the 3-4 link is expressed as a strong Rp relation there, {6, 7, 11}, between the 4-16 and the second 4-7.

The piano in mm. 11–13 produces its own descending wave (in thirds), and in addition to producing vertical 3-3s with the other instruments, the piano's horizontal segments yield pairs of tetrachords that link through Rp. The top line overlaps 4-2 (0124) with 4-21 (0246), linking strongly through a new n-1 common subset, {1, 3, 5}, a member of 3-6 (024). The bottom progresses from 4-2 to 4-22 (0247), linking weakly through (024). Both top and bottom lines progress from a more chromatic tetrachord to a less chromatic one: to a whole-tone tetrachord in the top voice, and a diatonic one in the bottom voice. Maybe the motion from chromatic to whole-tone (or diatonic) could be heard as reversing the progression from whole-tone to 4-18 (0147) that had just been heard in the flute at m. 11.

At m. 16, the regular wave alternation in quarter notes that opened "Mondestrunken" returns in the piano and flute, with a more complicated texture than that of the opening, and several different sets and set classes. The piano right hand begins m. 16 with the recognizable outward wave motive, <8, 4, 0>, 3-12 (048), but now follows it with <2, 11, 0, 5>, 4-13 (0136), portraying inward wave motion with an octatonic subset for the first time. If we include the piano's left hand in the analysis, the first quarter of m. 16 yields 5-26 (02458), a superset of the original inward 4-24, and the second quarter 6-Z17 (012478), an almost-octatonic hexachord. If, however, we consider the piano's right hand together with the flute, which alternates PCs 3 and 6 in a similar manner to the violin's accompanying line in the opening measures (see the dotted enclosures on the pitch-class map), the first quarter gives us 5-26 again, and the second quarter 6-Z13 (013467), a pure octatonic segment. The substitution of octatonic or almost-octatonic hexachords for what had been 6-Z44s at the beginning creates the effect of returning to the piece's initial alternating waves, but not getting all the way there. In m. 17, then, the flute and piano right hand produce 4-24 during the first quarter note and 6-Z44 on the second, with every pitch in its original register (but different timbres). This restores the music of the piece's beginning for a moment.

After the brief return, both flute and piano extend the incoming wave of m. 17's second beat through m. 18, in different ways, to prepare for the onset of the poem's second stanza and the melodrama's B section. The flute links <2, 10, 1, 7> of the original alternating pattern to <3, 0, 1, 9>, set class 4-18 (0147) to 4-12 (0236), through weak Rp using 3-3. This second tetrachord takes on a new and different rhythmic profile from the ubiquitous motive, seven even sixteenths after a sixteenth rest,[28] that has either portrayed alternating wave motions (when associated with <8, 4, 0, 2, 10, 1, 7>) or signaled the onset of longer incoming waves from the beginning of this piece. Now we hear triplet sixteenths that could possibly signify the faster-moving "longings" that skim across the spring flood of moonlight like water bugs.

The piano in mm. 17–18, after reproducing the <6, 3, 6> motive that the violin had originally introduced, pushes that line into an inner voice and places another chain of tetrachords above it in the top voice of the right hand. This new incoming wave no longer links different set classes together through weak Rp, but instead repeats the same set class, 4-16 (0157), three times. Though the passage *seems* sequential because of similar contours, it actually inverts {2, 4, 8, 9} through $T_8I$ to yield {11, 0, 4, 6}, and then transposes that by $T_9$ to get {8, 9, 1, 3}. Using the same set class rather than different ones linked by weak Rp gives this particular descending wave of moonlight a more focused quality than its predecessors, which will lead later on (in the retransition from B back to A′) to downward cascades that focus even more sharply by transposing exactly the same interval succession.

The accompanying voices to the piano's tetrachord chain create their own chain, which I commented on above when I mentioned how mm. 17b–18 reverse the succession of tetrachords 4-7 and 4-16 from the violin's incoming wave in mm. 12–13. But these two tetrachords also form the last part of a longer chain in the piano left hand that stretches back to the second beat of m. 15. I will pick it up on the downbeat of m. 17, where we hear an arpeggiated perfect fourth chord {1, 4, 6, 11}, set class 4-23 (0257), followed by the succession <1, 11, 9, 8>, set class 4-11 (0135).

---

[28] This rhythmic profile has been recognized by both Alan Lessem and Jonathan Dunsby as a recurring motive not only in "Mondestrunken" but throughout all of *Pierrot*, producing another bit of musical evidence for the work's cyclic status (in addition to the consistent use of "basic images" that I mentioned above and will elaborate through this chapter). See Lessem, "Text and Music in Schoenberg's *Pierrot Lunaire*," *Current Musicology* 19 (1975): 106–07; Dunsby, *Schoenberg: Pierrot lunaire*, p. 28.

Both set classes link to the following 4-16 (0157), {1, 6, 7, 11}, through Rp, the former through a strong Rp with {11, 1, 6}, 3-9 (027) as common subset, and the latter through a weak Rp with 3-4 (015) held in common. The {1, 6, 7, 11} on beat 3 of m. 17 then proceeds to two consecutive set classes 4-7 (0145), linking to the first through weak Rp with 3-4, and to the second through strong Rp with {6, 7, 11}, also a member of 3-4.

The only strand of the counterpoint in Example 6.5 that I have not described yet is the violin in mm. 15–18. It also creates a small chain of tetrachords, 4-1 (0123) moving to 4-4 (0125), which link through weak Rp using 3-1 (012). But with its longer note values, slurred tetrachords, and especially its descending leaps of <–14> in m. 16 and <–13> in m. 18, it seems to stand out from the rest of the texture. Its main function seems to be to provide a motivic preview of and transition to the beginning of the next section, the setting of the first two lines of stanza 2, illustrated in Example 6.6. In the B section, the violin is marked *hervor* ("bring out"). This leading voice begins with a single <–13> in m. 19, beat 2, then proceeds to swoop up and down in tetrachords that feature <–11>, <–13>, and <+11> prominently (these are boxed in the score, with their interval successions placed above the boxes). Comparing the ascending tetrachords to each other, as well as the descending ones, we can see that the pitch intervals expand and then mostly contract (like <–3, –11, –3> expanding to <–4, –11, –10> and then (mostly) contracting to <–1, –5, –13> in the descending tetrachords). The tetrachord set classes in the violin can also be understood as expanding and then contracting, starting with the second one: 4-2 (0124), 4-3 (0134), 4-3, 4-9 (0167), 4-12 (0236), 4-16 (0157) – a phenomenon reminiscent of the set-class expansions and contractions we discussed in Chapters 1 and 2.

But, though the adjacent tetrachords in the violin have a number of common n-1 subsets, the linking trichord between them is different in every case, and some tetrachords do not share a common trichord. (The one significant Rp relationship in the violin is a strong one around <7, 6, 10>, manifested by the ascending tetrachords in mm. 20 and 21 – which are not adjacent.) The emphasis has shifted, it seems, from portraying incoming waves through linked tetrachords to depicting the "longings" (Gelüste) that swim around in the spring flood, first increasing, then growing smaller. This swelling and shrinking can also be heard in the violin's contour, which alternates between precipitous falls and rises.

Other voices in the texture also follow the same pattern of growth, then contraction. The reciter's part is difficult to parse into tetrachords: a more natural segmentation yields both trichords and tetrachords, 3-1 (012), 4-9 (0167), 3-11 (037) for the first line of stanza 2, "Gelüste, schauerlich

Example 6.6 Schoenberg, "Mondestrunken," *Pierrot lunaire*, Op. 21, mm. 18b–23a, beginning of section B. Used by permission of Belmont Music Publishers and Universal Edition

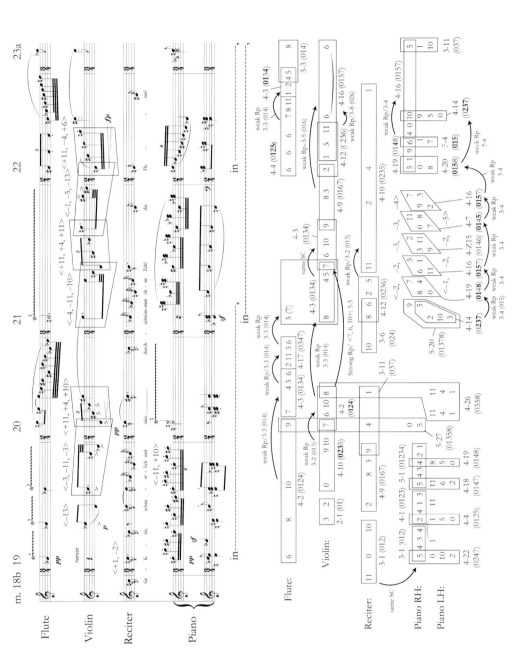

und süß," then 3-6 (024), 4-12 (0236), and 4-10 (0235) for the second line, "durchschwimmen ohne Zahl die Fluten!" The two lines contain an expansion of some of the intervals in the prime form ((012) to (0167)), followed by a contraction of some of the intervals ((0236) to (0235)). The general contour of both lines, rising up to the high points E5 and B4 and then descending, agrees with the picture of longings increasing and decreasing.

The piano breaks into the same two two-measure phrases as the voice, mm. 19–20 and 21–22 (unlike the flute and violin, which seem to create one continuous phrase through the passage). Parts of the piano's texture in both phrases contribute to the overall sense of expansion (not so much contraction), while others seem to develop specific aspects of the voice or other instruments. The right hand in m. 19 picks up the voice's 3-1 (012) on "Gelüste" and stretches it into larger and larger chromatic sets, 3-1, 4-1, 5-1. One of the interval sequences within the 5-1 sextuplet on beat 3 of m. 19 even recalls the ordered pitch intervals of "Gelüste": <+1, –2> is octave-complemented to <–11, +10>. We could say that one of the voice's original <+1, –2> "longings" has managed to swim through the rest of m. 19 in the piano, but expands intervallically as it does so. In contrast, the piano left hand in mm. 19–20 creates, together with the instruments and voice in some cases, a series of chords that (mostly) expand the adjacent intervals in their prime forms, starting with the second one, 4-4 (0125). The sequence reads 4-4, 4-18 (0147), 4-19 (0148), 5-27 (01358), 4-26 (0358); creating the adjacent prime-form intervals **113, 133, 134, 1223, 323**. I believe the progression from more closed to more open intervals is easy to hear in this chord succession, as it moves from chromatic and hexatonic subsets to diatonic ones.

The piano in mm. 21–22 can be heard as splitting into top and bottom lines and an underlying chord progression. The top line in m. 21, <9, 7, 5, 2, 11, 7>, expands its pitch intervals incrementally as it descends, <–2, –2, –3, –3, –4>, as does the same measure's "bass" line in the left hand, <0, 11, 9, 7, 2>, with ordered pitch intervals <–1, –2, –2, –5>. The right hand in m. 22 is less incremental, but is still mostly dependent on –4 intervals: <–4, –4, –3, –2, –4>. Here, the picture of descending, incoming waves of moonlight from part A is combined with the notion of gradual expansion of longings from part B. In addition, both hands of the piano in mm. 21–22 combine to create a chain of tetrachords in which almost every prime form holds 3-4 (015) as a common three-note subset (indicated in bold numbers). These are 4-14 (0**237**), 4-19 (**0148**), 4-16 (**015**7), 4-Z15 (0146, the only set that does not contain 3-4), 4-7 (**0145**), 4-16 (**015**7), 4-20 (**0158**), 3-4 itself, and 4-14 (0**237**). As most of the voices in the piano descend during these measures, the tetrachord almost-chain contributes to the portrayal of incoming waves of moonlight.

The one voice in Example 6.6 we have not discussed yet is the flute, which also produces chains of tetrachords linked by the same trichord subset, in this case, 3-3 (014), "Mondestrunken's" most common link. The first chain stretches from mm. 19–21, including 4-2 (**0124**), 4-3 (**013**4), 4-17 (**034**7), and ending in a tetrachord jointly expressed by the flute and violin at the beginning of m. 21, 4-3 (**0134**). The second chain begins on the F♯4 in m. 22 and links 4-4 (0**125**) and 4-3 (**0134**), ending with 3-3 itself. The flute's chains can be heard in the same way as before, as incoming waves of light (especially since the descending rhythmic motive of seven sixteenths from mm. 1–4 reappears in m. 20 as thirty-seconds). But they also partake of the rising and falling contour we heard in the violin and voice, which I associated with longings waxing and waning. Maybe both images can be heard as coexisting in this passage: increasing and decreasing longings, and waves overlapping and cresting at different times.

With m. 23, the first two lines of the poem return, "Den Wein, den man mit Augen trinkt, gießt nachts der Mond in Wogen nieder." It is to Schoenberg's credit, I think, that he did not choose to bring back a literal, simple repetition of the opening music at this point. Instead, he created what Michael Cherlin calls a "fantastic clockwork" in mm. 23–24 before recapitulating the opening in a much-intensified form in mm. 25–28.[29] Example 6.7 shows the brief clockwork, which pits triplets in the flute against duplets in the piano and violin *am Steg*.

If we separate flute from violin and piano in our segmentation on the basis of their rhythmic differences, what emerges are set-class and interval patterns that vary the immediately preceding music in different ways. The flute plays a chain of trichords, 3-5 (016), 3-7 (025), 3-9 (027), and 3-8 (026), each of which descends, that mostly link through the common interval-class 2 (except for the first two). These set classes progress from an octatonic subset to two diatonic subsets, and finally to a whole-tone subset, an expansion in the sense that the interval contents gradually sound more open. The ordered pitch intervals of these trichords, likewise, trace a pattern which generally expands, though the second trichord momentarily produces a smaller second interval: <–1, –5>, <–2, –3>, <–2, –5>, <–2, –6>.

As for the violin and piano, their sounding together in duplets over a sustained pair of notes encourages me to look at the vertical tetrachords created by them. In m. 23, they alternate set class 4-20 (0158) with other

[29] Cherlin, *Schoenberg's Musical Imagination*, p. 214.

Example 6.7  Schoenberg, "Mondestrunken," *Pierrot lunaire*, Op. 21, mm. 23–25a. Used by permission of Belmont Music Publishers and Universal Edition

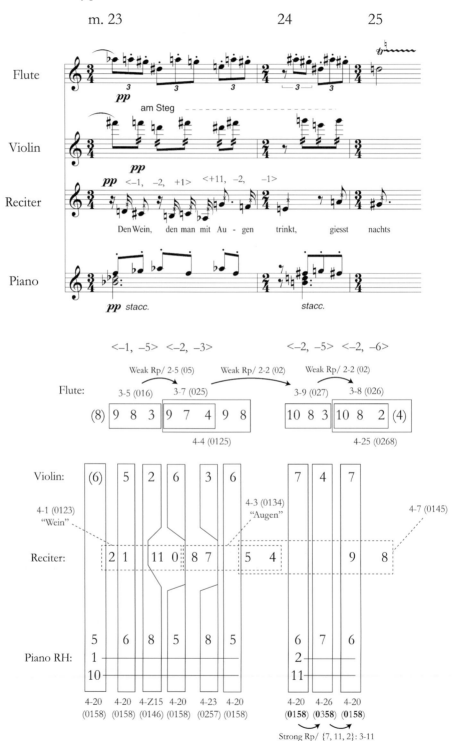

tetrachords that do not have a common n-1 subset with it, 4-Z15 (0146) and 4-23 (0257). In the following measure, as the 4-20 moves up by half-step, the tetrachord verticals alternate 4-20 with 4-26 (0358), which does have 3-11 in common with it as {7, 11, 2}. The reappearance of the n-1 common subset (quite audible in the piano as the G major triad) prepares us for the return of A material, chains of descending tetrachords, starting in m. 25.

Finally, the voice in mm. 23–24 is the one element of the texture that reprises the beginning of the piece – but it does so in a disguised way. The first four notes, setting "Den Wein, den man" again yields 4-1 (0123), the same set class that had set those words back in mm. 2–3, Lewin's "Wein" tetrachord. (Compare Example 6.7 with Example 6.2.) Likewise, "mit Augen trinkt" again receives 4-3 (0134), the "Augen" tetrachord, the set class that had set those words in mm. 3–4. But, *only* the set classes remain the same as in the earlier passage – making it necessary for us to admit the set class as an analytic tool if we want to claim that the earlier and later settings of the same words are related. The pitch class successions in mm. 23–24 are <2, 1, 11, 0> and <8, 7, 5, 4>, not related by ordered transposition or inversion to the <9, 11, 10, 8> and <9, 0, 11, 8> of mm. 1–2. Also, the ordered pitch-interval successions, given above the notes in the score, are very different in mm. 23–24, <–1, –2, +1> and <+11, –2, –1>, where the pitch intervals of mm. 2–4 had been <+2, –1, –2> and <+3, –1, –3>. This indicates that the notes of "Wein" and "Augen" have undergone reordering as well as transposition from the earlier to the later passage. Finally, the voice's tetrachord at mm. 23b–25a, covering the words "–gen trinkt, gießt nachts," yields 4-7 (0145), so that we can trace a set-class expansion in the voice even more clear than that happening simultaneously in the flute, 4-1 (0123) to 4-3 (0134) to 4-7 (0145).

In mm. 25–28, as I mentioned above, the ensemble returns to depicting the descending waves of moonlight from the piece's opening, but does so in a greatly intensified way. The passage, which creates a retransition to the A' section, is illustrated in Example 6.8. Both Michael Cherlin and Daniel Jenkins have already pointed out, the former with a brief description, the latter with a more detailed analysis, that Schoenberg cycles the original 4-24, 6-Z44 wave alternation (both piano and violin parts of mm. 1–4) down by major thirds here, so that the <8, 4, 0> descending augmented triad is projected on two structural levels and two transpositional levels simultaneously.[30] This technique of ornamenting all or part of the

---

[30] Cherlin, *Schoenberg's Musical Imagination*, pp. 214–15; Jenkins, "Schoenberg's Concept of 'ruhende Bewegung'," 98–100.

Example 6.8 Schoenberg, "Mondestrunken," *Pierrot lunaire*, Op. 21, mm. 25–28, retransition to A′. Used by permission of Belmont Music Publishers and Universal Edition

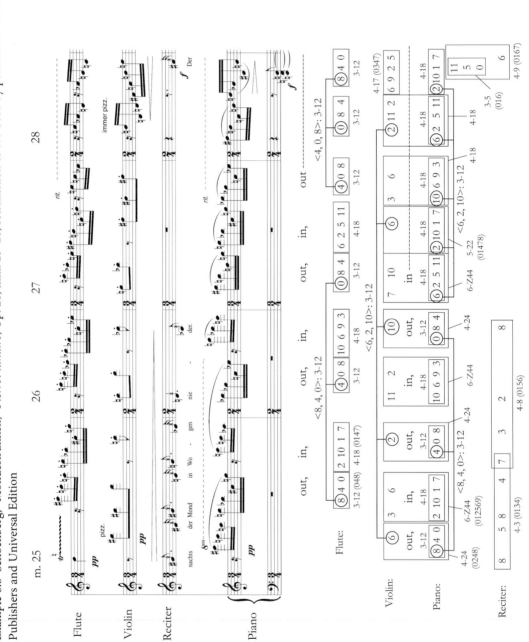

melodrama's principal motive with smaller copies of itself occurs elsewhere in *Pierrot*: Kathryn Bailey and I have commented on its use in "Nacht."[31]

My account will focus on how the alternating wave motion from the piece's beginning is both intensified and confused in this passage, to portray the growing inebriation of the poet as he takes in too much moonlight (a situation which will be described in the coming third stanza). The piano and violin in m. 25a begin with exactly the same pitches (an octave higher) and rhythms that they played in m. 1, and then transpose that out–in wave alternation down by major 3rd twice in mm. 25b–27a. These two voices alone project a clear picture of waves going out and in, while at the same time descending. On the second and third beats of m. 27 and the first beat of m. 28, the outward wave disappears from the piano and violin (as we shall see, it moves up to the flute part), and we hear only the inward part of the alternation. Both violin and piano are again transposing down by major 3rds, though the piano moves faster than the violin; so that they no longer create 6-Z44 on each beat, but 5-22 (01478) and 4-18 (0147) twice. However, these smaller sets are both subsets of 6-Z44, so that the progression can be heard to signify the same kind of extended incoming wave as we encountered repeatedly in the A section.

The intensification of the alternating wave motion in this passage is partly due to the flute part, which creates a canon with the right hand of the piano an octave lower and one quarter note later, from m. 25b through the second quarter note of m. 27. Its descending wave alternation is just as clear as that in the piano, but because of the rhythmic offset, its incoming 4-18 motives occur simultaneously with the outgoing 3-12 motives in the piano, and vice versa. This creates confusion as to whether the waves are moving in or out, which only grows greater on the third beat of m. 27 through m. 28, as the flute limits itself to the outgoing 3-12, again cycling down by major 3rd. While the piano and violin are extending an incoming wave, the flute extends an outgoing wave.

Another source of confusion is the passage's nearly total dependence on cycles of major 3rds, which both Cherlin and Jenkins emphasize – actually, two such cycles. The piano in mm. 25–26 and flute in mm. 25b–27a both use the <8, 4, 0> descending 3rd cycle, a middleground version of the original outgoing motive from m. 1, to govern the transpositions of their surface outward (3–12) and inward (4–18) waves. (These middleground

---

[31] Bailey, "Formal Organization and Structural Imagery in Schoenberg's *Pierrot Lunaire*," 102; Jack Boss, "Schoenberg on Ornamentation and Structural Levels," *Journal of Music Theory* 38/2 (Fall 1994): p. 214, fn 22; idem, "The Musical Idea and the Basic Image," 254, 258–60.

progressions are represented with circles and brackets above or below in the pitch-class map.) The flute in mm. 27b–28 switches to the middle-ground motive <4, 0, 8>, a rotation of the first cycle (and hidden repetition of the flute's surface motive on the third beat of m. 27), to control the transpositions of its outward wave motions. But at the same time, the violin throughout mm. 25–28 transposes its <–3, +3> motive according to a transposition of the first cycle, <6, 2, 10>; and when the piano switches to sequencing 4-18 incoming waves in mm. 27–28, it also uses <6, 2, 10> as its middleground. Thus, over the entire passage we hear a large-scale projection of <0, 2, 4, 6, 8, 10>, the $WT_0$ scale. Does this mean that we ought to perceive the whole retransition as outward wave motion (which is what whole-tone segments had signified earlier)? I prefer to hear it as an effect that mixes together middleground whole-tone outward motion with surface motives that alternate out and in, portraying a blurring of the poet's perspective. And, even though Jenkins uses this passage as an example of "ruhende Bewegung" because of all its sequences, I would argue that the canon, together with the simultaneous presentation of motives and set-classes that had signified outward and inward motion, creates a growth in intensity from the previous music. The sequences themselves, as a more focused presentation of the "wave" motives than the A section's chains of Rp-related tetrachords, contribute to the increased intensity. All this depicts overwhelming cascades of moonlight on which the poet is getting drunk (the topic of stanza 3, as I mentioned above).

Before we move on to stanza 3, however, I should say something about the voice part in mm. 25–28. It does not participate in the descending alterna-tions of 3-12 and 4-18 that the instruments are carrying on – but we can hear it as further extending the descent and gradual set-class expansion it had undergone in mm. 23–24. This is another way to portray the melodrama's basic image, which is exactly what the reciter is referencing here: "gießt nachts der Mond in Wogen nieder." In mm. 23–25a, as we already discussed regarding Example 6.7, the reciter had produced variations of the "Wein" and "Augen" tetrachords that yield the same set classes, 4-1 (0123) and 4-3 (0134), before moving on to 4-7 (0145). Her first tetrachord in m. 25 projects set class 4-3 (0134) again, followed by 4-8 (0156) in mm. 25b and 26. And the chord in the piano left hand at the end of m. 28, {11, 0, 5}, together with the voice's pickup note in the same location, PC 6, yields set class 4-9 (0167). As the reciter generally goes lower through mm. 25–26, we can hear her tracing the same kind of descending and expanding motion as was prevalent in both Examples 6.7 and 6.6.

Example 6.9 illustrates mm. 28b–32, the first two lines of stanza 3. This passage's most prominent feature is the rather abrupt introduction of

Example 6.9 Schoenberg, "Mondestrunken," *Pierrot lunaire*, Op. 21, mm. 28b–32, beginning of A′. Used by permission of Belmont Music Publishers and Universal Edition

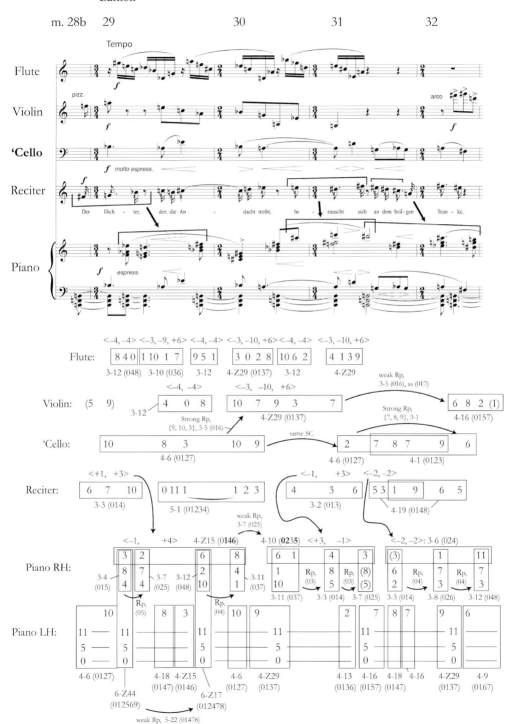

a new member of the ensemble, the 'cello, which Simms, Dunsby, and Brinkmann understand as representing the poet/composer.[32] Since the 'cello was Schoenberg's own instrument, these scholars claim or suggest that he, like Giraud before him, is here associating himself as modern artist with Pierrot (or, more likely, Hanswurst). Schoenberg, with characteristic efficiency, does this right away in his first melodrama, rather than waiting until the end of the first part of the cycle, as Giraud had.

I identified mm. 29–32 as the beginning of the A′ section previously, but the only features that support that reading are the wave motives from mm. 1–4, which were originally in the piano but are now in the flute and violin parts. As they had just previously in mm. 25–28, these out–in wave motions again overlap one another, and the one in the violin imitates the ones in the flute in augmentation. While the pitch-interval successions of the outgoing waves here are the same as in mm. 1–4 (and 25–28), those of the inward waves are changed. The motive had been <–4, –4> (out), <–4, –9, +6> (in) earlier, forming 3-12 and 4-18; but now the flute's first wave motion goes <–4, –4>, <**–3**, –9, +6>, ending with 3-10 (036), and the second and third, as well as the violin, go <–4, –4>, <**–3, –10**, +6>, creating 3-12 and 4-Z29 (0137). (The further significance of 4-Z29 will be discussed in the next paragraph.)

Every other voice in the texture of mm. 29–32 seems much more distantly related to the melodrama's opening, if related at all. The chords in the piano, and melodies in 'cello (doubled by the piano) and voice, sound like loud confusion, crashing and clashing – Schoenberg introducing himself as a modern composer, perhaps. But there is a logic underlying it all. The key to the passage, I think, lies in the set classes formed as verticals between the tenor voice in the 'cello and piano and the 3-5 (016) pedal, {11, 0, 5}, in Viennese Trichord voicing, in the bass voices. These are, in order, 4-6 (0127), 4-18 (0147), 4-Z15 (0146), 4-6 again, 4-Z29 (0137), 4-13 (0136), 4-16 (0157), 4-18, 4-16, 4-Z29, and 4-9 (0167). Obviously, they all relate to one another by strong Rp with 3-5 as the linking set, because {11, 0, 5} is part of all of them. And 4-18 is already familiar to us from its prominence in the A section as the final tetrachord of most of the incoming waves. But many of the other 3-5 supersets presented in the lowest voices of the ensemble play important roles as horizontal segments in A′: 4-6 (0127) occurs twice in the 'cello/piano melody, and then gives way to 4-1 (0123), related to it by strong Rp around 3-1 (012).

[32] Simms, *The Atonal Music of Arnold Schoenberg*, pp. 127–28; Dunsby, *Schoenberg: Pierrot lunaire*, p. 29; Brinkmann, "The Fool as Paradigm," p. 162.

The set 4-Z29 (0137) is created by the altered inward wave motions in the flute and violin in mm. 30–31. And 4-Z15 (0146) begins the top-voice melody of the right hand of the piano, which then leads to 4-10 (0235), related to it by weak Rp around 3-7 (025). Tetrachord supersets of 3-5, appearing as chords in the 'cello and left hand of the piano, also serve as starting points for horizontal chains of tetrachords like those in the A section, and those starting points are linked through their common 3-5 subset to the motive that either constituted or ended most of the incoming waves in the A section, <2, 10, 1, 7> or 4-18.

Another connection to the melodrama's opening can be found among the hexachords formed in mm. 29 in those places where the two hands of the piano strike chords together. The first of these, the second eighth of beat 1 of m. 29, forms set-class 6-Z44 (012569), the same SC that had been created by violin together with piano during the inward wave parts of mm. 1–4. This 6-Z44 links to the next large vertical chord on the second eighth of beat 4, 6-Z17 (012478), through weak Rp around set-class 5-22 (01478).

The piano right-hand melody, one of the tetrachord chains discussed above, is harmonized in trichords so that the set classes are mostly different from trichord to trichord. The pitch-class map shows that they, imitating the piano melody above them, form smaller Rp chains; groups of two or three trichords that share a common interval class. In m. 29, 3-4 (015) progresses to 3-7 (025), sharing (05). These are followed by 3-12 (048) and 3-11 (037), sharing (04). A group of three begins in m. 30b: 3-11 (037), 3-3 (014), and 3-7 (025), sharing (03), and another such group follows in mm. 31b–32: 3-3 (014), 3-8 (026), and 3-12 (048), sharing (04). (The emphasis on whole-tone trichords in m. 32 seems to match the right hand of the piano, which is descending through pitch classes <3, 1, 11>, SC 3-6 (024), at the same point.)

The voice in Example 6.9 seems to go its own way with respect to set classes, introducing harmonies like 5-1 and 4-19, not prominent elsewhere, at least in these measures. But it has another kind of connection with the melody in the piano's right hand, with which it shares several identical and similar pitch-interval successions (shown directly above the pitch-class sets in the PC map, and the related successions are bracketed in the score). The reciter's opening succession <+1, +3> on "Der Dichter" is answered almost immediately in rhythmic augmentation by <–1, +4> in the piano right hand, two similar pitch-interval sequences that belong to the same set class, 3-3 (014). Her succession <–1, +3> on "berauscht sich" in mm. 30–31 happens simultaneously with <+3, –1> in the piano, a reversal of the pitch intervals that again forms the same set class, 3-2 (013). Finally, the voice ("an dem heil –") and piano produce the same pitch-interval succession in mm. 31–32, <–2, –2>, 3-6 (024).

Thus, the opening of the A′ section, which initially sounds like familiar music (wave motions) in flute and violin, and a lot of seemingly unrelated confusion in the other voices, in fact has multiple harmonic and melodic connections between 'cello, piano, and voice themselves, and also between that trio and the flute and violin. The rest of the A′ section, shown in Example 6.10, continues and develops many of the same connections. In mm. 33–34, the violin, 'cello, and top line of the piano right hand again consist mostly of tetrachords with a single common n-1 subset; but instead of 3-5 (as in the previous measures) it is now 3-4 (015) that links 4-16 (0157), 4-7 (0145), and 4-11 (0135). In mm. 33b–34, 3-4 itself then appears in the right hand of the piano. The one tetrachord that does not contain 3-4 is 4-3 (0134), in the violin in mm. 33b and 34a. This tetrachord will prove to be important later, at m. 37, as the voice reiterates and varies its "Augen" motive one last time.

Though 3-5 is emphasized less in the instrumental lines here than previously, it definitely comes to the fore as a harmonic element, particularly in its Viennese Trichord voicing of perfect fourth above or below tritone, unordered pitch intervals <5, 6> or <6, 5>, in measures 33–35. The Viennese Trichord had been limited in mm. 29–32 to the bass-register ostinato, but in mm. 33–35 it moves up into the upper registers of the piano as well, and begins to proliferate. The right hand of the piano begins m. 33 with <6, 5>, which is answered on the second half of beat 2 in the left hand by <6, 5> again, followed by <5, 6> on the third beat of m. 33. Then in m. 34, both right-hand chords have unordered pitch intervals <5, 6>, and the second of them is accompanied by <6, 5> on the second beat in the left hand. Finally, the third tremolo in the right hand of the piano in m. 35 is <6, 7>, a close relative of the Viennese Trichord. The other right-hand and left-hand piano chords in these measures are mostly traditional major, minor, augmented, and diminished triads: 3-11 (037), 3-12 (048), and 3-10 (036), which do not form any kind of tonal progression, but rather link to and from the Viennese Trichords and each other by means of common interval classes (indicated by arrows between the chords on the pitch-class map).

The voice in the same measures, mm. 33–34, sets the words "Gen Himmel wendet er verzückt das Haupt." It also emphasizes 3-5 at its beginning – in fact, since the ordered pitch intervals in the voice alternate tritones and half-steps, <–1, –6, –1, –6, –1>, for the first two beats of m. 33, 3-5 overlaps with itself no less than four times. But at the end of the phrase, the reciter turns toward a $WT_1$ segment as the text speaks of Pierrot "turning his head ecstatically," <1, 5, 11, 3>, SC 4-21 (0246).

The voice's second phrase in mm. 35–36, "und taumelnd saugt und schlürft er den Wein," leans even further in the direction of whole-tone collections, beginning with 4-2 (0124) but then producing <0, 4, 2, 6>, 4-21 again, and <6, 4, 0, 10>, 4-25 (0268). These latter two tetrachords are members of the $WT_0$ collection, but $WT_1$ also plays an important role elsewhere in the texture: the 'cello on the second quarter of m. 34 starts a descent in long notes through five pitches of $WT_1$, <11, 9, 7, 5, 3>, finishing on the down-beat of m. 38. Perhaps it is possible to hear the flute's PC 1 on the second beat of m. 38 as continuing and completing the $WT_1$ scale.

So far, we have characterized the latter part of the A' section in terms of emerging harmonic and melodic trends; first, harmonic Viennese Trichords (with other versions of set class 3-5 in the voice), followed by melodic whole-tone collections and scales. The left hand of the piano in mm. 35–37 introduces a third emerging trend, this one more important for the musical form than the other two – the return of the outward and inward wave motions from the piece's beginning (these have been absent since the first beat of m. 31). These waves in mm. 35–37 repeat exactly the pitch-class succession of the beginning, <8, 4, 0>, <2, 10, 1, 7>. Unlike the beginning, however, they sound in the lower register of the piano here, and the first pair in mm. 34b–35 is offset rhythmically (it comes in two sixteenths too soon). The second pair of waves in mm. 35b–36, which is extended by a sequence of <2, 10, 1, 7> to <5, 1, 4, 10>, then corrects the rhythmic offset. It could be that the low register and rhythmic uncertainty represents Pierrot/Poet/Schoenberg "staggering" as he "sucks up and slurps" the waves of moonlight.

Another emerging trend worthy of mention, just before the final cadence, is the sudden profusion of members of set class 4-3 (0134) in mm. 37–38a. I pointed out at the beginning of our discussion of "Mondestrunken" (p. 275) that 4-3 is the set class that contains David Lewin's "Augen" motive, which had appeared directly after the 4-1 "Wein" motive in measures 2b–4. On p. 291, I showed that the return of the first two lines of the poem as the last two lines of the second stanza in mm. 23–24 seems to have motivated Schoenberg to bring back the set classes 4-1 and 4-3 in sequence, but *no other* characteristics of the "Wein" and "Augen" motives return, save their set classes. Here in mm. 36b–38a, the reciter repeats line 1 as the final line of the third stanza, "Den Wein, den man mit Augen trinkt." The 4-1 "Wein" motive is nowhere to be found in the voice part, since the reciter (as previously discussed) is descending through whole-tone 0 as she speaks of "the wine." But the tetrachord "den man mit Au –" does indeed produce 4-3, the set class of "Augen," and does so using the pitch intervals <–1, –3, +1>, not too distantly related to the

Example 6.10 Schoenberg, "Mondestrunken," *Pierrot lunaire*, Op. 21, mm. 32b–39.
Used by permission of Belmont Music Publishers and Universal Edition

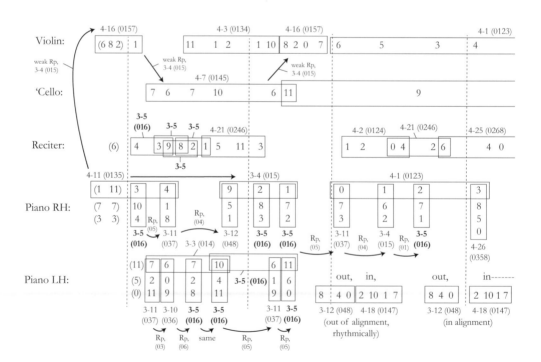

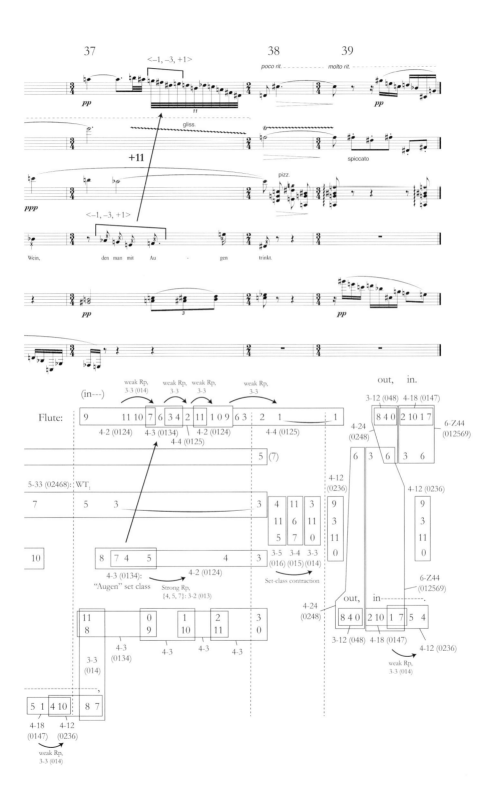

intervals of the original "Augen" in mm. 3–4, <+3, –1, –3>. In one way, the musical reference back to "Wein" and "Augen" in mm. 36–37 is more faint than the one in mm. 23–24 (only the "Augen" tetrachord remains), but in another way (the pitch intervals of "Augen") it seems closer to the original.

Together with the single 4-3 in the voice, the rising chromatic thirds in the piano in mm. 37–38a create multiple overlapping instances of 4-3. The other moving voice in m. 37, the flute (which enters in that measure after being silent for most of Example 6.10), reproduces as part of its long descending run not just set class 4-3, but the specific pitch-interval succession of the voice's 4-3, <–1, –3, +1>, as the first four notes of the eleven-note group. (The pitch-transpositional relationship between these motives is indicated on the musical score with brackets and an arrow.) The flute's 4-3, <7, 6, 3, 4>, links to the preceding set-class in its run, as well as the subsequent ones, through weak Rp around set class 3-3 (014), in the same manner as the descending waves of moonlight throughout section A.

In preparation for the final cadence, the 'cello plays a series of three pizzicato chords in m. 38, a summary of the principal set classes in this melodrama that have performed Rp linking functions between tetrachords. It orders them as a set-class contraction, 3-5 (016) to 3-4 (015) to 3-3 (014). This leads in m. 39 to the cadence, which returns to the material of mm. 1–4 – one out–in wave succession in the piano and violin (identical to the beginning), and a second one overlapping it in the flute and violin. The 'cello accompanies with an arpeggiated pizzicato chord that belongs to 4-12 (0236), a superset of 3-3, and the same set class that is formed by the extension of the piano's inward wave on beat 3 of m. 39. Thus, the piece circles back around to its basic image at the end, waves of moonlight going out, then in.

But, in reality, it never strayed too far away from that central image. We have seen that most of section A was devoted to creating extensions of the incoming waves through tetrachords linked by Rp around the same trichord set class (most often 3-3). Section B, as a contrasting section should, set aside the wave motions for a few measures to focus on portraying the "longings" which "swim through the flood," by means of expanding and contracting intervals and set classes, as well as alternating upward and downward contours. But the waves came back with a vengeance at m. 25, multiple sequences connected by middleground hidden repetitions of the outgoing wave, to create a retransition to A'. The final section again turned away from the basic image momentarily to focus on the Viennese Trichord and its supersets, then the whole-tone collection. But at the end, the wave motions and the "Augen" tetrachord returned to bring the piece back to its starting point – the portrayal of "wine coming down from the moon in waves." Thus we can say, confirming Schoenberg's own description of his text-setting process, that the whole piece indeed grows out of a visual image abstracted from the first two lines. At the same time, the music does react in several places to text later on in the poem, such as the portrayal of "longings" early in section B and Schoenberg's introduction of the 'cello at the beginning of A′ to represent himself as poet/composer.

## "Die Kreuze," No. 14

Schoenberg's final melodrama of part II also provides an excellent example of a piece that mostly elaborates a basic image drawn from the first two lines of text, but also reacts musically to modifications of that image introduced later in the poem. Its poem is given below, with my English translation:

| | |
|---|---|
| Heilge Kreuze sind die Verse, | Verses are holy crosses, |
| Dran die Dichter stumm verbluten, | On which poets silently bleed to death, |
| Blindgeschlagen von der Geier | Struck blind by a ghostly |
| Flatterndem Gespensterschwarme! | Fluttering swarm of vultures! |
| | |
| In den Leibern schwelgten Schwerter, | In their bodies swords reveled, |
| Prunkend in des Blutes Scharlach! | Showing off in the scarlet of the blood! |
| Heilge Kreuze sind die Verse, | Verses are holy crosses, |
| Dran die Dichter stumm verbluten. | On which poets silently bleed to death. |
| | |
| Tot das Haupt – erstarrt die Locken – | The head is dead – its curls are stiff – |
| Fern, verweht der Lärm des Pöbels. | Far away, the noise of the mob dies out. |
| Langsam sinkt die Sonne nieder, | The sun sinks down slowly, |
| Eine rote Königskrone. | A red, royal crown. |
| Heilge Kreuze sind die Verse! | Verses are holy crosses! |

I mentioned at the beginning of this chapter that "Die Kreuze" is in the same location, the end of the second part, in Schoenberg's twenty-one melodramas as "Les Croix" occupies in Giraud's fifty poems. (Refer back to Example 6.1.) The two poems play identical roles within the whole: they both represent the climax, the upper limit of grotesquerie, among Pierrot's real or imagined punishments for his crime of straying into atonality or Decadence. The poet/composer is nailed to the cross – his poem or piece – and suffers some of the same torments as Christ: the sword plunged into his side which brings an issue of blood, rejection by the crowd, and a crown, not of thorns here, but placed on his head by the setting sun. In addition, there is a new torment, the swarm of vultures that peck out his eyes; perhaps a metaphor for literary or music critics. At the end, he is no longer able to move or speak, "stumm," a picture of creative paralysis and death.

Schoenberg's basic image to represent this gruesome situation depends on a device he would adopt again and again later in his twelve-tone period – simultaneous vertical and horizontal symmetry. In his later music, such symmetry usually connotes perfection, sometimes even God's perfection,[33] but here, it produces the image of a cross which spans all twenty-two measures. The piece literally *is* a cross (illustrating the poem's first line in an unusually direct way): I will identify one principal vertical symmetry that creates a vertical cross stave for the whole piece, and most of the material from m. 1 returns in reverse order at the final cadence to create a horizontally symmetrical cross stave over the whole. I will also show that the piece's large cross contains a multitude of smaller ones in the first nine measures, as axes of vertical symmetry move around frequently and somewhat erratically in the first half of the piece, accompanied by similarly local horizontal symmetries. We can understand this as one way for Schoenberg to portray the idea that, as Simms puts it, "the composer will not quietly suffer the fate that the people have inflicted upon him" – he is alive and still moving around.[34] At m. 10, however, the piece introduces its main vertical axis, D4, as a pedal in the flute, and locks into that axis on the last quarter of m. 16 for much of the remainder, to represent the stiffness of the dead poet/composer and the utter finality of his situation. As a result of these local modifications to the piece's basic image, the form of the melodrama can be understood as binary – A for the first nine measures, the setting of stanzas 1 and 2, and B for the remainder, which sets stanza 3.

Our section-by-section tour of "Die Kreuze" begins with Example 6.11, the two chords that open the melodrama. David Lewin dubs them the "Kreuze" chords, pointing out that "they form a highly-characteristic (cross-like?) motto, which returns at the end."[35]

Lewin goes on to show that these chords contain two vertical pitch symmetries, one around the axes F♯ and G (or C and C♯), which he calls *i*, and a second around the axis G♯ (or D), which he calls *j*. In Example 6.11, we see that eight pitches of the "Kreuze" chords participate in vertical mirrors using the *i* inversion: four around F♯/G5 and four around F♯/G4, while the entire second chord and two pitches of the first participate in

[33] See chapters 5 and 7 of my book *Schoenberg's Twelve-Tone Music: Symmetry and the Musical Idea* for detailed accounts of how horizontal and vertical symmetry can represent perfection in the Piano Piece Op. 33a and *Moses und Aron*.

[34] Simms, *The Atonal Music of Arnold Schoenberg*, p. 129.

[35] Lewin, "Inversional Balance as an Organizing Force in Schoenberg's Music and Thought," *Perspectives of New Music* 6/2 (Spring–Summer 1968): 4–8.

Example 6.11 Schoenberg, "Die Kreuze," *Pierrot lunaire*, Op. 21, opening chords. Copyright © 1914, 1941 by Universal Edition AG Vienna, UE 34806. All rights reserved. Used by permission of Belmont Music Publishers and Universal Edition

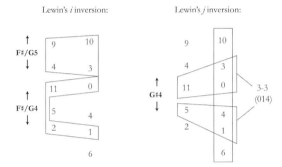

a single *j* inversion around G♯4. (Notably, two segments of this second mirror are members of set class 3-3 (014), which will continue to be a preferred segment for vertical mirrors in the rest of the piece.) As the melodrama progresses into its first four measures, shown in Example 6.12, the inversion around F♯/G becomes more prominent (which Lewin demonstrates) and is joined by a number of vertical symmetries around other axes (which he does not discuss, except for the one around E/F). A number of horizontal symmetries also appear and seem to grow in prominence gradually, which makes the "cross-like" quality of the opening chords more explicit.

The first of these horizontal symmetries involves the tenor voice of the "Kreuze" chords, <F4, F♭4>, which is reversed an octave lower as <E3, F3> in the bass on the second and third beats of m. 1 (the pitch-class map in Example 6.12 shows these as <5, 4> and <4, 5>). The succession <4, 5> then adds PC 1, and participates in two vertical symmetries: <4, 5, 1> in the piano's bass line against <7, 6, 10> on "– ge Kreuze" in the voice part is a pitch symmetry around a new axis, B3/C4. The bass's <4, 5, 1> also participates in a vertical pitch-*class* symmetry with <0, 11, 3> in the grace notes below it: PC 3 is an octave too low for pitch symmetry. (I represent pitch-class symmetries similarly to pitch symmetries in Example 6.12 and future examples, but instead of specific pitches between the up and down

Example 6.12 Schoenberg, "Die Kreuze," *Pierrot lunaire*, Op. 21, mm. 1–4, first stanza. Used by permission of Belmont Music Publishers and Universal Edition

arrows, the axes are given as pitch classes, G♯/D in this instance, and the symmetrical collections are either enclosed in dotted boxes or connected with dotted lines, as here. Non-symmetrical collections will be represented by a dotted enclosure without an axis.) The two successions <4, 5, 1> and <0, 11, 3> duplicate the pitch classes of the two 3-3 segments in the opening "Kreuze" chords (part of the *j* inversion). Finally, the grace notes themselves on beats 2 and 3 of m. 1 create a vertical pitch symmetry around F♯/G1, another instance of Lewin's *i* inversion.

As the piano texture thickens in mm. 1b–2 under the words "die Verse," new vertical symmetries appear, as well as a more substantial horizontal symmetry. The top stave of the piano begins in the pickup to m. 2 with a vertically symmetrical chord around G♯/A5. This is {11, 2, 3, 6}, SC 4-17 (0347), projected as unordered pitch intervals <3, 5, 3> from the bottom. It is followed in the remainder of m. 2 by {6, 7, 0} and {7, 0, 1}, pitch-interval stacks <5, 6> and <6, 5>, both Viennese Trichords and members of 3-5 (016), which together mirror vertically around A/B♭5. These symmetries are accompanied in the middle stave of the piano by {5, 9, 10, 1} progressing to {8, 11, 0, 4}, two members of 4-19 (0148) with pitch-interval stacks <3, 4, 4> and <4, 4, 3>. They mirror vertically around E/F4 (the third vertical symmetry that Lewin acknowledges in his article). They then *reverse* themselves temporally on the second and third beats of m. 2, with one note missing (the D♭4 from the first chord, but perhaps we can substitute the C♯5 in the piano's top stave for it). The middle stave in mm. 1b–2 contains a vertical symmetry that reverses itself to create an overarching horizontal symmetry – in other words, both kinds of symmetry occur together to form a cross. If we also consider the notes in the piano's bottom stave on the first beat of m. 2, the pitch-class symmetrical group {1, 5, 9}, which forms SC 4-19 as {9, 0, 1, 5} with the C4 in the middle stave directly above it, we have a configuration that Jan Gilbert called "4–19 with its repetitions [outlining] the shape of a cross."[36] Indeed, the {9, 0, 1, 5} in the middle could be understood as a vertical stave, surrounded by the horizontal symmetry of {5, 9, 10, 1} and {8, 11, 0, 4} and their reversal. (The use of SC 4-19 as a vertical cross stave between horizontally symmetrical shapes will recur in mm. 13–14.)

The cross imagery becomes less obvious in the next passage, mm. 2b–3a, as the activity moves to the lower register of the piano. But there are still prominent vertical and horizontal mirrors in this music that cross one another: the three trichords on the 4th beat of m. 2 and 1st and 2nd beats

---

[36] Jan Gilbert, "Schoenberg's Harmonic Visions: A Study of Text Painting in 'Die Kreuze'," *Journal of the Arnold Schoenberg Institute* 8/2 (1984): 123.

of m. 3, {4, 8, 9}, {2, 6, 10}, and {9, 1, 2}, have the unordered pitch-interval stacks <7, 4>, <4, 4>, and <7, 4>. The pitch-interval stacks create horizontal symmetry as a group, but the middle stack, <4, 4>, is vertically symmetrical itself, around G♭3. The third of these stacks extends into a B♭2, <1, 9, 2, 10>, to form the pitch intervals <4, 7, –4> (pitches and intervals reckoned from top to bottom), symmetrical around F/F♯3. And another vertically symmetrical stack around D♭3 follows on the fourth sixteenth of the second beat, <5, 5>.

After the introduction of the main two vertical symmetries of the piece, Lewin's *i* and *j*, in m. 1, the second and third measures have eschewed those two inversional axes for a number of others, signifying (in my reading) the poet/composer continuing to move around on the cross. But the passage in mm. 3b–4, which again moves up into the upper registers of the piano (creating a horizontally symmetrical registral contour over all of mm. 2–4), brings both *i* and *j* back, and *i* becomes especially prominent at the end of m. 4. Other pitch symmetries also appear, as well as symmetrical pitch-class sets. The third beat of m. 3 presents a set class 4-19 with a vertically symmetrical augmented triad as its bottom three notes, {2, 6, 10}, and follows this on the next two sixteenths with set-class 6-1, which is not arranged symmetrically by pitch, but can be understood more abstractly as a mirror around pitch classes 5 and 6. The fourth beat of m. 3 then produces the first of many descending cascades, consisting of the group (ordered from the top down) <4, 11, 8, 5, 0>, overlapping with <0, 7, 6, 1>. The first of these creates a mirror around G♯5, a *j* inversion, while the second balances around F♯/G4, an *i* inversion. Finally, we hear a symmetrical pitch-class set, {0, 1, 5, 6} (set class 4-8).

The voice, meanwhile, has kept itself separate from the piano's vertical and horizontal mirrors since m. 2, creating some of its own, as well as a strong Rp relation around {8, 9, 10}. But in its pickups to m. 4 and first beat of that measure, on the words "von der Geier," it produces the ordered pitch motive <7, 11, 3, 0>, yet another member of 4-19 (0148). That ordered pitch succession is then reversed in the piano's top voice an octave higher and a beat later (and ornamented), <0, 3, 11, (0), 7>. The <11, 3, 0>–<0, 3, 11> part of this horizontal mirror is particularly noteworthy. In the voice it sets the words "der Geier" (of vultures), but its interval patterns <+4, –3> and <+3, –4> and wing-shaped contours evoke the "butterfly" motive from melodrama No. 8, "Nacht," the initial phase in the series of punishments (and crimes) that make up Schoenberg's second part. In "Nacht," the poet/composer is smothered by giant black butterflies – again, his works – and rendered unable to speak or even breathe;

here he is pecked blind by another sort of creature with wings, and the
similarities between the two kinds of punishment inspire a motivic
parallel.

The piano texture accompanying the "vulture" horizontal mirror in mm.
3b–4 is full of vertical pitch symmetries around a variety of axes, with some
pitch-class symmetries. I will not detail them all, but one of this measure's
many descents is worth mentioning because it falls just short of creating
a symmetrical shape. On the second half of beat 1 and the first half of beat 2
of m. 4, in the lower two staves of the piano, we hear <0, 8, 7, 3>, pitch
intervals <–4, –1, 4>, symmetrical around G/A♭3 (again, the pitch classes
and intervals are listed from the top down in this descending figure). But
the downward cascade begins with the intervals <6, 5> above and finishes
with <–6> down below, so that the whole is not perfectly symmetrical. Not
too much later, on the second and third beats of the measure, we hear two
pairs of augmented triads, one in the top piano stave descending by half-
step (which provides accompanying voices for the piano's <0, 3, 11>
described above), and one in the middle piano stave ascending by half-
step. The upper pair is symmetrical around G/A♭5, the lower around F/
F♯4, and each of them forms different transpositions of set-class 6-20
(014589), which together exhaust the aggregate. I mentioned in
Chapter 1 that 6-20 was a favorite hexachord for Schoenberg and
a superset for both 3-3 and 4-19 – so it can be thought of as the source
for much of this melodrama's harmonic material.

The end of m. 4 is where Lewin's *i* inversion comes to the fore. On the
third and fourth beats, the upper and lower ends of the registral spectrum
in the piano produce pairs of intervals and collections that mirror vertically
around F♯/G4. On the third beat, <0, 1> in the upper voices on the first half
of the beat is answered by <1, 0> in the bass on the second half, a horizontal
mirror as well as a vertical one. On the fourth beat, the chord {0, 2, 6, 7} at
the top of the upper piano stave, pitch intervals <6, 2, 5> from the bottom
up, is answered by a configuration including {6, 11} and {1, 7} in the lowest
voices, producing the intervals <5, +2, 6>.

I analyzed mm. 1–4 in quite a bit of detail, to demonstrate that it is
filled with vertical and horizontal symmetries involving a variety of set
classes, and that several of them cross over one another to produce the
melodrama's basic image. These smaller crosses in mm. 1–4 squirm
around from one axis of symmetry to another, and are not yet locked in
to the main vertical axis that defines the piece's largest, overarching
cross. M. 5, the piano interlude between first and second stanzas, also
contains a multitude of vertical and horizontal symmetries, but many of
them involve members of the same set-class. Jan Gilbert calls this passage

Example 6.13 Schoenberg, "Die Kreuze," *Pierrot lunaire*, Op. 21, m. 5, piano interlude. Used by permission of Belmont Music Publishers and Universal Edition

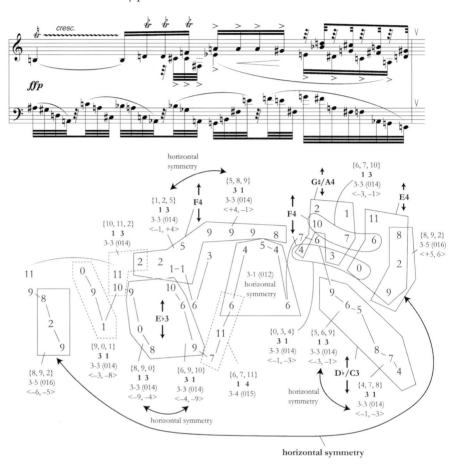

"a motivic hall of mirrors" and identifies the motive being reflected as set class 3-3 (014).[37]

My analysis of m. 5, shown in Example 6.13, shows that a horizontal pitch-class symmetry that does *not* involve 3-3 frames the measure, <8, 2, 9> beginning on the second thirty-second note in the left hand reflected by <9, 2-below-8> an octave higher in the right hand at the end of the measure.

Since everything is transposed up an octave, the two passages also create pitch-interval symmetry, <–6, –5> and <+5, 6>. These are Viennese Trichords again, interval stacks we have already seen reflected vertically

<hr>

[37] Gilbert, "Schoenberg's Harmonic Visions," 128.

in m. 2, and members of set class 3-5 (016). On the third beat of the measure in the left hand, we hear a horizontally symmetrical pitch sequence, <F♯3, E4, F4, E4, F♯3>, yielding set class 3-1 (012). But, as Gilbert claimed, the vast majority of the three-note segments that mirror one another in the piano interlude are members of 3-3 – most of them create vertically symmetrical pitch configurations and one is more abstract (denoted by dotted boxes on the left side of the pitch-class map). The more-abstract 3-3 mirror is the first one, descending <0, 9, 1> in the left hand on the second half of beat 1, and ascending <10, 11, 2> above it beginning the second beat mostly in the right hand. These trichords, because of pitch reordering, do not create vertically symmetrical pitch-interval successions: the first yields <–3, –8> and the second <1, +3>. But, their normal forms are inversions of one another, creating horizontal ordered pitch class interval symmetry (the first is a transposition of 034, the second of 014), which I illustrated by placing the adjacent intervals **3 1** and **1 3** in bold underneath the normal forms.

Most of the other 3-3 pairs in the passage do produce vertical pitch symmetries, however, and since all but one present their trichords one after another, they create horizontal pitch-interval symmetries at the same time, forming crosses within themselves. The left hand on beat 2 pairs <9, 0, 8> with <10, 6, 9>; these two 3-3s are symmetrical around E♭3 and form the pitch-interval succession <–9, –4>, (+14), <–4, –9>. On the second half of beat 2 and beat 3, the right hand (including one alto note) yields the overlapping trichords <2, 1, 5>, <5, 9, 8>; these successions balance their pitches vertically around the F4 in the middle, and form the horizontal pitch-interval sequence <–1, +4, +4, –1>. Also balanced around F4 are the first three notes of alto and tenor voices in beat 4, <10, 7, 6> and <4, 3, 0>. Since these 3-3s appear simultaneously rather than consecutively, we cannot speak of horizontal interval symmetry, but their interval successions still do reverse each other, <–3, –1> and <–1, –3>. The last six notes in the bass during beat 4 present one more pair of 3-3s balanced vertically around D♭/C3, <9, 6, 5> and <8, 7, 4>. Their interval succession is once again horizontally symmetrical, <–3, –1>, (–9), <–1, –3>. Finally, the two pairs of chords in the right hand on beat 4, <4, 10, 2>, <3, 7, 1> and <0, 6, 11>, <9, 2, 8>, each create pitch symmetry: the first pair balances set classes 3-8 (026) around G♯/A4, forming intervals <+6, 4> and <+4, 6>, and the second balances set classes 3-5 (016) around E4, forming <+6, 5> and <+5, 6>.

The continued proliferation of different vertical axes continues in the setting of stanza 2, mm. 6–10a, illustrated in Example 6.14, as the poem continues to speak of torments that a still living, moving poet/composer

Example 6.14  Schoenberg, "Die Kreuze," *Pierrot lunaire*, Op. 21, mm. 6–10a, second stanza. Used by permission of Belmont Music Publishers and Universal Edition

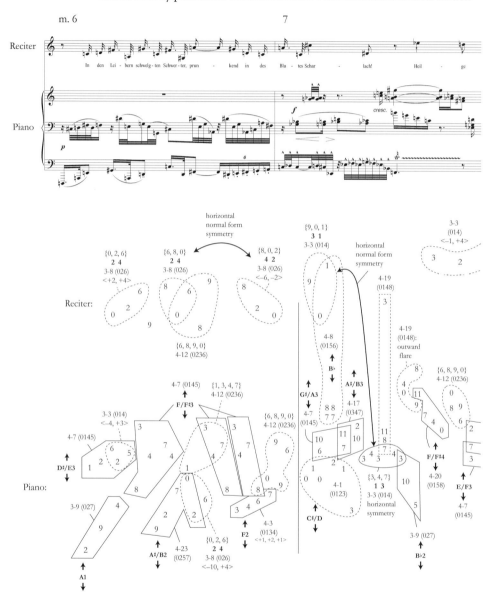

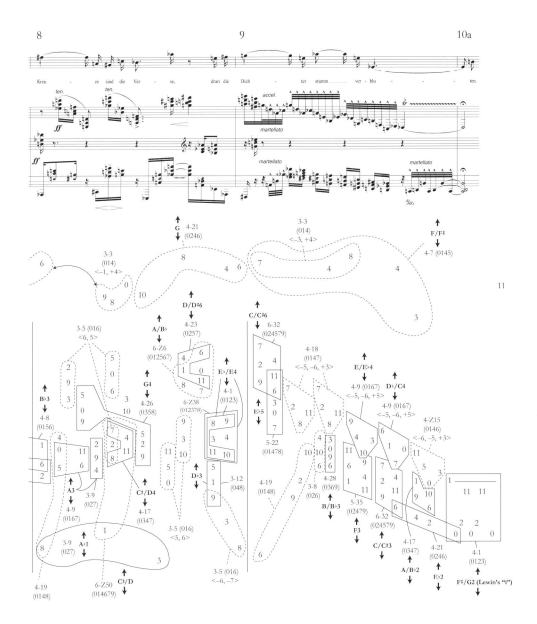

could endure – that is, swords reveling in his flesh. It seems like every measure of this passage changes its texture, as well as its strategy for expressing the melodrama's basic image, but they all depend on horizontal or vertical symmetry in some way. M. 6 is a counterpoint of three lines, voice plus tenor and bass lines in the piano. The piano's tenor line consists mostly of four-pitch figures that create vertical symmetry – the first, <1, 2, 6, 2, 5> balances around D♯/E3 (and ends with a vulture/butterfly motive, intervals <–4, +3>). This progresses to a tetrachord that occurs three times, the first involving repeated notes and making use of one of the left-hand bass notes, <8, 3, 4, 7, 4>, the latter two condensing the motive to <3, 4, 7, 8> and keeping it in the right hand. Since all four notes are fixed in pitch, G♯ or A♭2, D♯4, E3, and G3, the tenor figures all balance around F/F♯3.

The bass line in the piano's left hand begins on beat 1 of m. 6 with three of the pitch classes of m. 1's initial Kreuze-chord, <2, 9, 4>, forming set class 3-9 (027). This could be a way of marking the onset of the 2nd stanza, since these same three pitch classes appeared prominently at the beginning of stanza 1 and will return again as the lowest pitches of the final cadence (at the end of the 3rd stanza). After the first beat, the bass line mostly occupies itself with creating more vertical symmetries and trading a motive back and forth with the voice that Gilbert associated in her article with the vultures of m. 4.[38] But since this motive does not play much of a role in the music of that earlier measure, I prefer to call it the "sword" motive. I speak of set class 3-8 (026), which appears first in the voice in its prime form, <0, 2, 6> on "In den Lei –." The reciter follows this with a transposed and rotated version on "schwelgten Schwer –," <8, 0, 6>. The bass then takes over during the third beat of the measure, repeating <0, 2, 6> with a register transfer between the first two notes. Finally, the voice states 3-8 one last time as <8, 2, 0> on "– kend in des." This descending trichord could be understood as a horizontally symmetrical partner to the ascending <0, 2, 6> on the first beat, in contour and set-class if not specific intervals and pitches. Its normal form {8, 0, 2} also creates the more abstract horizontal ordered pitch-class interval symmetry that we remarked on in m. 5, with the preceding {6, 8, 0}. A superset of 3-8, 4-12 (0236) as {6, 8, 9, 0} and {1, 3, 4, 7}, fills in much of the rest of the texture of m. 6.

M. 7 then intensifies the texture by adding a third, soprano/alto, stave to the piano part. On the second and third beats of the measure, these higher voices create a shape that will become more prevalent in m. 8 – two voices flare outward in contrary motion, the contour of the original "Kreuze" chords, to a rhythm that also reminds us of the piece's opening, a sixteenth

[38] Gilbert, "Schoenberg's Harmonic Visions," 127–28.

off the beat to a longer value on the beat (quarter plus sixteenth). Here, Schoenberg (just as he did in "Mondestrunken") seems to be setting the return of the poem's first line, "Heilge Kreuze sind die Verse," with musical material that vaguely recalls the beginning, but does not repeat it literally. The outward wedge, <4, 8> in the soprano and <0, 9> in the alto, yields set class 4-19 (0148), the same chord that is created by all the voices together on the second half of beat 2. Set class 4-19 can also be understood as a reference back to the piece's beginning. At the beginning of m. 7, the tenor voices in the middle stave of the piano continue to produce tetrachords with vertical pitch symmetry around different axes (G♯/A3 and A♯/B3) and the bass again trades trichords back and forth with the reciter (this time, 3-3 (014)). The reciter's {9, 0, 1} on beat 1 and the bass's {3, 4, 7} on beat 2 are again horizontally symmetrical in the more abstract sense that the adjacent intervals of their normal forms reverse one another, **3 1** and **1 3**. And {3, 4, 7} itself can be heard as a horizontally symmetrical pitch succession with an extra ornamental note, <3, 4, (3,) 7, 4, 3>.

As I already mentioned, wedge shapes that evoke the opening chords become more prevalent in m. 8, as the reciter continues her repeat of the poem's first two lines. There are three of them, <7, 4> above <8, 11> on beat 2 in the bottom piano stave, <4, 6> above <1, 11> approaching beat 4 in the top piano stave, and <8, 9> above <11, 10> on beat 4 in the middle piano stave. All of them are pitch symmetrical, around C♯/D4, D/D♯6, and E♭/E4 respectively, and all are enclosed within (or overlap) larger groupings of notes that are either pitch- or pitch-class symmetrical. The latter two wedge outward, and both have the short–long rhythm characteristic of the piece's opening. Another configuration that has the short–long rhythm and pitch symmetry, but is not a wedge shape, is the six notes in the middle piano stave on the pickup to and downbeat of m. 8. All these groups recall the piece's opening in different ways, as do many of the other trichords found in m. 8: 3-5s voiced as Viennese Trichords and two 3-9s (027). Some of the 3-5s in m. 8 form a vertical symmetry of unordered pitch-interval stacks: the first three are voiced as <6, 5> followed by two more voiced as <5, 6>.

The texture changes again at m. 9, and this leads to one of the most interesting examples I have found in *Pierrot* of the basic image being modified to respond to words and concepts found later in the text, though here it might be more accurate to speak of a concept from the first two lines being presented in a more vivid way on the repeat. Specifically, Schoenberg's setting of the word "stumm" on the second half of beat 2 and the first half of beat 3 combines the basic image of "Die Kreuze" with that of "Mondestrunken," the descending waves of moonlight. The right hand of the piano under the word "Dichter" produces the sequence <7, 2, 8,

11> twice. In contour (descending for two notes, then turning up for the final note) and set-class (4–18), this motive matches the <2, 10, 1, 7> sequence that had represented incoming waves of moonlight in "Mondestrunken," the poet's inspiration. Neither the original <2, 10, 1, 7> nor this version, <7, 2, 8, 11>, is vertically pitch-symmetrical. Under the word "stumm," however, the piano right hand modifies the motive, so that the intervals, which had been <–5, –6, +3>, change to <–5, –6, +5>, and the set class becomes 4-9 (0167). This results in two tetrachords, <9, 4, 10, 3> and <6, 1, 7, 0>, that *are* vertically pitch-symmetrical – the first around E/ E♭4, the second around D♭/C4. As the reciter speaks of the poet's silence, the incoming waves of moonlight turn into vertical cross beams, the poet's inspiration and his work turn into a cross. The left hand of the piano at this same point (beat 2 second half, beat 3 first half) also plays vertically symmetrical configurations around different axes. And the descent culminates on the 4th beat of m. 9 and downbeat of m. 10 on {11, 0, 1, 2}, which balances vertically around F♯/G2 – Lewin's *i* inversion, which brings us back to the situation of the melodrama's beginning. The picture of the poet moving around on the cross, perhaps protesting his fate, but ultimately giving in to stillness and silence, together with the return of the first two lines of text, is expressed in mm. 6–9 in a number of ways.

But the onset of m. 10 begins a process that will ultimately lead to the most powerful portrayal in the melodrama of stillness while nailed to a cross. This is the B section's setting of stanza 3, the first five measures of which appear in Example 6.15.

As the flute, clarinet, violin, and 'cello enter in m. 10 on a quiet held note, stopping all motion for a moment, they create a sonority that *would* be pitch-symmetrical vertically around F4 if the 'cello were an octave higher. This is <3, 2, 8, 7> reckoned from the bottom up, SC 4-8 (0156), with the unordered pitch intervals <23 (a compound 11), 6, 11>. Then, the flute and clarinet both adjust downward, and eventually come to rest on the second half of the first beat of m. 11 on a second, five-note, sonority that is sustained much longer, until the second beat of m. 13. If we subtract the lower note of the 'cello's double stop, E♭2, which is in a different register from the rest of this chord, the top four notes are <6, 2, 11, 7> from the bottom up, SC 4-20 (0158). This chord consists of unordered pitch intervals <8, 9, 8>, and thus is vertically pitch-symmetrical around F♯/G4, Lewin's inversion *i*, similarly to the chord in the piano at mm. 9–10. This *i* inversion will be combined with others in the coming measures, but all of them will yield at the end of m. 16 to Lewin's *j* inversion around the pitch D4. (Of course, the flute in m. 11 is already starting to sustain D4 as a pedal

Example 6.15 Schoenberg, "Die Kreuze," *Pierrot lunaire*, Op. 21, mm. 10–14, third stanza, first part. Used by permission of Belmont Music Publishers and Universal Edition

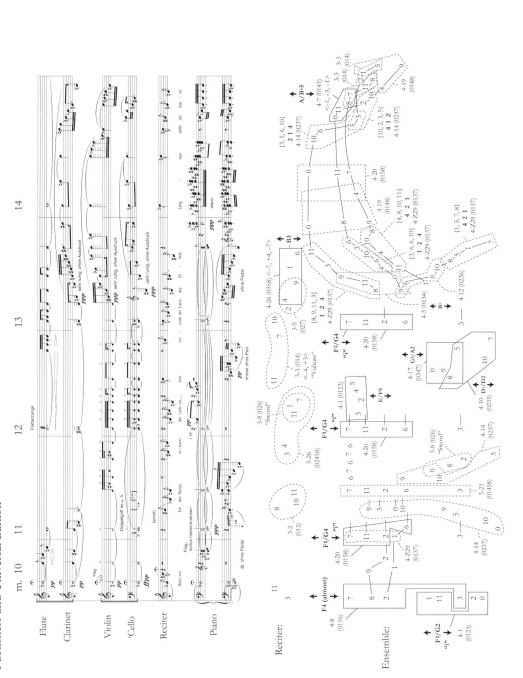

point, in anticipation of that pitch's emergence as m. 16's ultimate vertical axis.)

While the other instruments sustain their pitch-symmetrical <6, 2, 11, 7> (which, with the 'cello's lower note E♭2 added, forms {2, 3, 6, 7, 11}, SC 5-21, a superset of 4-19), the piano sustains a different chord as a harmonic in m. 11, <10, 0, 5, 9>, SC 4-14 (0237). This collection is neither pitch- nor pitch-class symmetrical, and has not been emphasized yet in "Die Kreuze," but it does offer a contrasting sonority to the 4-20 in the other instruments. The left hand of the piano doubles the tetrachord (to make the right-hand notes sound) in m. 11a, but in the second half of the measure it ornaments <9, 10, 0, 5> with <0, 8, 2>, a member of set class 3-8 (026), associated back in m. 6 with the sword motive. In the first half of m. 12, the piano's right hand adds a vertically symmetrical tetrachord around E/F5, and in the latter half, the piano's left hand overlaps two vertically symmetrical configurations that together contain {5, 9, 10, 0} as a subset. The upper collection, <8, 0-above-9, 5>, balances around G♯/A2, while the lower one, <8, 10, 5, 7>, balances around D♭/D2.

On the second beat of m. 13, the violin, clarinet, and 'cello begin to move from the pitches they had sustained since the beginning of m. 11. (The flute, however, continues to hang on to D4 obstinately, anticipating the vertical pitch axis that will "win out" in m. 16.) The trio of moving voices creates a horizontally symmetrical arch contour with two familiar tetrachords at its center. Within the rising part, all three voices project different members of set class 4-Z29 (0137). (This set class had appeared momentarily on the downbeat of m. 11, before the clarinet descended into the sustained <6, 2, 11, 7> 4-20 we discussed earlier.) The violin and clarinet create normal forms, {8, 9, 11, 3} and {3, 4, 6, 10}, that have the adjacent ordered pitch-class intervals **1 2 4**, while the 'cello's normal form, {4, 8, 10, 11}, yields the adjacent intervals **4 2 1**. In this way, these tetrachords create the same kind of abstract symmetry we saw back in m. 5, a symmetry of sets related by inversion within the same set class.

At the peak of the arch, all three voices together create first {0, 4, 8, 9}, SC 4-19 (0148) and then {11, 0, 4, 7}, SC 4-20 (0158). Of course, 4-19 reminds us of mm. 1b–2a in the bottom two piano staves, where that same set-class as a vertical stood in the middle of another horizontally symmetrical arch pattern, creating the melodrama's first complete cross shape. And 4-20 is the same set class that contains the vertically symmetrical sustained tetrachord of mm. 11–13. The contour then bends downward on the second, third, and fourth beats of m. 14, and the voices intertwine registrally to form tetrachords that were important earlier in the piece: 4-14 (0237), the piano harmonic from mm. 11–13 that creates its own abstract normal-form symmetry, as well as 4-7, 4-19, and 3-3. Before leaving the instrumental parts in mm. 13–14, it is important to point out that the piano in m. 13 balances the three rising voices with a descending eight-note run, which provides a vertically symmetrical contour to accompany the horizontal contour symmetry of mm. 13–14 in the violin, clarinet, and 'cello. The piano's run begins with 4-12 (0236), but ends with 4-Z29, the same tetrachord that is so prevalent in the rising lines directly above it.

The voice during mm. 11–13 does not participate in any of the symmetries that have just been described, but does refer to several motivic elements from earlier in the piece, and ends the second line of the third stanza with a tetrachord that is horizontally and vertically symmetrical, another cross shape. The motivic references come on the words "die Locken," which project SC 3-8, the "Sword" motive, and "fern verweht" ("in the distance dies out"), which produce not only the set class (3–3) but also the intervals, <–4, +3>, associated with the "Vulture" motive (as well as the butterfly motive from "Nacht" earlier in the collection). Then, "Lärm des Pöbels" is set to <4, 9, 1, 6>, a horizontally symmetrical interval succession <–7, +4, –7> that also produces vertical pitch symmetry around B3. "The noise of the mob" apparently constitutes a cross for Schoenberg as the poet.

It is easier to discuss the voice in mm. 14–15 and piano in m. 14 in connection with the next passage, mm. 14–17a, illustrated in Example 6.16a. The voice descends <–1, –3, –3, –4, –2, –1> underneath the descending clarinet and strings on "Langsam sinkt die Sonne nieder," portraying the setting sun. Meanwhile, the piano in m. 14 discovers a new way to create crosses – the right hand and left hand swap set classes, as well as several pitch-class sets. For example, on the third and fourth sixteenths of m. 14, {1, 4, 8} crosses from the right hand to the left, and {3, 6, 10} from the left hand to the right. A few other such crossings occur in the passage, indicated by arrows in the pitch-class map. As these trichords are exchanged between hands, some of them create vertically symmetrical larger sets around E5 and C♯5, and a bass line that begins <+1, +4, +1>, horizontally symmetrical around G4.

This leads in mm. 15 and 16a (first three beats) to a long descent in 'cello and piano, balanced in vertical contour symmetry against ascents in clarinet and violin, and the ever-present pedal D4 in the flute. The 'cello and piano parts here not only create numerous horizontal and vertical symmetries (together with the violin in some places), but allude to descents from earlier in the collection – the waves of moonlight in "Mondestrunken" and the descending butterflies in "Nacht."

Example 6.16a  Schoenberg, "Die Kreuze," *Pierrot lunaire*, Op. 21, mm. 13b–17a, third stanza, second part. Used by permission of Belmont Music Publishers and Universal Edition

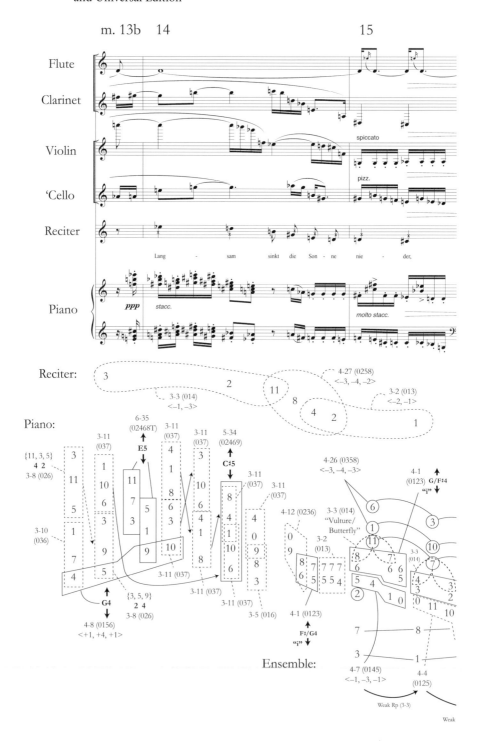

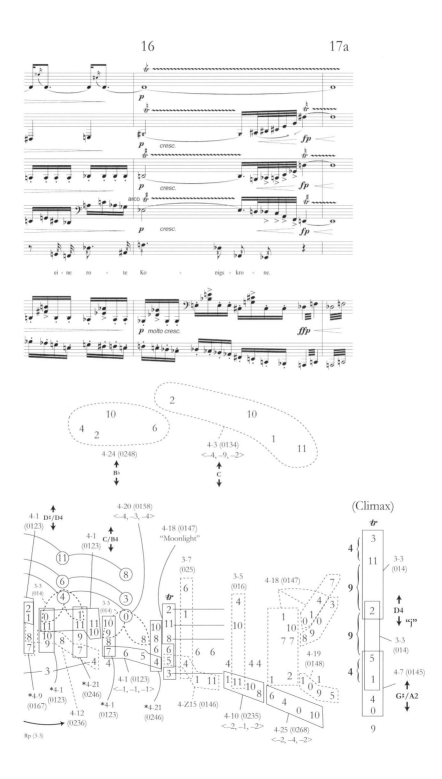

(The initial inspiration that brought on the poet/composer's turn to atonality, and the first stage of his punishment for doing so, both expressed as descents, continue to stick in his mind during his final punishment.)

Several horizontal symmetries arise between the accented higher notes in piano and 'cello on the second sixteenth of every beat in m. 15. The piano's top line, <6, 3, 11, 8>, and its next-highest line, <1, 10, 6, 3>, both create set class 4-26 (0358) as <−3, −4, −3>. The line created by the 'cello on its second sixteenths, <11, 7, 4, 0>, set class 4-20 (0158), flips the piano's intervals to create another horizontally symmetrical pattern, <−4, −3, −4>. Other horizontal symmetries occur in the left hand of the piano: <−1, −3, −1>, 4-7 (0145), on the first beat of m. 15; <−1, −1, −1>, 4-1 (0123), on the fourth beat; <−2, −1, −2>, 4-10 (0235), on the second beat of m. 16; and <−2, −4, −2>, 4-25 (0268), on the third beat. And vertical symmetry can be found among the 4-1 tetrachords that are created by 'cello and piano together in the middle of the texture on the first three beats of m. 15, as well as five tetrachords formed by 'cello, piano, and violin as vertical slices later in m. 15 (and marked with asterisks in Example 6.16a's pitch-class map), 4-9 (0167) as {1, 2, 7, 8}, 4-1 as {9, 10, 11, 0}, 4-21 (0246) as {7, 9, 11, 1}, 4-1 again as {7, 8, 9, 10}, and finally 4-21 as {4, 6, 8, 10}. Though these symmetrical verticals expand and contract to create different set classes, their axes of symmetry create a regular chromatic descent: B3/B♭3 (twice), B♭3, A3/A♭3, and G3. (Example 6.16b highlights these five tetrachords, showing their descending axes of symmetry and expanding and contracting unordered pitch-interval stacks.)

The 'cello and piano also provide multiple allusions to melodramas Nos. 8 and 1, as I mentioned above. The descending giant black butterflies of "Nacht" make their comeback in the 'cello on the first three sixteenths of all four beats in m. 15: <8, 11, 7>, <4, 7, 3>, <0, 4, 1>, <9, 0, 8>. All of them, save the third, replicate the interval succession of the original butterfly motto in "Nacht," <+3, −4>. (The third retrogrades it to <+4, −3>.) But the head notes of the first three butterflies, 8, 4, and 0, also bring back the same pitch classes that had been associated with descending waves of moonlight in "Mondestrunken." (When PC 9 follows at the head of the fourth butterfly, it forms SC 4-19.) The left hand of the piano in m. 15 recalls "Mondestrunken" in a different way, since the tetrachords starting on the first three beats, 4-7 (0145), 4-4 (0125), and 4-12 (0236), chain together through weak Rp with 3-3 (014) as a common subset, as had so many of the incoming waves in the first melodrama. As the piano's left hand progresses into m. 16, this Rp chain gives way to symmetrical tetrachords that contract and then expand, which I described earlier.

Example 6.16b  Detail of five verticals in m. 15, Schoenberg, "Die Kreuze"

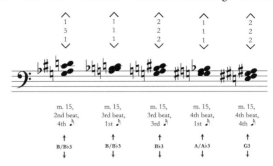

The clarinet, violin, and 'cello reach a temporary stopping point in their ascents and descents on the downbeat of m. 16, and sustain a trill for two beats, while the piano continues its descent. Together with the flute, who also begins a trill on the same beat, the main notes of the clarinet and strings, {8, 11, 2, 3}, create a member of the set class that was so prevalent in "Mondestrunken," 4-18 (0147), thereby continuing the passage's association with the image of descending moonlight for a moment. (If we add PCs 5 and 6 from the piano part, the downbeat of m. 16 yields SC 6-27 (013469), an octatonic subset.) M. 16's trill then leads on the third beat to rising figures in the clarinet and violin, balanced symmetrically with a falling figure in the 'cello – the clarinet and violin lines both give prominence to 4-18 again, while the 'cello descends through 4-19. During the trill and rising/falling figures, the voice descends on "Königskrone" to a PC-symmetrical set, 4-3 (0134) – its descent in pitch intervals reads <–4, –9, –2>.

All this leads inexorably to the fourth quarter of m. 16, which I understand to be the climax of "Die Kreuze," because it returns most of the voices to a vertical symmetry around D4, Lewin's *j* inversion from the opening, and "locks them in" at that location for much of the remainder of the piece. One could imagine the cross being dropped into its hole with a sickening finality at this point. At the same time, the work's largest, overarching cross begins to come into view. The pitch-class map shows that clarinet, violin, flute, and the right hand of the piano (not the 'cello or piano LH) form a vertically symmetrical interval pattern <4, 9, 9, 4> here, built from two of the intervals of the voice's descent in m. 16, and that pattern balances two set class 3-3s around the flute's D4 axis, {11, 2, 3} above and {1, 2, 5} below. This recalls the vertical on the downbeat of m. 1 and its pickup, the "Kreuze" chords, which had balanced two 3-3s, {11, 0, 3} and {1, 4, 5}, around *j*'s other axis, G♯4. Most of the lower voices reinforce the idea of vertical symmetry by creating their own pattern, <4, 9, 4>, from the C2 in the left hand of the piano up through the F3 in the piano's right hand, and including the 'cello's E2.

After traveling around to various axes of symmetry, the music finally falls back into one of its opening vertical symmetries, what has now become its principal one, on the fourth beat of m. 16, and stays there for much of the remainder. And this return to the *j* inversion after intervening material points forward to a horizontal mirror over the whole piece. From here to the end, depicted in Example 6.17, the instruments attempt to break out of the *j* inversion around D4 and are pulled back into it (mm. 18b–19), then manage to dislocate the vertical symmetry through the clarinet's escape up to A5 at the end of m. 19.

But in mm. 20–21, the flute presents an almost-horizontally symmetrical line that is punctuated by almost-vertically symmetrical chords in clarinet, violin, and 'cello – a shape whose general contour looks suspiciously like a cross. The final cadence in mm. 21–22 then presents several pitch-class sets and centers of inversion from the pickup to m. 1, m. 1, and the first part of m. 2 in reverse, completing and confirming the horizontal mirror that spans the whole. Let us examine these gestures in more detail.

For all of m. 17 and the first half of m. 18, the vertically symmetrical chord around D4 in the upper voices that was introduced on the last quarter of m. 16 sustains itself (in addition to the symmetrical chord around G♯/A2 in the lower voices), while the voice intones the poem's first line as the last line of stanza 3: "Heilge Kreuze sind die Verse." As we have seen before, the return of the first line of text motivates a return of some sort of musical material from earlier settings. In "Mondestrunken," line repeats were generally set by the same set classes, 4-1 and 4-3, but here, Schoenberg chooses ordered pitch-interval successions similar to those of the piece's beginning that generate new set classes. In m. 1, "Heilge Kreuze" had been set as <–1, –1, +4>, creating SC 4-2 (0124), but in m. 17, it expands to <–1, –1, +5>, SC 4-4 (0125). Likewise, "die Verse" in mm. 1–2 had been set as a simple neighbor figure, <+2, –1>, but in mm. 17–18 the intervals expand to <+4, –15>, an octave-compounded vulture/butterfly motive, portraying what the poet's creative output has turned into at this stage, an agent of torment.

As the voice falls silent, the clarinet, violin, and 'cello begin frenzied activity on the third and fourth beats of m. 18 that introduces two new axes of symmetry, C4 and A/B♭2, while the piano shifts to a vertically symmetrical projection of whole-tone collection 0 for these two beats, with A2 at its center. But the instruments are pulled back to the symmetries around the flute's D4 and low G♯/A2 of mm. 16b–18a, either on or just before the downbeat of m. 19 (marked by an asterisk in the pitch-class map). The clarinet, violin, and 'cello break out again on beats 1–3 of m. 19, and the piano joins them on the third beat, shifting back to the whole-tone 0 chord around A2. However, most of the instruments are yanked back to

Example 6.17 Schoenberg, "Die Kreuze," *Pierrot lunaire*, Op. 21, mm. 17–22, third stanza, third part. Used by permission of Belmont Music Publishers and Universal Edition

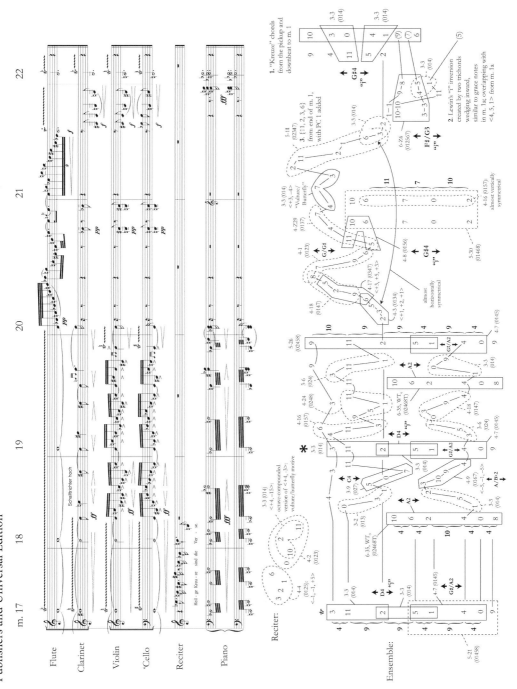

the chords of mm. 16–18 again on the fourth beat of m. 19, which sustains into m. 20 very briefly. The one exception is the clarinet, which, instead of returning to D♯5, leaps up to an A5, breaking the vertical symmetry in the top voices that had balanced set classes 3-3 around D4.

But this brief escape from symmetries characteristic of the beginning of the piece, specifically from the *j* inversion, does not last for long. In m. 20, the flute takes over, finally moving off its sustained D4 to spin out a line that rises and falls in contour twice over mm. 20–21. As it progresses, it reviews elements that played important roles in the melodrama: pitch-symmetrical and PC-symmetrical tetrachords, the "moonlight" chord 4-18, and a vulture/butterfly motive, <+3, –4>. But for our purposes, the most significant feature of the flute line is the comparison between its first four pitches in m. 20, <D4, E♭4, F4, G♭4>, and the last three in m. 21, <F♯4, E♭4, D4>. Except for the extra F4 in the first one, these two successions reverse one another at pitch, forming horizontal pitch symmetry. Halfway between them on the third and fourth beats of m. 20 stand two five-note chords in clarinet, violin, and 'cello. The bottom four notes in violin and 'cello create a vertical unordered pitch-interval stack that is also nearly symmetrical, <10, 7, 11>. As we saw in mm. 1–2 and again in mm. 13–14, a partially horizontally symmetrical line is crossing an interval stack, which here in m. 20 is almost symmetrical. The cross shape this creates on the pitch-class map is unmistakable.

The flute's descent on the first beat of m. 21, the right arm of mm. 20–21's cross, also participates in a process that will lead to the final cadence by confirming the suggestion of horizontal symmetry over the whole piece that was offered in mm. 16–18. Its descent reads <2, 11, 2, 1, 6, 3, 2>, which is nearly identical to the chord heard in the top staff of the piano on the pickup to m. 2, tied into the downbeat (look back at Example 6.12): {11, 2, 3, 6}. On the last two beats of m. 21, clarinet, violin, and 'cello take over, and their music includes an inward wedging pattern around F♯/G3 that David Lewin recognized as an instance of the *i* inversion, <10, 10, 9, 8> in 'cello and violin, <3, 3, 4, 5> in clarinet.[39] This corresponds to the wedge into F♯/G1 on beats 2 and 3 of m. 1, in the piano's grace notes. Also, the clarinet's PC 5 is supported by PC 1 in the 'cello, so that the two instruments together can be heard as playing <4, 5, 1>, the same motive that had appeared above the grace notes in the piano at m. 1. Finally, the two "Kreuze" chords return at the cadence, which again include the *i* inversion giving way to the *j* inversion. Four elements from the beginning of the piece, the "Kreuze" chords, <4, 5, 1>, a wedge into F♯/G, and {11, 2, 3, 6}, return at the end, but they return *in reverse order*.

---

[39] Lewin, "Inversional Balance in Schoenberg's Music and Thought," 6–7.

"Die Kreuze" thus projects its basic image over the whole melodrama by reversing at least four elements of its beginning at its final cadence, creating a large horizontal cross stave, while treating the *j* inversion, first around G♯4, later around D4 at m. 16, then around G♯4 again at the end, as its principal vertical symmetry, an upright cross stave for the whole. As it progresses through its text, however, it makes several modifications to that image to reflect the poem's changing situations. It allows its centers of vertical symmetry to move around haphazardly in the first nine measures, within an active piano texture (representing the poet still struggling against his fate), but then freezes first the texture in m. 10, and then the center of vertical symmetry in m. 16 (for the most part on D4), to portray the poet's inability to speak or move at the end. Along the way, Schoenberg also makes allusions to earlier melodramas in the collection when appropriate, portraying the descending waves of moonlight from "Mondestrunken" and the descending butterflies from "Nacht" to recall the poet's original inspiration, and his earlier punishments, in mm. 15 and 16.

## "O alter Duft," No. 21

The text of the last melodrama of *Pierrot lunaire*, with my translation, appears below:

O alter Duft aus Märchenzeit
Berauschest wieder meine Sinne!
Ein närrisch Heer von Schelmerein
Durchschwirrt die leichte Luft.

Ein glückhaft Wünschen macht mich froh
Nach Freuden, die ich lang verachtet.
O alter Duft aus Märchenzeit
Berauschest wieder mich!

All meinen Unmut gab ich preis,
Aus meinen sonnumrahmten Fenster
Beschau ich frei die liebe Welt
Und träum hinaus in selge Weiten . . .
O alter Duft – aus Märchenzeit!

O ancient scent from fairytale times,
you intoxicate my senses again!
A foolish host of roguish pranks
Buzzes through the gentle air.

A serendipitous wishing makes me glad
For joys that I have long despised.
O ancient scent from fairytale times,
You intoxicate me again!

All my displeasure I gave away,
From my sun-framed window
I freely view the beloved world
And dream out into blessed distances . . .
O ancient scent – from fairytale times!

Even though "Parfums de Bergame" does not come at the very end in Giraud's original collection, like "O alter Duft" does in Schoenberg's reduction of it (return to Example 6.1), both the original and its translation fall into that group of poems, the third group, that represents the poet returning to the Parnassian ideal – or (in Schoenberg's case) the composer going back to the musical style he had lived within before venturing forth into

Example 6.18  Schoenberg, "O alter Duft," *Pierrot lunaire*, Op. 21, final cadence, mm. 27–30. Copyright © 1914, 1941 by Universal Edition AG Vienna, UE 34806. All rights reserved. Used by permission of Belmont Music Publishers and Universal Edition

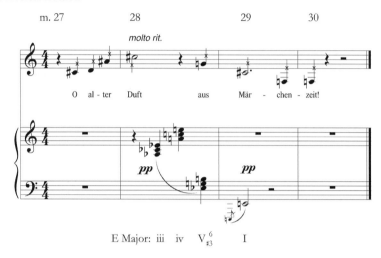

modernism. Functional tonality, in this case the key of E major, is the "ancient scent" that "again intoxicates" the composer's senses. Most of the discussions of "O alter Duft" in the literature assert that this melodrama is about some kind of return to tonality. For example, Reinhold Brinkmann refers to the final measures (Example 6.18) as "a veritable cadence in E (Major)," and tells us that this authentic cadence "has been prepared for throughout No. 21 by passages oriented toward E Major and in previous numbers by passages that lean toward this key (for example, Nos. 5, 6, 20)." He refers to Schoenberg's technique here as "Tonalität als Darstellungsmittel" – essentially the same concept as what I have been calling "specter of tonal function" for expressive (or representative) purposes in Chapters 4 and 5 of this book.[40]

However, this is not a simple successful return to the homeland of functional tonal writing after Schoenberg's reckless excursions into the foreign lands of atonality. After all, the *rondel* ends the same way as it began: "O ancient scent – *from fairytale times*." As others have done before me, I would like to claim that the basic image of "O alter Duft" portrays an *attempted* return to tonality that seems to work out for a brief moment; but tonality dissipates at the last minute, not reality, but only a "fairy tale." (As such, this melodrama's basic image is a descendant of that of Op. 19,

---

[40] Brinkmann, "The Lyric as Paradigm: Poetry and the Foundation of Arnold Schoenberg's New Music," in *German Literature in Music: An Aesthetic Fusion, 1890–1989*, ed. Claus Reschke and Howard Pollack (Munich: Wilhelm Fink, 1992), pp. 102–03.

No. 6, discussed in Chapter 5, which reaches up to the same key, E major, before being cast back down.) Brinkmann tells us about "O alter Duft's" final E major cadence (in a different article from the one previously mentioned): "the tonal language itself is understood as an 'as if' only. It alludes to the past and its beauty as a world that is lost and can only be remembered ... But at the same time the 'as if' does not allow a peaceful return."[41] Likewise, Jonathan Dunsby carefully warns us away from the "grandiose interpretation" that tonality has actually been "regained" in this final melodrama, and Bryan Simms refers to its E major as a "mock tonic."[42]

With respect to form, "O alter Duft" breaks into three sections that line up with the poem's three stanzas, without a substantial return of musical material at the beginnings of sections (instead, the main theme of mm. 1–2 returns at the *ends* of sections 2 and 3, to accompany the returns of the opening line of the *rondel*). Stephan Weytjens has pointed out that the ends of the first and second stanzas, as well as the beginnings of the second and third, are also marked at mm. 9–10 and 19–20 by a stepwise falling "cadential motive" in the piano and a "tutti chord" in the flute, clarinet/ bass clarinet, and strings. (The beginnings of second and third stanzas are also signaled by tempo markings: returns to the original tempo after a *poco ritard.*)[43] Because of the relative lack of returning motivic or harmonic material at the beginnings of the second and third sections, I will call them A (mm. 1–9), B (mm. 10–19), and C (mm. 19–30).

My analysis of No. 21, rather than discussing the whole melodrama as I did previously, will focus on those three places where the first line of the *rondel* appears, the beginning of the A section and the ends of the B and C sections. In each of these locations, E major (or, in one place, D major) is established by all or most voices in the texture, produces either a half or authentic cadence, and then quickly vanishes – usually because of the intrusion of either symmetrical pitch collections, or trichords and tetrachords characteristic of other melodramas in the cycle, such as 4-19 (0148) and 3-3 (014). The first appearance of the melodrama's motto, mm. 1–6, appears in Example 6.19. Weytjens points out that this passage, the opening two lines of the poem, breaks into two three-measure phrases, one for each line.[44] As the reader can see from the middle level of Example 6.19, a Schenkerian graph consisting of many (but certainly not all) notes in the texture, the first

[41] Brinkmann, "The Fool as Paradigm," p. 159.

[42] Dunsby, *Schoenberg: Pierrot lunaire*, p. 72; Simms, *The Atonal Music of Arnold Schoenberg*, p. 129.

[43] Stephan Weytjens, "Text as a Crutch in Arnold Schoenberg's 'Pierrot lunaire' Op. 21?" (PhD dissertation, University of Leuven, 2003), pp. 417–18.

[44] Ibid., p. 421.

Example 6.19 Schoenberg, "O alter Duft," *Pierrot lunaire*, Op. 21, mm. 1–6, beginning of A section. Used by permission of Belmont Music Publishers and Universal Edition

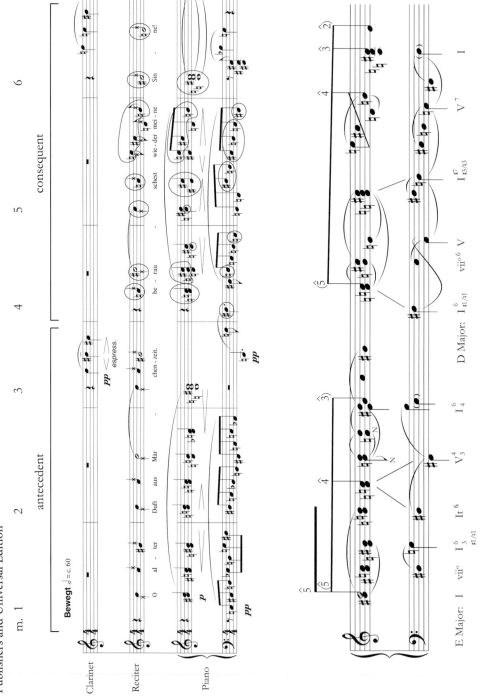

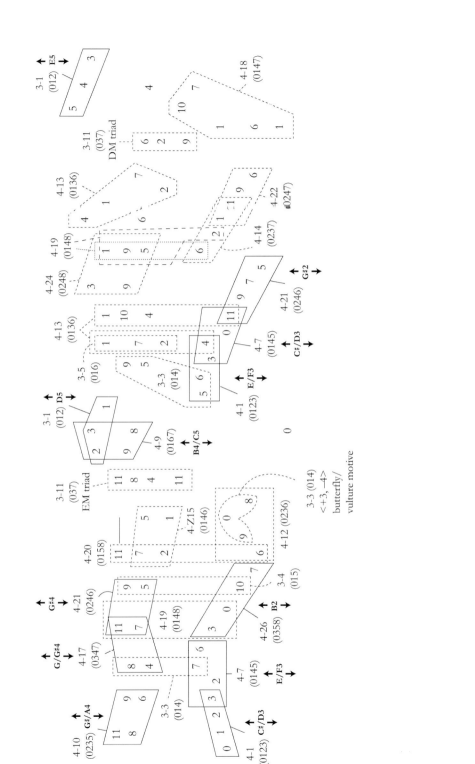

phrase progresses $\hat{5}$–$\hat{4}$–$\hat{3}$ to an imperfect authentic cadence in E major at m. 3, and the second phrase begins similarly, reaching $\hat{3}$ above I$_4^6$ in D major on the downbeat of m. 6 before moving on to $\hat{2}$ on the third beat.

In neither phrase, however, do we have a simple, unclouded ornamentation of the tonal middleground. In mm. 1–3, though the voice and right hand of the piano fit quite well into my graph (allowing for G♮ as a split third or neighbor, and F♮ as a neighbor), most of the left hand's notes do not. Four of them can be heard to provide weak support for the right hand's structure: E♭ on the third beat of m. 1, if respelled as D♯, could be the root of a vii° chord substituting for V, and G♮ on the fourth beat could serve as part of a tonic split-third chord. D♯ on the downbeat of m. 2 could be combined with F♮ and A in the right hand a beat later to form an inverted Italian sixth chord pointing toward the tonic, and F♯ on the third beat of that same measure could be heard as that altered dominant changing into a V$_3^4$.

But the majority of the pitches in the left hand of mm. 1–2 push against the tonal resonances above them, creating collections that return the listener to the atonal sound world of the previous melodramas. The bottom level of Example 6.19, a pitch-class map, shows that m. 1's left hand overlaps two pitch-symmetrical tetrachords, <0, 1, 2, 3>, which balances around C♯/D3, and <3, 2, 7, 6>, balanced around E/F3. The two set classes formed are 4-1 (0123) and 4-7 (0145). In m. 2, the bass line continues with a third symmetrical set around B2, <3, 0, 10, 7>, forming set class 4-26 (0358), and finishes with <6, 9, 0, 8>, a non-symmetrical configuration belonging to SC 4-12 (0236). The use of three pitch-symmetrical tetrachords recalls "Die Kreuze," of course, while three of the four set classes represented were common elements in both "Mondestrunken" and "Die Kreuze." The last three pitch classes of m. 2 in the left hand, <9, 0, 8>, create another familiar motive, <+3, –4> in pitch intervals, the "butterfly" motive from "Nacht" that reappeared in "Die Kreuze" to represent vultures. In addition, several familiar atonal sounds result when the left hand combines with the tonal prolongation in the right: {4, 7, 8}, set class 3-3 (014), on the fourth beat of m. 1; {11, 0, 3, 7}, 4-19 (0148), on the first beat of m. 2; {5, 9, 10}, 3-4 (015), on the second beat; and {6, 7, 11, 2}, 4-20 (0158), on the third beat.

But all the conflicting material suddenly disappears on the downbeat of m. 3, leaving a second-inversion tonic triad in E to resonate for one quarter note. Second-inversion triads are normally unstable in traditional tonal contexts; but in this context, after overcoming two measures of dissonant static in the bass, the I$_4^6$ gives us the definite impression that a goal has been reached. Almost immediately, however, the clarinet enters with conflicting information – the fairy tale of tonal arrival gives way to the reality of more dissonance. By itself, the clarinet creates <2, 3, 1>, a symmetrical collection around D5 belonging to SC 3-1 (012); and with the voice it creates {8, 9, 2, 3}, wedging out from B4/C5 and belonging to 4-9 (0167).

The second phrase, mm. 4–6, follows the same trajectory from conflict between dissonant and consonant materials to a clear arrival on a tonic 6/4, followed quickly by further conflicting information. This time, however, the pattern plays out a whole step lower in D major, and both hands of the piano mix consonant with dissonant pitches in m. 4, progressing to mostly consonant ones in m. 5 – unlike mm. 1–3, where the left hand had carried most of the dissonance and the RH most of the consonance. The Schenkerian graph in the middle level of Example 6.19 explains mm. 4–6 as $\hat{5}$–$\hat{4}$–$\hat{3}$ above $I^6$–$vii^{o6}$–$V$–$I\sharp^7$–$V^7$–$I$, allowing for split thirds on the first two tonic triads. The first part, $I^6$–$vii^{o6}$–$V$, is supported by a little over half of m. 4's pitches (10 of 17 to be exact; circled in the score). The pitches that do not participate, and some that do, form pitch-symmetrical tetrachords in the left hand again (three of them in mm. 3b–5a), as well as familiar atonal trichords and tetrachords in the vertical dimension: 3-3, 3-5 (016), and 4-13 (0136).

In m. 5, the final $I^{\sharp 7}$–$V^7$ seems to emerge out of its dissonant surroundings, as seventeen out of a total twenty-three pitches (again circled in the score) contribute to the Schenkerian graph. They form a tonic major seventh with split third on the first two beats of m. 5, followed by an unfolded $V^7$, with passing B in the bass, on the second two beats. Conflicting symmetrical sets are at a premium in m. 5, though it should be pointed out that the $I^{\sharp 7}$ with split third contains two 4-19s, {1, 5, 6, 9} and {9, 1, 2, 5}, and other characteristic atonal tetrachords can be found within the measure by grouping notes within the piano right hand alone. The left hand in m. 5, on the other hand, overlaps diatonic tetrachords, 4-14 (0237) and 4-22 (0247), owing to the emphasis on D major scale elements we have already discussed. In general, m. 5, like mm. 1–2, creates a definite tonal impetus toward the tonic $\begin{smallmatrix}6\\4\end{smallmatrix}$ that sounds alone for an eighth note on the downbeat of m. 6, relatively stable in its context. But again it proves to be a chimera, as the piano left hand intrudes on the second eighth of beat 1 with a very familiar atonal tetrachord, 4-18 (0147), which had represented moonlight in "Mondestrunken"; the clarinet complicates matters even further by playing a symmetrical 3-1; and the voice continues on beyond $\hat{3}$ to $\hat{2}$, attempting to move to a half cadence while the piano right hand continues stubbornly to sustain the tonic triad.

The last two lines of stanza 1 or end of the A section (mm. 7–9; not illustrated) then continue the conflict between D major on the one hand

and pitch-symmetrical collections and familiar atonal set classes on the other. The D major triad is prominent in the right hand of the piano at m. 7, and strongly suggested by the voice in m. 9, while the chord that enters in woodwinds and strings to mark the end of the stanza in m. 9 and continues through mm. 10–11 is symmetrical around E♭4, SC 5-22 (01478). The first two lines of stanza 2 or beginning of the B section in mm. 10–13 (again not illustrated; consult the score) return to E major at the beginning of m. 12, as the reciter begins to speak of returning to joys that she has long despised. The right hand of the piano and voice in mm. 12–13 especially lead the ear back to the home key, but an A♭–G♭–F♭ sequence in the left hand of m. 13 (enharmonic for $\hat{3}$–$\hat{2}$–$\hat{1}$) also helps. As before, a number of the other notes in the texture conflict with this tonal reading – but relatively few in mm. 12–13.

The re-establishment of E major then leads to the return of lines 1 and 2 as the last two lines of stanza 2, mm. 14–19a, illustrated in Example 6.20.

As I mentioned at the beginning of my analysis, the main theme of mm. 1–3a returns in mm. 14–16a to accompany the text refrain. In the piano, mm. 14–15 are identical to mm. 1–2, but placed an octave higher, while the voice part changes slightly, but remains securely within the orbit of E major, alternating between *sol* and *fa*. In m. 16, the voice again progresses *sol–fa–mi* (as it had in m. 3), while the piano plays the E: I$^6_4$ in the same register as m. 3, arpeggiating its lower two notes. All the conflicts between right and left hands of the piano, followed by the moment of clarity on E major tonic, that we heard in mm. 1–3 are recapitulated exactly in mm. 14–16a. Here, however, there is an additional voice: the flute. Unlike the clarinet in earlier measures, the flute actually *strengthens* the impetus toward E major on m. 16's downbeat in one way – moving from *la* and *ti* in m. 15 to *do* (with a downward register transfer, to match the piano's) in m. 16. At the same time, the pitch-class map shows that the addition of the flute and changes to the voice increase the number of vertical hexatonic subsets, characteristic *Pierrot* sonorities such as 4-19 (0148) and 4-20 (0158). Paradoxically, the alterations to the main theme in m. 14-16a support both sides of the conflict: the tonal reading, if one listens horizontally, and the atonal reading, if one listens vertically.

The arrival back home in E major in m. 16 after two measures of conflict proves to be a fantasy yet again, as the 'cello intrudes on m. 16's second beat with the same pitch classes the clarinet had used in m. 3, <2, 3, 1>, creating a pitch-symmetrical trichord 3-1 around D4 by itself, and combining with the voice to produce a pitch-symmetrical tetrachord around F/F♯4, <2, 3, 8, 9>; as before, a member of SC 4-9 (0167). The downbeat of m. 17 presents another pitch-symmetrical 4-9 in the piano, this time {1, 2, 7, 8} with the vertical unordered pitch intervals <6, 5, 6>, an overlapping of Viennese Trichords; as we have seen, one of the most characteristic atonal collections in Op. 21. As we progress through m. 17, however, the piano and voice gradually move away from symmetrical collections back in the direction of functional tonality – accumulating members of the dominant seventh chord in E major as the measure progresses (circled on the musical score). This motion culminates at the beginning of m. 18 with what could be considered a V7 with split third – the viola plays the minor third in $V^4_3$ on the downbeat, but the bass clarinet enters with the major third spelled enharmonically on beat 2, changing the chord momentarily to $V^6_5$. (This reading, of course, depends on the reciter's ability to touch securely, if ever so briefly, on the pitch B3 as the root of the dominant chord.)

As we have seen at line endings a number of times in the previous music, this slightly obscure half cadence is then made even more obscure by the instrumental entries following it. The bass clarinet in m. 18 briefly doubles the chord root B, but then continues on into an arpeggiated SC 3-3 (014), whose B♭ and G♮ cloud any sense of dominant arrival. The flute and 'cello enter at the end of m. 18 with yet another pitch-symmetrical collection, {5, 8, 10, 1}, belonging to 4-26 (0358), adding more dissonant pitches to the $V^7$. In summary, both phrases in Example 6.20, mm. 14–16a (corresponding to the first line of the refrain) and 16b–19a (corresponding to the second line), create the same trajectory we saw in mm. 1–3 and 4–6: a conflict between dissonant and consonant pitches gives way to a moment of clear arrival on the tonic (or less clear arrival on the dominant), which is then almost immediately obscured by more dissonant material. We hear the aural equivalent of the basic image, again and again: making the arduous journey home, seeming to arrive for just a moment, only to realize it was all a dream.

The beginning of stanza 3, the C section, in mm. 19–22 can be heard as pointing toward tonic in E major at m. 19, particularly the lower two voices of the piano's right hand. The music then progresses in the direction of the subdominant in mm. 21 and 22, but with dissonant additions, as always. (The voice on the downbeat of m. 21 and right hand of the piano on the first two beats, the right hand of the piano on the second beat of m. 22, the viola line progressing up from E3 to A3 and C4 on the second through fourth beats, and the voice's A4–G♯4 on the third beat of m. 22 all gently nudge the listener part of the way toward A minor.) For space's sake, I chose not to illustrate mm. 19–22; my music example (Example 6.21) begins in m. 23 instead and runs until the final cadence, corresponding to the last three lines of stanza 3. It begins with an anticipation of the return of

Example 6.20 Schoenberg, "O alter Duft," *Pierrot lunaire*, Op. 21, mm. 14–19a, end of B section. Used by permission of Belmont Music Publishers and Universal Edition

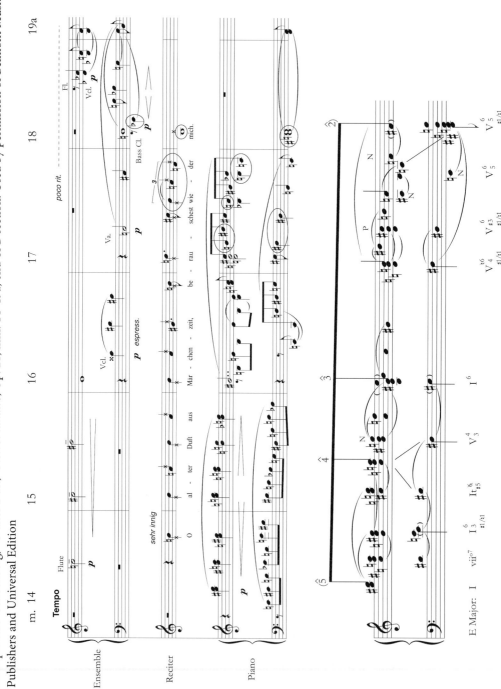

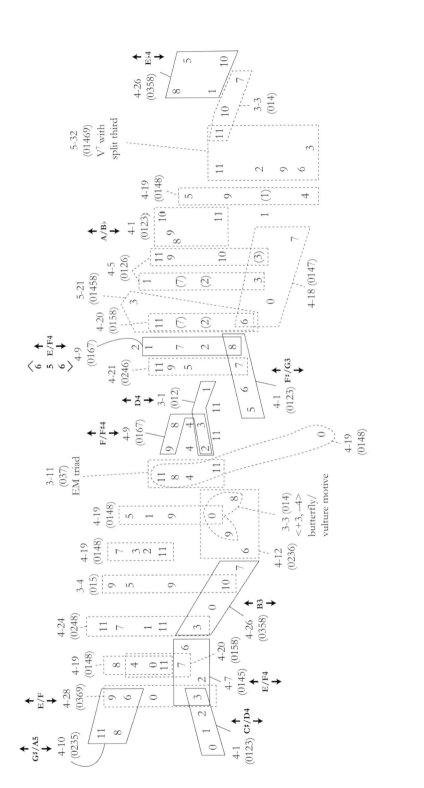

Example 6.21  Schoenberg, "O alter Duft," *Pierrot lunaire*, Op. 21, mm. 23–30, end of C section. Used by permission of Belmont Music Publishers and Universal Edition

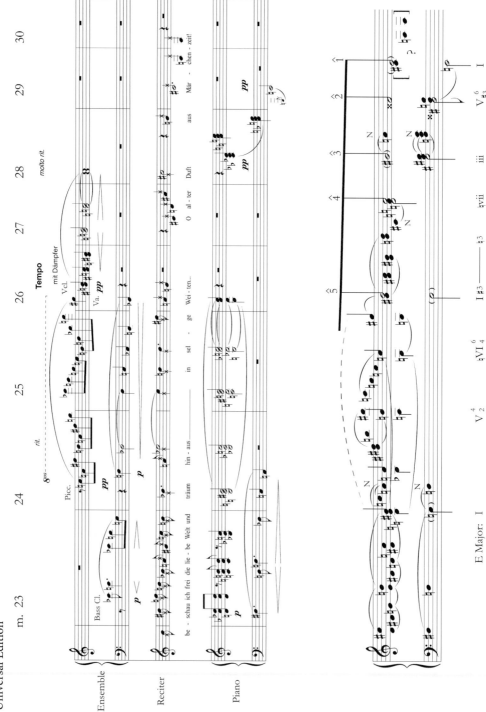

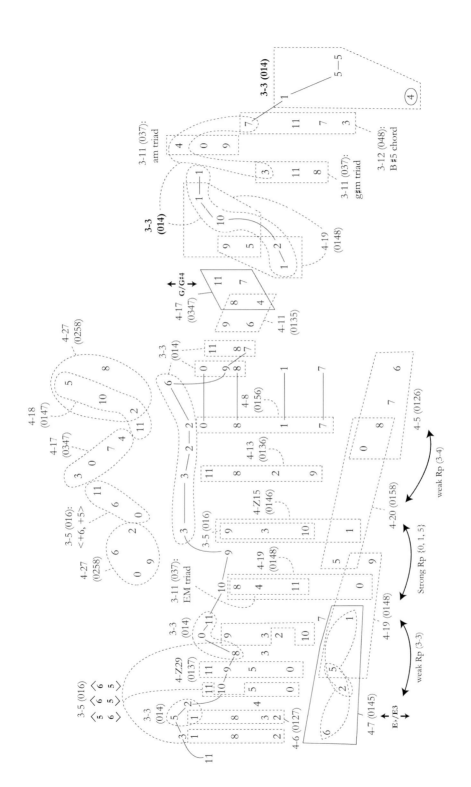

the main theme, setting the words "I freely view the beloved world and dream out into blessed distances."

The anticipatory passage in mm. 23–26a begins, as so often in previous passages, with characteristically atonal sounds and pitch-symmetrical collections battling to be perceived against hints of E major. The right hand of the piano in m. 23 provides several characteristic atonal sounds, three Viennese Trichords, members of SC 3-5 (016). The first of them utilizes the unordered pitch intervals <6, 5>, and the second and third invert that configuration to <5, 6>. The left hand of the piano, meanwhile, begins with pitch classes <6, 2, 5, 1>, which overlap two butterfly/vulture motives, pitch-symmetrical around Eb/E3, and a member of 4-7 (0145). This tetrachord overlaps with the descending <5, 1, 0, 9>, a member of SC 4-19 (0148), but then the piano's left hand falls silent as the bass clarinet picks up the bass line in mm. 24–25: <5, 1, 0, 8>, also descending. The latter succession belongs to set class 4-20 (0158): not symmetrical, but related to the immediately preceding piano tetrachord through strong Rp around {0, 1, 5}. Thus, ways of arranging and relating tetrachords characteristic of both "Mondestrunken" (strong Rp) and "Die Kreuze" (pitch symmetry) are evident in mm. 23–25.

Meanwhile, diatonic segments in E major appear in some of the prominent voices in m. 23. The bass clarinet begins with Eb4–E4–Eb4, an enharmonic spelling of *ti–do–ti*; the voice on the last two beats of the measure intones *fa–mi–le–sol*; and the top voice of the piano's three Viennese Trichords could be heard as *la–sol–fa* if the Db5 is spelled as C♯. All this leads quite convincingly to a relatively clear statement of the E major tonic 6/4 chord on the downbeat of m. 24 in the piano right hand, with *mi* as its top voice. This momentary tonic arrival is clouded somewhat by dissonant notes in the voice and piano left hand, though; and the continuation in mm. 24 and 25 in the piano right hand, voice, and piccolo moves away from tonality and back in the direction of characteristic atonal sets again. The piano's right hand, sometimes doubled by the voice an octave higher, opens up in contrary motion outward in these two measures (perhaps a registral portrayal of the blessed distances being referred to?), and all three of its chords after the E major triad are either Viennese Trichords or supersets of them: 3-5 (016) as unordered pitch intervals <5, 6> in the second half of m. 24, 4-13 (0136) as <5, 6, 3> on the downbeat of m. 25, and 4-8 (0156) as <6, 7, 4> in the second half of m. 25. During these same measures, the piccolo adds an arpeggiation of 3-5 as well as two other characteristic atonal sets, 4-18 (0147) and 4-17 (0347), and two 4-27s (0258), both of them dominant seventh chords, but neither supportive of E major as tonic. The "blessed distances" the reciter speaks of certainly seem to grow more distant from the notion of tonality as a guiding force.

But with the final repeat of line 1 in mm. 26–30, the main theme of mm. 1–2 returns our ears once again to the E major orbit, and sets up for the work's most definitive cadence in the home key – which is then turned aside one last time – as the reciter intones the words "from fairytale times." The Schenkerian graph in the middle of Example 6.21 represents this definitive cadence through an *Urlinie* descent from mm. 26–29; in a way, similar to the final descent in Schoenberg's Op. 2, No. 2 song, described back in Chapter 1. The members of the descent itself are mostly intact (in some register, not necessarily the obligatory one) as well as the opening and closing chords, but several of the internal chords are unexpected. The $\hat{5}$ is harmonized by the same tonic split third chord that begins all the reiterations of the main theme, $\hat{4}$ by a minor vii chord on D♮, $\hat{3}$ by a minor iii chord (respelled as A♭ minor). After an upper neighbor A♮, harmonized by minor iv, the cadence progresses to $V_{\sharp3}^{6}$ under $\hat{2}$, the raised fifth F$_\times$ respelled as a G♮, and $\hat{1}$ (as well as I) appears on the downbeat of m. 29, in the guise of a bare octave, E1-E2. Unusual as it is, this cadence has been recognized by Brinkmann and others as the melodrama's clearest statement of E major.[45]

However, as I mentioned above, this final cadence is turned aside one last time to create the most definitive musical portrayal of the basic image. Schoenberg accomplishes this rather subtly and gently by means of the voice part, which sets two small phrases against the cadence in piano and strings; the first ascending on "O alter Duft," the second descending on "aus Märchenzeit." The first phrase, <1, 2, 10, 1>, arpeggiates set class 3-3 (014), and rises to a C♯5 to conflict with the F4 and A4 (from the natural vii chord under $\hat{4}$) that resonate at the beginning of m. 28. The second, <7, 1, 5>, conflicts with the piano's E arrival by placing first C♯4 against it (momentarily suggesting an ending on the vi chord)[46] and finally the more dissonant F3. With E, both C♯ and F form 3-3 again, so that the

[45] Brinkmann's harmonic analysis of the final cadence, on p. 103 of "The Lyric as Paradigm," only includes the final three chords, iv, $V_{\sharp3}^{6}$, and I, which he labels S, D, and T in the Riemannian functional manner. In footnote 17 (p. 121) of the same article, he explains the chord on the last quarter note of m. 28 in the same way as I do: "E♭-G-B, spelled as B-D♯-F$_\times$, is a dominant with raised fifth."

[46] This arrival on C♯4 at the downbeat of m. 29, together with its upper octave C♯5 a measure earlier (together with similar emphases on C♯ at the melodrama's beginning), motivates Richard Kurth to suggest a different tonally ambiguous reading of the final measures: E major and C♯ major as co-equals in an instance of "suspended tonality." See Kurth, "*Pierrot lunaire*: Persona, Voice, and the Fabric of Allusion," pp. 132–34.

two diversions from E major tonality both create what is probably *Pierrot lunaire*'s most common atonal trichord: the mirage of tonal arrival dissipates and the atonal reality that had characterized most of the twenty-one melodramas wins out in the end. Tonality's ancient scent as "fairytale," indeed.

Thus *Pierrot lunaire* ends as it began: portraying through sound a visual image abstracted from the first lines of the poem's text – at the beginning, intoxicating waves of moonlight that sometimes come in too far; at the end, a journey home in which the desired arrival turns into a mirage at the final moment. In the middle, we "see" (with our ears) the poet/composer nailed to the vertically and horizontally symmetrical cross. Together with the other eighteen melodramas, these sound pictures illustrate the story of the artist who strays into modernism then tries, though unsuccessfully, to return home. Though I could not analyze the remaining numbers here to prove that all of them grow out of visual images, I have the strong hunch that many, if not all, do – especially since attempts to analyze other numbers such as "Nacht," "Parodie," "Der Mondfleck," and "Eine blasse Wäscherin" in similar ways have been successful.

Instead of exploring *Pierrot* and its dependence on the basic image further, then, my final chapter will briefly review the ways in which musical idea and basic image, together with tonal references for expressive purposes, both structure and enliven the pieces from Schoenberg's atonal *oeuvre* that we have examined in this book. I believe these ways of organizing constitute a thread that connects every piece in Schoenberg's middle period, so that they enable me to characterize his compositional development as more steady and consistent than has been portrayed in the past. But if his atonal music in fact developed coherently along the lines I have presented, what motivated him to make the transition to twelve-tone music?

# 7 Summary, and the Way Forward to Twelve-Tone Music

This book started off with an argument against Ethan Haimo's assertion that Schoenberg's middle-period music ought not to be called "atonal." In response, I showed how the Schenkerian contrapuntal structures that were still in effect (though harmonized differently) during Schoenberg's tonal period literally unravel in a work such as Op. 11, No. 1, which compels us to give that music a label reflecting such a radical shift. I also demonstrated in Chapter 1 how motivic and set-class relations, traditional musical form, and – most importantly – the conflict, elaboration, and resolution of the musical idea serve, in the absence of tonal contrapuntal structures, to produce a coherent and unified statement in Op. 11, No. 1.

As my book progressed, it also continually pushed back against a second assertion made by Haimo, as well as numerous other scholars. This is the notion that Schoenberg's music made a sudden detour in the summer of 1909 away from motivic networks and processes as well as musical form and other means of large-scale coherence, before gradually finding its way back beginning in 1911 with the Op. 19 Little Piano Pieces, in 1912 with parts of *Pierrot lunaire*, or in 1913 with *Die Glückliche Hand*. Haimo refers to this detour as "New Music," while Joseph Auner calls it the "intuitive aesthetic."[1] One of the main purposes of my book is to counter such portrayals of Schoenberg's atonal period as discontinuous or even haphazard, pushed in wildly different directions by motivations such as trying to keep up with Webern and his other students. Instead, I want to understand the compositions of 1908–12 as connected by the constant guiding presence of complete or incomplete musical ideas and/or basic images, not to mention the gradual re-emergence of functional tonality as an expressive device after its rejection in 1908 as the guarantor of large-scale coherence.

To this end, I described both Op. 11, Nos. 1 and 2 as manifestations of musical idea, in which the stages of the idea line up with the parts of some traditional form (truncated sonata-rondo, ABA′CA″, in the first; ABA′ in the second). In both pieces, certain motivic and harmonic elements appear in the initial A section and conflicting elements in a large B section or small b subsection, and that conflict is elaborated through the course of the piece,

---

[1] Haimo, *Schoenberg's Transformation of Musical Language*, p. 349; Auner, "Schoenberg's Aesthetic Transformations," 106.

with a resolution coming just before and also during the final return of A. I pointed out that the motivic material in Op. 11, No. 2 is derived from that of the first piece, but is more fragmented – short phrases as opposed to themes. This tendency toward fragmentation then continues in Piece No. 3, which could possibly be organized into a loose version of rondo form around three similar-sounding sections (Brinkmann's A, F, and L) – but in general, the shortness of all eighteen sections of the piece and the jagged textural, registral, and dynamic contrasts from one section to the next provide some support for the idea that traditional form is cast aside. Contrary to the conventional wisdom, however, motives and motivic processes are *not* cast aside in Op. 11, No. 3. The piece is built from two processes that are both motivic and harmonic, one that incrementally expands the intervals between adjacent pitch classes in prime forms, and a second that follows different voicings of SC 4-19 with an arrangement, <–4, –1, –3>, that explains that set class as derived from Op. 11, No. 1's motto, <–3, –1>. These two processes conflict with one another for the first part of the third piece, but eventually the set-class expansion process crowds out the explanatory one without any real synthesis between the two, characterizing Op. 11, No. 3 as an incomplete musical idea. Since both processes in No. 3, as well as the motives and harmonies that participate in them, have roots in Op. 11, No. 1, and were also reflected in Op. 11, No. 2, I characterized the three pieces of Op. 11 as a cycle.

The book then took a step backward in time, to consider two of Schoenberg's Op. 15 songs, Nos. 7 and 11, some of his first atonal compositions. These were found to provide good examples of the other way of organizing the whole that seems to span Schoenberg's atonal period (and is also present in his tonal and twelve-tone music, I believe), what I call "basic image." "Angst und Hoffen" translates into pitch and rhythm the image of the poet's face turning alternately toward fear and hope, while his body first shrinks and then expands to emit sighs, a picture abstracted from the first two lines of the text. Likewise, "Als wir hinter" builds out from its third line "was our felicity quite what we dreamed?" to create a faint, clouded memory of two bodies lightly brushing together, maybe uniting sexually, followed by a more solid image of their union at the end. This second basic image, with its uncertainty that is elaborated, striven against in an attempt to remember, and finally resolved, parallels the stages of a musical idea, and Schoenberg manifests both image and idea in the song through different ways of realizing common subsets between tetrachords, and relationships between rhythm and meter.

Another piece that scholars point to as an exemplar of Schoenberg's supposed amotivic style is his monodrama *Erwartung*, Op. 17.

In Chapter 4, I argued that *Erwartung* not only repeats and develops melodic motives (<D, F, C♯> as <+3, +8> among many others), but also gives them representative functions, in the manner of leitmotives (<D, F, C♯> represents the lover's dead body, for example). Further still, it expands the notion of leitmotive to include set classes and groups of set classes. But even more importantly for our present discussion, the leitmotives of *Erwartung*, through their gradual cumulations, participate in the projection of an extended basic image that is perceptible despite the continually changing moods on the piece's (and libretto's) surface – a double emergence of, first, the lover's dead body, and, second, the woman's realization that she will never see him again. The latter emergence cumulates in a quotation from an earlier Schoenberg song, "Am Wegrand" – not only the rhythms and intervals of the quotation but also the harmonic context, D minor tonic. Though functional tonality has ceased to be the main organizing force in *Erwartung*, it returns here as a text-painting device: D minor as the key of desolation.

My analyses of three Op. 19 piano pieces in Chapter 5, then, characterized them not as returning to more traditional ways of organizing after the sharp detour into "New Music," but as continuing to develop the organizational schemes Schoenberg had used in the immediately preceding years by applying them to pieces of much smaller scale. All three are based on miniature versions of traditional forms: a three-part strophic form (with variation) in No. 2, rounded binary in No. 3, and sonata in No. 6. But in Nos. 2 and 3, the form assists with the projection of the musical idea, in different ways – the hexatonic collection pulls its opponents into synthesis with itself in No. 2, while the diatonic collection prevents it from doing so in No. 3. And in No. 6, the miniscule sonata manifests both an incomplete musical idea and a basic image, in which Schoenberg, attempting to follow in Mahler's footsteps, strives to reach up to an E major cadence but is pushed back down toward atonality.

Likewise, I portrayed *Pierrot lunaire* not as a transitional piece in which some melodramas are still "intuitive" and others return to more traditional notions of motive and form, but rather as the high point in the development of the basic image as background organizational scheme. In each of the melodramas I studied, Nos. 1, 14, and 21, a visual image abstracted from the first two lines, that is, the repeating element in the *rondel*, motivates and controls the pitch and rhythmic processes of the piece. In "Mondestrunken," the descending waves of moonlight translate into cascades of tetrachords that either chain through Rp relations or transpose themselves in ornamentation of the descending augmented triad in the middleground. In "Die Kreuze," the image of the cross on which the poet hangs motivates vertical and horizontal symmetries that cross one another, around different axes of vertical symmetry at the piece's beginning (as Pierrot squirms around), but eventually locking into the mirror around D and A♭ near the end (as he becomes still and lifeless). Finally, in "O alter Duft," the basic image portrays the poet (or composer) attempting to return home to his older style but being thwarted at the last minute. This motivates multiple approaches to authentic and half cadences that are clouded by dissonant voices immediately following the cadence, another example of tonality used as an expressive device, rather than as the agent of coherence.

In these ways, my book characterizes Schoenberg's pre-twelve-tone atonal music as a continuous development that uses a limited number of organizational methods to create long-range coherence in each and every piece. Though I do admit that works such as Op. 11, No. 3 and *Erwartung* could be understood as dispensing with traditional musical form, both "intuitive" works I studied *preserve motivic processes*; the former using processes in conflict to project an incomplete musical idea, the latter using leitmotives and leitmotivic pitch-class sets to fill out an extended basic image. Now, such a view of Schoenberg's music from summer 1909 to 1911 is, of course, incompatible with the notion that "Away with motivic work-ing!" was a compositional manifesto for Schoenberg at that time, the position that Haimo and others maintain.[2] But I have already explained in Chapter 2 and elsewhere[3] that I believe Schoenberg's oft- and mis-cited exclamation to Busoni, "Away *from* motivic working," was no manifesto, but rather a bit of hyperbole, part of an attempt to convince Busoni to perform the Op. 11 Piano Pieces without rescoring them.

In the same way, my view of the music from 1909 to 1911 appears to contradict statements Schoenberg made in his diary and letters during 1911 and 1912 about the waning of his creative abilities, statements that others have cited to support their case that the supposed amotivic style was a compositional dead end for him. For example, this from his Berlin diary, written on Mar. 12, 1912:

> I had already considered the possibility that I might never compose again at all. There seemed to be many reasons for it. The persistence of my students, who are always at my heels trying to outdo what I offer, puts me in danger of becoming their imitator, and it keeps me from calmly building on what I have already attained. They always raise everything to the tenth power. And it

[2] Haimo, *Schoenberg's Transformation of Musical Language*, pp. 346–49.
[3] Boss, "Away With Motivic Working? Not So Fast: Motivic Processes in Schoenberg's Op. 11, No. 3."

works! It is really good. But I don't know whether it is necessary. So I am
forced to decide all the more carefully whether I must compose now as
before.[4]

But I suggested in Chapter 5 that Schoenberg's equivocation about whether
and how to keep composing may have been motivated as much by other
concerns as by any dissatisfaction he felt with the musical style he had
adopted. In this case, he seems to be admitting to a bit of jealousy about his
students' successes (primarily Webern?). There is no direct reference to the
abandonment of motivic working here, but only a vague allusion to the
difficulty of keeping up with his students because of certain advanced
aspects of their musical style. Finally, it is important to note that the
diary entry appeared in March 1912, more than a year *after* the composition of Op. 19, which many scholars have interpreted as the first step back
from the supposed abyss of amotivicism and free form, and simultaneously
with the beginning of Schoenberg's composition of *Pierrot lunaire*. This
suggests that the equivocation this diary entry describes may not have been
brought on by "New Music" alone, since Schoenberg had already begun
correcting that problem (if it was indeed a problem) when he wrote it.

   There is one more Schoenberg quotation, however, that seems to contradict the interpretation of his pre-twelve-tone atonal music I presented in
this book: the well-known passage from "Composition with Twelve Tones"
where he explains his motivations for developing the twelve-tone style
(here abbreviated):

> The first compositions in this new [atonal] style were written by me around
> 1908 and, soon afterwards, by my pupils, Anton von Webern and Alban Berg.
> From the very beginning such compositions differed from all preceding
> music, not only harmonically but also melodically, thematically, and
> motivally . . . New colorful harmony was offered; but much was lost.
>    Formerly the harmony had served not only as a source of beauty, but, more
> important, as a means of distinguishing the features of the form . . .
> Establishing functions demanded different successions of harmonies than
> roving functions; a bridge, a transition, demanded other successions than
> a codetta; harmonic variation could be executed intelligently and logically
> only with due consideration of the fundamental meaning of the harmonies.
> Fulfillment of all these functions . . . could scarcely be assured with chords
> whose constructive values had not as yet been explored. Hence, it seemed at
> first impossible to compose pieces of complicated organization or of great
> length.

---

[4] Arnold Schoenberg, *Berliner Tagebuch*, ed. Josef Rufer (Frankfurt: Propyläen, 1974),
   pp. 33–34; cited by Bryan Simms in *The Atonal Music of Arnold Schoenberg*, p. 113.

> A little later I discovered how to construct larger forms by following a text
> or a poem. The differences in size and shape of its parts and the change in
> character and mood were mirrored in the shape and size of the composition,
> in its dynamics and tempo, figuration and accentuation, instrumentation and
> orchestration. Thus the parts were differentiated as clearly as they had for-
> merly been by the tonal and structural functions of harmony.
>
> ... After many unsuccessful attempts during a period of approximately
> twelve years [1908–1920?] I laid the foundations for a new procedure in
> musical construction which seemed fitted to replace those structural differ-
> entiations provided formerly by tonal harmonies.
>
> I called this procedure Method of Composing with Twelve Tones Which
> are Related Only with One Another.[5]

From the vantage point of thirty-three years later, Schoenberg describes
his venture into atonality in 1908 as an exciting exploration of new, "colorful" harmonies that was ultimately unsuccessful, and which necessitated
a new direction around 1920. The problem, he says, was that it was
impossible for him to regulate all these new harmonies; to determine
which chords and progressions were appropriate for the different functions
of different parts of a traditional form: transitions, closing sections, etc.
This made it impossible for him to write extended pieces. After a while, he
discovered the expedient of using a text to motivate the pitch and rhythmic
structure (perhaps this is an allusion to what I have called "basic image"?),
making longer compositions possible if the text was long enough – but that
too eventually proved to be unsatisfactory for a composer steeped in the
absolute music tradition. Finally, the twelve-tone method proved to be an
acceptable solution, because it enabled him to imitate some of the form-
defining features of tonal music, while remaining within an atonal context.

Any fan of Schoenberg's pre-serial atonal music (among which I number
myself) should find quite a bit to argue against in this quotation. There are
analytic observations I have made in numerous places in this book that
directly contradict his claims about not being able to support formal
function with the new motivic and chordal materials. For example, consider the incremental ordered pitch-interval expansion interrupted by
other kinds of motivic development in the first eleven measures of Op.
11, No. 1, which characterizes that piece's large A as a three-part opening
section, or the sudden, extreme motivic, rhythmic, and registral changes
at m. 12 that mark B as a contrasting section (see, again, Chapter 1,
pp. 22–28). Or, "Die Kreuze's" ability to mark the two parts of its binary

---

[5] Arnold Schoenberg, "Composition with Twelve Tones (1)" (1941), in *Style and Idea*,
   pp. 217–18.

form with textural and instrumental changes that reinforce the move from multiple axes of symmetry to a single axis (mostly) in m. 10 (Chapter 6, pp. 316–18). "Die Kreuze's" binary form would be clearly perceptible on musical grounds, even if the text were absent. At the most basic level, I am not comfortable with Schoenberg's characterization of his atonal music in this quotation as "many unsuccessful attempts." The pieces we have explored in this book, *every one* of them in my estimation, surely must be counted among his masterpieces, because of the way each projects its form as well as its idea or image.

So if Schoenberg's turn toward the twelve-tone style was not motivated by the inadequacies of his atonal music as he claimed, what motivated it? Why was the composer not satisfied with continuing to write in the style of *Pierrot lunaire* and the Op. 19 miniatures? My conviction is that there were two main forces driving Schoenberg toward the twelve-tone approach, both of them intensifications of tendencies that already display themselves in his pre-twelve-tone atonal music. Scholars in English and German who describe his transition from atonal to twelve-tone music, such as Ethan Haimo, Bryan Simms, and Jan Maegaard, all refer to both forces.[6] They are: 1) Schoenberg's growing tendency to circulate through the chromatic scale in a regular manner, without repeating pitch classes, "regular circulation of the aggregate" or "aggregate cycles" as we will call it, and 2) a growing inclination to make the opening phrase or section of the piece, the *Grundgestalt*, serve as the only source for everything that follows. Schoenberg admits to both tendencies himself, in other essays reprinted in *Style and Idea* (1984). In "Composition with Twelve Tones (II)," written in 1948, he gives a rationale for the regular circulation of the aggregate:

> The construction of a basic set of twelve tones derives from the intention to postpone the repetition of every tone as long as possible. I have stated in my *Harmonielehre* that the emphasis given to a tone by a premature repetition is capable of heightening it to the rank of a tonic. But the regular application of a set of twelve tones emphasizes all the other tones in the same manner, thus depriving one single tone of the privilege of supremacy.[7]

And in "Linear Counterpoint" (1931) he explains the other driving force, the desire to make every subsequent note and rhythm in a piece answerable to its *Grundgestalt*:

---

[6]  Haimo, *Schoenberg's Serial Odyssey*, chs. 3 and 4; Simms, *The Atonal Music of Arnold Schoenberg*, chs. 7 and 8; Maegaard, *Studien zur Entwicklung des dodekaphonen Satzes*, Book I, pp. 80–119, Book II, pp. 489–574, Notenbeilage, pp. 53–103.

[7]  Schoenberg, *Style and Idea*, p. 246.

> There is a higher level, and it is at this level that one finds the question which
> needs answering in order to arrive at the postulate: "Whatever happens in
> a piece of music is nothing but the endless reshaping of a basic shape." Or, in
> other words, there is nothing in a piece of music but what comes from the
> theme, springs from it and can be traced back to it; to put it still more severely,
> nothing but the theme itself. Or, all the shapes appearing in a piece of music
> are foreseen in the "theme."[8]

I said above that both forces that drove Schoenberg toward the twelve-tone
style were already present in his pre-serial atonal music, in less-intense
manifestations. Every one of the atonal pieces we studied in this book
introduces pitch and rhythmic material in the opening measures, which
then becomes the source for much, if not all, of what follows. Even an
"intuitive" work such as Op. 11, No. 3 presents both of its warring motivic
processes in the opening five measures (which I called the *Grundgestalt* in
Example 2.13), and almost every section following m. 5 varies material
from that opening in some way. And the pieces that I called manifestations
of "musical idea" develop their opening material in an even more elaborate
and dramatic manner. For example, Op. 11, No. 1 produces motives
derivable from the original motto <–3, –1>, what I called motive *a*, in its
opening A section (motive *x* arises as a link between *a* motives, and *y* as the
inversion and repetition of motive *a*'s second interval; see Example 1.7).
But soon after the onset of B (Example 1.8), we hear motives and chords
that are more difficult to "trace back" to motive *a*, such as <+5, +6> and
<+4, +4, +9>, motives *b* and *c*. The core of the musical idea in Op. 11, No. 1,
then, consists of the strategy Schoenberg uses in the final A″ section (and
the retransition to it) to show how the foreign elements of B can, in fact, be
understood as "reshapings" of motive *a* and its variations in the A section.
(See Example 1.9.)

The tendency toward regular circulation of the aggregate can also be
seen in Schoenberg's pre-serial atonal music, though it is much less prevalent than dependence on a *Grundgestalt*. We saw one brief example in
"Die Kreuze," in m. 4 (Example 6.12), where {0, 3, 4, 7, 8, 11}, one
transposition of set-class 6-20, appears in the right hand of the piano on
beat 2, overlapping with the complementary transposition, {1, 2, 5, 6, 9, 10},
in the left hand on beats 2 and 3. But this little passage is engulfed by
numerous others that repeat pitch classes before the surrounding aggregate
is completed. An example from a piece closer to Schoenberg's transition to
twelve-tone music (1913), the introduction to the Op. 22 song "Seraphita,"
extends the aggregate circulation technique using complementary forms of

[8] Ibid., p. 290.

6-20 to two measures, mm. 14–15, and approaches it in a gradual manner.[9] (See Example 7.1.)

On the downbeat of m. 12, the violins produce a hexachord (SC 6-Z19), which is one PC different from a version of 6-20 we will encounter in m. 14, {0, 1, 5, 6, 8, 9} rather than {0, 1, 4, 5, 8, 9}. The 'cellos and trombones then provide the other six pitch classes {2, 3, 4, 7, 10, 11}, in the middle part of m. 12, but not without repeating pitch classes 5, 6, and 9 too soon for a regular aggregate cycle. On the fourth beat, we hear another chord in the violins, SC 6-18, which is two off from the complement of {0, 1, 4, 5, 8, 9}: {0, 2, 5, 6, 7, 11} rather than {2, 3, 6, 7, 10, 11} – thus m. 12 also fails to create an aggregate cycle in the violins alone. In m. 13, we hear two hexachords in violins and descending pizzicato 'cellos that are, again, one PC removed from complementary forms of 6-20: {0, 3, 4, 7, 8, 10} instead of {0, 3, 4, 7, 8, 11}, and {1, 2, 5, 6, 9, 11} rather than {1, 2, 5, 6, 9, 10}. In this case, however, the two chords are complements of each other, both members of SC 6-31, and so they do create an aggregate cycle, just not using complementary forms of 6-20. Beat 4 of m. 13 then presents another hexachord in the violins that is one PC off from a member of 6-20, forming 6-Z44 instead; {2, 3, 6, 9, 10, 11} rather than {2, 3, 6, 7, 10, 11}.

All these approximations of SC 6-20, two of which form an aggregate, then lead to regular alternations between {0, 1, 4, 5, 8, 9} in the violins and {2, 3, 6, 7, 10, 11} in the clarinets that create two aggregate cycles, one in m. 14 and one in m. 15. In the second part of m. 15, however, the piece turns away from cycling through the aggregate: each eight-note chord in the violins and trombones contains pitch class 0, and several of them have other common tones linking them.

We have seen that Schoenberg's pre-serial atonal music does demonstrate incipient tendencies to derive subsequent pitch material from its *Grundgestalt* and to cycle through the aggregate, but these tendencies by no means account for every note. It is possible, then, to understand the transition from Schoenberg's atonal style to his twelve-tone style as motivated by his striving to bring more of the musical texture under the control of these two principles. I will not present a complete account of this transition in this chapter: Haimo, Simms, and Maegaard have produced step-by-step timelines with detailed study of sketches and complete pieces already. Instead, I will limit myself to describing two representative examples that show the increasing influence that aggregate circulation and *Grundgestalt* exerted over Schoenberg's music.

---

[9] Bryan Simms refers to these measures multiple times in *The Atonal Music of Arnold Schoenberg* as a step in the direction toward more regular cycling through the aggregate. See pp. 144, 176, and 186.

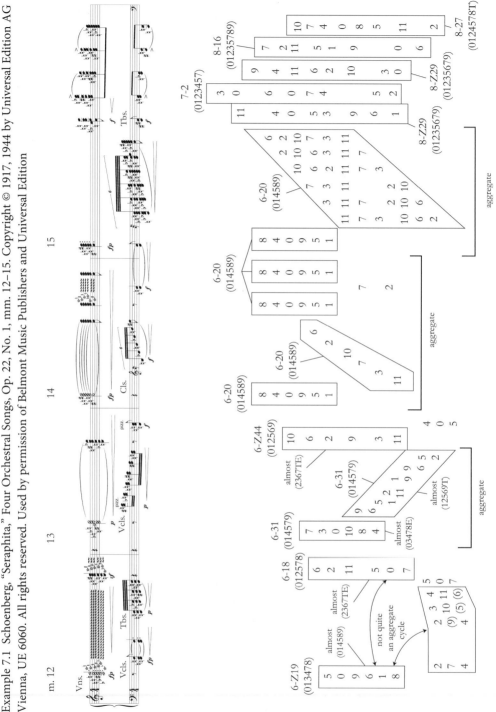

Example 7.1 Schoenberg, "Seraphita," Four Orchestral Songs, Op. 22, No. 1, mm. 12–15. Copyright © 1917, 1944 by Universal Edition AG Vienna, UE 6060. All rights reserved. Used by permission of Belmont Music Publishers and Universal Edition

We will begin with a sketch from 1914, of a Scherzo movement from an unfinished Symphony. Schoenberg claimed in 1937, in a letter to Nicolas Slonimsky, that this movement was his first step in the direction toward twelve-tone music.[10] And Haimo, Simms, and Maegaard all give this unfinished piece the distinction of being Schoenberg's first to use a twelve-tone pitch row and to develop it in some of the ways that would become characteristic in his later music – including the highlighting of invariant segments between row forms. But they also all recognize that the twelve-tone *Grundgestalt* accounts for only a small part of the texture in this Scherzo.[11] The opening twelve measures of the movement, transcribed from sketch page MS 93_U 395 at the Arnold Schönberg Center in Vienna, can be found in Example 7.2. (A facsimile of the sketch itself can be found in Example 7.3.)

The leading voice in mm. 1–5a, 6 unison first clarinets, plays a twelve-tone pitch row through twice: <2, 7, 3, 9, 8, 4, 5, 11, 0, 6, 1, 10>. The accompaniment, three trumpets, consists of three chords that cannot be explained as contiguous row segments. But the last two chords do have a distant relationship to the row: both are Viennese Trichords, members of set class 3-5 (016), which appears no less than five times as segments of the row. The row's final 3-5, <0, 6, 1>, has the same ordered pitch intervals, <+6, −5>, as the unordered pitch intervals of the two Viennese Trichords.

After m. 5b, the accompaniment drops out, and the clarinets start to develop their line, turning back toward techniques resembling Schoenberg's atonal music and abandoning strict twelve-tone writing. First we hear a fragment consisting of the row's first eight notes, then two hexachordal successions, <6, 0, 10, 7, 9, 0> and <8, 4, 0, 9, 11, 1> (which is repeated). The second of these has been recognized by Haimo as containing a reordering of five notes from the original row:[12] actually, the whole hexachord can also be heard as taking row order positions **3-10**, leaving out two of them (**6** and **9**), and reordering the rest. In addition, both hexachords contain "head motives," <6, 0, 10, 7> and <8, 4, 0, 9>, that relate in ways typical of Schoenberg's earlier music to salient tetrachords in the tone row. The succession <6, 0, 10, 7> forms set class 4-Z15 (0146), the Z-relative of 4-Z29 (0137), produced by the row's final tetrachord <0, 6, 1, 10>. The two tetrachords also link through three common tones, a strong Rp

---

[10] This letter is cited in Haimo, *Schoenberg's Serial Odyssey*, p. 42.

[11] Haimo, *Schoenberg's Serial Odyssey*, pp. 42–45; Simms, *The Atonal Music of Arnold Schoenberg*, p. 159; Maegaard, *Studien zur Entwicklung des dodekaphonen Satzes*, Book II, pp. 524–25.

[12] Haimo, *Schoenberg's Serial Odyssey*, p. 47.

Example 7.2 Schoenberg, Scherzo from Symphony (1914–15), mm. 1–12a. Used by permission of Belmont Music Publishers

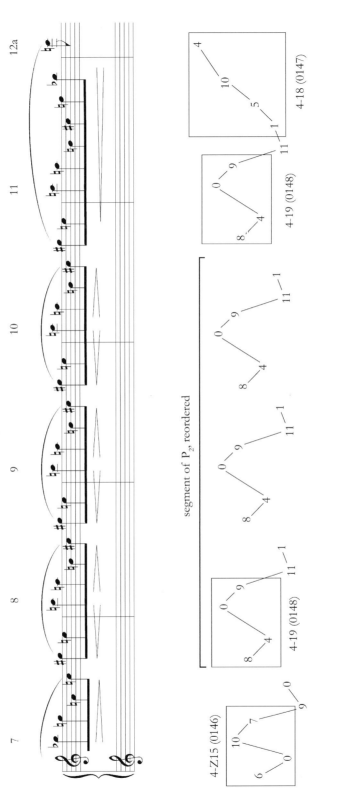

segment of $P_2$, reordered

Example 7.3  Schoenberg, Sketch MS 93_U 395 for the Scherzo movement of
a Symphony (1914), mm. 1–34. Used by permission of Belmont Music Publishers

relation (an important feature of our "Mondestrunken" analysis in
Chapter 6). As for <8, 4, 0, 9>, it is a member of set class 4-19 (0148),
a favorite tetrachord of Schoenberg's in his middle period, which also occurs
between the last three notes of the row and the first note of its repetition, <6,
1, 10, 2>, in mm. 2b–3a. The relation between these two tetrachord segments
is made more hearable by their similar contours: down, up, down.

In mm. 12–23, not just the tone row but also its further developments
in mm. 5–12 are transposed up a perfect fourth, to $P_7$, and played by six E♭

Example 7.4  Detail from sketch page MS 93_U 380 for the Scherzo, Symphony (1914), showing retrograde-invariant segment between $P_2$ and $I_2$. Used by permission of Belmont Music Publishers

clarinets. And in mm. 23–25, six second clarinets launch the same process a perfect fourth lower than the original, $P_9$, but only get as far as one repetition of the tone row. After this, they are joined by the first clarinet section in m. 25, which plays the repeated row at its original level $P_2$, thus in parallel fourths,[13] and the E♭ clarinet section comes back in at m. 27, playing the further developments of mm. 5b–8 at the perfect fourth above, together with the other two clarinet sections, resulting in parallel perfect fourth chords.

In a way, Schoenberg has made the basic shape of his Scherzo account for all of the first thirty measures, if we understand this *Grundgestalt* as all of m. 1–12 – two row repetitions plus their fragmentations and variations in the subsequent measures. This material is transposed up a perfect fourth, down a perfect fourth, and at the end of the second transposition all three transpositions are combined. But within the transposed sections themselves, the technique shifts from row repetition to a more flexible type of variation, reminiscent of Schoenberg's atonal music. As a result, regular circulation of the aggregate occurs only in a few places.

I mentioned above that this Scherzo also contains the first instance in which Schoenberg recognized and made use of invariant segments between row forms (this process of discovery is described in detail by Fusako Hamao).[14] On another sketch page, MS 93_U 380, the top left corner of which is reproduced in Example 7.4, he sets down the pitch row at $P_2$ and its pitch inversion $I_2$, and brackets order positions **5-8** in the inverted row, <0, 11, 5, 4>, which create a retrograde invariance with the corresponding positions in $P_2$, <4, 5, 11, 0>.

Later on the same sketch page, he copies out $P_2$ again, and places "X"s above order positions **5-8**, to indicate their possible removal to make an

---

[13]  The second clarinets do diverge from $P_9$ at one point in this passage, the fourth eighth note of m. 26, creating a single tritone: this may have been an error.

[14]  Fusako Hamao, "On the Origin of the Twelve-Tone Method: Schoenberg's Sketches for the Unfinished *Symphony* (1914–1915)," *Current Musicology* 42 (1986): 32–45.

eight-tone row, <2, 7, 3, 9, 8, 6, 1, 10>. He then reorders the last three notes to form <2, 7, 3, 9, 8, 1, 10, 6> in mm. 32–34, the bottom right corner of Example 7.3's sketch, and creates what Jan Maegaard calls "stretto harmony" from the new eight-tone row.[15] I transcribed and analyzed these measures in Example 7.5, highlighting the four-voice stretto in piccolo, flutes, and clarinets at a distance of one quarter note.

An important byproduct of this imitation is the alternation of two vertical tetrachords, {2, 3, 8, 10} and {1, 6, 7, 9}, designated A and B in my example. (The sketch also indicates, using shorthand on stave 3, alternating four-note chords using the same pitch classes in oboes and bassoons, taken from an earlier sketch, MS 93_U 381. I provided these chords to the right of the main sketch.) Chord A belongs to set class 4-16 (0157) and B to set class 4-Z29 (0137), the same set classes as the first and last tetrachords of the original row – so that Schoenberg has here discovered a way to make the *Grundgestalt* control both the vertical and the horizontal dimensions of the piece (he would use a similar technique many years later in mm. 21–22 of the first movement of the Fourth String Quartet).[16] Meanwhile, the excised notes from $P_2$, <0, 11, 5, 4>, in the order they appear in $I_2$, are added to the texture in percussion and harp.

Already in 1914–15, Schoenberg has found a way to make much of the subsequent music dependent on the first twelve pitches and their variations. But not all of the music can be understood yet as closely derived from the twelve-tone *Grundgestalt*, and the Scherzo has not yet achieved regular circulation of the aggregate, though it comes close in certain passages, such as the opening four measures and mm. 32–34. To accomplish his dual purposes, Schoenberg would need to continue to develop the concept of *Grundgestalt* beyond a row of pitches, to something more abstract – a series of pitch classes. Free changes in register would enable him to repeat the same collection of pitch classes, its transpositions and inversions, without monotony. Though other works in the intervening years would also take steps in this direction (Simms discusses a fragment for a piano piece from 1918),[17] Schoenberg reaches a culmination in this regard with the fourth piano piece of Op. 23, of which the opening fourteen measures were written in 1920 (the

---

[15] Maegaard, *Studien zur Entwicklung des dodekaphonen Satzes*, Book II, pp. 524–25.

[16] Ethan Haimo and Bryan Simms also discuss the relationship between vertical harmony in mm. 32–34 of the Scherzo and the first and last tetrachords of the tone row. See Simms, *The Atonal Music of Arnold Schoenberg*, p. 162 and Haimo, *Schoenberg's Serial Odyssey*, pp. 48–52.

[17] Simms, *The Atonal Music of Arnold Schoenberg*, pp. 182–83.

Example 7.5  Schoenberg, Scherzo from Symphony (1914–15), mm. 32–35. Used by permission of Belmont Music Publishers

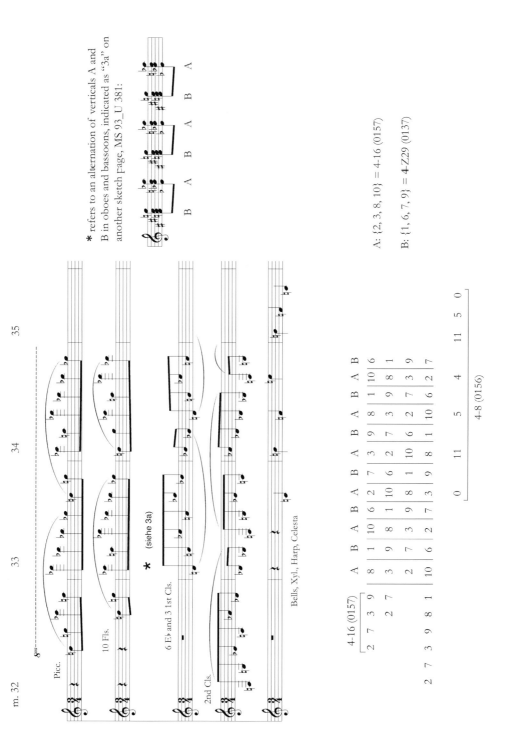

Example 7.6  Schoenberg, Piano Piece Op. 23, No. 4, autograph MS 17, composer's analysis of mm. 1–7. Used by permission of Belmont Music Publishers

piece was completed in 1923). This is one of the few pieces for which the composer himself provided an analysis, in which he circled three hexachords and one group of ten notes at the beginning (shown in Example 7.6): A, C, D, and B.[18]

Schoenberg then proceeded to mark both complete reiterations of A and partial reiterations of all four groups, up to m. 14. Numerous scholars have claimed that the content of these groups (and, occasionally, the ordering of A) can be shown to account for every note in the movement (but they

---

[18] The autograph manuscript page reproduced here can be found on the Arnold Schönberg Center website at: http://archive.schoenberg.at/compositions/manuskripte.php?werke_id=192&id_quelle=652&id_gatt=&id_untergatt=&herkunft=allewerke.

disagree on how that accounting should work).[19] In Example 7.7a and b, I show how the first 7½ measures of the piece could be derived from Schoenberg's hexachords A, C, and D, if we allow for register transfer, as well as reordering in most cases. (I relabeled the three hexachords as $A_3$, $B_2$, and $C_0$ – the subscript indicates the starting PC in each hexachord.)

Measure 1 presents hexachord $A_3$ in its definitive order, <3, 11, 10, 2, 4, 7>, and in a V-shaped contour that it will retain in many of its later iterations. We hear Hexachord $B_2$ crossing it in m. 1a, which, with its vertical grace-note trichord, has no definitive order. For the sake of my pitch-class map, I have ordered the vertical part from top to bottom, yielding <2, 10, 5, 0, 9, 1>. At the end of m. 1, we find Hexachord $C_0$, which has the ordering <0, 8, 10, 6, 9, 5> if verticals are counted top down. In m. 2, Simms suggests two transformations of source hexachords (which Schoenberg did not indicate in his analysis; instead this measure contains his fourth source group, the ten-note one).[20] The right hand presents Hexachord $C_0$ transposed up a half-step, thus $C_1$, <1, 9, 11, 7, 10, 6>, and reordered, while the remainder of the texture overlaps it in two notes with an ordered transposition of the first hexachord, $A_1$: <1, 9, 8, 0, 2, 5>. The picture becomes more complex in m. 3, but Schoenberg comes to our aid by labeling three fragments as "A2" in his sketch, by which he means the last five notes of what I call $A_3$, <11, 10, 2, 4, 7>. One "A2" appears below the E4 in the middle voice on the last sixteenth of beat 1: this pitch actually begins a rotated version of $A_8$: <4, 3, 7, 9, 0, 8>, which also includes notes in the bass and soprano voices. A second "A2" appears below B3 on the last sixteenth of beat 2; this points to the last five notes of $A_3$ itself, <11, 10, 2, 4, 7>. Finally, Schoenberg's "A2" also appears below the E♭3 in the bass at the beginning of beat 2: this calls our attention to a reordered trichord fragment of $A_3$, <3, 7, 10>, starting on E♭3 that is beamed together, which could be heard as completing the <4, 2, 11> that sounds on the first beat (I interpreted PC 1 on the first beat as connecting up with the $A_1$ in m. 2). The other notes in m. 3 can be understood as a reordering of $A_5$, originally <5, 1, 0, 4, 6, 9>, in the soprano and alto, and a reordering of $A_6$, <6, 2, 1, 5, 7, 10>, in the lower voices at measure's end.[21]

[19] Some examples include Haimo, *Schoenberg's Serial Odyssey*, pp. 77–78; Simms, *The Atonal Music of Arnold Schoenberg*, pp. 192–96; Maegaard, *Studien zur Entwicklung des dodekaphonen Satzes*, Book II, p. 503, Notenbeilage, pp. 70–71; Martha Hyde, "Musical Form and the Development of Schoenberg's Twelve-Tone Method," 99–110; Kathryn Bailey, *Composing with Tones: A Musical Analysis of Schoenberg's Op. 23 Pieces for Piano* (London: Royal Musical Association, 2001), pp. 73–99.
[20] Simms, *The Atonal Music of Arnold Schoenberg*, p. 193.
[21] Simms also recognizes the $A_6$; see *The Atonal Music*, p. 193.

Example 7.7a  Schoenberg, Piano Piece Op. 23, No. 4, mm. 1–3. Copyright © 1923 (Renewed) by Edition Wilhelm Hansen. This arrangement Copyright © 2018 by Edition Wilhelm Hansen. International copyright secured. All rights reserved. Used by permission of Hal Leonard LLC

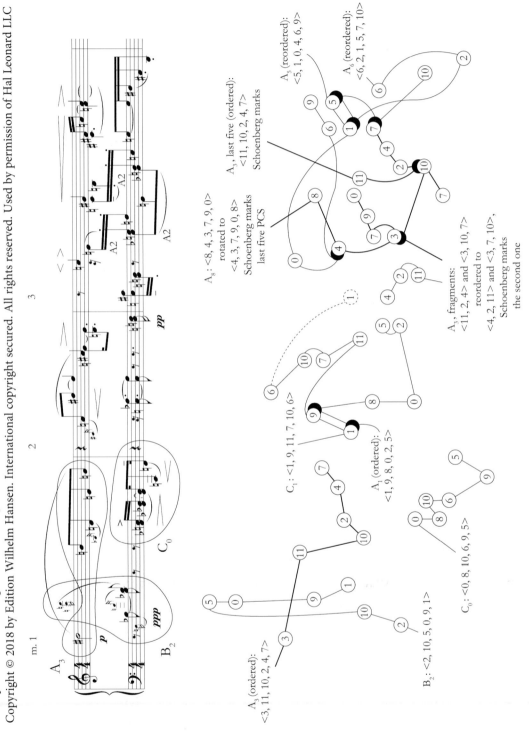

Example 7.7b  Schoenberg, Piano Piece Op. 23, No. 4, mm. 4–7a. Used by permission of Hal Leonard LLC

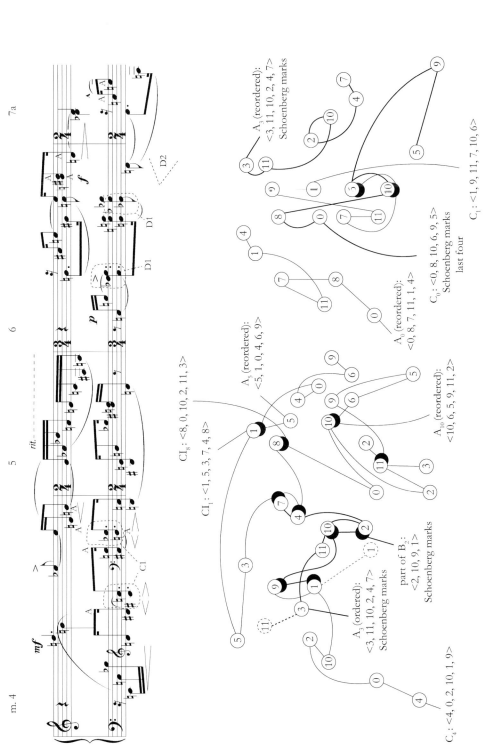

In a similar way to m. 3, our understanding of how the source hexa-chords are manipulated in mm. 4–5 is enhanced by Schoenberg's mark-ings. He places "A" next to five of the six pitch classes of $A_3$ in the latter part of m. 4: this calls our attention to a manifestation of the original hexachord that preserves contour and order (except for one vertical), but not register, and which is hidden behind the surface of the music. His other marking in this measure encloses the verticals A4-above-C♯4 and B♭3-above-D3 and labels them "$C_1$" (which is equivalent to parts of our hexachord $B_2$). This alerts us to the presence of a fragment of $B_2$, <2, 10, 9, 1>, which is presented in retrograde. Other hexachord transformations present in mm. 4–5a are $C_4$: <4, 0, 2, 10, 1, 9>, with the middle dyad reversed, at the beginning of m. 4; the inversion of C transposed to start on PC 1 ($CI_1$: <1, 5, 3, 7, 4, 8>), and reordered to form the soprano voice up to the D♭5 in m. 5; and $CI_8$: <8, 0, 10, 2, 11, 3>, whose reordering accounts for the A♭4 on the second sixteenth of m. 5, as well as all the left-hand notes in the sixteenth pickup to m. 5 and the first beat of that measure. In the latter part of m. 5, Martha Hyde calls our attention to a reordered $A_5$: <5, 1, 0, 4, 6, 9> in the right hand and a reordered $A_{10}$: <10, 6, 5, 9, 11, 2> in the left.[22]

Finally, in mm. 6–7a, Schoenberg's markings as well as more recent analyses help us decipher the passage in similar ways. Schoenberg places "A" next to, again, five notes of a reordered $A_3$ at the end of m. 6 and beginning of m. 7. He also boxes or brackets A♭3-above-C3 on the second beat of m. 6, G♭3-above-B♭2 on the third beat, and <F2, A1> from mm. 6b–7a, and labels the first two dyads "D1" and the last one "D2." "D" is his name for our hexachord $C_0$, and some of these pitches do indeed present a reordered version of <0, 8, 10, 6, 9, 5>. (PCs 8 and 0 for Hexachord $C_0$ in my pitch-class map come from the last sixteenth of beat 2, instead of the beginning of that beat.) In addition to Schoenberg's attributions, Kathryn Bailey has identified the rest of the hexachords in these measures: $A_0$, <0, 8, 7, 11, 1, 4>, reordered to create the first part of m. 6, and $C_1$, <1, 9, 11, 7, 10, 6>, intertwining with $C_0$ in the verticals on the last sixteenth of beat 2 and first eighth of beat 3.[23]

I have just presented an exhaustive account of the ordered, reordered, transposed, and inverted source hexachords in the first 6½ measures of Op. 23, No. 4 – mainly to drive home the point that a freer use of register, defining the series in terms of pitch *class* rather than pitch, together with reordering, enabled Schoenberg to create a wider variety of shapes while still making everything accountable to the three *Grundgestalten*. But Op.

[22] Hyde, "Musical Form and the Development of Schoenberg's Twelve-Tone Method," 106.
[23] Bailey, *Composing with Tones*, pp. 80 and 83.

23, No. 4 did not enable its composer to progress any further toward his other goal, regular aggregate cycles. Soon after July 1920, he would attempt to solve that problem definitively as well, by using a row containing all twelve pitch classes; so that he combined the twelve-tone pitch *ostinati* of works like his 1914–15 Scherzo with his redefinition of *Grundgestalt* as a pitch-class series in Op. 23, No. 4 and other works. The fifth piece of Op. 23, the Waltz, for example, consists of repetitions and retrogrades of a row of twelve pitch classes. But that piece was written in February 1923; another composition based on the repetitions of a twelve-tone pitch class row, its inversions and their retrogrades, had appeared almost two years before that, in July 1921. I am speaking of the Prelude from the Suite, Op. 25 – a work whose twelve-PC *Grundgestalt* divides into tetrachords that overlap with one another frequently, but still enables regular aggregate cycles in many places (not all). Schoenberg also assigned "tonic" and "dominant" function to its two prime row transpositions, $P_4$ and $P_{10}$, in his sketches, giving himself the opportunity to mimic the form-building functions of key areas, just as his "Composition with Twelve Tones" quotation said he wanted to do. And, through its tearing down and building up of symmetrical pitch-class structures, the Prelude also enabled Schoenberg to project the problem, elaboration, and solution of the musical idea in a completely new way.

But the detailed study of *how* the Prelude, Op. 25 does all those things – as well as how some of its successors develop their *Grundgestalten* into comprehensible forms that manifest the musical idea in a myriad of ways – is the topic of another book.[24]

[24] Jack Boss, *Schoenberg's Twelve-Tone Music: Symmetry and the Musical Idea.*

# Bibliography

Adorno, Theodor W. *Philosophy of New Music*, trans., ed. and with an introduction by Robert Hullot-Kentor. Minneapolis: University of Minnesota Press, 2006.

Auner, Joseph. "Schoenberg's Aesthetic Transformations and the Evolution of Form in *Die glückliche Hand*," *Journal of the Arnold Schoenberg Institute* 12/2 (November 1989): 103–28.

    *A Schoenberg Reader: Documents of a Life*. New Haven: Yale University Press, 2003.

Bailey, Kathryn. *Composing with Tones: A Musical Analysis of Schoenberg's Op. 23 Pieces for Piano*. London: Royal Musical Association, 2001.

    "Formal Organization and Structural Imagery in Schoenberg's *Pierrot lunaire*," *Studies in Music from the University of Western Ontario* 2/1 (1977): 93–107.

Bailey Puffett, Kathryn. "Structural Imagery: *Pierrot lunaire* Revisited," *Tempo* 60/237 (2006): 2–22.

Barkin, Elaine. "Play it AS it Lays," *Perspectives of New Music* 17/2 (Spring-Summer 1979): 17–24.

    "(a song of ing)," *In Theory Only* 6/1 (November 1981): 40.

    Untitled essay (on Schoenberg's Opus 19, No. 6), *In Theory Only* 4/8 (February-March 1979): 18–26.

Benjamin, William. "Abstract Polyphonies: The Music of Schoenberg's Nietzschean Moment," in *Political and Religious Ideas in the Works of Arnold Schoenberg*, ed. Charlotte M. Cross and Russell A. Berman. New York: Garland, 2000, pp. 1–39.

Berger, Arthur. "Problems of Pitch Organization in Stravinsky," *Perspectives of New Music* 2/1 (1963): 11–42.

Boge, Claire. "Poetic Analysis as Part of Analysis Pedagogy," *In Theory Only* 12/3–4 (1992): 47–67.

Boss, Jack. "'Away with Motivic Working'? Not So Fast: Motivic Processes in Schoenberg's Op. 11, No. 3," *Music Theory Online* 21/3 (September 2015). www.mtosmt.org/issues/mto.15.21.3/mto.15.21.3.boss.html.

    "The Musical Idea and the Basic Image in an Atonal Song and Recitation of Arnold Schoenberg," *Gamut* 2/1 (2009): 223–66.

    "'Musical Idea' and Motivic Structure in Schoenberg's Op. 11, No. 1," in *Musical Currents from the Left Coast*, ed. Jack Boss and Bruce Quaglia. Newcastle-upon-Tyne: Cambridge Scholars, 2008, pp. 258–83.

    "Schoenberg's Op. 22 Radio Talk and Developing Variation in Atonal Music," *Music Theory Spectrum* 14/2 (Fall 1992): 125–49.

    "Schoenberg on Ornamentation and Structural Levels," *Journal of Music Theory* 38/2 (Fall 1994): 187–216.

*Schoenberg's Twelve-Tone Music: Symmetry and the Musical Idea*. Cambridge: Cambridge University Press, 2014.

Brinkmann, Reinhold. *Arnold Schönberg, Drei Klavierstücke Op. 11: Studien zur Frühen Atonalität bei Schönberg*, vol. 7 of Beihefte zum Archiv für Musikwissenschaft. Wiesbaden: Franz Steiner Verlag, 1969.

"The Fool as Paradigm: Schoenberg's *Pierrot lunaire* and the Modern Artist," in *Schoenberg and Kandinsky: An Historic Encounter*. Amsterdam: Harwood Academic, 1997, pp. 139–68.

"The Lyric as Paradigm: Poetry and the Foundation of Arnold Schoenberg's New Music," in *German Literature in Music: An Aesthetic Fusion: 1890–1989*, ed. Claus Reschke and Howard Pollack. Munich: Wilhelm Fink, 1992, pp. 95–129.

Buchanan, Herbert H. "A Key to Schoenberg's *Erwartung* (op. 17)," *Journal of the American Musicological Society* 20/3 (Autumn 1967): 434–49.

Burkholder, J. Peter. *All Made of Tunes: Charles Ives and the Uses of Musical Borrowing*. New Haven: Yale University Press, 1995.

Busoni, Ferruccio. *Ferruccio Busoni: Selected Letters*, trans., ed., and with an introduction by Antony Beaumont. New York: Columbia University Press, 1987.

Cherlin, Michael. "*Pierrot Lunaire* as Lunar Nexus," *Music Analysis* 31/2 (2012): 176–215.

"Schoenberg and *Das Unheimliche*: Spectres of Tonality," *Journal of Musicology* 11/3 (Summer 1993): 357–73.

*Schoenberg's Musical Imagination*. Cambridge: Cambridge University Press, 2007.

Christensen, Thomas. "Schoenberg's Opus 11, No. 1: A Parody of Pitch Cells from *Tristan*," *Journal of the Arnold Schoenberg Institute* 10/1 (June 1987): 38–44.

Cinnamon, Howard. "Tonal Elements and Unfolding Nontriadic Harmonies in the Second of Schoenberg's *Drei Klavierstücke*, Op. 11," *Theory and Practice* 18/2 (1993): 127–70.

Cogan, Robert and Pozzi Escot. *Sonic Design*. Englewood Cliffs, NJ: Prentice-Hall, 1976.

Dahlhaus, Carl. *Nineteenth-Century Music*, trans. J. Bradford Robinson. Berkeley and Los Angeles: University of California Press, 1989.

DeLio, Thomas. "Language and Form in an Early Atonal Composition: Schoenberg's Op. 19/2," *Indiana Theory Review* 15/2 (Fall 1994): 17–40.

Domek, Richard. "Some Aspects of Organization in Schoenberg's *Book of the Hanging Gardens*, Opus 15," *College Music Symposium* 19/2 (Fall 1979): 111–28.

Dunsby, Jonathan. *Schoenberg: Pierrot lunaire*. Cambridge: Cambridge University Press, 1992.

Dunsby, Jonathan and Arnold Whittall. *Music Analysis in Theory and Practice*. New Haven: Yale University Press, 1988.

Falck, Robert. "'Fear and Hope': A Look at Schoenberg's Op. 15, No. VII," *Canadian Association of University Schools of Music Journal* 7 (1977): 91–105.

Forte, Allen. "Concepts of Linearity in Schoenberg's Atonal Music: A Study of the Opus 15 Song Cycle," *Journal of Music Theory* 36/2 (1992): 285–382.

   "Context and Continuity in an Atonal Work," *Perspectives of New Music* 1/2 (Spring 1963): 72–82.

   "The Magical Kaleidoscope: Schoenberg's First Atonal Masterwork, Opus 11, Number 1," *Journal of the Arnold Schoenberg Institute* 5/2 (1981): 127–68.

   *The Structure of Atonal Music.* New Haven: Yale University Press, 1973.

Frisch, Walter. *The Early Works of Arnold Schoenberg, 1893–1908.* Berkeley and Los Angeles: University of California Press, 1993.

George, Stefan. *The Works of Stefan George Rendered into English*, trans. Olga Marx and Ernst Morwitz. Chapel Hill, NC: University of North Carolina Press, 1949.

Gilbert, Jan. "Schoenberg's Harmonic Visions: A Study of Text Painting in 'Die Kreuze'," *Journal of the Arnold Schoenberg Institute* 8/2 (1984): 116–30.

Goldsmith, Ulrich K. *Stefan George: A Study of His Early Work.* Boulder, CO: University of Colorado Press, 1959.

Gostomsky, Dieter. "Tonalität – Atonalität: Zur Harmonik von Schönbergs Klavierstück Op. 11, Nr. 1," *Zeitschrift für Musiktheorie* 7/1 (1976): 54–71.

Greenbaum, Matthew. "Dialectic in Miniature: Arnold Schoenberg's Sechs Kleine Klavierstücke Op. 19," *Ex Tempore* 14/2 (Spring-Summer 2009): 42–59.

Guck, Marion. "*A noir – à miroir*: Past Senses Reverses Nests (A Priori?)," *In Theory Only* 2/10 (January 1977): 29–34.

Haimo, Ethan. "Atonality, Analysis and the Intentional Fallacy," *Music Theory Spectrum* 18/2 (Fall 1996): 167–99.

   "Schoenberg's *Pierrot Lunaire*: A Cycle?," in *Pierrot Lunaire: Giraud/Hartleben/ Schoenberg*, ed. Mark Delaere and Jan Herman. Louvain: Peeters, 2014, pp. 145–55.

   *Schoenberg's Serial Odyssey: The Evolution of his Twelve-Tone Method.* Oxford: Clarendon Press, 1990.

   *Schoenberg's Transformation of Musical Language.* Cambridge: Cambridge University Press, 2006.

Hamao, Fusako. "On the Origin of the Twelve-Tone Method: Schoenberg's Sketches for the Unfinished *Symphony* (1914–1915)," *Current Musicology* 42 (1986): 32–45.

Harrison, Daniel. *Pieces of Tradition: An Analysis of Contemporary Tonal Music.* New York: Oxford University Press, 2016.

Heneghan, Áine. "Schoenberg's Compositional Philosophy, the Three Piano Pieces, and his Subsequent *Volte-Face*," in *Musical Currents from the Left Coast*, ed. Jack Boss and Bruce Quaglia. Newcastle-upon-Tyne: Cambridge Scholars, 2008, pp. 299–314.

Hicken, Kenneth. "Tonal Organization in Schoenberg's Six Little Piano Pieces, Op. 19," *Canadian University Music Review* 1 (1980): 130–46.

Hyde, Martha. "Musical Form and the Development of Schoenberg's Twelve-Tone Method," *Journal of Music Theory* 29/1 (Spring 1985): 85–143.

Jenkins, J. Daniel. "Schoenberg's Concept of 'ruhende Bewegung'," *Theory and Practice* 34 (2009): 87–105.

Knight, Russell C. "Operand Set Theory and Schoenberg's *Erwartung*, Op. 17," PhD dissertation, University of California at Santa Barbara, 2008.

Kurth, Richard. "*Pierrot lunaire*: Persona, Voice, and the Fabric of Allusion," in *The Cambridge Companion to Schoenberg*, ed. Jennifer Shaw and Joseph Auner. Cambridge: Cambridge University Press, 2010, pp. 120–34.

    "Pierrot's Cave: Representation, Reverberation, Radiance," in *Schoenberg and Words: The Modernist Years*, ed. Charlotte M. Cross and Russell A. Berman. New York: Garland, 2000, pp. 203–41.

Larson, Steve. "A Tonal Model of an 'Atonal' Piece: Schönberg's Opus 15, Number 2," *Perspectives of New Music* 25/1–2 (Winter–Summer 1987): 418–33.

Leichtentritt, Hugo. *Musical Form*. Cambridge, MA: Harvard University Press, 1951.

Lerdahl, Fred. "Atonal Prolongational Structure," *Contemporary Music Review* 4 (1989): 65–87.

Lessem, Alan. *Music and Text in the Works of Arnold Schoenberg*. Ann Arbor: UMI Research Press, 1979.

    "Text and Music in Schoenberg's *Pierrot Lunaire*," *Current Musicology* 19 (1975): 103–12.

Lewandowski, Stephan. "'A Far Higher Power,' Gedanken zu ideengeschichtlichen Vorgängermodellen der Pitch-Class Set Theory," *Tijdschrift voor Muziektheorie* 15/3 (2010): 190–210.

Lewin, David. "Inversional Balance as an Organizing Force in Schoenberg's Music and Thought," *Perspectives of New Music* 6/2 (Spring–Summer 1968): 1–21.

    "Klumpenhouwer Networks and Some Isographies that Involve Them," *Music Theory Spectrum* 12/1 (Spring 1990): 83–120.

    "Re: The Intervallic Content of a Collection of Notes, Intervallic Relations between a Collection of Notes and Its Complement: An Application to Schoenberg's Hexachordal Pieces," *Journal of Music Theory* 4/1 (Spring 1960): 98–101.

    "Some Investigations into Foreground Rhythmic and Metric Patterning," in *Music Theory: Special Topics*, ed. Richmond Browne. New York: Academic Press, 1981, pp. 101–37.

    "Some Notes on *Pierrot Lunaire*," in *Music Theory in Concept and Practice*, ed. James M. Baker, David W. Beach, and Jonathan W. Bernard. Rochester, NY: University of Rochester Press, 1997, pp. 433–57.

    "Some Notes on Schoenberg's Opus 11," *In Theory Only* 3/1 (April 1977): 3–7.

    "Toward the Analysis of a Schoenberg Song (Op. 15, No. XI)," *Perspectives of New Music* 12/1–2 (1973–74): 43–86.

    "Transformational Techniques in Atonal and Other Music Theories," *Perspectives of New Music* 21/1–2 (Autumn 1982–Summer 1983): 312–71.

    "A Tutorial on Klumpenhouwer Networks, Using the Chorale in Schoenberg's Opus 11, No. 2," *Journal of Music Theory* 38/1 (Spring 1994): 79–101.

"A Way into Schoenberg's Opus 15, Number 7," *In Theory Only* 6/1 (November 1981): 3–24.

Lubet, Alex. "Vestiges of Tonality in a Work of Arnold Schoenberg," *Indiana Theory Review* 5/3 (Spring 1982): 11–21.

Maegaard, Jan. *Studien zur Entwicklung des dodekaphonen Satzes bei Arnold Schönberg*, 3 vols. Copenhagen: Wilhelm Hansen, 1972.

Mailman, Joshua Banks. "Schoenberg's Chordal Experimentalism Revealed through Representational Hierarchy Association (RHA), Contour Motives, and Binary-State Switching," *Music Theory Spectrum* 37/2 (Fall 2015): 224–52.

Marsh, Roger. "'A Multicolored Alphabet': Rediscovering Albert Giraud's *Pierrot Lunaire*," *Twentieth-Century Music* 4/1: 97–121.

McKee, Eric. "On the Death of Mahler: Schoenberg's Op. 19, No. 6," *Theory and Practice* 30 (2005): 121–51.

Morrison, Charles. "Syncopation as Motive in Schoenberg's Op. 19, Nos. 2, 3 and 4," *Music Analysis* 11/1 (1992): 75–93.

Neidhöfer, Christoph. "Atonalität und *Transformational Analysis*: Zu einigen verborgenen (und nicht so verborgenen) Strukturen in Schönbergs *Klavierstück* op. 11, 3," in Jahrbuch 2008/09 des Staatlichen Instituts für Musikforschung Preußischer Kulturbesitz, ed. Simone Hohmaier. Mainz: Schott, 2009, pp. 53–73.

Norton, Robert E. *Secret Germany: Stefan George and His Circle*. Ithaca: Cornell University Press, 2002.

Ogdon, Will. "How Tonality Functions in Schoenberg's Opus 11, Number 1," *Journal of the Arnold Schoenberg Institute* 5/2 (1981): 169–81.

Payette, Jessica. "Seismographic Screams: *Erwartung's* Reverberations through Twentieth-Century Culture," PhD dissertation, Stanford University, 2008.

Perle, George. *Serial Composition and Atonality*. Berkeley and Los Angeles: University of California Press, 1962.

Raessler, Daniel M. "Schoenberg and Busoni: Aspects of Their Relationship," *Journal of the Arnold Schoenberg Institute* 7/1 (1983): 7–27.

Raff, Christian. *Gestaltete Freiheit: Studien zur Analyse der frei atonalen Kompositionen A. Schönbergs – auf der Grundlage seiner Begriffe*, Sinefonia, vol. 5. Hofheim: Wolke, 2006.

Reich, Willi. *Schoenberg: A Critical Biography*, trans. Leo Black. New York: Praeger, 1971.

Roig-Francolí, Miguel A. "A Theory of Pitch-Class Set Extension in Atonal Music," *College Music Symposium* 41 (2001): 57–90.

Schmalfeldt, Janet. *Berg's Wozzeck: Harmonic Language and Dramatic Design*. New Haven: Yale University Press, 1983.

Schoenberg, Arnold. "Analysis of the Four Orchestral Songs Op. 22," trans. Claudio Spies, *Perspectives of New Music* 3/2 (Spring–Summer 1965): 1–21.

*Arnold Schönberg, Fünfzehn Gedichte aus "Das Buch der hängenden Gärten" von Stefan George, für Gesang und Klavier*, with afterword by Theodor W. Adorno. Wiesbaden: Insel-Bücherei no. 683, 1959.

*Berliner Tagebuch*, ed. Josef Rufer. Frankfurt: Propyläen, 1974.

*Fundamentals of Musical Composition*, 2nd edn, ed. Gerald Strang and Leonard Stein. London: Faber & Faber, 1970.

*Pierrot lunaire, Op. 21, The Book of the Hanging Gardens, Op. 15*, with Jan DeGaetani, mezzo-soprano, The Contemporary Chamber Ensemble, Arthur Weisberg, conductor, and Gilbert Kalish, piano, © 1990 by Elektra Nonesuch, Elektra Nonesuch 9–79237-2, compact disc.

*Structural Functions of Harmony*, rev. ed. Leonard Stein. New York: Norton, 1969.

*Style and Idea:* Selected Writings of Arnold Schoenberg, rev. paperback edn, ed. Leonard Stein, trans. Leo Black. Berkeley and Los Angeles: University of California Press, 1984. Includes: "Composition with Twelve Tones (1)" (1941), "Hauer's Theories" (1923), "Linear Counterpoint" (1931), "New Music: My Music" (*c.* 1930), "New Music, Outmoded Music, Style and Idea" (1946), "On revient toujours" (1948), "Problems of Harmony" (1934), "The Relationship to the Text" (1912).

*Theory of Harmony*, trans. Roy E. Carter. Berkeley and Los Angeles: University of California Press, 1978.

Simms, Bryan. *The Atonal Music of Arnold Schoenberg, 1908–1923*. New York: Oxford University Press, 2000.

Stein, Deborah. "Schoenberg's Opus 19, No. 2: Voice-Leading and Overall Structure in an Atonal Work," *In Theory Only* 2/7 (October 1976): 27–43.

Steuermann, Eduard. "*Pierrot Lunaire* in Retrospect," *Journal of the Arnold Schoenberg Institute* 2/1 (October 1977): 49–51.

Straus, Joseph N. *Introduction to Post-Tonal Theory*, 3rd edn. Upper Saddle River, NJ: Pearson Prentice-Hall, 2004.

*Introduction to Post-Tonal Theory*, 4th edn. New York: Norton, 2016.

"Voice Leading in Set-Class Space," *Journal of Music Theory* 49/1 (Spring 2005): 45–108.

Stuckenschmidt, Hans Heinz. "Opus 19, Nummer 3: Eine Schönberg-Analyse," *Orbis musicae* 1/1 (Summer 1971): 88–90.

*Schoenberg: His Life, World and Work*, trans. Humphrey Searle. New York: Schirmer Books, 1978.

Theurich, Jutta. "Der Briefwechsel zwischen Arnold Schönberg und Ferruccio Busoni," in *Arnold Schönberg – 1874 bis 1951: Zum 25. Todestag des Komponisten*, ed. Mathias Hansen and Christa Müller. Berlin: Akademie der Künste der DDR, 1976, pp. 55–58.

Travis, Roy. "Directed Motion in Schoenberg and Webern," *Perspectives of New Music* 4/2 (Spring–Summer 1966): 85–89.

Tymoczko, Dmitri. *A Geometry of Music: Harmony and Counterpoint in the Extended Common Practice*. New York: Oxford University Press, 2011.

Väisälä, Olli. "Concepts of Harmony and Prolongation in Schoenberg's Op. 19/2," *Music Theory Spectrum* 21/2 (Fall 1999): 230–59.

van den Toorn, Pieter. *The Music of Igor Stravinsky*. New Haven: Yale University Press, 1983.

Vilain, Robert. "*Pierrot Lunaire*: Cyclic Coherence in Giraud and Schoenberg," in *Pierrot Lunaire: Giraud/Hartleben/Schoenberg*, ed. Mark Delaere and Jan Herman. Louvain: Peeters, 2014, pp. 127–44.

von Massow, Albrecht. "Abschied und Neuorientierung – Schönbergs Klavierstück op. 19, 6," *Archiv für Musikwissenschaft* 50/2 (1993): 187–95.

von der Null, Edwin. *Moderne Harmonik*. Leipzig: F. Kistner & C. F. W. Siegel, 1932.

Wen, Eric. "Bass-Line Articulations of the *Urlinie*," in *Schenker Studies 2*, ed. Carl Schachter and Hedi Siegel. Cambridge: Cambridge University Press, 1999, pp. 276–97.

Weytjens, Stephan. "Text as a Crutch in Arnold Schoenberg's 'Pierrot lunaire' Op. 21?" PhD dissertation, University of Leuven, 2003.

  "Text as a Crutch in Schoenberg's *Pierrot Lunaire*?" in *Pierrot Lunaire: Giraud/Hartleben/Schoenberg*, ed. Mark Delaere and Jan Herman. Louvain: Peeters, 2014, pp. 109–24.

Whitney, Kathryn. "Schoenberg's 'Single Second of Maximum Spiritual Excitement': Compression and Expansion in 'Erwartung,' Op. 17," *Journal of Music Theory* 47/1 (Spring, 2003): 155–214.

Williams Jr., Edgar Warren. "A View of Schoenberg's Op. 19, No. 2," *College Music Symposium* 25 (1985): 144–51.

Youens, Susan. "Excavating an Allegory: The Texts of *Pierrot Lunaire*," *Journal of the Arnold Schoenberg Institute* 8/2 (1984): 94–115.

# Index

*By the same author*

# Schoenberg's Twelve-Tone Music
## *Symmetry and the Musical Idea*

In the *Music since 1900* series
*Winner of the 2015 Wallace Berry Award from the Society for Music Theory*

Jack Boss takes a unique approach to analyzing Arnold Schoenberg's twelve-tone music, adapting the composer's notion of a "musical idea" – problem, elaboration, solution – as a framework and focusing on the large-scale coherence of the whole piece. The book begins by defining "musical idea" as a large, overarching process involving conflict between musical elements or situations, elaboration of that conflict, and resolution, and examines how such conflicts often involve symmetrical pitch and interval shapes that are obscured in some way. Containing close analytical readings of a large number of Schoenberg's key twelve-tone works, including *Moses und Aron*, the Suite for Piano Op. 25, the Fourth Quartet, and the String Trio, the study provides the reader with a clearer understanding of this still-controversial, challenging, but vitally important modernist composer.

> "Future scholars interested in following Boss's lead will benefit immeasurably from his careful analyses, his synthesis of previous scholarship, and, perhaps most of all, the provocative questions his work raises." **Zachary Bernstein**, *Journal of Music Theory*

> "Densely informative and richly detailed, Jack Boss's monograph on Schoenberg's twelve-tone music is the product of an impressive thirteen years of analytical work, itself drawing on a career-spanning engagement with Schoenberg's music. The sincerity of the project is unquestionable and Jack Boss communicates both expertise and laudable passion." **Andrew J. Chung**, *Current Musicology*

> "Boss's groundbreaking book provides a new and illuminating methodology for understanding, exploring, and appreciating Schoenberg's music." **Joe Argentino**, *Music Theory Online*

HB ISBN: 978 1 107 04686 3
PB ISBN: 978 1 107 62492 4
OC ISBN: 978 1 107 11078 6

Available for purchase on Cambridge Core
Also available in paperback and hardback formats from www.cambridge.org